About the Book and Editors

This book presents important case studies highlighting social, economic, political, and biological dimensions of environmental degradation in the Third World. Focusing on areas identified as experiencing or at risk for deterioration, the studies are drawn from nearly every continent and cover most of the larger ecosystems of the Third World, including arid and semiarid rangelands, tropical rain forests, steep-sloped mountains and hills, tropical river basins, and coastal lowlands. The authors use local data to examine, test, and refine larger explanatory models and theories, showing how comparisons of case-specific data can sharpen our knowledge about resource use in areas at risk. In doing so, the authors address two critical questions: How can land degradation processes be identified and how can the human role in land degradation be separated from the effects of climate and other natural actions?

Peter D. Little is senior research associate at the Institute for Development Anthropology. **Michael M Horowitz** is director of the Institute for Development Anthropology and professor of anthropology at SUNY-Binghamton.

MONOGRAPHS IN DEVELOPMENT ANTHROPOLOGY

Under the General Editorship of
DAVID W. BROKENSHA
MICHAEL M HOROWITZ
and
THAYER SCUDDER

Sponsored by the Institute for Development Anthropology

Anthropology and Rural Development in West Africa, edited by Michael M Horowitz and Thomas M. Painter

Lands at Risk in the Third World: Local-Level Perspectives, edited by Peter D. Little and Michael M Horowitz, with A. Endre Nyerges

Anthropology of Development and Change in East Africa, edited by David Brokensha and Peter D. Little (forthcoming)

Anthropology and Development in North Africa and the Middle East, edited by Muneera Salem-Murdock and Michael M Horowitz (forthcoming)

Lands at Risk
in the Third World:
Local-Level Perspectives

edited by Peter D. Little
and Michael M Horowitz,
with A. Endre Nyerges

Foreword by Gilbert F. White

Westview Press / Boulder and London

Monographs in Development Anthropology

This Westview softcover edition is printed on acid-free paper and bound in softcovers that carry the highest rating of the National Association of State Textbook Administrators, in consultation with the Association of American Publishers and the Book Manufacturers' Institute.

Copyright © 1987 by the Institute for Development Anthropology

Published in 1987 in the United States of America by Westview Press, Inc.; Frederick A. Praeger, Publisher; 5500 Central Avenue, Boulder, Colorado 80301

Library of Congress Cataloging-in-Publication Data
Lands at risk in the Third World.
  (Monographs in development anthropology)
  Bibliography: p.
  Includes index.
  1. Land use, Rural—Environmental aspects—
Developing countries. I. Little, Peter D.
II. Horowitz, Michael M, 1933– . III. Series.
HD1131.L37 1987   333.73'13   86-51423
ISBN 0-8133-7311-5

Composition for this book was created by conversion of the editors' word-processor disks.
This book was produced without formal editing by the publisher.

Printed and bound in the United States of America

(∞) The paper used in this publication meets the requirements of the American National Standard for Permanence of Paper for Printed Library Materials Z39.48-1984.

6   5   4   3

Contents

Foreword

Gilbert F. White

A perplexing, central issue in all programs for agricultural development is whether or not production can be gained or maintained without decreasing the resource base. This problem applies to all lands, but especially to Third World areas where incomes and food production per capita are perilously low. Since the great wave of enthusiasm for economic development efforts that began shortly after World War II, it has been posed in a variety of ways, ranging from convictions that the earth had already exceeded its carrying capacity (Vogt 1948), through more cautious predictions that large areas would be irrevocably threatened by the year 2000 unless drastic measures were taken (Council on Environmental Quality and Department of State 1980), to arguments that substantial population increases could be accommodated so long as certain prescriptions were followed (Repetto 1985; Simon and Kahn 1984).

The papers in this volume address one segment of analysis bearing on this issue that is basic to its resolution and that all too often is neglected in appraising development activity and prospects. The neglected sector comprises the effects of social structure, social process, and culture history on the practices leading to resource deterioration. We know far more about technologies to increase crop or forest production and about the diffusion of what we hope are improved practices than about their consequences— when they are applied at particular times and places under particular social circumstances—for the basic resources of land, water, and air.

Recent interest in development in the Third World has turned attention to why so many well-intentioned programs have gone wrong and to where either economic success or failure has led to environmental deterioration. This volume provides invaluable new information and insights on both, and on how they are related, in specific areas of Africa, Asia, and Latin America. All these areas are experiencing a welter of appraisal and self-examination concerning development programs, although with the exception of some recent publications many of these analyses are circulated only within funding organizations. The United Nations Environment Programme, for example, is sponsoring a review of why the ambitious 1977 plan of action to combat desertification led to such disappointing results. Under-standing the conditions and histories of specific projects and areas is essential to such appraisal.

In appraising the burgeoning experience and in asking its relevance for future programs, there may be value in trying to place it in the context of four other streams of thought. These have to do with global trends in livelihood and dependence, with the environmental effects of land trans-formation, with the difficulties of predicting program outcomes, and with risks in addition to land degradation that farmers and herders face.

One important set of agricultural and health statistics suggests that in the face of growing population, per capita food production has more than kept pace, and life expectancy has continued to increase in most parts of the Third World (Holdgate, Kassas, and White 1982). While production has been threatened in some areas, it has gained in others. Africa, of course, is the major exception, but even there the shortfalls in food production are generally traced to socioeconomic and political causes rather than to deficiency in land resources. These conditions are linked in complex ways with the increasing interdependence of people in the Third World through flows of funds, commodities, labor, and information. Interdependence has fostered stability in some quarters and instability in others. Its circumstances are changing rapidly, and there is reason to question the supposition that the same set of external conditions of market, technology, or social structure will long prevail in any area in exactly the same mix.

A second current of investigation is directed at the precise character of change in soil fertility when land use is transformed. The interrelations of soil structure, soil biota, plant cover, nutrient cycling, and water movement are exceedingly complex. It is difficult to discern how they are affected by alterations in grazing or cultivation practices, plants, nutrients, pesticides, herbicides, fungicides, and the water cycle. Estimates of the consequences of soil erosion for long-term productivity of a given soil type, for example, do not come easily, and even more complicated are judgments as to the extent to which they are reversible (Wolman, in press). Caution needs to be exercised in defining what is meant by "degradation" or "deterioration" or "improvement," and in estimating how lasting or reversible they may be.

A third stream of thought is related to the notion of resilience in ecosystems, and the corollary difficulty of predicting how they will respond over time to manipulation (Holling 1978). Increasingly, scientists are questioning the confidence attaching to the post-1969 practice of environmental impact assessment. They argue that there are so many unknowns in the processes affected and so many surprises in store for most presumably well-planned improvement projects that the prudent program should emphasize flexibility and capacity to respond to surprise as the unexpected unfolds.

Land degradation is only one of the hazards a herder or farmer encounters in seeking optimal use of land. Its effects generally are slower to become evident than drought, flood, or any of the other environmental extremes, but they may be more lasting. Studies in recent years of how people cope with those hazards have tended to examine how individuals choose among the kinds of behavioral adjustments open to them, and how the choices are affected by information, perception of the hazard, and numerous social constraints (Burton, Kates, and White 1978; Hewitt 1983). One of the theories growing out of such studies is that societies in transition are especially prone to losses from extreme events, but may in time develop a different, more stable response. This suggests that the period when both the agricultural system and the resource base are especially vulnerable to disruption may be during rapid transition, as often is found in development programs.

All four of these streams of thought are strengthened by the kinds of analyses reported in this volume. The degradation phenomena need to be viewed in a world perspective of increasing interdependence that may promise short-term gains at risk of long-term losses, and that may change rapidly. Degradation processes require very careful description from physical and biological standpoints, and may be either accelerated or reversed by social programs. Among the various factors that decrease confidence in predicting the impacts of land transformation, none is more deserving of careful study than the set of factors involved in social structure, social process, and culture history. And the periods of transition in local systems may be seen as times of especially high vulnerability to both short- and long-term disturbance. No simple solutions neatly point the way to truly sustainable development, and certainly none will evolve without genuine understanding of all these factors as they are at work in each agricultural environment.

References

Burton, Ian, Robert W. Kates, and Gilbert F. White
    1978   The Environment as Hazard. New York, NY: Oxford University Press.
Council on Environmental Quality and Department of State
    1980   The Global 2000 Report to the President. 3 vols. Washington, DC: Government Printing Office.
Hewitt, K., ed.
    1983   Interpretations of Calamity from the Viewpoint of Human Ecology. Boston, MA: Allen and Unwin.
Holdgate, Martin, W., Mohammed Kassas, and Gilbert F. White, eds.
    1982   The World Environment, 1972–1982. Dublin: Tycooly International.
Holling, C. S., ed.
    1978   Adaptive Environmental Assessment and Management. Chichester: John Wiley and Sons.
Repetto, Robert, ed.
    1985   The Global Possible: Resources, Development, and the New Century. New Haven, CT: Yale University Press.
Simon, Julian L., and Herman Kahn, eds.
    1984   The Resourceful Earth: A Response to Global 2000. Oxford: Basil Blackwell.

Vogt, William
    1948   Road to Survival. New York, NY: William Sloane Associates.
Wolman, M. G., et al., eds.
    In press   Land Transformation in Agriculture. SCOPE (Scientific Committee on
            Problems of the Environment), No. 32. Chichester: John Wiley and Sons.

Acknowledgments

This book is based on the proceedings of the conference "Lands at Risk in the Third World" held at the Security Mutual Life Insurance Company in Binghamton, New York, 10–12 October 1985. We are grateful to Mr. Robert M. Best, Chairman of Security Mutual, for graciously lending us his superb meeting facilities.

The conference was conducted under the auspices of the Clark University/ Institute for Development Anthropology (IDA) Cooperative Agreement on Human Settlement and Resource Systems Analysis, funded by the Office of Rural Development, the Science and Technology Bureau, Agency for International Development. Bob Walter and Eric Chetwynd of the Office of Rural Development deserve special thanks for their support.

Several members of IDA's staff assisted in this effort. Vivian Carlip and Sylvia Horowitz copyedited the entire manuscript and supervised its transformation for computer-generated typesetting. The chapters on Latin America were read and commented on by Michael Painter. Vera Beers, Kate MacQueen, and Cynthia Woodsong proofread the manuscript and provided some last-minute typing.

Our greatest debt of appreciation goes to the contributors, who displayed considerable forbearance through often several requested revisions.

Peter D. Little
Michael M Horowitz

Introduction:
Social Science Perspectives on
Land, Ecology, and Development

Peter D. Little and Michael M Horowitz

An Awareness

A claimed "environmental crisis"—an assertion that the capacity of the habitat to sustain life is at risk in many, perhaps most, Third World countries—has moved to the center of the development dialogue. While no region appears to be immune from degradation, the most vulnerable areas include arid and semiarid rangelands, tropical rain forests, steep-sloped mountains and hills, tropical river basins, and coastal lowlands. Most of the discussion about degradation in the development literature focuses on biological and climatic factors, but there is also a resurgent awareness of the pertinence of socioeconomic and political processes. Specialists from both natural and social sciences are contributing to the discussion, although as yet an ecological perspective drawing on both has rarely informed the policies and actions of governments and aid agencies. Especially disturbing is the latter's recurrent assumption that a major cause of long-term environmental decline is "traditional practice"—whether by herders or farmers—without attempting to understand the changing contexts within which those practices occur, without appreciating that the objectionable practices are often of very recent origin, and often without recognizing that the proposed development alternatives may worsen rather than retard or reverse the decline.

While there is a general consensus among scientists and often among local people (see Messerschmidt's description in this volume of Nepalese elders pointing to the loss of forests) that considerable environmental degradation is taking place in the Third World, there is far less agreement on its causes and on its duration and direction. The uncertainties derive from the lack of persuasive theory linking social and biophysical processes and of adequate longitudinal data on ecological processes for all but a handful of the world's habitats (Blaikie 1984; Horowitz and Little 1986). Without adequate theory and data it is difficult to distinguish the effects of natural erosion and climatic fluctuations from those caused by human actions, and therefore official policy responding to the crisis tends to be ill-informed.

What have become clear recently are the reciprocating impacts of environmental and social well-being, such that declines in environmental productivity seem to correlate with marked reductions in producer income, labor availability, and consumption. These, in turn, contribute to practices that further degrade the landscape. Ecological changes, then, are symptomatic of more general social and political economic transformations occurring throughout the rural Third World.

Anthropology and Lands at Risk

For the most part, anthropologists have not made prominent contributions to the environmental debate until quite recently. In America, Boasian anthropologists seemed to fear that an examination of a dynamic relationship between habitat and culture would be read as an embracing of a previously rejected environmental determinism. Though Wissler (1938) and Kroeber (1939) related their culture areas to large geographic regions, environment was accorded only a passive, limiting, or "possibilist" function (cf. Herskovits 1951:159). In Britain, with the significant exception of Audrey Richards (1932, 1939), for whom "social environment and its ecological underpinnings [became a] life's work" (Gladstone 1986:345),[1] and possibly a few others (e.g. Forde 1963), the emphasis on functional integration and equilibrium rendered the notion of dynamic adaptation irrelevant and nonproblematic. Classical evolutionists such as White (1949) in America and Childe (1951) in Britain also rejected a causal role for environment. In a famous footnote to his treatise on cultural evolution, White wrote:

> Both organism and culture—and consequently the behavior resulting from the interaction of these two factors—are of course affected by the natural environment. But in the problem which confronts us now we are concerned only with the relationship between man and culture. The environmental factor may therefore legitimately be considered a constant and as such be omitted from our consideration (1949:199).

The effective participation of anthropologists in ecological studies awaited the post-World War II adoption in the discipline of two scientific paradigms: cultural ecology and cultural historical materialism. Both these schools began to flourish in the 1960s and 1970s (Barth 1961; Scudder 1962; Meillassoux 1975), although their antecedents may be found in the 19th and early 20th centuries (Marx 1973; Steward 1938; 1963). Cultural ecology directed anthropologists' attention to the material basis of social life, and in particular to the relationship between a productive technology and its environment. Once it was appreciated that environments as well as cultures change— sometimes abruptly as in earthquakes (Oliver-Smith 1986), sometimes more slowly as a consequence of such human actions as deforestation and river basin development—the relationship between technology and habitat was seen as necessarily dynamic and adaptive. How, it began to be asked, could technological change serve to maintain an adequate subsistence in the face of environmental deterioration or population growth (cf. Boserup 1965)?

Historical materialists illuminated for anthropology the critical relationship between technology and the social organization of production, and the ways in which local organizations were articulated with larger regional, national, and world political economies. Without necessarily embracing the entire significance claimed for historical materialism by some of its practitioners, a growing number of anthropologists today are to some degree concerned with the relationships among environment, technology, and modes of production.[2]

While much of the discussion about these interrelationships may be primarily of academic interest, the various arguments have clear potential for influencing policy. For example, both the occurrence and the causes for desertification on rangelands have been subject to a good deal of debate since some anthropologists and ecologists began to challenge the attribution of environmental degradation uniquely or largely to pastoral practice (cf. Horowitz 1979, 1986; Sandford 1983). Prior to that challenge, development planners seemed unanimously to favor actions such as sedentarization, stock reduction, and increased off-take rates that, despite their being universally resisted by pastoral producers, were deemed necessary to reverse the untoward ecological effects of open-range grazing. Certain systems for classifying tropical forest and farm lands, used by planners to design agricultural programs, also have been subject to recent scrutiny. Dourojeanni (1984) shows how three land-use surveys conducted in the same area of Peru in 1981 generated radically different results, providing "scientific" bases for opposing land-use policies: a World Bank-sponsored study indicated that only 5 percent of the region should be committed to forest; a Peruvian government study recommended a forest cover of about 50 percent; and a USAID-sponsored study proposed that 65 percent of the region be forested. The corresponding recommendations about clear-cut agriculture in annual crops were respectively 42 percent, 17 percent, and 8 percent. In consequence, a "scientific" study can be invoked in support of almost any land use policy.

A specifically *development* anthropology, based largely on a materialist approach, emerged out of what was perceived at the time as an environmental crisis—the sudano-sahelian drought of 1968–1974. Both the British colonial service and the United States Agency for International Development and its precursors had involved anthropologists in development activities before that date,[3] and anthropologists were occasionally employed on short-term missions at the World Bank. But it was the coincidence of the drought and of the orientation towards rural development in the 1973 "new directions" in American foreign aid policy that revived and greatly expanded a role and career tracks for anthropologists in government, and prompted departments to explore curricula that would better prepare their graduates for non-academic employment. As Horowitz and Painter (1986:3) commented, however, the re-entry of anthropologists into development in the mid-1970s did not imply a homogeneity of viewpoint between them and their employers:

There is a certain irony in the receptivity to anthropologists that resulted from New Directions in AID. Planning and financing agencies continued to view the actions of rural peoples as *traditional* (i.e., not rational), and as obstacles to development. They employed anthropologists with the hope that traditional ways could be overcome—changed. Most anthropologists, on the other hand, rejected tradition as an explanatory tool, and looked at it rather as the result of specific opportunity structures in which rural populations were situated. These anthropologists repeatedly demonstrated through their research and analysis that rural communities were neither static nor irrationally opposed to change, but were dynamic, open-ended, and receptive to those changes that promoted their welfare and entailed reasonable risks. Anthropologists argued that the obstacles to development were largely external in nature. These obstacles included natural factors to be sure: climate, soil quality, geomorphologic formation, ecology, etc.; but the obstacles that received the greatest attention were political—the external control of systems and economic decision-making, and their impact on rural populations.

In the early post-sahelian-drought period, efforts began to focus on ways in which theories, methods, and findings of anthropology and other social sciences might effectively be applied to the formulation of development policies and to the planning and evaluation of development programs and projects. It became clear quickly that social scientists also had a great deal to learn from their involvement with development, especially as they were confronted with substantive problems with which few of them had much prior direct experience. A substantial number of these problems had strong environmental components, and anthropologists found themselves participating in efforts calling for improved use of rangelands, irrigation and dryland farming systems, forests and savanna woodlands, lake and river basins.

The Conference

The editors of this volume have their major field experiences in research on pastoral production systems in semiarid rangelands of East and West Africa. In attempting to understand these systems we have been frequently drawn to studies from other ecological zones. Often these studies were by anthropologists, but a substantial number of them were conducted by geographers, economists, and other social scientists. Analyses of resource use in the Amazonian tropical lowlands (Hecht 1984; Moran 1983), of soil erosion and deforestation in southeast Asia (Blaikie 1984), of rangeland degradation in the Middle East (Spooner and Mann 1982), and of environmental decline in the Andes (Collins 1984) reflected processes similar to those we observed in Africa. Examinations of lands at risk almost all acknowledged recent changes in social and ecological parameters (Bourgeot 1981; Thomson 1985; O'Brien 1983; Bunker 1985) that require new approaches to understand contemporary environmental change. We decided to bring to the Institute for Development Anthropology some of the contemporary thinking about human-environment relations in a conference held in Binghamton in October 1985. In selecting conference participants, emphasis was given to persons who had conducted long-term fieldwork in an area identified as experiencing or risking environmental degradation.

The conference had three objectives. The first was an empirical presentation of local-level data on ecology and resource management. What could these data contribute to our understanding of such large environmental processes as desertification and soil erosion? What conclusions do comparisons of these case-specific data allow us to draw about resource use in areas considered to be at risk? Second was an exploration of several social science approaches to examining resource management. What are current theories dealing with land use and ecology, and what is their relevance to the analysis of specific problems? Last was a treatment of the very notion of "environmental risk" itself as problematic; that is, we felt that the determination of an environment at risk should be the product or outcome of analysis, and not an a priori assumption. While the fragility of certain environments has widely been assumed—as in the oft-stated "fragile sahelian habitat," leading to the elaboration of possibly inappropriate policies and actions (such as forced destocking of the range)—the conferees asked two questions: how can the process of land degradation be identified and operationalized, and how can the human role in that degradation be disaggregated from the effects of climatic and other natural actions?

Neither the conference nor this book has achieved consensus on these issues. The objective is merely to contribute to the debate over relationships among environment, society, and development, and not to resolve it. The studies included here refer to locations in the Caribbean, South America, Africa, and Asia, and cover many of the larger ecosystems found in the Third World. The unifying perspective among these studies is an emphasis on *localized* data used to examine, test, and refine larger explanatory models and theories. Many of these issues have implications well beyond the analysis of natural resource use, a point that is brought out by Collins who draws upon debates in development theory and peasant studies to confront ecological change.

The Book

The following chapters present case studies highlighting social, economic, political, and biological dimensions of environmental degradation. The authors are all social scientists whose approaches to the analysis of environmental issues might differ from those of a biological or natural ecologist, but who nonetheless attempt to integrate ecological materials in their analyses. We do not pretend, however, that the biological and biophysical dimensions of environmental change and degradation are fully treated herein; only that an emphasis on the social, economic, and political dimensions is also essential to ultimate understandings and corrective actions.

The chapters deal with a number of cross-cutting issues and with recurrent themes, making it difficult to allocate them to neatly differentiated sections.

There are four general themes, however, that seem especially salient and that we have utilized in defining major sections of the book: (1) models of resource management; (2) the role of the state; (3) changing rights to land and other resources; and (4) local management strategies.

Models of Resource Management

Several theoretical approaches to resource management and ecological change are presented in this book. They include, *inter alia,* models based on political economy perspectives, household production, indigenous knowledge and resource use, and biology. While the authors demonstrate divergence in theoretical orientation, most try to relate theory to a body of empirical data based on long-term fieldwork. The contributions in this section of the book suggest ways of moving beyond the particulars of specific geographic areas to more general understandings that can be applied in discrepant societies and environments.

In the first chapter, Collins examines the significance of economic diversification for ecological change and finds that as farmers diversify into wage employment and other nonfarm activities, they have less time properly to manage agricultural lands. A process of environmental decline sets in when farmers must work off the farm to maintain household subsistence, but do not generate enough income for farm investment to compensate for the loss of labor. Collins proposes a household model that focuses on the importance of labor and asks two related and significant research and policy issues: (1) what is the availability of labor in rural areas? and (2) what economic changes in these areas are altering the allocation and value of labor? The basic change identified is a process of semiproletarianization: producers are partly incorporated into labor markets, while continuing "to produce food and other products for their own use" (p. 34, n1). Semiproletarianization results in the paradox of rural land and labor shortages occurring simultaneously, a phenomenon that challenges the frequent assumption of low opportunity costs for peasant labor. Collins uses her model to examine a number of cases where diversification led to environmental decline, citing examples in Peru and Jamaica, where labor shortages resulted in improper management of coffee farms (Peru) and agricultural terraces (Peru and Jamaica), increasing the rate of soil erosion in these areas.

Schmink and Wood seek to establish a "political ecology" of resource use that incorporates the concepts of surplus, social class, the state, and ideology, arguing that earlier approaches focused too narrowly on man-environment relationships to the exclusion of political variables. The authors use their model to analyze environmental change in the Amazonian basin (Brazil), looking at patterns of resource use among Indians, *caboclos,* immigrant peasants, and commercial ranchers. While the impact of both Indians and caboclos on the environment is modest, peasants and commercial ranchers follow land-use strategies that, although economically rational in the short-term, are ecologically damaging. The immigrant peasants, who overcultivate and thereby degrade their small plots to earn needed cash, come into conflict with the wealthy rancher class, which wishes to transform the forests into grazing land for cattle. The peasant/capitalist conflict results in frequent peasant moves along the frontier, which gives rise to the description of their farming system as "shifted cultivation." This whole system is reinforced by a national ideology of "growthmania" that in the Amazon pays only token attention to the environmental consequences of economic expansion, especially by ranches and other commercial enterprises. The theme of inappropriate resource use in "frontier" areas, and its subtle or not so subtle support from the state, also is found in chapters by Moran (Brazil), Lopez (Philippines), Anderson (Philippines), M. Painter (Bolivia), and Bedoya (Peru).

Spooner, in his chapter, reminds us that indigenous uses of the environment are not always harmonious, and that to see them as balanced might be interpreted as a form of ethnocentrism. He identifies such a view as a form of "biocentrism," in which observers place themselves in the role of stewards of someone else's nature. Spooner argues that the analyst needs to examine the perspectives of each actor in the ecosystem—the plant, the animal, and the human—since what may be optimal for one actor may not necessarily be optimal for others. He, like Messerschmidt in a later chapter, places human values and meaning at the core of human ecological studies and asks that we understand the production goals, knowledge, and management techniques of the indigenous people before examining other components of the ecosystem. Traditional Baluch herders of Pakistan, the case study referred to by Spooner, had as a primary production goal the maintenance of those social relationships required to reproduce the system. In this context, conserving resources was not a goal. Whether this necessarily leads to environmental degradation is a matter of some debate and, according to the author, unlikely to be resolved with our present knowledge.

Moran demonstrates that neither local social systems nor microecologies of agrarian systems are well understood by development planners. Using the Amazon basin case, the author shows that considerable local variation in soil, climatic, and vegetation characteristics is obscured when data are aggregated in planning exercises. An agricultural definition of degradation, measured by the loss of agricultural potential in terms of declines in soil fertility, is used to examine farmer settlements and decision-making in the Amazon. Moran examines soil characteristics in detail and establishes criteria for determining the risk of fertility degradation, thereby providing parameters a planner can use to decide whether to open a territory to land clearing. The chapter has wider significance, however, showing relationships among soil and plant characteristics, cultivation techniques, and even history (the Iberian frontier tradition) that make an area prone to degradation. The ecological framework that Moran develops has particular relevance to "new lands" colonization where farmers are resettled with little knowledge of the local ecology and appropriate farming techniques.

The Role of the State

The chapters in the previous section point to the importance of reconciling the role of the state in models of ecological change. Governments can influence agrarian systems and ecology directly, via large-scale infrastructure projects (Horowitz and Salem-Murdock, Salem-Murdock, and Merrey) and settlement programs (Anderson, Lopez, Moran, and Schmink and Wood), or in more subtle ways, through price policies (M. Painter, Bedoya, and Whitney) or the subsidization of certain technical "packages" (T. Painter, Little, and Brush). The chapters in this section examine government and donor-funded projects, programs, and policies that have resulted in environmental change. In many cases, these outside interventions, rather than local management or ecological processes per se, have tilted previous balances toward a more destructive use of the land. Although governments and donors often appear as culprits in this book, there are cases where seemingly sound government- and donor-sponsored efforts to improve natural resource use are under way (Messerschmidt) or being contemplated (T. Painter).

Horowitz and Salem-Murdock explore in their chapter a donor program to retard desertification in White Nile Province, Sudan. They argue that the approach, calling for the introduction of forestry in local grazing systems, is unlikely to succeed without an understanding of the social context of resource abuse supplementing biological information. Resource problems in the study area are of recent origin, following the disruption of a roughly balanced system by rapid population increase, the construction of the Jebel al-Awliya Dam, and the expansion of state-sponsored irrigation. These changes have led to increased demands on the economy, increased social differentiation, and the impoverishment of the majority of the rural population. While formerly the two zones, river banks and sandy uplands, were exploited by agro-pastoralists on a seasonal basis, the dam and associated irrigation displaced herds from the riverine area. Displaced herders, now unable to survive solely on the produce of their herds and millet fields, have settled close to the river to take advantage of new employment opportunities. Their concentration (and the concentration of herds and fields) in the sandy uplands bordering the alluvium has led to degradation and overuse of the land. Echoing a theme of Collins's and Little's chapters, the authors find that diversification of livelihood strategies puts local producers in a bind: they are unable properly to manage their production activities because they have to divert labor and other resources to wage employment, but wage employment is too uncertain and poorly compensated to provide for household reproduction on its own. Given the constriction of their previous territories, it is unlikely that the local population will support the removal of still more land for forestry projects.

Whitney examines, also in the Sudan, the relationship between increased energy demands and rural deforestation. The chapter complements the local-level analysis of forestry issues given by Horowitz and Salem-Murdock, in that it sets out the national context of these issues. Whitney demonstrates that the exploitation of wood for fuel in the Sudan far exceeds the "allowable cut"—the amount that can be cleared and regenerated each year. A considerable portion of forest clearing is related to the need to supply cheap fuel for rapidly growing urban centers that are clearly favored over the rural areas by government policies. Whitney explores a number of alternatives, such as more fuel-efficient cook stoves, but argues that these are at best palliative. His proposal is to tap another locally available resource, an aquatic weed, as a source of energy to replace fuelwood and charcoal. Although unlikely to be a panacea for energy and environmental problems in the Sudan, it does suggest a low-technology solution that might prove appropriate under certain conditions.

T. Painter also addresses land use and environmental problems in semiarid Africa, switching the focus to dryland agriculture in the West African Sahel. Few geographic regions have been characterized in the literature as being more "at risk" than the Sahel. Painter points out, however, that in the case of the sudano-sahelian zone of Niger, agricultural development programs have been uniformly planned and implemented with little concern for natural resources. After the publicity of the 1968–1974 sahelian drought, donor-funded projects were hurriedly pushed through the government system, with little sensitivity to the variety of microecologies and agrarian production systems in the region. The result was the promotion of monolithic productivity packages that were counter-productive even in the short term. Despite a profusion of donor spending in the 1970s and early 1980s, cereal yields per land unit actually declined during the period. What is needed, according to Painter, are locally adjusted conservation techniques to shore up Niger's depleted resource base and bring land back into production.

M. Painter discusses the environmental implications of the San Julian (Bolivia) Colonization Project, arguing that while the project has addressed many of the questions that plague resettlement, problems remain that minimize its success. When analyses examine the project's relationship to the wider regional and national economies, these constraints become apparent. The terms of exchange between the settlers and the national economy are unfavorable, resulting in the overuse of land to counteract declining real agricultural incomes. Farmers are unable to increase production beyond a certain point, due to shortages of labor and capital, and the techniques they do use are environmentally destructive. Exploring themes in Collins' and Horowitz and Salem-Murdock's chapters, Painter shows that the increased impoverishment of the local population diminishes their ability to invest in land improvements.

Changing Rights to Land and Other Resources

Several chapters document the dynamic relationship between land tenure systems and environmental processes. Rapid social and economic change often creates ambiguities over rights to land and other resources, thereby facilitating the conditions for natural resource abuse. Under a context of uncertainty, politically powerful groups, as witnessed in the Philippine examples (Lopez and Anderson), are able to manipulate rules to claim land and overexploit resources. The authors in this section explore the theme of land tenure in natural resource systems, providing evidence of its importance and of cases where recent tenure changes have had dire ecological consequences.

The competition between African herders and farmers for land and water, a recurrent motif in the Africanist literature, is ventilated in the chapter by Little. Using materials from Kenya, he explores three models of land-use conflicts in rangelands: (1) the encroaching farmer; (2) the cultivating herder; and (3) the absentee herd owner. While the second stems from economic pressures to diversify, the first and third models are facilitated by ambiguities over land rights that allow certain groups to control part of the range for private use. Little notes that the problem of the herder/farmer conflict has often been analyzed in terms of farmers taking prime lands from pastoralists, with the result that pastoralists are obliged to overuse the remaining range. This narrow view fails to properly account for land alienation by local elites, for herding and other purposes, and by herders beginning to cultivate, both processes occurring internally (although they are clearly related to events in larger political arenas). These problems of land conflicts—encroaching farmer, cultivating herder, and absentee herd owner—reflect some of the political problems now experienced by pastoralists in Kenya. At the state and regional levels, pastoralists lack the power to stop agriculturalist encroachment or the alienation of range by absentee herders. At a more local level, they are experiencing sedentarization both of the rich stock owners and also of the poor, each for very different reasons but with the same effect—local rangelands are being overused. In his conclusion, Little examines some of the policy options that are available to alleviate land use conflicts in Kenya.

Ibrahim also explores the theme of pastoral/agricultural land use, in this case with reference to the Sudan. He argues that changes in farming practices, particularly sedentarization by herders and the transgression of the agronomic boundary, are as much to blame for the 1984–85 drought disaster in the Sudan as the rainfall deficit. Huge areas of savanna woodland have recently been cleared for large-scale mechanized farming, while the population has expanded greatly and requires more land to feed itself. As a result of these changes, excessive cultivation, based on traditional techniques, is occurring around permanent water points in semi-arid areas— those areas where rainfall is too low to consistently support millet farming and where soils when denuded of vegetation are susceptible to deflation and water erosion. Pastoralists, in turn, are forced into even more marginal habitats where overgrazing is now occurring. Thus, the people of the central Sudan face a paradox. They are hungry because they do not control enough food. As a result, they are compelled to do the very thing, that is to plant millet beyond the agronomic boundary, that will degrade their resources and reduce their future yields.

The chapter by Lopez looks at the political context of land tenure changes on the Philippine island of Palawan. Many of the island's land use problems derive from a highly differentiated tenure system that favors immigrants, large-scale farmers, and private and public corporations at the expense of indigenous peoples whose ancestral rights to land are not legally acknowledged, and who are compelled to intensify their swidden systems on remaining land, thereby facilitating erosive processes. Government policy, by classifying their lands as public domain, legitimizes settler and other encroachment. Thus Palawan has become the "frontier" for Philippine society, comparable to what the Amazon has been for Brazil (see Moran and Schmink and Wood). Only recently the Palaw'an, under the instigation of a Peace Corps Volunteer, have tried to fend off encroachment by the establishment of land-leasing community foundations. In 1985 one foundation was seeking a communal land lease that could serve in the future as a legal/organizational model for other Palaw'an communities.

Anderson also examines land tenure and use problems in the Philippines, paying particular attention to deforestation in the uplands and coastal zone. He describes the disruptive policies of the Marcos regime that allowed indiscriminate clear-cutting of forests by individuals and corporations, forced swidden farmers to abandon shifting cultivation, and denied tribal peoples their customary rights to land. Supplementing Lopez's discussion of Palawan land use problems, Anderson draws on social and environmental data from several different regions of the Philippines, including Luzon, Negros, and Panay. While cautious in assessments of future trends, he points to recent changes in national leadership and national forestry programs (that currently emphasize agroforestry systems) as positive signs for small farmers and for those concerned about the environment.

Local Management Strategies

Farmers, herders, and other rural producers possess a wealth of knowledge about local ecology, a variety of strategies for surviving under stressful conditions, and a range of institutions for overcoming labor and other resource shortages. These knowledges, strategies, and institutions influence, to a great extent, how local people manage their physical environment. The chapters in this section explore the richness and variety of local management systems, many of them currently under considerable stress. An important theme of these chapters is the inherent tension between local systems and those regional, national, and international interests that wish to transform them.

Brush documents the process by which Andean farmers of Peru have been able to maintain a relatively stable production system under conditions of population increase, rapid economic change, and outmigration. He suggests that the capacity of mountain ecozones to sustain large numbers of producers has been underestimated, and that the "claimed" widespread environmental degradation of the Andes is not substantiated by existing data. By analyzing one key component of the Andean agricultural system—potato production—he shows that the diversity of species and management practices makes problematic general statements about the effects of steep slope farming on the environment. Certain traditional practices of Andean farmers, like "sectoral" fallowing, conserve the environment, while others are damaging.

Brush recommends that agricultural development programs in the Andes implement technologies that incorporate the traditional practices of diversity, zonal differentiation, and communal management.

Bedoya also discusses agriculture in Peru, but with a specific focus on soil erosion and deforestation in Peru's upper Huallaga valley. This is an area of the upper jungle that has experienced massive farmer settlement along three frontiers: Tingo Maria (1940s and 1950s), Aucayacu (1960s), and Tocache and Uchiza (1970s). To measure land use problems in these three frontier areas, Bedoya employs an index of soil-use intensity that distinguishes between intensive and extensive farming systems. The shortening of fallow periods in response to land shortage, and shifts to such lucrative crops as tea, coffee, and coca result in the overuse of certain agricultural lands, and the need to clear-cut protected forest areas. Bedoya concludes that future calculations of land available for settlement should exclude forested areas.

Nyerges brings our attention to the West African savanna, arguing for a reevaluation of the region's ecology and development potential. In contrast to the view of policy-makers, including those at the World Bank, the Guinea savanna is not capable of absorbing large numbers of immigrants from drought-prone zones such as the sahel. The presence of tsetse and black flies (the vectors for trypanosomiasis and onchocerciasis, respectively), erratic rainfall, and low soil fertility inhibit large-scale agricultural settlement. Nyerges suggests that development programs build on already existing technologies and production potentials of resident populations, rather than advocate new settlements and agricultural systems.

In her chapter on the New Halfa irrigation scheme, Salem-Murdock suggests that the differential production goals of different social classes are responsible for widespread water and soil degradation in the area. While serious environmental changes are going on in terms of water supply, other degradation is caused by the wealthy in this area, who have preempted most of the resources and are exploiting them for short-term gain. Their practice is to mine rented land until it is depleted and then to rent new land. The social differentiation in the area, which is the basis of many of the scheme's problems, predates the scheme but has been accelerated by it. Salem-Murdock reflects a theme of Wood and Schmink's, as well as of other chapters in the book, that the different interests of classes, in terms of land use and conservation, have to be taken into account in land-use planning and development programs.

Like the Sudan, Pakistan has some of the largest irrigation schemes in the world, many of which are facing problems of reduced water supply and salinization. Merrey, in his chapter on the Indus basin, discusses these problems in the context of a village where he conducted long-term fieldwork. He points to the presence of a highly centralized management structure, unable to respond to local needs and problems, as a major cause of irrigation problems in the area. Using a model derived from systems theory and originally applied to ancient hydraulic civilizations, he finds that centralization of water controls in the Indus basin results in supply fluctuations, causing waterlogging and salinization. Because water supply decisions are under the control of engineers 200 km from the farms, the system is not based on farmer demands for water but rather on supply directives issued out of Lahore. The system at the local level is inherently unstable because management does not respond to local ecological problems.

Messerschmidt analyzes forest degradation in Nepal, where the rate of deforestation is now proceeding at 25 percent per decade. He attributes the cause of degradation to a combination of flawed forest policies, population pressure, and a fragile environment. Drawing on his work as an anthropologist for a community forestry program in the country, he argues that the most hopeful management options are based on incorporation of indigenous management techniques. This can be achieved through a method of "village dialogue" that solicits the knowledge of local leaders and farmers, local organizations, and traditional rules regulating forest use, in the planning of forestry programs. He provides considerable detail on local management techniques and ethnographic method by which they can be discovered and incorporated. Messerschmidt paints an optimistic picture of what can be done to arrest environmental deterioration in the Third World when local knowledge and resources are used.

A Final Note

A recurrent theme of this volume is that environmental decline in the Third World is intricately related to problems of land tenure, poverty, and ill-advised policies and development programs. An anthropological analysis of natural resource abuse concerns itself as much with rules and policies governing access to resources, as it does with their actual use. A first step toward addressing the situation is to improve our understandings of its causes, consequences, and nature. The chapters do not provide immediate solutions to environmental deterioration in the Third World. They do offer data and suggest analyses that might lead to more sensible policies and programs for environmental action, and they demonstrate the perils that result when such socioeconomic materials are ignored.

Notes

1. "When Max Gluckman reviewed [Richard's] book . . . he praised *Hunger and Work* and *Land, Labour and Diet*, particularly for isolating and highlighting the most acute problem for Bemba women, that of contingency planning under dearth conditions during the long and dangerous weeks before the new millet ripened annually" (Gladstone 1986:342).

2. Exceptions are found among the more consistently idealistic anthropologists, such as Edmund Leach, who has recently reiterated his objection to the search for historic and economic patterns or regularities: "There are no 'laws' of historical process; there are no 'laws' of sociological probability. . . . Anthropologists who

imagine that, by the exercise of reason, they can reduce the observations of the ethnographers to a nomothetic natural science are wasting their time" (1982:51–52).

3. One writer notes that during the 1950s the U.S. International Cooperation Administration was the largest employer of anthropologists in America, but by the early 1970s "only a handful remained" (Hoben 1982:354).

References

Barth, F.
   1961   Nomads of South Persia. Bulletin No. 8. Oslo: Universitets Ethnografiske Museum.
Blaikie, P.
   1984   The Political Economy of Soil Erosion in Developing Countries. London: Longman.
Boserup, E.
   1965   Conditions of Agricultural Growth. Chicago, IL: Aldine.
Bourgeot, A.
   1981   Pasture in the Malian Gourma: Habitation by Humans and Animals. *In* The Future of Pastoral Peoples. J. Galaty, D. Aronson, P. Salzman, and A. Chouinard, eds. Pp. 165–182. Ottawa: International Development Research Centre.
Bunker, S.
   1985   Underdeveloping the Amazon: Extraction, Unequal Exchange, and the Failure of the Modern State. Urbana, IL: University of Illinois Press.
Childe, V. G.
   1951   Man Makes Himself. New York, NY: New American Library.
Collins, J.
   1984   The Maintenance of Peasant Coffee Production in a Peruvian Valley. American Ethnologist 11:413–438.
Dourojeanni, M.
   1984   Potencial y Uso de los Recursos Naturales: Consideraciones Metodológicas. *In* Población y Colonización en la Alta Amazonía Peruana. Consejo Nacional de Población and Centro de Investigación y Promoción Amazónica, eds. Pp. 110–121. Lima: Consejo Nacional de Población and Centro de Investigación y Promoción Amazónica.
Forde, C. D.
   1963   Habitat, Economy, and Society: A Geographic Introduction to Ethnology. New York, NY: E.P. Dutton and Co.
Gladstone, J.
   1986   Significant Sister: Autonomy and Obligation in Audrey Richard's Early Fieldwork. American Ethnologist 13:338–362.
Hecht, S.
   1984   Cattle Ranching in Amazonia: Political and Ecological Considerations. *In* Frontier Expansion in Amazonia. M. Schmink and C. Wood, eds. Pp. 366–398. Gainesville, FL: University of Florida Press.
Herskovits, M.
   1951   Man and His Works. New York, NY: Alfred A. Knopf.
Hoben, A.
   1982   Anthropologists and Development. *In* Annual Review of Anthropology. Volume 11. B. J. Siegel, A. R. Beals, and S. A. Tyler, eds. Pp. 349–375. Palo Alto, CA: Annual Reviews Inc.

Horowitz, M. M
  1979   The Sociology of Pastoralism and African Livestock Projects. AID Program Evaluation Report No. 4. Washington, DC: Agency for International Development.
  1986   Ideology, Policy, and Praxis in Pastoral Livestock Development. *In* The Anthropology of Rural Development in West Africa. M. Horowitz and T. Painter, eds. Pp. 251–272. Boulder, CO: Westview Press.
Horowitz, M. M, and P. D. Little
  1986   African Pastoralism and Poverty: Some Implications for Drought and Famine. *In* Drought and Hunger in Africa: Denying Famine a Future. M. Glantz, ed. Cambridge: Cambridge University Press, forthcoming.
Horowitz, M. M, and T. Painter
  1986   Introduction: Anthropology and Development. *In* The Anthropology of Rural Development in West Africa. M. M Horowitz and T. Painter, eds. Pp. 1–8. Boulder, CO: Westview Press.
Kroeber, A. L.
  1939   Cultural and Natural Areas of Native North America. University of California Publications in American Archaeology and Ethnology 48:1–242.
Leach, E.
  1982   Social Anthropology. New York and London: Oxford University Press.
Marx, K.
  1973   Grundrisse (translated by M. Nicolaus from the 1857–1858 edition). London: Penguin Books.
Meillassoux, C.
  1975   Femmes, Greniers et Capitaux. Paris: Librairie François Maspero.
Moran, E. F., ed.
  1983   The Dilemma of Amazonian Development. Boulder, CO: Westview Press.
O'Brien, J.
  1983   The Political Economy of Capitalist Agriculture in the Central Rangelands of Sudan. Labor, Capital and Society 16:8–32.
Oliver-Smith, A.
  1986   The Martyred City: Death and Rebirth in the Andes. Albuquerque, NM: University of New Mexico Press.
Richards, A.
  1932   Hunger and Work in a Savage Tribe: A Functional Study of Nutrition among the Southern Bantu. London: Routledge and Kegan Paul.
  1939   Land, Labour and Diet in Northern Rhodesia: An Economic Study of the Bemba Tribe. London: Oxford University Press.
Sandford, S.
  1983   Management of Pastoral Development in the Third World. Chichester: John Wiley & Sons.
Scudder, T.
  1962   The Ecology of the Gwembe Tonga. Manchester: Manchester University Press.
Spooner, B., and H. S. Mann, eds.
  1982   Desertification and Development: Dryland Ecology in Social Perspective. London: Academic Press.
Steward, J.
  1938   Basin-Plateau Aboriginal Sociopolitical Groups. Washington, DC: United States Government Printing Office (US Bureau of American Ethnology. Bulletin 120).

   1963   Theory of Culture Change. Urbana, IL: University of Illinois Press.

Thomson, J. T.
   1985   The Politics of Desertification in Marginal Environments: The Sahelian Case. *In* Divesting Nature's Capital. H. J. Leonard, ed. Pp. 227–262. New York, NY: Holmes and Meier.

Wissler, C.
   1938   The American Indian: An Introduction to the Anthropology of the New World. 3rd Edition. New York, NY: Oxford University Press.

White, L.
   1949   The Science of Culture: A Study of Man and Civilization. New York, NY: Grove Press.

PART ONE

Models of Resource Management

1

Labor Scarcity
and Ecological Change

Jane L. Collins

Introduction

Six years ago, at a conference on Production on Hill Lands in Latin America, economist Carmen Diana Deere and anthropologist Robert Wasserstrom suggested that the vast majority of smallholding producers in Latin America were part-time farmers who divided their productive activity between their lands and animals and a variety of off-farm, income-generating activities. They argued that while off-farm sources of income were important to all farmers who participated in these activities, they were particularly significant for the poorest stratum of peasants. The question raised by their analysis, and addressed to a broad audience of policy-makers, was: should development programs—and particularly those on less fertile lands—emphasize a policy of employment, or one that builds on the capacities of smallholders as farmers? It was their contention that labor invested in the improvement of agricultural productivity would come at the expense of a decline in income from waged employment or commercial activity (Deere and Wasserstrom 1980).

The policy issue raised by Deere and Wasserstrom has been frequently addressed but not resolved. It turns on questions related to the availability of labor in rural areas, and the nature of processes of economic change occurring in these contexts. It forces anthropologists to test their theories of peasant economy, rural class structure, and the value of labor to peasant households, against the difficult realities of semiproletarianization. Most importantly, it requires a careful look at models of social change that have implicitly linked "participatory" development to small-scale technologies and labor-intensive cultivation.

This chapter examines the significance of processes of semi-proletarianization[1] for ecological change. It seeks to identify crucial linkages between problems of labor availability and destructive land-management strategies. It also attempts to identify questions that must be answered when we introduce technological improvements and conservation measures in smallholder agriculture.

The chapter begins by defining the nature of the labor scarcity that affects many contemporary rural communities, and examines its relationship to strategies of economic diversification, seasonal and temporary migration, and the terms of trade faced by rural households. The second section examines the major debates over labor availability that have emerged in the work of economists and anthropologists concerned with rural development. In reviewing these debates, the lack of congruence between models of labor dynamics and empirical studies is striking, and the role of particular models in justifying specific agricultural or agrarian policies is revealed. The remainder of the chapter identifies the policy dilemmas that arise in attempts to introduce conservation measures when peasants are "part-time" farmers. In addition to presenting briefly a case study from the eastern slopes of the Peruvian Andes, it draws on the experience of two recent attempts to introduce improved land management techniques to rural producers—one in Jamaica and the other in Peru.

In view of the frequent assumption that labor is the resource most freely available to small farmers in developing nations, the questions raised in this chapter may seem to contradict some of our basic intuitions about the nature of rural poverty. Yet a careful reading of the available literature reveals that the crises of reproduction increasingly experienced by rural households in many parts of the world involve a complex relationship between declining terms of trade, intensification of production, and migration and off-farm labor. As producers attempt to maintain constant levels of income and to allocate labor between new and old forms of economic activity, ecological decline is not an uncommon result (Bernstein 1977). Individual decisions designed to insure sufficient income from year to year may have negative effects when multiplied by large numbers of producers and taken over the long-term. For this reason, theories of labor availability or demographic trends framed at the national level can provide only a part of the picture needed to explain the relationship between labor dynamics and ecological decline in rural areas, and must be supplemented by the analysis of producer decisions at the local level.

The Nature of Labor Scarcity in Rural Areas

Deere and Wasserstrom based their analysis on ten empirical studies investigating the income base of small farmers in Latin America. The average percentages of income derived from off-farm salaried employment in the studies they reviewed ranged from 6 percent in one study conducted in Colombia to 89 percent in Chamula, Mexico. Five of the ten studies showed more than 50 percent of income to be derived, on the average, from off-farm employment, and seven showed an average income from wages of 30 percent or more. The proportion of income from off-farm salaries was highest for families whose plots were characterized as *minifundio*, and dropped markedly for higher income families (1980:155). In Bolivia, for example, only 27 percent of total income was derived from agriculture on farms of one hectare or less, as compared to 67 percent on properties of more than 5 hectares (ibid.:157).

Wage work is not, however, the only activity that takes peasants off the farm. Numerous studies have documented the multiplicity of activities in which many rural households engage. Deere and de Janvry (1979) found that northern Peruvian peasants obtained nearly half (48.6 percent) of income from the sale of labor power, 12.5 percent from commerce, 7.1 percent from artisanry, and 7.5 percent from remittances sent by family members. Only the remaining one-quarter of income was provided by agriculture and animal husbandry (ibid.:607). In the southern highlands of Peru, Figueroa found that the average family obtained 14 percent of monetary income from the sale of crops, 23 percent from sale of livestock, 23 percent from artisanry and commerce, and 40 percent from the sale of labor power (1984:49).

This diversification of activities represents an attempt on the part of rural families to increase levels of income absolutely, as well as to accommodate the risk inherent in individual activities. Speaking of southern Peru, Guillet (1981:12) noted:

> Another mechanism for reducing risk is based on the need to control variability across sectors of the economy. One finds, in this regard, the combination within households of several forms of productive activity in addition to "classically" peasant production. These forms include: seasonal labor for wage opportunities in highland cities, coastal cities and colonization zones in the humid tropics. Others include the sale of dairy products, taxi and trucking enterprises, cattle fattening, pig breeding, artisanry and a host of other small-scale activities. . . . It is a major means of spreading risk across economic sectors and geographical space and securing alternative sources of income.

Economic diversification does serve to increase income and to mitigate risk. The fact that integration into a poorly paid seasonal labor force can solve problems for peasants explains in part their compliance with an exploitative system. Nevertheless, recognition of these facts does little to explain the circumstances under which a diversified subsistence strategy becomes necessary, the way in which rural families become involved in specific types of activities, or the impact of their participation on institutions and communities. Diversification strategies are often devised in response to crises, providing income to meet short-term subsistence needs.

Land pressure is an important trend related to the search for off-farm employment. In a comprehensive survey of landlessness and near-land-lessness in Latin America, Lassen (1980:11–12) provides illustrative data. Her calculations of landless and near-landless families as a proportion of rural households ranged from 55 percent in Costa Rica to 85 percent in Guatemala and Bolivia. Excluding the landless population, and calculating only the percentage of farms too small to support a family, Lassen found rates that ranged from 22 percent in Brazil to 93 percent in Peru. The figure exceeded 50 percent in Colombia, Ecuador, Venezuela, El Salvador, Guatemala, Honduras, the Dominican Republic, and pre-revolutionary Nicaragua.

While land scarcity and labor scarcity might appear to be in contradiction, they actually may occur together. First, land scarcity may arise from processes of land transfer and encroachment as well as demographic growth. Secondly, whatever the cause of land scarcity, the downward pressure it exerts on household income may force productive members into other activities, or to leave rural areas permanently. There is no guarantee that demographic growth and rural exodus will balance one another in the end. The latter depends on a complex of factors including the availability and reliability of alternative work, the skills such work requires and the possibilities of acquiring them, the recruitment and employment practices of industries involved, cultural definitions and expectations of work, and a range of market forces. Stier (1977) has described the twin dynamic of population increase and labor migration in a Cuna community of Panama, and the negative impacts that excessive out-migration has had on agriculture.

Another factor that may force rural families to diversify their production is the decline in the terms of trade they experience. A variety of secular economic trends as well as specific policy measures make it highly likely that, over time, small farmers will experience a relative decline in the prices received for their production compared to those they must pay for consumer goods and inputs. This is particularly true if one considers the relationship of price to the labor embodied in a product. When faced with this dilemma, a family's options are limited. They may intensify production insofar as labor resources are available. They may decrease consumption. Or they may seek to diversify production in order to maintain constant levels of income (Bernstein 1977).

All forms of diversification obviously do not have the same impact on rural households. The activities adopted require different levels of labor investment and of skill, which means that they may draw on the family's diverse labor resources in different ways. Children can peddle food and gather grasses for basketry, for example, while the elderly may weave and spin and take over tasks of child care.

Migration has the greatest potential effect on rural households, since it actually removes productive members for some length of time. The migratory process may take a range of forms, from permanent exodus, to seasonal movements tied to the demands of industry and agriculture, to temporary trips designed to provide quick cash in a crisis. Temporary and seasonal migration may be engaged in freely, or may be motivated by the solicitations of labor recruiters who often use debt obligations as a means of procuring workers (Bedoya 1982; Scott 1976). Seasonal migration almost inevitably requires reallocation and adjustment of productive responsibilities (Brush 1977; Deere 1976; Collins 1986).

In a recent attempt to introduce soil conservation measures as part of an Integrated Rural Development project in Jamaica, researchers noted that 20 percent of the farmers secured the bulk of their livelihood through non-agricultural means. Thirty-four percent labored off-farm as their principal source of income (USAID 1978a:95). Labor was mentioned as a constraint to production, even by owners of very small farms of less than one acre (USAID 1978b:102). Project personnel suggested that "any program of expansion of output that requires additional labor is likely to encounter labor problems" (ibid.:95). In a similar vein, an attempt to reintroduce techniques for terracing hillsides in Peruvian communities was forced to consider that "the Peruvian farmer is weighed down by a multiplicity of possible activities: commerce, artisanry, seasonal wage labor in mining and construction, etc." (USAID 1984a[2]:2).

The recognition of these problems allows us to pose a series of questions for policy. Is it possible that, as actions are taken to improve production and marketing conditions, labor will be drawn back in to rural communities, and the less lucrative of off-farm activities will be left aside? Or does the attempt to improve the productive base of small farmers simply perpetuate their poverty, slowing their movement into more rapidly growing spheres of the economy? In order to address these issues, it will be helpful to review a few of the models that have shaped current thought on the role of rural labor in developing economies and to examine the bases of their assumptions.

Visions of Labor Surplus and Scarcity in Agricultural Research

The debate over labor surplus and scarcity began with the publication of "Economic Development with Unlimited Supplies of Labour" by W. A. Lewis in 1954. In this article, Lewis was doing more than proposing a pre-existing "natural" surplus of labor in developing economies. He was establishing a model of dual economy in developing nations that would pervade economic thinking for years to come. Lewis' basic proposition was that the economies of developing nations could be viewed as possessing two sectors. The first was a low productivity subsistence sector, where both the intensity and remuneration of labor were determined by custom or "tradition," and where there was no reliance on hired labor or the use of reproducible capital. The second was a more productive modern capitalist sector. In the traditional sector, according to Lewis:

> population is so large relative to capital and natural resources that there are large sectors of the economy where the marginal productivity of labour is negligible, zero or even negative. . . . The family holding is so small that if some members of the family obtained other employment, the remaining members could cultivate the holding just as well (of course they would have to work harder) (1954:141).

Because of this situation, Lewis reasoned that rural areas could provide a steady stream of unskilled labor for nascent industry. Individuals would seek urban employment as long as the wage rate in the capitalist sector was some 30–50 percent higher than their conventional subsistence income.

Because of the size of population relative to resources, this transfer of labor could be accomplished without reducing levels of production in the subsistence sector.

Lewis' model has been subjected to three kinds of criticisms over the years. First, agricultural economists have faulted him for his implicit neglect of agriculture as a motive force in economic growth. It was clearly Lewis' assumption that growth would be concentrated in the industrial sector, with agriculture's share of the economy progressively declining.

A second set of criticisms have been methodological/empirical in nature, and they have attempted to determine, through various kinds of measurements, whether a surplus of labor "actually exists" in agriculture. Most of these studies have proceeded by calculating the labor requirements of various crops per hectare, multiplying by the number of hectares, and dividing by the available labor force in a community or region. As Brush (1977), Connell and Lipton (1977), and Maletta (1978) have noted, many of the initial attempts at such measurement were crude and unrealistic. They did not consider the many subsidiary tasks necessary for the reproduction of family and community such as maintenance of infrastructure and tools, craft production, the keeping of barnyard stock, as well as daily tasks of water and firewood collection, cooking, child care, and walking to and from fields. They also ignored socially necessary investments of labor in community meetings or labor projects, rituals and festivals, and other forms of service.

In recent years, a greater sophistication in measurement of labor inputs has been achieved. In particular, there has been a movement away from the use of culture-bound notions of employment and "underemployment" and toward more flexible and culturally relevant measures of labor utilization (Connell and Lipton 1977). Nevertheless, even with relatively crude measurement procedures, early researchers often found labor requirements in agriculture to be high relative to available labor supply (Warriner 1955; Paglin 1965; CEEB 1970; Hopper 1965; Mathur 1964).

Some researchers attempted to test the notion that labor could be removed from agriculture without decreasing productivity by looking at historical instances where a large proportion of the rural labor force had in fact been removed by events such as famine or epidemic. This was the approach of Schultz (1964) and of examples cited by Boserup (1965). Both of these authors concluded that the removal of labor led to productivity decline, and in Boserup's examples, to a reversion to less intensive methods of cultivation.[2] A review of attempts to measure labor availability produced in the 1960s concluded:

> To date there is little reliable evidence to support the existence of more than token—five percent—disguised unemployment in underdeveloped countries as defined by a zero marginal product of labor and the condition of *ceteris paribus* (Kao et al. 1964:141).

A third criticism of Lewis' model has been based on evidence of a more historical nature. The dual-sector model assumes that labor surplus in subsistence production becomes significant with the emergence of a labor market. Expansion in the capitalist sector continues until earnings in the two sectors are equated. The movement of labor from agriculture to industry is viewed as part of a spontaneous and beneficial process that rationalizes the allocation of productive forces and results exclusively from the free choice of individuals in the marketplace.

Researchers such as Arrighi (1970) and Scott (1976) have challenged the notion that labor dynamics in developing economies are determined solely by market mechanisms. These authors argue that under colonialism, the creation of a labor market was accomplished through a variety of open and concealed forms of compulsion. Contrary to Lewis' suggestion, they say that labor supplies available to the industrial sector actually moved from a condition of scarcity in early periods of capitalist development, to one of abundance in later years. This was a result not of market forces, but of a variety of extra-economic measures designed to "free" labor from subsistence production and to create practices of wage employment.

The historical critique, in revealing the social and political forces that have shaped labor availability in the past, raises questions about how such extra-economic forces affect contemporary rural communities. Political repression, debt bondage, and racial, cultural, and gender-based barriers to economic participation still shape the opportunities for rural households. The intervention of the state in production or commercialization—or the monopolization of aspects of these processes by elites—is not unusual, but is the norm in many rural areas. Finally, new types of economic activities may bring into play divergent definitions of work, the workday, and of acceptable conditions of labor. All of these factors shape the "availability" of labor.

Because the labor-surplus hypothesis incurred powerful critiques, the ensuing debate generated new insights into rural labor dynamics. Much discussion emerged, for example, around the issue of the seasonality of labor inputs in agriculture. Early observers were uncertain whether an "appropriate" year-round labor force should be calculated on the basis of levels necessary to meet peak demands, or whether the "seasonal unemployment" this would imply was a negative factor. The work of Rosenstein-Rodan (1957) was influential in distinguishing between "removable" and "fractional" disguised underemployment. In the case of the former, unused labor was concentrated in sufficiently large blocks of time that it could be withdrawn for productive purposes. Fractional disguised underemployment, on the other hand, represented idle hours or days scattered unpredictably throughout the year. This kind of "idleness" did not provide a basis for the removal of productive workers.

A second issue clarified by the debate was related to the ceteris paribus conditions imposed on models of the agricultural sector by early economists. These models were built on the assumption that both technology and labor investments in agriculture would be unchanging. Works like that of Boserup (1965) demonstrated that techniques of agricultural production were altered under population pressure—even in the absence of technological advances—

and that these changes could imply a heavier utilization of labor in the rural environment. The Green Revolution technologies of the 1960s and 1970s, with their supposed characteristics of divisibility and scale neutrality, further fueled the notion that rural agricultural regimes could, in the course of their development, absorb even greater quantities of labor.

Development Policy and Visions of Labor Availability

Divergent visions of the rural labor situation supported radically different kinds of policy measures. Lewis' initial work, and those that built upon it in the 1950s, provided a theoretical basis for investment in the industrial sector. They did so by promising a cheap and easily available labor supply for urban-industrial growth and by denying the productive potential of agriculture. With the establishment of the first large agricultural research centers in the 1960s, new theories were needed that supported investments in rural areas. Schultz (1964) assisted in this endeavor by providing a vision of the rural cultivator as "efficient-but-poor," and argued that the development of new technologies for small farmers would bring significant efficiencies.

The labor surplus debate thus provided a forum for arguing the relative merits of what have been called "peasant-biased" and "landlord-biased" improvements in agriculture. The use of heavy machinery and mechanized processing was supported by the view that labor in rural areas was scarce, potentially scarce, or at least not as abundant as had previously been suggested. Bedoya (1981), for example, describes how claims of labor scarcity supported the purchase of large tractors for land clearing in the Peruvian *selva* despite the destructive impact of such equipment on tropical soils. The links between theory and policy were more complex than this, however. As Jorgensen (1969) has pointed out, arguments asserting rural underemployment could be used to support land reform, and assertions to the contrary could serve to deny its necessity. Intentionally and unintentionally, theories of labor availability fueled a debate over who, within the context of rural class structure, should be supported by development programs and policies.

Models of labor surplus persisted in the 1960s and 1970s despite the growing empirical evidence that it was not a significant feature of rural economies. In part, this could be explained by the visibility of world population growth and by the overpopulation observable at national levels. It was difficult for researchers to separate the fact of demographic growth over large regions from the demographic and production dynamics of rural communities. Given the high rates of population growth in developing nations, it seemed inconceivable that complex interrelationships between population growth and population movement could give rise to regionally and temporally specific problems of labor scarcity.

Most importantly, a link was established between the empirical question of labor availability and questions related to the scale of development.

Notions of abundant labor provided support for models of peasant-based, small-scale development that many researchers and groups felt to be the most viable strategy for improving agricultural production. A vision of labor surplus thus became tied to those approaches to development that promoted labor-using, rather than labor-saving technologies.[3]

The Seasonal Migration of Aymara Cultivators

The kinds of knowledge required accurately to assess rural labor availability, and the kinds of problems that can arise in the course of such work, can be illustrated by a case drawn from fieldwork conducted in the southern Peruvian department of Puno in 1980.[4] The Aymara-speaking farmers who live on the northern shore of Lake Titicaca practice the intensive cultivation of hardy high-altitude crops. About one-third of the region's population supplements its agricultural production by growing coffee on the eastern slopes of the Andes. Others become involved in wage labor and commerce in the southern highlands, or migrate seasonally to the Peruvian coast. The Aymara represent a case where the diversification of economic activities on and off the farm has stretched labor resources to the limit.

It is not difficult to understand why the Aymara have adopted off-farm economic activities. Their lands are quite small (averaging less than one hectare of cultivable land per family) and they face unfavorable markets for the sale of their highland produce. They took up lowland coffee cultivation in the 1930s—in response to a decline in markets for wool and food and to social conflicts in the region that gave rise to repression and violence against rural cultivators. While the search of Aymara families for off-farm productive opportunities is not difficult to explain, two related questions have proven more challenging. Why do the families involved not settle permanently on their coffee lands in the lowland valleys, and why—in contrast to their careful land management techniques in the highlands— do they use their coffee lands in a manner that leads to rapid deterioration? The answers to these two questions are closely related and reveal the linkages between terms of trade with the larger economy, labor scarcity, and processes of ecological decline.

While the soils of the eastern slopes of the Peruvian Andes are chemically poor, their physical condition has been described by soil scientists as adequate, and as exhibiting a well-developed structure permitting good aeration and rapid water absorption. Sustained yields of perennial crops should be possible when producers apply soil management techniques that diversify species, maintain soil cover, and provide for the restoration of soil fertility (Ríos 1979). Nevertheless, highland Aymara cultivators have not implemented basic practices of soil conservation. They monocrop their coffee, without providing the necessary shade; they do not intercrop annuals to maintain soil cover; and they weed extensively around the coffee bushes twice a year, leaving the soil virtually bare. Significant soil erosion has resulted, and migrants have already been forced to abandon their coffee plots in the higher reaches of the lowland valley.

The Aymara do not lack knowledge of principles of lowland cultivation; they have been producing in Tambopata for more than three generations, and before that time many families worked on rented land or as wage laborers in the lowland valleys of northern Bolivia. They do not lack the inclination to conserve soil resources in their home communities, where they practice techniques of plowing, terracing, irrigation, and fertilization. A careful assessment of their labor investments over an annual cycle, however, reveals that most migrant households are currently using their labor resources to the limits of availability. Given the intensive nature of agricultural production in the highlands, greater investments of labor in coffee cultivation are not possible (Collins 1984).

The failure of families to give up their highland plots for permanent residence in the lowlands can be traced to the action of market forces and government policies in recent history. A shift to settlement was actually under way for a brief period in the 1950s, but was undercut by a series of events. First, producers began to question the security of their claims to land when the government declared its land records a shambles and required all cultivators to have their plots resurveyed and to resubmit their petitions for title. Second, the world market price of coffee dropped sharply in 1960 from the levels maintained throughout the 1950s. Third and most importantly, in 1962, the government supported the establishment of a marketing cooperative that subsequently took charge of the commercialization of coffee, and which gave the state indirect control over coffee prices, transport, the amount of land that could be cultivated, and credit availability.

The convergence of these three factors made it impossible for families to obtain incomes from coffee production that were sufficient (and sufficiently secure) to maintain themselves throughout an annual cycle and to reproduce themselves over time. Thus, they retained coffee production as an off-farm component of their highland-based productive system. While the potential income from highland crops was always lower than that from coffee sales, the former provided a secure food supply that could be supplemented by more highly remunerative off-farm activities (Painter 1984).

Today, members of highland families travel to lowland valleys during the three to four months of the dry season and for brief periods after their highland crops are in the ground. These absences have made highland production more difficult for those who remain, straining relationships of labor exchange within kin groups and communities (Collins 1986). They have resulted in a decline in ritual and ceremonial participation and in the production of craft goods—a phenomenon noted earlier by Brush (1977) for northern Peru. The degree to which these stresses will undermine the long-term viability of highland production is not yet known.

The most immediate consequence of the overtaxing of labor resources has been the lack of attention to soil conservation in the lowlands. Because of their short periods of lowland residence, the Aymara cannot cultivate annual crops along with their coffee. Because they are only in the valley for brief periods, they attempt to control secondary growth through intensive weedings at these times. Appropriately diversified agroforestry systems would require investments of labor that are simply not available to them. Thus, the destruction of valley soils continues—over half of the lands suitable for coffee production have already been exhausted. Not only is a potentially important productive region rendered unusable, but highland families are losing an important component of their diversified productive regimen.

It is easier to explain the decisions already made by small-scale producers than to predict the direction of change. Understanding the role played by labor scarcity in this situation makes it clear that the introduction of conservation practices in the lowlands will not succeed unless coffee income can be raised to meet socially determined subsistence requirements, making full-time residence in the valley possible. Producers would also have to be assured that the government would not again revoke their titles, and cropping systems would have to be diversified so that families would not be completely dependent on the world market price of a single commodity. What we do not know, however, is the level to which incomes would have to be raised in order to make this an attractive option; and the degree of risk that families would find acceptable, given the fact that they would be relinquishing direct control over their food supply. These are the kinds of questions that currently require analysis based on an understanding of the diversified productive regimens of small farm families, and of the labor requirements that these regimens impose.

Soil Conservation in Jamaica and Peru: Policy Dilemmas

Two cases in which development agencies have attempted to introduce soil conservation measures to rural producers provide an opportunity to evaluate their experience in terms of labor availability: The Government of Jamaica/USAID Second Integrated Rural Development Project conducted in the Two Meetings and Pindars River watershed areas from 1977 to 1983; and The Peru Soil Conservation Project, which supports the construction of soil-conserving terraces in eleven regions of Peru. This project was initiated in 1980 and should continue through 1986. Both projects provide ample documentation of labor availability.

Integrated Rural Development in Jamaica

The goal of the Two Meetings/Pindars River project was to improve the standard of living of small hillside farmers in rural Jamaica. Its philosophy was that if productivity could be improved, and soil loss decreased, farm labor could be more fully utilized and young people would be attracted back into agriculture. The soil conservation component of the Integrated Rural Development Project (IRDP) promoted the construction of a variety of forms of terraces and drainage systems over 17,700 acres.

An evaluation of the project by Blustain (1982) revealed the cost of these measures to be quite high. Machine-built terraces cost approximately 1100

Jamaican dollars per acre,[5] and hand-built terraces from J$1249 to J$2800 (including the cost of hired labor). Maintenance costs also proved to be a problem. Maintenance of two acres of appropriately configured landscape would require an annual investment of 49 days of labor, or J$392. Blustain notes:

> It could be argued that there are times of the year when there is little agricultural work to be done and when the farmer's own opportunity cost is close to zero; these seasons, it could be claimed, would be good times to spend on maintenance. Yet most of the repair work is required during the rainy seasons, when terrace walls or the risers on ditches have a tendency to erode away. And it is these times that are also the peak season for agricultural work (1982:31).

Another problem in obtaining the labor for maintenance stemmed from the fact that the out-migration of young people had left a relatively elderly population, some of whom were simply unable to perform the heavy work of terrace construction and repair.

In the early stages of project implementation, the issue of labor availability proved central in the analyses of small-farm production. One farmer survey revealed that more than 50 percent of farmers with less than a single acre of land reported problems hiring and retaining labor, and complained about the high wage rates they had to pay. When farmers were asked to identify constraints to production based on their own assessments, labor availability proved as large a problem for those with lands under five hectares as for those with 50 hectares or more (USAID 1978a).

The study of small farmers related these problems of labor availability to the fact that the principal means of livelihood for small farmers was non-agricultural. Thirty-four percent of those surveyed said that non-agricultural activities or off-farm labor was their *principal* source of income. Project researchers noted that it seemed easier for farm families to adjust their labor force by sending some members to engage in off-farm work, and to make up for their absence with hired labor, than to attempt to adjust their farm program. They concluded that "it is an inevitable consequence of such diversification that some enterprises are not well managed" (1978a:97).

Because project participation was heavily subsidized (75 percent) many farmers participated in the initial stages of construction. By accepting project subsidies at the accepted wage rate, and paying somewhat less, they could actually make money on the construction process. Once constructed, however, the terraces were not maintained. Labor availability interacted with a range of other constraints to make such maintenance undesirable. Because the farmers did not hold clear title to their land, they feared that soil conservation measures might encourage the landlord to reclaim it. The vegetables produced on terraces did not have a good marketing outlet, and thus were frequently wasted. Price fluctuations were marked. The investment of 49 days' labor per year at an official wage rate of J$392 had to be compared to the average per capita income of J$306 (including the value of subsistence production).

Investments of labor or cash in maintaining terraces were unlikely to repay the producer (Blustain 1982).

While the project's assumption—that investing in soil conservation and improving productivity would draw labor, and particularly young labor, back to the land—may prove sound in some cases, in the Jamaican case, there was a failure accurately to assess whether the gains in agriculture were sufficient to offset the forgoing of other sources of income or the expenses of hiring outside labor.

Soil Conservation in Peru

The Soil Conservation Project initiated by USAID in the Peruvian high-lands sought to develop and apply conservation technologies that would prevent erosion, increase productivity, and improve the standard of living in rural areas. The technology chosen was the use of various forms of terraces. Terracing has a long history in the Peruvian Andes, but the practice has fallen into disuse in many contemporary communities. The basic premise of the Soil Conservation Project was that producers had to be convinced of the value of the terracing techniques. Thus, a decision was made to avoid using any but the mildest of incentives, and a large proportion of project resources were devoted to extension work that would adequately explain and promote the terracing program (USAID 1984b).

As in the case of Jamaica, the personnel involved in the Soil Conservation Program recognized that labor availability was a constraint. Booklets designed for workers who would be promoting the technology noted that:

> Many agriculturalists will emerge convinced of the value of the technique, but not necessarily its adaptability to their parcels, believing that they will not have the technical support, *necessary labor,* proximity to markets or highways, or soil fertility that characterized experimental plots (USAID 1984a:[1]5, translation and emphasis mine).

Project documents indicate that attention was given to the diversification of productive regimens and to off-farm labor requirements among project participants. Project surveys investigated the kinds of non-agricultural work in which families engaged, the extent of seasonal migration outside the community, and the availability of offspring to assist in productive work. The results of these investigations were instructive. Fifty-five percent of families had no children or only one child to help with production, and only 20 percent had more than two. Only ten percent of families engaged in non-agricultural activities on the farm, while 24 percent were involved in seasonal migration. These figures were presented in aggregate form for the eleven participant communities; it is not unreasonable to expect that there would have been substantial variation from one region to another.

Project personnel paid careful attention to labor availability because the labor requirements of terracing were heavy. Most were concentrated in the initial stages of construction. Absorption terraces, for example, required an average of 742 days/hectare to construct; they were projected to last, however, for 20 years with minimal maintenance. Because the terraces could only be worked with footplows and not with animal traction, production on treated lands required approximately 6 percent more labor per year than traditional hillside farming. The increases in yields obtained on terraced land were striking, however. The difference between treated and control fields of potatoes was 43 percent where the control land was fertilized, and 142 percent where it was not.

While project personnel were sensitive to alternative demands on the labor of producer families, diffusion of the technology was said to depend on convincing families to reorganize their time to accommodate the new practices. Field staff were encouraged to gauge implementation plans to the migratory schedule of the community. In communities with many migrants they were instructed to organize women's groups to conduct as much of the work as possible. Migrants were also encouraged to return on weekends to perform the initial tasks of construction. Project documents recommended that traditional practices of labor exchange and community labor be drawn upon to mobilize labor resources, and disseminators of the technology were trained in the various forms of cooperation and labor mobilization that characterized Andean communities.

Like the IRDP in Jamaica, the Soil Conservation Project assumed that if the productivity and sustainability of agriculture were improved, labor would be withdrawn from many of the other activities in which it was invested. The project was designed to build on the capacities of smallholders as farmers, and to improve their productive base in agriculture. Labor scarcity, while a complicating factor in implementation, was viewed as a product of rural poverty rather than a cause.

The success of the Soil Conservation Project remains to be evaluated. The considerations introduced to this point, however, suggest that rural families will accept the new practices, maintaining and using them after project staff leave, if they can sell the additional production at a rate that will offset the gains forgone in off-farm labor. The degree to which this is a possibility will clearly vary from community to community. Where economic diversification and engagement in off-farm activities have not reached massive levels, the necessary additional labor might be generated if families simply work longer and harder, or draw on the practices of communal work and labor exchange. In other communities, however, it may be necessary to abandon one or more non-agricultural activities.

On the other side of the equation, acceptance will depend on whether there is a viable market for the crops produced, on the transport costs involved, and on the market value of the crops appropriate for production. For some families, terracing could represent a way of maintaining their agricultural base as well as contributing to the urban food supply. For others it may be an impediment to participation in activities that better meet their income needs.

Summary and Conclusions

This chapter has raised a series of issues that can contribute to a more precise evaluation of the dynamics of labor availability in rural communities. In contemporary communities, the question cannot be understood apart from the processes of semiproletarianization that are affecting rural households. Family members may be involved in subsistence production one month, petty commerce another, and seasonal migration to sell their labor power during the dry season. The need to participate in these diverse activities is frequently related to a diminishing land base or to declining terms of trade.

This dynamic may lead to problems of labor scarcity. Labor scarcity may, in turn, lead to patterns of poor resource management, thus creating a vicious circle of impoverishment. As natural-resource quality declines, families must struggle even harder to maintain constant levels of income. In consequence, still more labor may be drawn away from the farm.

While rural families devise diversified economic strategies with creativity and resourcefulness, they are often powerfully constrained in their endeavors. The seasonality of agricultural employment, the piece-work rate paid for such jobs, monopsonistic marketing structures, "cheap food" policies, and the lack of access to basic technical and financial services are only a few of the obstacles they face in their attempts to meet their basic needs. These features of the rural environment are linked not to development planning per se, but to the demands of commercial enterprises for cheap labor or the requirements of urban centers for cheap food.

Theoretical treatments of labor surplus and scarcity have frequently been tied to specific policy concerns, justifying a particular factor mix for innovations in agriculture. Of particular relevance here, the notion of labor surplus became tied in the 1960s to theoretical trends that favored support for small-farm agriculture. This turn of events led many researchers to assume, a priori, that labor-intensive innovations were preferable in rural areas. The complex and often contradictory pressures experienced by rural households as a result of their integration into wage and commodity markets were thus ignored.

The issue of labor availability cannot be resolved on the basis of national demographic trends or of abstract two-sector models of rural economies. It requires determination in specific regional and temporal contexts. This does not mean that any intervention in production must be preceded by detailed measurements of labor investments and supply, although more research of this type is needed. What it does mean is that we must become more sensitive to the problems of labor allocation that can arise, their ecological and social "symptoms," and their relationship to various forms of economic diversification. We must be able to recognize communities stressed by the growing need to seek off-farm activities, and land that is poorly managed as a result of strategies to meet short-term needs.

Once labor scarcity is identified, and its roots and consequences explored, the issue for policy is whether the greatest benefit may be obtained by more adequately filling the employment needs of migrants off the farm or by strengthening the resource base and productivity of rural families. This cannot be determined globally, but will depend on the nature of opportunities available in specific contexts. There will be some cases, as the soil conservation projects in Peru and Jamaica anticipated, where increasing the productivity and profitability of rural farms will end seasonal migration and will draw labor back to the home community. To determine whether this will occur, however, we must be able realistically to compare the returns to investments in measures to conserve soil and improve productivity not only against their immediately measurable costs, but also against the income that will be forgone. And, if programs are to be truly participatory, we must ask rural families to help us assess the relative gains and risks over the short and long term, rather than engaging in elaborate promotional campaigns.

As both of these projects recognized, however, labor scarcity is not a *cause* of rural poverty. It is but one of the dilemmas experienced by rural households as they confront larger structural problems of declining terms of trade, land scarcity, state intervention in production, competition with commercial farmers, and oppression by rural elites. It provides a point of entry, however, into the web of contradictions experienced by small producers in the disarticulated (de Janvry 1981), and often stagnated, rural economies of developing nations—economies where land scarcity and labor scarcity can exist side by side, and where rapid population growth can lead to insufficient hands to work the fields.

Notes

1. Semiproletarian is used here to refer to individuals who are partially incorporated into labor markets, and who continue to produce food and other products for their own use.

2. In addition to Lewis, some of the major proponents of the notion of labor surplus (in its various forms) were Ranis and Fei (1961), Georgescu-Roegen (1963), Nurske (1953) and Dovring (1967). Many of those attempting empirically based critiques of the concept are listed above.

3. There are many reasons for suggesting that support for small farmers was and is a rational strategy. These include various measures of small farm productivity and efficiency, the income-distribution benefits of such an approach, and the political and economic stability that a small farming regimen is believed to provide. The point, however, is that for many researchers, labor surplus lost its status as a question that could be empirically investigated in particular regions and specific historical circumstance, and became an article of faith associated with a particular development model.

4. The research on which this account is based was funded by an Inter-American Foundation Learning Fellowship for Social Change, 1979–80.

5. In December 1983, 3.43 Jamaican dollars equalled US$1.00.

References

Arrighi, Giovanni
    1970   Labour Supplies in Historical Perspective: A Study of the Proletarianization of the African Peasantry in Rhodesia. Journal of Development Studies 6(3):197–284.

Bedoya, Eduardo
    1981   La destrucción del equilibrio ecológico en las cooperativas del Alto Huallaga. Lima: Centro de Investigación y Promoción Amazónica Serie Documento no. 1.
    1982   Colonizaciones en la ceja de selva a través de enganche: El caso Saipai en Tingo Maria. *In* Colonización en la Amazonia. Lima: Centro de Investigación y Promoción Amazónica.

Bernstein, Henry
    1977   Notes on Capital and Peasantry. Review of African Political Economy 10:60–73.

Blustain, Harvey
    1982   Resource Management and Agricultural Development in Jamaica: Lessons for a Participatory Approach. Ithaca, NY: Cornell University Special Series on Resource Management No. 2.

Boserup, Ester
    1965   The Conditions of Agricultural Growth. Chicago, IL: Aldine.

Brush, Stephen
    1977   The Myth of the Idle Peasant. *In* Peasant Livelihood. Rhoda Halperin and James Dow, eds. Pp. 60–78. New York, NY: St. Martin's Press.

CEEB (Convenio para Estudios Económicos Básicos)
    1970   Primera estimación del subempleo de la PEA agrícola en áreas rurales, por meses, provincias y regiones. Lima: CEEB.

Collins, Jane
    1984   The Maintenance of Peasant Coffee Production. American Ethnologist 11(3):413–38.
    1986   The Household and Relations of Production in Southern Peru. Comparative Studies in Society and History, forthcoming.

Connell, John, and Michael Lipton
    1977   Assessing Village Labour Situations in Developing Countries. Delhi: Oxford University Press (prepared for the World Employment Programme of the International Labour Organization).

Deere, Carmen Diana
    1976   Rural Women's Subsistence Production in the Capitalist Periphery. Review of Radical Political Economics 8(1):9–17.

Deere, Carmen Diana, and Alain de Janvry
    1979   A Conceptual Framework for the Empirical Analysis of Peasants. American Journal of Agricultural Economics 61:601–611.

Deere, Carmen Diana, and Robert Wasserstrom
    1980   Ingreso familiar y trabajo no agrícola entre los pequeños productores de América Latina y el Caribe. Paper presented to Seminario Internacional sobre la producción agropecuaria y forestal en zonas de ladera en América Latina. Turrialba, Costa Rica.

de Janvry, Alain
    1981   The Agrarian Question and Reformism in Latin America. Baltimore, MD: Johns Hopkins University Press.

Dovring, Folke
  1967   Unemployment in Traditional Agriculture. Economic Development and
          Cultural Change 15(2):163–175.
Figueroa, Adolfo
  1984   Capitalist Development and the Peasant Economy in Peru. New York, NY:
          Cambridge University Press.
Georgescu-Roegen, N.
  1963   Economic Theory and Agrarian Economics. Oxford Economic Papers
          12:1–40.
Guillet, David
  1981   Surplus Extraction, Risk Management and Economic Change Among Pe-
          ruvian Peasants. Journal of Development Studies 18:3–24.
Hopper, W. D.
  1965   Allocation Efficiency in Traditional Indian Agriculture. Journal of Farm
          Economics 47:611–24.
Jorgensen, Dale
  1969   The Role of Economic Development: Classical versus Neoclassical Models
          of Growth. *In* Subsistence Agriculture and Economic Development. Clifton
          Wharton, ed. Pp. 320–47. Chicago, IL: Aldine.
Kao, Charles, Kurt Anschel, and Carl Eicher
  1964   Disguised Unemployment in Agriculture: A Survey. *In* Agriculture in
          Economic Development. C. Eicher and L. Witt, eds. Pp. 129—44. New
          York, NY: McGraw-Hill.
Lassen, Cheryl
  1980   Landlessness and Rural Poverty in Latin America: Conditions, Trends and
          Policies Affecting Income and Employment. Special Series on Landlessness
          and Near-Landlessness No. 4. Ithaca, NY: Cornell University.
Lewis, W. A.
  1954   Economic Development with Unlimited Supplies of Labour. Manchester
          School of Economic and Social Studies 22:139–91.
Maletta, Héctor
  1978   El subempleo en el Perú: Una visión crítica. Apuntes 8:3–48.
Mathur, A.
  1964   The Anatomy of Disguised Unemployment. Oxford Economic Papers
          16:161–93.
Nurske, Ragnar
  1953   Problems of Capital Formation in Underdeveloped Countries. London:
          Oxford University Press.
Paglin, M.
  1965   Surplus Agricultural Labor and Development. American Economic Review
          55:815–32.
Painter, Michael
  1984   Changing Relations of Production and Rural Underdevelopment. Journal
          of Anthropological Research 40:271–92.
Ranis, Gustav, and John Fei
  1961   A Theory of Economic Development. American Economic Review
          51:533–65.
Ríos, Raúl
  1979   Development of Integrated Agricultural, Livestock and Forestry Production
          Systems in Tropical Peru. Paper presented to Workshop on Agro-Forestry
          Systems in Latin America, Turrialba, Costa Rica: Centro Agronómico
          Tropical de Investigación y Enseñanza.

Rosenstein-Rodan, P. N.
   1957   Disguised Unemployment and Underemployment in Agriculture. Monthly
           Bulletin of Agricultural Economics and Statistics (Rome: FAO) 6:1–7.
Schultz, Theodore
   1964   Transforming Traditional Agriculture. New Haven, CT: Yale University
           Press.
Scott, C. D.
   1976   Peasants, Proletarianization and the Articulation of Modes of Production:
           The Case of Sugar Cane Cutters in Northern Peru. Journal of Peasant
           Studies 3(3):321–341.
Stier, Frances
   1977   Effects of Demographic Change on Agriculture in an Eastern San Blas
           Community: Preliminary Report. Manuscript, files of the author.
USAID
   1978a   The Small Farmer in Jamaican Agriculture: An Assessment of Constraints
           and Opportunities. Report of the Agriculture Sector Assessment Team of
           the Office of International Cooperation and Development to USAID/
           Jamaica and to the Ministry of Agriculture, Jamaica.
   1978b   The Small Farmer in Western Portland and Eastern Saint Mary (Jamaica).
           Vol. 2. Bases for an Integrated Rural Development Program. Report of the
           Agriculture Sector Assessment Team of the Office of International Coop-
           eration and Development to USAID/Jamaica and to the Ministry of
           Agriculture, Jamaica.
   1984a   Estratégias de promoción en las comunidades y caserios andinos: Para la
           conservación de suelos en el Perú. Programa Nacional de Conservación
           de Suelos y Aguas. Convenio USAID/Ministerio de Agricultura no. 527-
           0220.
   1984b   El impacto de la conservación de suelos y aguas en el desarrollo del agro
           en la sierra peruana. Program Nacional de Conservación de Suelos y
           Aguas en Cuencas Hidrográficas. Convenio Peru-AID no. 527-0220.
Warriner, Doreen
   1955   Land and Poverty in the Middle East. London: Royal Institute of International
           Affairs.

2

The "Political Ecology" of Amazonia

Marianne Schmink and Charles H. Wood

The growing concern over the negative environmental impact of recent expansion of population and economic activity into the Brazilian Amazon basin has raised important questions about the relationship between the natural environment and socioeconomic behavior. Fiscal policies designed to attract the expertise of private firms to the Amazon region have induced rampant land speculation and the rapid expansion of unproductive pastures rather than the expected "rational" use of natural resources. Small-farmer colonization schemes, plagued by institutional failures and market bottlenecks, have been unable to absorb a significant portion of the Brazilian migrants seeking to settle the region. Land titling procedures remain confused, and, as a result, ranchers, squatters, and miners use indiscriminate forest removal as a means to assert their claims. The increasing rate of deforestation in Brazil is especially worrisome in light of the importance of tropical forests as a source of biological diversity and of potentially useful products. Persistent violence and conflicts over land, and a growing pattern of concentration of landholdings, have repeatedly required military intervention to prevent open warfare. Indigenous groups and other long-standing inhabitants of the region have been on the losing side of most of these confrontations. Not only are their lands being taken away, but their well-adapted resource management strategies have been ignored by development planners. Attempts to protect indigenous groups and to preserve portions of the forest from intrusion have met with modest success in Brazil. At the same time, continued frontier expansion poses a formidable challenge to those who seek to minimize the disruption of the Amazonian ecosystem. Why have so many development plans and protective environmental efforts gone awry?

We can begin to answer this question by noting that the goals of environmental policy (conservation and long-term sustainability) are fundamentally at odds with the goals of expanded production and short-term accumulation. Unmitigated ecological disasters are often hailed as resounding economic and political successes. By the same token, such resource management projects as conservation efforts that strictly "quarantine" the natural environment, thereby depriving people of economic sustenance and businesses of profit, may entail unacceptable, and potentially disruptive, social and political costs.

In the socioeconomic and political context within which resource management projects must be carried out, the principle of private profit and expanded production far outweighs that of biophysical sustainability and environmental conservation. Hence, it is hardly surprising that the goals of ecologically sound projects premised on assumptions of sustainability are consistently subverted by the mechanics of a social system based on the laws of accumulation. It follows, also, that explanations for this "subversion" cannot be attributed solely to the familiar list of factors: insufficient knowledge and technical training, poorly informed public policy, the self-interest of particular social groups, population increase, and so on. Although these considerations are certainly relevant to project failure, they are themselves the result of much broader phenomena. As we will argue in this chapter, a society's prevailing form of economic production and class structure, and the manner in which diverse economic groups battle for ideological and policy advantage within the state apparatus, are crucial considerations in the process of designing resource management projects and in formulating strategies to carry them out.

In the first section we present a model of the sociopolitical system that can be used to analyze the processes pertinent to understanding the human use of natural resources. The framework, drawn from the perspective of political economy, shows the relationship between surplus production, social class, the function of the state in promoting private accumulation, and the role of ideology in public discourse and development planning. In order to demonstrate the relevance of these concepts and relationships to the study of resource management, we extend the political economy framework to address the specific issue of land use patterns in the Brazilian Amazon. This approach, which we have called "political ecology," illustrates how economic and political processes determine the way natural resources have been exploited in frontier regions of northern Brazil.[1]

The concluding section applies these insights to the practical problem of how to create programs to alter the ways in which resources are exploited. We argue that both the design of intervention projects and the strategies to implement them must be formulated on the basis of a thorough assessment of a society's overall political economy. We propose that the design of policy interventions follow an explicit agenda by which the desiderata of a proposed resource-use model (based on an assessment of both ecological and social factors) is weighed against what can be feasibly accomplished in a given setting (based on an analysis of existing resource-use systems, differences in socioeconomic and political power, and the conflicts and trade-offs these imply).

The Political Ecology of Amazonian Development

Distinct forms of sociopolitical organization are based on different production principles. For our purposes two types are of special importance: those based on subsistence, or simple reproduction, and those based on expanded production and private accumulation. The relevance to political ecology stems from the markedly different implications the two forms of organization have in terms of human appropriation of the natural environment.

Simple Reproduction

In some societies, such as certain indigenous groups in Amazonia, the goal of production is subsistence. Such groups operate beyond the reach of the market economy and produce no significant surplus. Internal social differentiation follows kinship and distinctions of age and gender that together define a division of labor legitimated by the norms, values, and beliefs of a well-adapted world view (culture). In some cases ceremonial obligations (e.g., communal feasts) act as "leveling mechanisms" that impede individual accumulation. In some hunting and gathering societies people shun the accumulation of material possessions for the simple reason that it hinders efficient mobility. In nearly all instances exchanges through kinship networks serve to redistribute goods throughout the group, thereby enhancing collective survival.

Peasant producers, though connected to national markets, follow a similar subsistence strategy. The basic organizing principle is the maximization of security and the minimization of physical expenditure (Chayanov 1966; Forman 1975). Peasants trade or sell a portion of their crop to obtain or purchase necessities that they cannot themselves produce. Labor inputs are calculated on the basis of expected family needs, which often contain a monetary referent. But the acquisition of cash is destined primarily for household consumption requirements rather than for purposeful investment in expanded production for profit.

Between peasant and Indian lies the purely Amazonian figure of the *caboclo*—in Spanish, *ribereño* or *mestizo* (Moran 1974; Wagley 1968)—a racially mixed population that grew with the migration into the region during the rubber boom. The traditional caboclo subsistence pattern combines the harvest of forest products with some agriculture, hunting, and fishing. Links to the market exist but are mostly based on the *aviamento* system. Creditors, or *aviadores*, advance food, tools, gunpowder, and goods such as kerosene and salt in exchange for rubber or Brazil nuts.

Sustenance strategies developed by subsistence producers may be simple in their goals but they are highly complex in their interaction with the natural environment. For example, the Northern Kayapo in Brazil recognize eight major ecological zones and two types of transitional zones near their main village (Posey 1985). Similarly, the Panaillo Shipibo of Peruvian Amazonia, studied by Bergman (1980), use nine biotopes for their diverse forms of agriculture and other zones for fish and game. This diversity minimizes the potential for environmental degradation and is well suited to tropical rain forest ecology. Practiced over extensive territories under conditions of low population density, these systems have been sustainable over hundreds of years. Because subsistence needs are finite, simple technology is used and population size is small, and because kin-based systems of exchange ensure the provision of society as a whole, the human impact on the natural environment is minimal.

Subsistence societies, whose activities have only a minimal impact on the natural environment, approximate steady-state economies. This need not imply that indigenous groups are in complete harmony with all aspects of the ecosystem. The very diversity of their strategies implies a wide range of environmental disturbances and is likely to lead to undue pressure on specific resources at specific moments. The relatively small scale of the economy, however, impedes wholesale disruption of the recycling process that is central to the stability of the tropical forest ecosystem.

The traditional riverside dweller, or caboclo, shares with indigenous adaptations a finely tuned diversity developed over centuries of occupation of the Amazonian ecosystem. In one study, for example, caboclos recognized at least 40 different local "resource units" within which they differentiated "vertical levels" of terrestrial, arboreal, and aquatic resources (Parker et al. 1983:183). As late as 1970, more than half the population of Brazil's Amazon region still depended on a combination of forest extraction, horticulture, hunting, and fishing for their sustenance (Pinto 1980:87). Caboclo social relations, however, are different from those found in indigenous systems. Isolated caboclo families or small clustered settlements are the rule rather than communal labor and land allocation systems like those of indigenous kin and clan groups.

Peasant producers (as distinct from the traditional caboclo) are recent newcomers to Amazonia, primarily attracted to the region by road construction projects that opened up new territories for occupation. As outsiders, they bring to the region agricultural practices familiar to their places of origin but sometimes poorly adapted to the intricacies of rain forest ecology. More importantly, however, their relationship to natural resources is subject to severe socioeconomic and political constraints within which they struggle to survive on the frontier. The concentration of land ownership, for example, relegates small farmers to plots smaller than subsistence size, causing them to overcrop their meager holdings out of sheer necessity. This tendency is exacerbated by economic pressures deriving from credit systems, exploitation by middlemen in the commercialization process, and the unequal terms of trade inherent in the market linkages to the larger economy (Collins 1986). Similarly, the lack of secure title and the precarious de facto hold over land mean that reinvestment in erosion control, fertilizer, and irrigation are both costly and irrational (see the discussion of class conflict below). Contrary to official planning documents, such as Brazil's *Second Development Plan for Amazonia* (SUDAM 1976), peasant producers are not inherently "predatory."

Their relationship to land and natural resources is socially, economically, and politically constrained.

To summarize, indigenous groups, caboclos, and peasants share, to a greater or lesser extent, a production system oriented primarily to simple reproduction. Beyond this general similarity, important distinctions exist with regard to their respective appropriation of natural resources. The complex adaptive strategies developed by indigenous peoples who have little connection to the market lie at one end of the continuum. At the other are peasant producers, with more specialized production methods and stronger ties to market networks and the money economy, while traditional Amazonian caboclos and market-oriented native producers fall somewhere in between.

Pressures for surplus production immediately disrupt the balance that characterizes production systems geared to simple reproduction. For example, the demand for turtle eggs and meat during the colonial period destroyed the traditional mechanisms by which local populations had previously managed the turtle population (Smith 1974). Rapid depletion of turtle and manatee populations not only deprived the indigenous population of sources of oil and meat, but also seriously disrupted the riverine ecosystem (Bunker 1985:64). The influx of migrants during the rubber boom at the turn of the century led to increased pressures for agricultural production, and pushed inhabitants from their floodplain settlements to the dry *terra firme*, a more fragile ecosystem. The intricate technologies by which they had managed the floodplains (*várzea*) were virtually lost (Ross 1978). More recently, demand for animal pelts threatened jaguar and cayman populations as indigenous and caboclo populations responded to outside market opportunities.

Expanded Production and Private Accumulation

Once an increase in labor productivity makes a surplus possible, the stage is set for a struggle over how this surplus will be distributed. We speak of a class society when one subgroup of the population relies on institutionalized mechanisms (as opposed, say, to plunder) to garner surplus that they did not themselves produce. Social classes are thus defined by the particular way surplus product is created and accumulated, the structure of which is historically variable. Slavery, medieval feudalism, and modern capitalism have in common the existence of surplus, yet in each case the system of production and distribution—and, therefore, the society's class structure—are markedly different.

Unlike other forms of social organization, capitalism is an inherently expanding system. The engine of this continual expansion is the market competition between producers who privately own the means of production. When one producer adopts a new technology, others are forced to follow suit if they are to survive in the marketplace. In this way there is built into the system a constant need for individual firms to advance technology and productivity, tendencies which, in a competitive market environment, necessarily spread throughout the economy.

Expanding capitalist production tends to subordinate, and in some cases eradicate, noncapitalist forms. As noted earlier, the penetration of market linkages into indigenous societies violates the principle of simple reproduction and can disrupt the delicate balance noncapitalist groups have with the natural environment. Similarly, the ever-increasing quantity of cheap commodities produced by the dynamic capitalist sector undermines the economic viability of artisans, craftsmen, and small farmers. These structural transformations can have negative implications for land use when peasant producers are relegated to plots too small to provide for subsistence needs, and when they are forced to over-exploit their meager resources merely to stay alive (see M. Painter in this volume).

Within capitalist firms the logic of expanded production is inherently degrading to land and other resources. So long as governments do not interfere through regulatory mechanisms, the natural environment can (indeed, must) be exploited for maximum short-term gain. This is especially true in Amazonia where the viability of long-term investments is in doubt. Ranchers destroy the tropical forest with little regard for wildlife or indigenous groups. Sawmills harvest only highly valuable mahogany trees, causing ranchers and peasant farmers simply to burn all other types of wood. Mining companies, as well as individual placer miners, pollute streams in the search for gold and other valuable metals.

The point is that environmental degradation is an eminently rational process, at least insofar as the short-term needs of capital are concerned. It follows that attempts to intervene in the manner in which natural resources are exploited run counter to the interests of powerful economic groups. Such groups wield considerable influence within the legislative and planning bureaucracies of the state. Dominant economic groups also command the financial and intellectual resources to mold public opinion and to limit the universe of political discourse to a range of options favorable to their interests. We can therefore anticipate that resource-management projects, or environmental policies that increase production costs to private capital (and hence reduce the rate of profit), will meet with predictable opposition from the representatives of particular sectors of the economy and from their spokesmen in the political arena.

Identifying the class structure of a society or a regional economy is thus more than a taxonomic exercise. Such an analysis reveals, among other things, the constellation of interest groups with which any intervention policy must contend. As we will argue in the conclusion, the ability to recognize sources of political opposition (and support) is essential to formulating and implementing projects designed to alter existing forms of resource use.

Social Class and Conflict

In nonmonetary, kin-based indigenous societies oriented to subsistence production, land is held communally and cannot be sold to outsiders. Because of the diversity of land-use strategies, the size of their territories must be far larger than the amount equivalent to one farm plot per family. Tribal lands are increasingly coveted as the frontier expands into the region. The technical complexity of indigenous resource management goes unappreciated because it does not produce a significant market surplus. Non-natives thus complain that indigenous groups monopolize enormous land areas on which they produce nothing of use to the nation. Even with the official protection of Brazil's Indian Statute, passed in 1973, tribal territories continue to suffer incursions by squatters, ranchers, loggers, miners, road construction crews, and others. Yet the reserves on which the indigenous groups are now confined are far more limiting than the vast areas over which many of them traditionally moved. As they are forced to adopt more sedentary, less diverse adaptive systems, Indians may begin to lose the capacity for long-term sustainability.

Other traditional Amazonian social groups, such as caboclos, are also threatened by the struggle over land. While their ecology has much in common with indigenous societies, caboclos lack the cultural and political distinctiveness that has constituted a measure of defense (however limited) for native groups. Caboclos are invisible within the "empty spaces" development policy seeks to occupy, and their vast ecological knowledge is ignored in colonization attempts (Moran 1981). Although often caboclo populations have occupied riverside lands for years, even for generations, they are so far removed from the legal requirements to make good their claims that they are seldom able to defend them from outsiders. Struggles over access to Amazonian land are therefore likely to replace the diversity of caboclo adaptations with the simplified agricultural systems imported from other parts of Brazil.

An even more direct threat to Amazonian forests emerges from the struggle for land between squatters and investors. For both, clearing the land of forest is the first step to establishing land rights. This is the most rational strategy even when the future of any productive endeavor is in doubt. The fact that the two groups compete for access to the same areas not only increases social tension and violence in frontier areas, it also accelerates the rate of deforestation as claims are continually pushed forward. It is in this case that the environmental effects of class conflict in Amazonia are most dramatic.

The "rationality" of rampant land clearing by investors and squatters is based on the logic of economic behavior that characterizes each of the two systems of production. On the one hand, capitalist investors have moved into the Amazon from southern Brazil, attracted by the generous program of fiscal incentives offered by the government and by the prospect of acquiring large amounts of land as a hedge against inflation, a means of diversifying their portfolios, and an outlet for profits that could not be remitted abroad. Conditions for investors were so attractive that the profits to be made bore little relationship to productive investments. For these "speculative fronts" (Sawyer 1984:194), land as a means of production was secondary to its function as a "reserve of value" and as a means of obtaining access to other forms of wealth associated with land in the Amazon region: lumber, minerals, cheap credit, and fiscal incentives (Silva 1980:47). Since the land itself rapidly increased in value regardless of its productivity, the seemingly reckless forest destruction was for these investors the most rational economic strategy.

The small farmer migrants were primarily attracted by the prospect of owning their own land. They came from other regions of Brazil where profound changes in agricultural systems were under way: expulsion from earlier frontier areas, the breakdown of traditional tenant and sharecropping relationships, the increasing mechanization of agriculture, and the concentration of landownership. Most have few other options but to move to the frontier, clear a plot of land, and hope to hold on to it. Yet in the history of frontier movement in Brazil, a "demographic" front of small farmer migrants is later dispossessed by the "economic" front of investors who appropriate the value created by these farmers (Foweraker 1981). Selling and moving on, in response to threats from the other party in land conflicts, constitutes the so-called "land rights industry" (*indústria da posse*) that is the only way migrants can accumulate cash in the frontier setting. Myers (1980) refers to these migrants as "shifted cultivators" and labels them the greatest threat to tropical forests because of their numbers. As wave follows wave in particular areas, land is cleared successively until the possibilities of forest regeneration are remote. The rational behavior of these migrants, within the limited range of options open to them, not only degrades the forest environment but undermines the prospects for their own productive endeavors. Strategies to improve the collective capabilities of smallholders to manage their resources and defend their tenure rights could help to stabilize small-scale agriculture in already occupied areas. But agrarian reform, and other measures carried out beyond Amazonia's borders, would be the most effective policies to relieve pressures on forest lands (Goodland 1980; Spears and Ayensu 1984:16–17).

Markets and Surplus Extraction

While local and regional markets may foster economic self-sufficiency of peasants and natives, national and international markets often exhibit a "boom or bust" pattern that tends to impoverish the region. As indigenous groups are drawn into the larger market system, they have access to new supply sources and consumer outlets, but face competition from other (usually better-off) producers. They begin to lose their subsistence orientation and to overexploit the forest resources. This rational response by individuals to market incentives can lead to the degradation of commonly held property.

Most development programs for the Amazon stress the need to link the region to national markets (Goodland 1985:27). This is the primary justification for roads and other infrastructural investments. Subsistence-level production that does not create surplus is irrelevant to the criteria imposed by growth-oriented development approaches (Alvim 1980:34; Painter et al.

1984:9); nor does an orientation to local or regional markets, to increase self-sufficiency, justify settlement of new lands. Instead, development policies have favored large-scale producers of export crops, to the detriment of small-farmer agriculture. Precisely these industrial groups are responsible for most of the forest clearing (Browder 1985). Yet some productive systems, such as pasture for cattle, are profitable only through speculation on the land market (Hecht 1985), even with hefty government subsidies (Browder 1985).

Small farmers who produce food crops are unable to reap adequate returns on the market; they also end up overexploiting their natural resource base. Amazonian colonists are hampered by initial poverty, unfavorable market integration, and institutional relationships (credit, technical assistance, titling) that often lead to a cycle of indebtedness and environmental degradation (cf. Collins 1986). The need for cash both leads to off-farm activities that compete with resource management, and forces farmers to intensify short-term production through shortened fallows or monocropping, especially in pasture.

If farmers have a good harvest they are likely to lack adequate transportation and storage systems, and to face prices controlled by middlemen. If prices go high enough to compensate for the costs of production, their products are still unable to compete with goods produced elsewhere, where costs are lower. As a result, most frontier areas import, rather than export, food. Small farmers rarely have the capital to invest in inputs that might counteract the adverse environmental effects of their agricultural enterprises, and even if they did, to do so would be irrational, given the insecurity of land tenure and the poor market prospects. The overexploitation of land, leading to degradation of soils, is a rational short-term solution to the market-oriented production that drains capital from the producer. For these reasons, many conservationists advocate the improvement of intensive forms of subsistence agriculture as a complement to the market orientation of most development projects (Goodland 1980:12).

The State and Civil Society

Analysts often assume that the malfunctioning of the market system and the violence associated with land conflicts are due to an ineffective presence of the Brazilian state in regulating frontier occupation. Such a view rests on an implicit notion of the state as a neutral arbiter of competing interests. Social tension and bureaucratic inefficiencies are attributed to imperfections in the execution of this moderating role. Studies that make this point call for greater knowledge and resources, or changes in personnel and administrative procedures (e.g., Spears and Ayensu 1984:77).

The political economy approach adopts a more structural perspective, emphasizing the causal relationships between a society's economic base—the form of production and the associated class structure—and the legal institutions and administrative agencies of the state. The primary function of the Brazilian state is to maintain the existing structure of production and distribution, and to ensure the reproduction of the conditions for continued (or enhanced) private accumulation, rather than to act as an objective arbiter of conflicting claims. The model need not endorse a strict determinism (characteristic of earlier studies) between the needs of private capital and the behavior of public institutions. Indeed, if there were perfect correspondence between the interests of dominant economic classes and the role of the modern state there would be no possibility of alternative policy, and, by extension, little purpose in this chapter.

Contemporary perspectives on the role of the state continue to endorse its class-based character, yet at the same time move away from the idea of a mechanical relationship to the economy (for a review, see Carnoy 1984). Quite apart from meeting the needs of economically powerful groups, the state must also, to one degree or another, attend to the interests of a much broader sector of society if it is to protect its own position. The concept of "relative autonomy" (Althusser and Balibar 1968) labels this indeterminacy between the economic and the political, without altogether abandoning the strong influence of the former over the latter. It provides a way to conceptualize the "degrees of freedom," or the "political openings" that allow us to promote alternative initiatives while, at the same time, retaining a healthy respect for the power that threatened economic groups wield within the realm of politics, planning, and public administration.

The recent development experience in the Amazon amply illustrates the class bias of the Brazilian state. The most consistent trend has favored large investors, beginning with programs of fiscal incentives instituted in 1966. These policies sought to transfer systems of production from other regions of Brazil into the Amazon region, to fill the "empty spaces" where Indians and caboclos carry out their peculiarly Amazonian economic activities. Thus the goal of favoring dominant economic interest groups and their particular systems of production led to the imposition of economic models that were ecologically irrational, if politically rational.

In the 1970s, the government also sponsored some tandem activities oriented to the settlement of small farmers via the Transamazon colonization scheme and the Polonoroeste project in Rondonia. Again, the initiative was motivated by a political need to respond to pressures, this time to small farmers in the drought-ridden northeast or those being pushed out of earlier frontier areas in southern Brazil. Investors wielded their influence through the Association of Amazonian Entrepreneurs to undermine these initiatives. They successfully pushed the arguments that small farmers were a predatory, ecological hazard as well as a retrograde influence standing in the way of progress. Ironically, large-scale cattle ranching was promoted as the proper "vocation" for the region. Yet because pasture deteriorated so quickly, conversion of new forest was more profitable than rehabilitation of existing pasture (Goodland 1980:2). The combination of rising inflation rates and government-sponsored road-building programs made land values in the region increase rapidly even if productivity was declining. The productive capacity of land was secondary to its potentials for resale and for obtaining access to federal subsidies and such other forms of wealth as minerals and lumber (Hecht 1985).

The political strength of these entrepreneurial groups is such that the policies favoring pasture investments have changed little. The Second National Development Plan restricted the fiscal incentives for cattle ranches to certain areas of the Amazon where large-scale ranches already predominated (Hecht 1985:673), but this turned out to represent only a temporary setback for large investors, since the next policy initiative gave priority to private colonization projects. The new approach meant, in effect, abandoning the earlier commitment to public distribution of land to poor farmers in favor of procedures that would permit private firms to purchase large tracts and sell subdivided plots to migrants with economic resources. This sudden shift from one policy constituency to another was in large part responsible for the increase in land conflicts between squatters and investors in some parts of Amazonia.

In retrospect, it is hard to point to any of these development strategies as being very successful in the Amazon. The Transamazon scheme was rapidly abandoned after being beset by a variety of problems (Moran 1981; Smith 1982; Wood and Schmink 1978). Private colonists seem to do little better, as the purchase of land and the costs of establishing a farm leave them as decapitalized as the official colonists (Butler 1985). Neither have large investors delivered on their promises: while some enterprises are productive, the economics of investment in the region has encouraged most to make their profits through market manipulation or through speculation in land or short-term capital markets (Hecht 1985; Browder 1986). The government has been left with a legacy of persistent tensions over land that has required increasing military intervention (Schmink 1982). The failure of land regulatory agencies to resolve these problems has given way to "crisis colonization" schemes, directed by the military intelligence establishment. These programs have relied on massive distribution of smaller plots of land in order to accommodate a larger number of settlers and quickly remove disputed land from the public domain. Officials in these agencies admit that the smaller lots are probably not viable over the long term, but their concern is primarily political, not ecological. The strategy has increased population pressure and accelerated the land market in areas of greatest tension.

That politics prevails over technical considerations is often attributed to the lack of adequate understanding of tropical ecology. Such a conclusion presumes that cognitive understanding—this time on the part of government planners—is the determining factor in land use planning, a conclusion not borne out by the evidence. In Brazil, for example, a blue-ribbon commission in 1979–1980 proposed a comprehensive plan for the zoning of the Amazon. The project constituted the first attempt to plan on the basis of technical, scientific criteria. When the plan was made public, adverse reaction from political and economic groups, who viewed it as a threat to their interests in the region, promptly killed the initiative. The short history of the zoning plan attests to the fact that expertise, although a necessary component of effective project design, is hardly sufficient. However well-conceived a project may be on technical grounds, its success is contingent on a receptive political environment.

Global Interdependence

Having stressed the economic and political nature of development and land policy, we must further note that the content of those policies is often stimulated or constrained by factors that lie well beyond Brazil's borders. The Amazon, for example, has been tied to the world economy since the sixteenth century. The extraction of forest products, especially the harvest of natural latex in the late nineteenth and early twentieth centuries, was associated with the demand for commodities in other parts of the world. As Bunker (1985:25) notes, extractive systems are inherently unstable. In most cases, per unit costs tend to rise as the scale of extraction increases, since commodities must be sought in more distant and difficult locations. Rising costs mean that sources elsewhere are substituted, leading to economic decline. The "boom and bust" cycles that shook Amazonia created little in the way of social or ecological structures capable of fostering long-term development compatible with the regional environment.

During the early period of Brazil's industrialization, the Amazon was essentially a backwater region. But the aggressive road-building schemes of the 1950s and 1960s, linked to the expanding automobile industry in southern Brazil, soon ended the region's isolation. Beginning in the 1960s explicit government policies sought to transfer the capital generated in southern industry to the Amazon region, hoping to create additional export earnings. Notions of the Amazon as a producer of cheap food, as a "safety valve" for excess population, or a "resource frontier" for export, indicate the various roles the region was to play in the overall development plan of Brazil (and of most other Amazonian countries). These imperatives were a response to the transformations and socioeconomic dislocations in the country's economy and to its new role in the world economic system.

In the 1980s the foreign debt burden has placed severe constraints on economic planning possibilities of many Latin American countries, especially Brazil. Under the crisis circumstance there is little choice but to view the region as a potential source of export commodities (including lumber, gold, iron ore, and other minerals) to be plundered as rapidly as possible, and as the site of vast development projects (such as Carajas and Polonoroeste) by which new foreign loans may be floated. Conversion of land from food crop to export crop production in other parts of Brazil also contributes to the migrant stream into Amazonia because it leads to land concentration and the expulsion of former food producers. Yet the most promising export crops, such as coffee and cacao, are still subject to price fluctuations on the world market. Furthermore, in the short- and medium-term it seems unlikely that the massive state projects will provide a solution to the debt problem (Mendes 1985:46; Pinto 1982). Given the constraints imposed by the debt situation, however, economic policy must concentrate on the short-term export possibilities to the detriment of a more sustainable long-term strategy.

On the positive side, recent experience has shown that pressures from international lobby groups can influence the direction of land-use policies. The prestige of the international scientific community and the political lobbying of conservation organizations have helped to create support for initiatives within Brazil to evaluate the appropriateness of land-use models. The outstanding example is that of the World Bank's explicit recognition of environmental issues and indigenous rights as lending criteria. Especially important is the Bank's willingness to back up these conditions with effective material sanctions (as in the case of the Polonoroeste project in Rondonia). These actions may set a precedent for other lenders and provide some concrete lessons in political strategy.

Ideology

Class societies evolve belief systems that morally justify existing social and economic arrangements and, hence, preserve the privileges of dominant groups. There is thus an economic and a political side to the formation of idea-systems that, once produced, become weapons in the clash of social interests (Wolf 1982:390). We use the term "ideology" to refer to such ideas, noting their functional relationship to the organization of production and distribution and to the interests of particular social classes.

In the nineteenth and early twentieth centuries, when Brazil was a thoroughly agrarian society, landed elites embraced Ricardo's law of comparative advantage, which saw in the export of agricultural commodities the road to wealth and progress. The ascendance in the 1930s of new economic and political groups, whose fortunes were bound to urban-based manufacturing, forged a different development strategy that put exclusive faith in the expansion of industrial production. The present-day "growth-mania" for which Brazil is internationally known began during this period, and was later formalized by growth models (from Keynes to Rostow) that sought to maximize annual aggregate real output (GNP—gross national product).

The single-minded obsession with increasing GNP, and an uncritical faith in the idea that growth would lead to the Rostovian notion of "economic takeoff," put environmental concerns squarely in the category of transitory social costs. Brazil's representative to the 1972 Stockholm Conference on the Human Environment explicitly held this view (Goodland 1985:5). The United States, England, and Japan, he claimed, had already polluted the environment and, so doing, became developed. Brazil, he argued, could ill afford the "luxury" of environmental preoccupations until the country reached a similar stage.

The accepted growth paradigm is invoked by specific groups whenever they find its precepts compatible with their interests. For the social scientist, this basic principle goes a long way in clarifying the content of the debate in the sphere of Amazonian development policy. Fiscal and credit incentives for cattle ranching, the switch to private rather than public colonization schemes, investment in large-scale projects—all of these initiatives and many others are justified on the grounds of their contribution to GNP.

It is the power of ideology that makes the validity of these arguments, and their respective project manifestations, seem thoroughly self-evident. Calls for a more equitable distribution of land or income, programs to set aside large tracts of land for indigenous groups, proposals to pay attention to environmental degradation—any ideas or policies that run counter to assumptions embedded in dominant ideology (and which threaten the position of vested interest groups) at best receive little attention. At worst, the ideas are labeled "subversive" and their proponents silenced by the repressive arm of the state (Schmink 1982).

Even environmental reasoning can be a useful weapon in the struggle to bend state policy to the needs of private accumulation. The *Second Development Plan for Amazonia (1975-1979)*, for example, was heavily influenced by the political pressures brought to bear by business interests. The Plan explicitly disavowed the government's earlier commitment to small-farmer colonization projects in favor of the more "rational" and "less predatory" form of occupation to be achieved by backing private entrepreneurs. According to the Plan, the "indiscriminate migration" to the region of poorly educated groups who employ rudimentary technology, far from contributing to the development of the Amazon, only "exacerbates ecological damage to natural resources" (SUDAM 1976:13). By implication, large-scale, highly technical investments by private business are rational, non-predatory and ecologically sound. This argument was bolstered by studies that showed that pasture actually improved soil nutrients, a claim that has not withstood more detailed research (Jordan 1985; Hecht 1985).

The end of the Brazilian miracle in the mid-1970s, the economic decline of the 1980s, and the gradual opening up of political debate during this period stimulated the beginnings of a conservation movement in Brazil. Growing popular concern was reflected in the creation of a Special Environmental Secretariat and the passage of a comprehensive National Environmental Policy in 1981 (Goodland 1985:5). A number of parks and reserves have been established, and the environmental impact of some major development projects is now being monitored. These are important steps, although their impact on the overall pattern of deforestation has so far been small. A sobering economic climate and a return to a democratic political system make this a propitious time to reformulate current development models so that land occupation and resource use in Amazonia will become more consistent with long-term sustainability.

Any attempt to modify the manner of exploiting the natural environment must necessarily confront both structural and ideological opposition. Ideas are never "innocent." Mental conceptions, including belief systems, morality, philosophy, and law, either reinforce or challenge existing social and economic arrangements. And they do so actively, as biased participants in sociopolitical intercourse. From these sets of assumptions it follows that development and resource management initiatives that seek to moderate the biophysical degradation inherent in unchecked economic accumulation can prevail only if strategically promoted on the basis of a realistic assessment of the strengths and the vulnerabilities of the projects' material and ideological opponents.

Policy Scenarios

To summarize, in modern social systems characterized by expanded production, the way in which natural resources are exploited is largely determined by the imperatives of private accumulation. Associated with a given structure of production and accumulation is a complex array of social classes and interest groups, each possessing varying degrees of social power. Compared to subordinate classes, those groups that occupy positions of wealth and privilege also command a greater voice in the realm of politics and public policy. Hence, the institutions and agencies of the state, as well as the corresponding ideological assumptions that justify state action (or inaction), tend to cater to the needs of the dominant classes.

Environmental policies and resource management projects that seek to protect the long-term sustainability of the biophysical system often run counter to the logic of private accumulation and, as a consequence, to the interests of powerful social actors. Thus, any attempt to modify the human exploitation of the natural environment in ways that entail the redistribution of costs and such benefits as access to resources and to forms of production must inevitably contend with a wide range of economic, political, and ideological factors. It is our contention that we can enhance the chances of successful intervention if these sociopolitical considerations are explicitly incorporated into the design and the execution of environmental policy.

The methodological agenda we propose begins with defining a specific policy goal(s) for a particular place. The objective may be environmental (conservation of species) or socioeconomic (small-farmer production) or, as is often the case, may simultaneously include several different goals. Indeed, Amazon development policies have often endorsed conflicting goals, as noted earlier. The failure squarely to address the potential conflicts in goal definition has predisposed many costly programs to failure. In the case of the Transamazon colonization project, for example, the fundamental contradiction between social goals (distribution of land to resource-poor settlers) and economic objectives (increasing agricultural production) was a major, and ultimately fatal, flaw in the project design. While administrators selected colonists on the basis of region of origin, large family size, lack of other property, and individual need, evaluators later assessed project success in terms of performance in agricultural production. The latter form of success was more adequately predicted by other factors, such as previous management experience and ownership of durable goods (Moran 1981).

A clear definition of policy goals, and the choices, contradictions, and trade-offs they imply, is ultimately a political question, one that will be determined in the broader socioeconomic arena. Nonetheless, a careful screening of initial goals will help to identify the areas where choices or compromises will be required.

The second step in the strategy is to examine the existing system of resource exploitation in the area to be affected by the proposed policy. The procedure involves what Vayda (1983) calls a "progressive contextualization." It begins by focusing on significant human activities or people/environment interactions (e.g., land clearing, timber cutting, mining, hunting), and then explains such interactions by placing them within progressively wider contexts. The process starts with an analysis of a specific activity performed by particular people in a given place, then traces the causes and the effects of these activities outwards. In so doing the strategy is committed to the holistic premise that an empirically observed behavioral phenomenon can be understood only if the particular event is seen as part of the larger social, economic, and political context.

We believe (in contrast to Vayda, who shuns the use of any a priori framework) that the concepts and relationships comprising the political economy perspective are useful in organizing this "contextualizing" analysis. The analysis makes use of economics, history, and the social sciences to investigate the various forms of economic activity in a given region, to identify the social groups involved in each activity, and to understand how these groups appropriate different aspects of the natural environment. A political economy perspective further draws attention to the relationships between different social groups and to the potential for conflicts which, in turn, may have important consequences for the natural environment. The investigation at this stage also relies on ecology and the natural sciences to specify the environmental impact of the forms of extraction and production associated with the various economic activities.

The third step is to analyze the content of project goals in relation to what is known about existing systems. Which elements of those systems seem to be compatible with the goals defined at the outset, and which would have to be changed? Such questions must be addressed even in the absence of complete information about either the social or physical sphere. It is therefore useful at this stage to proceed by proposing alternative scenarios, each of which implies a different set of recommendations. The range of acceptable divergence from project goals should also be defined. Tools such as the concept of carrying capacity may be useful in defining the limits of policy options, provided they integrate both socioeconomic and environmental variations (Fearnside 1986).

We can expect the policy recommendations derived from alternative scenarios to affect in different ways the material interests of the social groups associated with the existing organization of production. The fourth step, therefore, is to "map" the sociopolitical structure, identifying the classes and interest groups likely to be helped or hurt by the recommended change in resource use. At this stage, consultation with planners, with the local population, and with others likely to be affected by the proposed scenarios (such as bankers and exporters) will provide crucial information. The potential interactions, conflicts, and trade-offs identified in the earlier assessment of existing resource-use patterns will point to key areas of concern at this stage. Issues of growth versus sustainability, large versus small enterprises, public versus private sector, and redistribution versus accumulation must be scrutinized in relation to the policy choices at hand. If the goal is creation of stable regional markets, should incentives for large cattle enterprises oriented primarily to markets outside the Amazon be phased out? Are there ways to incorporate different goals, which benefit distinct social groups, into a more complex approach? An important aspect of this stage is to assess the magnitude of the economic, political, and ideological resources available to potential supporters and opponents of the proposed policy alternatives. If competing or conflicting policy objectives are to be addressed, institutional mechanisms must be found to support the claims of less-powerful constituencies, such as peasant and native groups.

The final step in formulating an intervention strategy can be thought of as a bargaining process. On one side are the desiderata of a proposed resource-use model that has been refined and assessed through the approach outlined above. Weighed against the defined objectives are the ecological, economic, and sociopolitical obstacles to the changes required to achieve them. Actual policy is the outcome of a process of successive compromises. Initial concessions are made to the interest groups over which one has no control, and to the major constraints that cannot be changed. Each modification of this type will require a reevaluation of goals, outcomes, and costs. The final stage will be reached when the intervention strategy is within the range of feasible options. What can be realistically endorsed will depend on the assessment of the resources available, on the relative strengths of the various interests arrayed on both sides, and, in general, on the prospects for success given anticipated obstacles. By avoiding the abstractions of "ideal" or "optimum" goals, such a pragmatic view of the evaluation of policy scenarios provides the basis for the tough choices and creative thinking required to improve development policy in the Amazon and elsewhere.

Notes

1. Others have called for a "political ecology" perspective (e.g., Hjort 1982) but no one, to our knowledge, has developed one.

References

Althusser, Louis, and Etienne Balibar
   1968   Reading Capital. London: Verso.
Alvim, Paulo de T.
   1980   Agricultural Production Potential of the Amazon Region. *In* Land, People and Planning in Contemporary Amazonia. Françoise Barbira-Scazzocchio, ed. Cambridge: Cambridge University, Centre of Latin American Studies, Occasional Publication No. 3.

Bergman, Roland W.
　1980　Amazon Economics: The Simplicity of Shipibo Indian Wealth. Dellplain Latin American Studies, No. 6. Ann Arbor, MI: University Microfilms.
Browder, John O.
　1985　Subsidies, Deforestation and the Forest Sector in the Brazilian Amazon. Washington, DC: Report to the World Resources Institute.
　1986　Logging the Rainforest: A Political Economy of Timber Extraction and Unequal Exchange in the Brazilian Amazon. Ph.D. dissertation, University of Pennsylvania.
Bunker, Stephen G.
　1985　Underdeveloping the Amazon. Urbana, IL: University of Illinois Press.
Butler, John R.
　1985　Land, Gold and Farmers: Agricultural Colonization and Frontier Expansion in the Brazilian Amazon. Ph.D. dissertation, University of Florida.
Carnoy, Martin
　1984　The State and Political Theory. Princeton, NJ: Princeton University Press.
Chayanov, A. V.
　1966　The Theory of Peasant Economy. Homewood, IL: Richard D. Irwin.
Collins, Jane L.
　1986　Smallholder Settlement of Tropical South America: The Social Causes of Ecological Destruction. Human Organization 45:1–10.
Fearnside, Philip M.
　1986　Human Carrying Capacity of the Brazilian Rainforest. New York, NY: Columbia University Press.
Forman, Shepard
　1975　The Brazilian Peasantry. New York, NY: Columbia University Press.
Foweraker, Joe
　1981　The Struggle for Land. Cambridge: Cambridge University Press.
Goodland, Robert J. A.
　1980　Environmental Ranking of Amazonian Development. *In* Land, People and Planning in Contemporary Amazonia. Françoise Barbira-Scazzocchio, ed. Pp. 1–20. Cambridge: Cambridge University, Centre of Latin American Studies, Occasional Publication No. 3.
　1985　Brazil's Environmental Progress in Amazonian Development. *In* Change in the Amazon Basin, Vol. I: Man's Impact on Forests and Rivers. John Hemming, ed. Pp. 5–35. Manchester: Manchester University Press.
Hecht, Susanna B.
　1985　Environment, Development and Politics: Capital Accumulation and the Livestock Sector in Eastern Amazonia. World Development 13:663–684.
Hjort, Anders
　1982　A Critique of "Ecological" Models of Pastoral Land Use. Nomadic Peoples 10:11–27.
Jordan, Carl F.
　1985　Nutrient Cycling in Tropical Forest Ecosystems. New York, NY: Wiley.
Mendes, Armando Dias
　1985　Major Projects and Human Life in Amazonia. *In* Change in the Amazon Basin, Vol. I: Man's Impact on Forests and Rivers. John Hemming, ed. Pp. 44–57. Manchester: Manchester University Press.
Moran, Emilio F.
　1974　The Adaptive System of the Amazonian Caboclo. *In* Man in the Amazon. Charles Wagley, ed. Pp. 136–159. Gainesville, FL: University of Florida Press.

1981   Developing the Amazon. Bloomington, IN: Indiana University Press.
Myers, Norman
1980   The Primary Source. Tropical Forests and Our Future. New York, NY: Norton.
Painter, Michael, Carlos A. Perez-Crespo, Martha Llanos Albornóz, Susan Hamilton, and William L. Partridge
1984   Colonización y desarrollo regional: lecciones de San Julián, Bolivia. Binghamton, NY: Institute for Development Anthropology.
Parker, Eugene, Darrell Posey, John Frechione, and Luiz Francelino da Silva
1983   Resource Exploitation in Amazonia: Ethnoecological Examples from Four Populations. Annals of Carnegie Museum 52(8):163–203.
Pinto, Lúcio Flávio
1980   Amazônia: No Rastro do Saque. São Paulo: Hucitec.
1982   Carajás, O Ataque ao Coração da Amazônia. Rio: Editora Marco Zero.
Posey, Darrell A.
1985   Native and Indigenous Guidelines for New Amazonian Development Strategies: Understanding Biological Diversity through Ethnoecology. *In* Change in the Amazon Basin, Vol. I: Man's Impact on Forests and Rivers. John Hemming, ed. Pp. 156–181. Manchester: Manchester University Press.
Ross, Eric
1978   The Evolution of the Amazon Peasantry. Journal of Latin American Studies 10:193–218.
Sawyer, Donald R.
1984   Frontier Expansion and Retraction in Brazil. *In* Frontier Expansion in Amazonia. Marianne Schmink and Charles H. Wood, eds. Pp. 180–203. Gainesville, FL: University of Florida Press.
Schmink, Marianne
1982   Land Conflicts in Amazonia. American Ethnologist 9:341–357.
Silva, Jose Graziano da
1980   A porteira já esta fechando? Revista Ensaios de Opinião. March.
Smith, Nigel J. H.
1974   Destructive Exploitation of the South American River Turtle. Association of Pacific Coast Geographers 36:85–101.
1982   Rainforest Corridors: The Transamazon Colonization Scheme. Berkeley, CA: University of California Press.
Spears, John, and Edward S. Ayensu
1984   Sectoral Paper on Forestry. World Resources Institute, Global Possible Conference. Resources Development and the New Century.
SUDAM (Superintendência do Desenvolvimento da Amazônia/Superintendency for the Development of the Amazon)
1976   II Plano de Desenvolvimento da Amazônia: Detalhamento do II Plano Nacional de Desenvolvimento (1975–1979). Belém: SUDAM.
Vayda, Andrew P.
1983   Progressive Contextualization: Methods for Research in Human Ecology. Human Ecology 11(3):265–281.
Wagley, Charles
1968   Amazon Town. A Study of Man in the Tropics. New York, NY: Alfred A. Knopf.
Wood, Charles H., and Marianne Schmink
1978   Blaming the Victim: Small Farmer Production in an Amazon Colonization

Project. Studies in Third World Societies, Publication Number 7, "Changing Agricultural Systems in Latin America." Pp. 77–93.

Wolf, Eric R.
  1982   Europe and the People Without History. Berkeley, CA: University of California Press.

3

Insiders and Outsiders in Baluchistan: Western and Indigenous Perspectives on Ecology and Development

Brian Spooner

We have generally become used to the idea that ethnographers are a part of what they study. They live in the community they study and participate in the events and (ideally) in the social and cultural processes which they analyze and interpret. They cannot stand either theoretically or methodologically outside what they study—even though we do not perhaps all of us always manage to follow through with the implications of this condition.

The evolutionary ecologist knows implicitly that his professional activity, like all other human activity, takes place within the evolutionary process. But his orientation towards his subject matter tends to be very different from that of the ethnographer. Other investigators, and particularly economists and development planners, study unequivocally from without—they translate the laboratory-objectivity tradition of Western scientific method into the field. The growing emphasis on popular participation in development planning and implementation draws attention to these differences of orientation. In this chapter a case from Baluchistan will be used to illustrate the significance of the difference.

Ecology and Ethnography

We use the word "ecology" in two senses. It was coined to denote the scientific study (*-logia*) of "household" (*oiko-*) relations in and between communities, in and between biological populations, and between them and their physical environment. It has come to be used also for sets of those relations themselves. We often confuse these two meanings.

Ecology as a type of study has been pursued in various paradigms, most particularly a systemic "ecosystems" paradigm, and (more commonly in recent years) an evolutionary paradigm. In either of these paradigms it has been understood mainly as a natural science, deriving historically from biology, and using natural-science assumptions and models. Where social scientists have talked ecology—calling it cultural ecology, human ecology, or anthropological ecology—in their studies of human activities in relation to their natural matrix, they have explicitly borrowed concepts from biological ecology, and have talked in terms of adaptation, niche, etc. They have been concerned with the problem of explaining how human activities and experience are caused, conditioned, or affected by natural processes and conditions, rather than the other way round. Having no concepts that apply to both sides of the equation, physical-biological and human-cultural, they have tried applying concepts borrowed from the biological side.[1] Whether they begin from systemic or evolutionary assumptions, they run into similar problems: on the one hand we have not yet found a way to relate ethnographic data to evolutionary models; on the other, although for a time we had great hopes for systemic models of society, we have become disillusioned with them.

For this reason a serious dilemma underlies the attempts of biological ecologists, development planners, and anthropologists to work together in specific projects. This dilemma vitiates most ecologically oriented work related to development. (It is worth noting that in the past it has also had the effect of separating ecological anthropologists theoretically from their colleagues.) The dilemma is rarely faced. Whatever the focus of their work, biological ecologists tend implicitly to include human activity and its effects in their studies. However, as biologists they cannot treat human activity on the same level as the activity of other species, because as fellow human beings they impute values and intentions to it. Perhaps partly for this reason, they tend to treat it as intrusive.

There is good reason for them to treat human activity as intrusive. The organization of human activity commonly transcends the boundaries of ecosystems or habitats, and cannot therefore be usefully analyzed in terms of the ecologists' universe of study. Although human societies and cultures may be products of biological evolution, social and cultural processes do not fit into ecological systems or "communities." But ecologists' reasons for treating human activity as intrusive are more complicated than this, and not always entirely explicit: if they can manage to exclude it, there is nothing to prevent them from formulating their problems, hypotheses, methods, and solutions with the objectivity that is de rigeur in the Western scientific tradition. If they admit the presence of human activity on a level with other (nonhuman) activities, they find themselves in the position of having to deal with members of their own species (if not their own actual "population" or "community"), with whom, unlike the members of other species in their universe, they are unavoidably related (in the sense that their objectivity is compromised) by differences of interests and values—essentially, that is, by a political and moral (rather than a scientific) relationship (cf. Tucker 1977). They avoid this problem by treating all human activity as extraneous to the ecosystem. By thus reserving scientific objectivity for themselves they deftly condemn as beyond the pale all human opinion that differs from theirs.

Natural scientists are untrained to deal scientifically with questions of politics and morals. Social scientists *are* prepared for questions of politics and morals, but with rare exceptions do not adequately understand ecology. Not even those rare exceptions have yet proposed how to integrate the essential positivist objectivization of ecological science (which sees science as extra-cultural and absolute) with the semiotic approaches of social science (which see scientific arguments, like all other arguments, as socially and culturally conditioned or filtered), in order to arrive at a somewhat humbler and more practical scientific ecology that would not treat human activity as intrusive. Ignoring the problem has led many (including many social scientists) to the general conviction that we know what all human beings should think and do in relation to the productivity of the renewable natural resources to which they have access, irrespective of the legitimate interests of other people in those resources.

To return to the initial distinction between objective ecology and ecological analysis: unlike ecological reality, ecological analysis is (like ethnographic description) not absolute but relative; it is relative to the social and cultural experience of the scientist. Although the ecologists' situation is far less obvious, they are in fact as much a part of what they are studying as are ethnographers of what they are studying. The identity of Western (as well as non-Western but Western-trained) ecologists derives from their place in their own society, and their society's position in the world, as well as from ideas from the cultural repertoire of their society which presently include (for example) positive thoughts about stewardship of nature ("we are responsible to God and to future generations for the condition of the natural world") and negative thoughts about the destructiveness of the "frontier mentality" ("there will always be more out there for us to exploit to our advantage").[2]

It is not too difficult to grasp and to explain the possibility of cultural variation in ecological orientation. We have become accustomed to the idea that different people from different cultural backgrounds have different values and consequently are likely to have different perceptions of nature and of their relation to it. But the ability to appreciate social differences seems to lie deeper in our cultural consciousness. Though we recognize them instinctively, we repress them, or at best proceed on the assumption that they are artificial and easily overcome, whereas in fact the more we seek to overcome them, the more they control our daily lives. Our feelings towards nature and the natural environment turn out to be a reflection of the way we relate to other people. Our ecological values are to a large extent a function of our social values.

This social dimension of ecology obscures our view of development problems. It is therefore on social variation in relation to territory and natural resources that I shall focus in the remainder of this chapter.

Ecology and Social Context

Social variables have to do with interests. Interests relate to individuals and to groups. In some cases (especially in the West) individual interests tend to take priority over group interests. In other cases (especially in some tribal societies—*pace* Hardin) group interests may take precedence over individual interests. Every ecological issue involves a range of different interests, representing conflict between individuals within a group, and between groups, between insiders, and between insiders and outsiders.

The classic case of an ecological issue between insiders and outsiders is the issue between "us" and "them," between the ecologist-consultant and the indigenous community. Mary Douglas, who has done more than anyone to sensitize us to the social mainspring of human experience, puts it this way:

> Unlike tribal society, we have the chance of self-awareness. Because we can set our own view in a general phenomenological perspective, just because we can compare our beliefs with theirs, we have an extra dimension of responsibility. Self knowledge is a great burden (1975:230–231).

If we are to acknowledge the burden that Douglas identifies, we must take account of the fact that statements about ecology are not just right or wrong. Apart from being objectively right or wrong, they have different meanings, more or less significant, according to whether one is a member of the ecological community in question or not, and (if one is a member) according to the particular position in that community that one occupies. Both the habitat and the ecological future look very different according to whether one is a hunter in a small closely knit society; or a dry-farmer, a pastoralist, or an irrigator in a society that may also include people with different resource interests; or a steel worker in a modern complex society, where one is not committed to a particular occupation or a particular relationship to the natural environment, but may (perhaps unconsciously) feel locked into a particular economic class. Just as there is more than one recognized valid interpretation of a modern industrial economy (the differences correlate with different political ideas about the ideal economy), so the ecosystem may look very different according to the niche one occupies within—or outside it.

For comparison let us imagine ourselves in Disneyland. Take the case of a gazelle in an open steppe ecosystem. Although everything is indeed connected to everything else (cf. Commoner 1971:29), the survival interests of grasses and forbs, shrubs, herbivores, and predators are obviously in conflict. The ecologist stands outside the system but bases his research design implicitly on certain interrelated assumptions about productivity and diversity. However objective his research design, the ecologist is led by his assumptions to discriminate against the interests of individual creatures in favor of the survival of what he perceives as "the system." The survival of the system may, of course, be in the long-term best interests of the totality. It is definitely not, however, in the best interests of all the component species, let alone of all the living individuals, some of whom will inevitably sooner or later fall prey to predators. A reduction in the number of predators would, therefore, be in the best interests of some at least of the living herbivores. Similarly, a reduction in the number of herbivores would be in the best interests of many living plants.

If a gazelle could produce a study of the same ecosystem, we might expect the results to differ from those of the ecologist, inasmuch as they would, as a matter of course, be based on different values, which would derive from a different social situation. The gazelle's assumptions would of course not be disinterested. A member of the system, such as the gazelle, whose personal interests are at stake, would argue for his own survival first. But what about the ecologist? The ecologist can argue in terms of the survival of species and of the system, because survival on that level suits his own social values best. Both arguments may be equally objective and scientific, but differ on grounds of morals and personal interest, which are socially relative. The conflict between them is always in the end resolved politically, as a function of the difference in power of the individuals or the communities or the populations in question (cf. Spooner 1982a:7). Social scientists will also recognize here the familiar problem of the actual individual versus the abstract society. However, the issue of the conflict of interest between the cheetah, the gazelle, and the shrub is introduced in order to clarify the difference of interests between the Western-trained ecologist and the nomad, the horticulturalist, or the irrigator, each in relation to (not an ecosystem, but) all the other human, biological, and physical factors that impinge on their lives. A particular case from the Third World will show the significance of this argument for problems of development (standard of living) and ecology (habitat and natural resources).

A Case Study from Baluchistan

Baluchistan is the western province of Pakistan. The name comes from the Baluch, who comprise the majority of the population throughout most of the province, as well as in the neighboring province of Iran and the adjoining part of southern Afghanistan. The total population is estimated tentatively at four million. In all three countries the territory is arid and poor, and has remained for many centuries in comparative isolation from the major economic and political centers of the region. Baluch identity is symbolized in their language and oral literature and code of honor. Otherwise they are a heterogeneous collection of tribes of various origins, and the land they inhabit varies from high plateau with cold winters to subtropical coastal lowlands. They live by a mixture of dry and irrigated agriculture and pastoralism. Community organization varies between extremes of highly stratified villages (often in the past dominated by strong forts) and small egalitarian nomadic groups.

In Makran, the southwestern division of the province of Baluchistan in western Pakistan, and across the border in Iran, the nomadic pastoralists play a particularly significant social role. Their continued activity provides a communications network among the settled village communities and symbolizes for those communities the values that support traditional Baluch identity. They contribute significantly, that is, to both the logistics and the morale that are essential to the continued viability of Baluch society in the area. Unfortunately, these variables do not show up in either economic or ecological analysis.

Nomads are important for the local economy, both for what they produce and as a source of seasonal labor. They bring milk products to the local market, and they supply the necessary labor for the date harvest in the villages—the most important event in the traditional agricultural cycle, which coincides in late summer with the slack season in the pastoral cycle. They are also agricultural producers themselves. Much of the subsistence-crop production of the area depends on unpredictable river flow and runoff, which only the nomads know how to use. Small pockets of soil scattered throughout the area produce crops when a downpour happens to bring water by—if a nomad is there to channel and apply it. Although no one in the towns wants to live that life anymore, the idea of it remains an important cultural value: nomadic life is still thought of as the genuine Baluch life, which embodies the authentic Baluch virtues of honesty, loyalty, faith, hospitality, asylum for refugees, and so on.

There are no reliable figures to indicate how many of the Makran population of some 230,000 are now nomadic, nor how many of those who are nomads by socialization still spend most of the year in tents or other temporary dwellings with their families and flocks rather than taking one of the modern options of wage labor in the (until recently) booming Gulf Emirates, or wage labor in towns outside the province. We may estimate, conservatively, over 50,000.

The significance of the nomads for the future development of Makran far outweighs their numbers or their economic contribution. They are the only people who use or are ever likely to use some 90 percent of the territory of Makran. Without them the greater part of the population would be marooned in isolated oases, which on their own do not have the resources to be economically independent, and with increasing dependence on outside subsidies would gradually lose population to more attractive opportunities outside the province. With the nomads, the Baluch population as a whole forms an interdependent social and cultural, as well as economic and political, network covering the whole of the area. As long as the nomads are there, the whole of the area continues to be inhabited by people who consider it to be their territory. If the nomads leave, the settled population will see itself simply as an economically disadvantaged appendage of the national economy. As long as they remain, the total population shares a conception of ethnic provincial autonomy.

The nomads depend on the primary productivity of the semidesert and desert areas which cover the greater part of the territory. Traditionally they make no improvement in either the pasture or the watering resources. Based on comparison with other areas of similar climate and soils, ecologists evaluate most of this rangeland as severely degraded. Their evaluation is made without reference to the fact that the Baluch continue to make a living out of it, and without the possibility of direct comparison with earlier data. It is an outsider's evaluation, which focuses on the vegetation rather than on the evolving process of interaction between the vegetation and the pastoralists.

Pastoral activity is an essential component of the Baluch economy, and it contributes significantly to the social interaction and the culture of the province. Range science condemns Baluch pastoral practice. But no one has yet shown how the principles of range science might be integrated with the social conditions of this type of situation. The national economy is intruding more and more into the life of the area, helped by programs financed by USAID. A major consequence of these programs is increasing dependence of the population on the national and regional economies. For the time being, however, the pastoralist sees his main interests in continued exploitation of the range, of localized runoff, and of the socioeconomic resources of the scattered settlements of the area. The farmers in the settlements depend both on the pastoralists and on the outside economy. Loss of the pastoralists would significantly reduce the viability of most of the settlements. The pastoralists can use help, but what they need is not enforced improvement of their range through enforcement of Western range science principles, but defense against the effects of the national economy. The best defense would probably be in the form of management by government of the terms of trade, manipulating prices in such a way as to reinforce local values, instead of subverting them.

Western range ecology, as its name implies, starts with the range. The range scientist is the self-designated steward of the plant communities of the Baluch's range. According to the principles of this science, no more herbivores should be allowed onto the range than can graze without degrading its plant communities. The pastoralist, on the other hand, sees range, domesticated animals, and people in interdependent interaction. It would probably not be too much of an oversimplification to characterize this view as one that would emphasize the convenience of the family group in the context of its social matrix. The nomad's first priority is to avoid disruption of his social relations. If this would mean reduction of the productivity of the range for future generations, that is of secondary importance. In these times of rapid change, who knows what future generations will need?

However, there is evidence to suggest that the range has remained in its current "degraded" state for a long time, over a century (Hughes-Buller and Minchin 1906–1907), and we do not have convincing evidence that current *trends* are adverse. Unfortunately, no one will finance the studies that would be necessary to establish what the trends are. Such studies—which would construct an insider's ecology—would need to focus on interactions of pastoral technology, animal behavior, and plant communities over a period of time (cf. Nyerges 1982).

Comparable Cases

Such cases of insider's ecology are beginning to appear. In Africa pastoralists have the reputation of seeking to maximize numbers of animals.

Recent work by Sandford (1982 and in press) has provided a rational basis for this emphasis in range-science terms by synthesising accumulated existing information on what might be called indigenous range-management practices. Cossins (in press), using data gathered by ILCA (International Livestock Centre for Africa) research teams, has demonstrated that many pastoral systems in sub-Saharan Africa are also in fact more efficient in terms of productivity per hectare than ranching systems in either developing or developed countries. But as Legesse (in press) has shown in his study in northern Kenya, in order to understand what is going on ecologically among the Boran and the Gabra pastoralists, it is necessary to study the interdependence of their two sets of activities. What we need more than anything else, however, is some reconstruction of what has actually happened in the relationship between pastoralists and their resources over a significant period of time. Cassanelli is probably the first historian to work in the historical ecology of pastoralists. He brings the skills of an historian to bear on the problem, without the biases of either the ecologist or the anthropologist (in press).

In each of these cases there are obviously several different ways of defining the universe of reference—each producing different results. The Western ecologist wants primary productivity at the expense (if necessary) of current livelihood—on the assumption that we are otherwise sacrificing the livelihood of future generations to the interests of the living, and that we should not do that. The Baluch pastoralist sees market centers and agriculture as a resource on a level with the range. He wants more in return for his product, but his first priority is the security of his social life. Else he will think of leaving his niche. The range ecologist considers that the local range, and therefore also the global resource base, would be better off if the pastoralist would leave his niche. The Baluch farmer sees the nomads as a resource. He wants to keep them where they are; otherwise only economic subsidies will keep him where he is.

It would be easy to add examples of other forms of land use. A similar case could be made in the much more complex situation of the Punjabi irrigator (Spooner 1984b:28–39). But perhaps more interesting here is the case of the Susu in northwestern Sierra Leone (Nyerges 1985). Susu swiddeners do not have enough labor to produce an adequate food supply, though shortage of labor leads them to clear plots inadequately, with the result that the degradation of the forest proceeds at a slower pace than might otherwise be the case; recurrent famine keeps population and the labor force down; they cannot intensify to produce more food, because of insufficient labor; they cannot reduce labor inputs and de-intensify to fit labor availability, because they dare not risk lower production of food. But we cannot help them, because if we introduce labor or technology from outside, what we introduce will have a higher value for them than the local resources and they will degrade faster and have less interest in conserving local resources.

Since people do not fit easily into ecosystemic frames of reference, the shift from a systemic to an evolutionary paradigm in ecology has helped us to develop ways of incorporating local interests and points of view into ecological analsyis. However, in case I may have appeared to argue that social relativism is more important than global survival, let me in concluding emphasize that this is not my view. As I stated at the beginning, ecology is real; but ecological analysis derives from a particular social and cultural (and perhaps even ideological) position. To return to the Bambi-like example: without human intervention the gazelle population would probably never expand to the point where it disrupts the eco-"system." Malthusian factors would take care of them first. But human populations, having culture, are not always restricted by Malthusian pressures. On the contrary, they are often able to act out the scenarios of Marx and Boserup, and have done so periodically from the Neolithic up to the Green Revolution.

Furthermore, human beings, having culture, have rights—not only human rights but civil rights. We scientists and consultants learn our science and our morality in two different arenas. When we mix them we do so as amateurs. If we stand outside the ecosystem (as we do in the case of the gazelle and the Baluch) we artificially keep morality out of the discussion. In fact, however, every ecological question that involves human activity is not only an ecological question, but also both a moral question and a political question. Development has tended to ignore the political and moral dimensions of ecological (among other) problems, and has concentrated on the scientific and technological solution of the problem qua objectified ecological problem only. In the long term it cannot be done. The ecological dimension of the problem will be resolved only as part of a comprehensive resolution of the whole problem, including its moral and political dimensions. The primary productivity of the rangelands of Baluchistan must be taken care of not by ecologists but by politicians, using ecological among other information, at the level of national planning, adjusting the terms of trade so as to reinforce local values insofar as they are politically and morally desirable, making economic planning an instrument of social planning rather than a victim of ecological planning.[3]

Notes

1. It is not pertinent here that some of these concepts, such as "community," were originally derived from social studies. This borrowing has been written up by Rapport and Turner (1977) and Richerson (1977).

2. Passmore (1974a) reviews the history of these various attitudes towards nature in our own history in a book that helps in many ways to "remove the rubbish" (Passmore 1974b) from our everyday thinking about ecology.

3. This essay builds on three earlier essays in which I argue that (a) ecology is relative (1982b), (b) assessments of the ecology of dry lands should be assessments of the evolving relationship between human culturally organized activities and natural processes (1982a), and (c) the relationship between a population and its territory may be as valuable and as fragile as the ecosystem, and perhaps should be given planning priority over the ecosystem (1984a). My aim here has been to show how, without giving in to cultural relativism with regard to ecological analysis, there may

be a valid ecologically relevant local point of view that would direct our attention to more fruitful development objectives.

References

Cassanelli, Lee
　In press　Historical Perspectives on Pastoral Development: Examples from the Somali and the Maasai, Eastern Africa. *In* The Developing World: Challenges and Opportunities. Proceedings of the Second International Rangelands Congress, Adelaide, 1984. Brian Spooner, ed.

Commoner, Barry
　1971　The Closing Circle. New York, NY: Knopf.

Cossins, N. J.
　In press　The Productivity and Potential of Pastoral Systems. *In* The Developing World: Challenges and Opportunities. Proceedings of the Second International Rangelands Congress, Adelaide, 1984. Brian Spooner, ed. (See also ILCA Bulletin No. 21, pp. 10–15.)

Douglas, Mary
　1975　Implicit Meanings. London: Routledge and Kegan Paul.

Hughes-Buller, R., and C. F. Minchin
　1906–1907　Makran and Kharan. Volumes 7 and 7A of Baluchistan District Gazetteer. Bombay: Time Press.

Legesse, Asmarom
　In press　Gabra and Boran Pastoral Ecology. *In* The Developing World: Challenges and Opportunities. Proceedings of the Second International Rangelands Congress, Adelaide, 1984. Brian Spooner, ed.

Nyerges, A. Endre
　1982　Pastoralists, Flocks and Vegetation: Processes of Co-adaptation. *In* Desertification and Development: Dryland Ecology in Social Perspective. Brian Spooner and H. S. Mann, eds. Pp. 217–248. London: Academic Press.
　1985　Swidden Agriculture and the Savannization of Forests in Sierra Leone. Paper presented at 84th Annual Meeting of the American Anthropological Association.

Passmore, John
　1974a　Man's Responsibility for Nature. New York, NY: Scribners.
　1974b　Removing the Rubbish. Encounter 42(4):11–24.

Rapport, D. J., and J. E. Turner
　1977　Economic Models in Ecology. Science 196:367–373.

Richerson, Peter J.
　1977　Ecology and Human Ecology: A Comparison of Theories in the Biological and Social Sciences. American Ethnologist 4:1–26.

Sandford, Stephen
　1982　Pastoral Strategies and Desertification: Opportunism and Conservatism in Dry Lands. *In* Desertification and Development: Dryland Ecology in Social Perspective. Brian Spooner and H. S. Mann, eds. Pp. 61–80. London: Academic Press.
　In press　Traditional African Range Management Systems. *In* The Developing World: Challenges and Opportunities. Proceedings of the Second International Rangelands Congress, Adelaide, 1984. Brian Spooner, ed.

Spooner, Brian
  1982a Rethinking Desertification: The Social Dimension. *In* Desertification and
        Development: Dryland Ecology in Social Perspective. Brian Spooner and
        H. S. Mann, eds. Pp. 1–24. London: Academic Press.
  1982b Ecology in Perspective: The Human Context of Ecological Research. In-
        ternational Social Science Journal 34:396–410.
  1984a Nomads in a Wider Society. Cultural Survival Quarterly 8(1):23–25.
  1984b Ecology in Development: A Rationale for Three-Dimensional Policy. Tokyo:
        United Nations University.
Spooner, Brian, ed.
  In press The Developing World: Challenges and Opportunities. Proceedings of
        the Second International Rangelands Congress, Adelaide, 1984.
Spooner, Brian, and H. S. Mann, eds.
  1982 Desertification and Development: Dryland Ecology in Social Perspective.
        London: Academic Press.
Tucker, William
  1977 Environmentalism and the Leisure Class: Protecting Birds, Fishes, and
        Above All Social Privilege. Harpers 255(1531):49–67.

4

Monitoring Fertility Degradation of Agricultural Lands in the Lowland Tropics[1]

Emilio F. Moran

Introduction

The analysis of lands at risk has tended to take a macro perspective that reflects the justifiable fear of environmental degradation on a worldwide scale that we all face in the biosphere. However, this concern with the conservation of natural habitats and the maintenance of the productive capacity of agricultural lands should not obscure the lack of preciseness common in the use of terms such as "fragile lands," "soil degradation," and "lands at risk." While these terms are legitimately used to point to the need for conservation, they should be more precisely defined in order to maintain the credibility of the scientific community in policy circles. This is not an easy task to accomplish, given the range and variation of relevant factors, including soil types, crop species, crop varieties, microhabitats, and microclimates.

In this chapter I present a preliminary assessment of the parameters that might serve as measures of the risk of fertility degradation, defined as a 50 percent decline in agricultural productivity from first-year yields, that is posed by different kinds and uses of the agricultural lands in the humid tropics. A great deal more data is needed, as is a great deal more communication among specialists to sharpen the parameters defined and chosen herein.

The humid tropics encompass areas of the world with high temperature and humidity, a dry season of less than four consecutive months, and a cover of tropical forest vegetation. One and a half billion hectares of the earth's surface are included in the humid tropics, of which 45 percent are in tropical America (Sánchez 1987). The soils of tropical America tend to conform more closely to the stereotype of acid, low-nutrient conditions than do those of Africa or Asia (Table 4.1). Soil degradation is probably more severe in Africa because of the large areas of semiarid tropics with long dry seasons and limited soil cover. In the Amazon, degradation focuses on

TABLE 4.1   Distribution of Soils of the Humid Tropics Based on
            Dominant Soil Type in FAO Maps at a Scale of 1:5
            Million (in million hectares)

Soil Orders	Americas	Africa	Asia	Total	Percent
Oxisols	332	179	14	525	35
Ultisols	213	69	131	413	28
Inceptisols	61	75	90	226	15
Entisols	31	91	90	212	14
Alfisols	18	20	15	53	4
Histosols	4	4	23	31	2
Spodosols	10	3	6	19	1
Mollisols	–	–	7	7	–
Vertisols	1	2	2	5	–
Aridisols	3	1	1	5	–
TOTAL	673	444	379	1,496	100

Source: Based on Sánchez (1987).

acidity and fertility, rather than on soil erosion, surface crusting, and other
forms of severe soil degradation that occur but to a much lesser extent.
Table 4.2, for example, shows that about 81 percent of the soils of Latin
America are acidic and low in nutrients—as compared with 56 percent of
Africa's and 38 percent of Asia's. By contrast, as much as 33 percent of
humid tropical Asia has soils of moderately high base status, as compared
with only 12 percent of humid tropical Africa and 7 percent of tropical
America (National Research Council 1982). In short, there are significant
differences between the soils of Latin America, Africa, and Asia that ought
to be noted in making assessments as to their fragility or risk of degradation—
rather than lumping all of these areas as if they represented the same kind
of risk.

TABLE 4.2 Distribution of Soil Grouping (in percent)

	Americas	Africa	Asia	World
Acid, low fertility soils (Oxisols, Ultisols, dystropepts)	81	56	38	63
Moderately fertile, well-drained soils (Alfisols, Vertisols, Mollisols, andepts, tropepts, fluvents)	7	12	33	15
Poorly-drained soils (aquepts)	6	12	6	8
Very infertile sandy soils (psamments, Spodosols)	2	16	6	7
Shallow soils (lithic Entisols)	3	3	10	5
Organic soils (Histosols)	1	1	6	2
TOTAL	100	100	100	100

Source: Sánchez (1987).

Physical/Chemical Elements in a Definition of Lands at Risk

An important volume evaluating the state of knowledge on tropical forests chose the title *Fragile Ecosystems* (Farnworth and Golley 1974). In that volume the conference participants emphasized the importance of working toward a sustained yield of products useful to man without degradation of the productivity, richness, and long-term viability of ecosystems. This is the ecologists' meaning of environmental degradation: a loss of natural habitat, whether to agriculture, pasture, mines or settlement. It is not the meaning I nor many others follow in talking about degradation. It is best always to clarify whether the subject is "environmental degradation," "fertility degradation" (the meaning used in this chapter), or "soil degradation" (referring to compaction, erosion, etc.).

One of the most instructive conclusions of the Farnworth and Golley volume refers to the relevance of climate as a variable. Macroclimatic data, for example, suggest that the action of temperature patterns is of relatively little significance for plants and animals, given that mean temperature fluctuations are well within the range of tolerance of most tropical organisms (1974:11). The study goes on to warn, however, that these macroclimatic data are largely irrelevant to the issue, since within localized areas there can be major temperature fluctuations that significantly affect the ecology of the plants and animals found there. This warning could be extended to most of the current discussion of the fragility of the humid tropics, which is over-reliant on macroclimatic and aggregate data sets that lump the considerable variation of these regions and obscure the environmental realities. Indeed, it might be argued that one of the reasons for the inability of governments to stop current rates of deforestation and to monitor soil fertility degradation is due to the insensitivity of policy-makers to the variation present in the areas they are supposed to be managing—as well as their sometimes compromised position as actual beneficiaries of the process of deforestation through their alliance with logging companies and large-scale ranchers.

Effects of Initial Conditions

Soils of the humid tropics vary a great deal in physical and chemical characteristics, and it must be recognized that these initial characteristics constrain the agricultural potential of tropical lands in different ways. The initial characteristics of soils form the first set of things that are worth examining in determining the overall risk of fertility degradation. There may be soils that pose such serious constraints to cultivation (or whose constraints cannot be adequately corrected at current levels of capitalization or technology) that clearing them of forest is a conscious contribution to environmental, soil, and fertility degradation.

A recent assessment of the distribution of soil constraints in the humid tropics summarized in Table 4.3 shows that while most of the soils are indeed nutrient-poor (64 percent overall), they are less subject to low effective cation exchange capacity than generally thought (11 percent overall), and they present less erosion potential than many other areas (17 percent overall—except for Asia, where 33 percent of humid tropical soils occur in slopes of over 30 percent). In addition, the medium to high fertility soils that are found in the humid tropics do not occur in a small number of patches, but rather appear throughout the regions. Laterite tends to occur in high promontories, and is thus unlikely to be farmed, because they are preferred sites for settlement. Areas of high erosion potential (i.e., steep slopes) occur throughout the humid tropics, and they would generally serve the population better as forests than as agricultural land, except on the gentle slopes where contour planting can accommodate the high rates of rainfall. Some of the best Alfisols of the Amazon occur in precisely these kinds of undulating landscapes. There are some 207 million hectares of

TABLE 4.3   Distribution of Soil Constraints in the Humid Tropics
            (in percent)

Soil Constraint	Americas	Africa	Asia	Humid Tropics
Low nutrient reserves	66	67	45	64
Aluminum toxicity	61	53	41	56
High P fixation	47	20	33	37
Acid, not Al toxic	11	22	33	18
Slopes over 30 percent	18	5	33	17
Poor drainage	11	14	19	13
Low ECEC	8	20	5	11
Shallow depth	7	4	12	7
No major limit	3	2	2	3
Shrink/swell	1	1	2	1
Allophane	1	-	2	1
Acid sulfate soils	-	1	3	1
Gravel	-	1	1	1
Salinity	-	-	2	-
Sodic Soils	1	1	-	-
TOTAL	100	100	100	100

Source: Sánchez (1987).   Table based on Sánchez, Couto and Buol
(1982).

TABLE 4.4   Main Soil Constraints in the Amazon under Native
            Vegetation

Soil Constraint	Million Hectares	% of Amazon
Phosphorus deficiency	436	90
Aluminum toxicity	353	73
Drought stress	254	53
Low potassium reserves	242	50
Poor drainage/flood hazard	116	24
High phosphorus fixation	77	16
Low cation exchange capacity	64	13
High erodibility	39	8
No major limitations	32	7
Slopes of over 30 percent	30	6
Laterite hazard if subsoil exposed	21	4

Source: Based on Cochrane and Sánchez (1982), cited in Sánchez
(1987).

well-drained soils in the Amazon occurring on slopes of less than 8 percent
(Cochrane and Sánchez 1982).

The major soil constraints in the humid and lowland tropics appear to
be low nutrient reserves, aluminum toxicity, high phosphorus (P) fixation,
acidic soils, soils on slopes above 30 percent, and areas of low effective
cation exchange capacity. Table 4.4 illustrates how the Amazon fares in this
list of constraints. In addition, I will discuss briefly the impact of land-
clearing methods and other constraints coming from the socioeconomic
systems present in the contemporary Amazon.

Phosphorus Deficiency. Phosphorus deficiency has been found in 90 percent
of Amazon soils, and 50 percent of Amazon soils have low reserves of
potassium. These low levels of nutrients pose serious constraints to cultivation. Normally, the release of nutrients to the soil in swidden farming
provides sufficient amounts of these nutrients to obtain one or two crops

on the dominant Oxisols and Ultisols, longer on the medium-to-high-fertility Alfisols and Inceptisols, without fertilization. A good soil-covering crop and crops that do not make excessive demands on these nutrients might extend the number of cropping seasons. Cereal and grain legumes take up 10–35 kg P/ha depending on whether yields are 1 or 8 tons per hectare. "Root crops are high extractors of phosphorus" in the order of 35–40 kg P/ha, with the exception of sweet potatoes and yams (Sánchez 1976:263–264). Bananas are low phosphorus extractors, but high potassium extractors. Tree crops remove little phosphorus in the harvested parts (in the order of 2 kg P/ha) and the nutrient cycling of these crops probably provides most of their phosphorus requirements (Sánchez 1976:263–264). The choice of crop, therefore, plays a major role in the sustainability of the agricultural system and on its continuing requirements for nutrients. Critical levels for P vary between crops, but less than 2 ppm of available P in the soil is generally associated with low yields even for relatively undemanding crops. Approximately one-half the soils of Amazonia are below this figure, while 90 percent are below 7 ppm of available P (Cochrane and Sánchez 1982:170).

In general, any sustained cultivation will have to plan on fertilizer applications. This last point must be emphasized since it is common in conservationist and anthropological writings to suggest that if the soils cannot be farmed in a sustained manner without fertilizers, then the system is inappropriate. There are no soils on earth that can be cultivated for extended periods of time without replenishing the nutrients removed (Buol and Sánchez 1984). This can be done by incorporating animal and plant waste into the soil, or by use of inorganic fertilizers. Given the thinness of the organic horizon in most of the humid tropics, organic fertilizers coming from plant and animal residues offer numerous advantages over inorganic ones. In very intensive systems, with plentiful labor and nearby markets to absorb production, such a strategy should work well—as it did in many areas of Asia, although inorganic fertilizers are dominant today. It is less likely to succeed, however, in areas of low demographic density far removed from markets capable of absorbing the higher production. Research on tolerance to low levels of available phosphorus is still in its infancy in the humid tropics and future findings may show that low levels of application can result in relatively good yields in the years ahead. All things being equal, crop varieties and species with lower available phosphorus requirements should be chosen to reduce the rates of depletion of initial P and to reduce fertilizer requirements.

High Phosphorus Fixing Capacity. There are 77 million hectares of soils in the Amazon that are both deficient in phosphorus and have a high fixation capacity. Fortunately, this areal extent constitutes only 16 percent of the Basin. These are soils that fix large quantities of phosphorus into relatively insoluble forms. The more acid soils also have higher phosphorus fixation capacities, as do those with higher topsoil clay content—an indirect effect of the iron and aluminum oxide contents found in the clay fraction of red and yellow soils (Sánchez 1976:260).

TABLE 4.5   Critical Levels of Aluminum Saturation and Soil pH
            for a Number of Crops

Area	Crop	<50% max yield		90% max yield	
		pH	Aluminum saturation (%)	pH	Aluminum saturation (%)
Brazil[a]	Maize	-	-	5.3-5.6	<10
Puerto Rico[b]	Maize	4.4	50	5.0	<15
United States[c]	Maize	4.5	60	5.1	<40
Philippines[d]	Maize	4.4	46	5.0	<20
Brazil[a]	Soybean	-	-	5.6	<10
Puerto Rico[e]	Soybean	5.0	20	5.6	<10
United States[c]	Soybean	4.9	40	5.6	<20
Puerto Rico[f]	Sugarcane	4.4	50	5.0	<10
United States[c]	Cotton	5.0	45	6.0	<7
Uganda[g]	Cotton	-	-	5.3	0
Puerto Rico[b]	Green bean	4.3	50	5.2	<10

[a]Soares et al. 1975.   [b]Abruña et al. 1975.   [c]Kamprath 1970.
[d]Samonte and Ocampo 1977.   [e]Abruña et al. 1978.   [f]Abruña and
Vicente-Chandler 1967.   [g]Foster 1970.

Reprinted from E. Kamprath, "Soil Acidity in Well-drained Soils of
the Tropics as a Constraint to Food Production," in IRRI/Cornell,
Soil Related Constraints to Food Production in the Tropics, Los
Banos, Philippines: International Rice Research Institute, 1980,
p. 182, by permission of the publisher, IRRI.

Aluminum Saturation. It is sometimes difficult to differentiate between
the effects of high aluminum saturation and low phosphorus availability in
acid soils of the humid tropics (Sánchez 1976:269). "Aluminum is known
to precipitate phosphorus in root cell walls and cytoplasmic membranes as
aluminum phosphates." Thus, species capable of transporting phosphorus
faster may escape this precipitation and can be more tolerant of high
aluminum levels (Sánchez 1976:270). Sweet potatoes, rice, and corn seem
to be tolerant of low phosphorus levels, as are tropical pasture legumes
such as *Stylosanthes humilis* and *Centrosema pubescens.* However, significant
differences between varieties of rice have been found (Salinas and Sánchez
1976:156). Table 4.5 illustrates the critical levels of aluminum saturation
and soil pH for a number of crops. To achieve a 90 percent maximum yield,
aluminum saturation can be no higher than 10 to 20 percent, whereas the
yields decline to 50 percent of maximum with aluminum saturation between
40 and 60 percent, depending on the crop (Kamprath 1980:180–181). There

are wide varietal differences in tolerance to aluminum saturation and soil acidity, and this constitutes one of the most important research areas in coping with this constraint to food production.

Three-quarters of Amazon soils have aluminum toxicity problems, and aluminum saturation is the main reason behind the acidity of soils. Swidden burning provides a corrective for this acidity, but the pH starts declining again with time. Another workable solution is to choose soils for cultivation that have higher pH and little or no aluminum saturation. Populations long familiar with the microecosystems of Amazonia have been known to use vegetative criteria in choosing soils with pH above 6.0 with uncanny accuracy (Moran 1977, 1981, 1984). Liming or working with aluminum tolerant plants can also lead to extension of the period before abandonment.

The relationship between soil pH and aluminum saturation is a close one (see Figure 4.1) since aluminum is precipitated at a pH between 5.5 and 6.0 (Sánchez 1976:224). Oxisols and Ultisols tend to be high in percentages of aluminum saturation, whereas Alfisols tend to be low. Poor crop development is directly correlated with aluminum saturation (see Figure 4.2). Acid soil infertility is due to aluminum toxicity, calcium or magnesium deficiency, or manganese toxicity. The most common cause is aluminum toxicity, which directly injures the root system by restricting root development.

Aluminum tends to accumulate in the roots and impede the translocation of calcium and phosphorus to the tops of plants, thereby accentuating calcium and phosphorus deficiencies (Sánchez 1976:231). Although the exact critical level varies from crop to crop and between varieties, 60 percent aluminum saturation is generally associated with significant ill effects on root growth. Only certain crops that evolved in the humid tropics appear to be able to perform well in the 60 to 75 percent aluminum saturation level (e.g., upland rice, cassava, mango, cashew, cowpeas, pineapple, and some tropical pasture legumes).

Manganese becomes very soluble at pH values lower than 5.5. A soil solution concentration between 1 and 4 ppm of manganese is a desirable goal. It might require liming to maintain desirable levels and avoid toxicity resulting from oversupply.

Low Cation Exchange Capacity. About 64 million hectares or 15 percent of the Amazon Basin has effective cation exchange capacity (ECEC) values below 4 milliequivalents (meq)/100 g. At these low levels, many nutrient cations are rapidly lost by leaching, a loss that causes nutrient imbalance problems. Raising ECEC to 4 ppm can be accomplished by liming with oxide layer silicate systems and by increasing soil organic matter content. In Oxisols and Ultisols, the maintenance of organic matter is almost synonymous with the maintenance of ECEC (Sánchez 1976:155). The role of organic fertilizers becomes evident in the management of this deficiency.

So far we have discussed only the constraints posed by the initial characteristics of acid soils of the lowland tropics. In addition to these constraints, numerous others are posed by the types of human intervention brought to bear upon these natural resources. Most critical in this regard

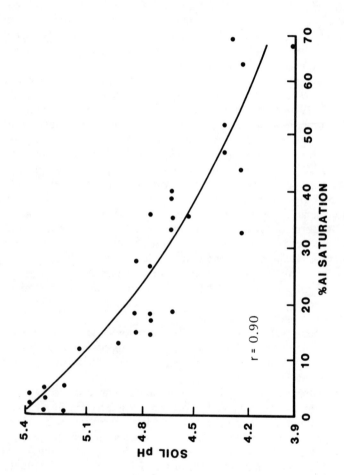

Fig. 4.1 Relationship Between Soil pH and Aluminum Saturation in Eight Ultisols and Oxisols of Puerto Rico.

Source: Abruña et al. (1975); Sánchez (1976:225).

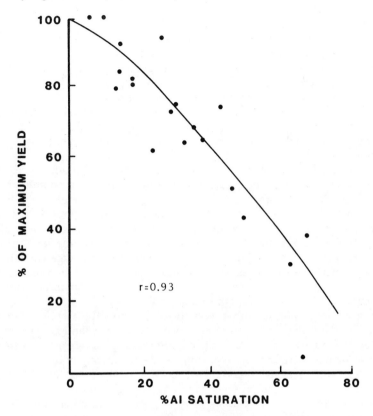

Fig. 4.2 Relationship Between Aluminum Saturation
Levels and Snap Bean Production.

Source: Abruña et al. (1975); Sánchez (1976:231).

appear to be the choice of land-clearing method, the crops chosen, and the management of the land.

Effects of Cultivation
and Other Management Practices

There is a recurrent tendency in social science and environmentalist writings to blame either initial macro-environmental conditions or the existing political/economic systems for the destruction of humid tropical ecosystems (Meggers 1971; Uhl 1980, 1983; and Foweraker 1981; to name but a few). These treatments tend to aggregate Amazonian ecosystems in a manner that submerges the existence of large areas where the typical constraints mentioned in this chapter—low P reserves, high P fixation, low ECEC, high aluminum saturation, and steep slopes—are not present. Such treatments tend also to discuss poor rural peoples as a lumpenpeasantry or lumpen-proletariat, rather than as a highly diverse population with a broad range of goals. The exploiter class is treated in a similarly simplified manner, as if all capitalists agreed on how best to achieve their goals, and as if there were no important contradictions faced by individual capitalists between personal and economic choices that impinge upon their behavior.

In almost any single area of the humid tropics today, a highly diverse population devises strategies and experiments with ways to produce and exchange, seeking personal benefits from these choices. The differences in action represent the range of capacities, both personal and economic, that each possesses rather than some philosophic choice, although even this cannot be ruled out. The evidence, for example, strongly implies that in the Amazon region anyone entering the frontier would move towards cattle ranching at the earliest opportunity rather than cultivating the land. This will be true whether the individual is a poor peasant or a large capitalist. That the former often engages in subsistence agriculture is a result of a temporary capital constraint. Those peasants who succeed in accumulating capital rapidly move towards pasture and cattle.

Such a strategy reflects both a scarcity of labor in the frontier, and a historical southern Iberian tradition in which control over land is the surest guarantee of families' abilities to control labor and capital when and if they become available. It reflects a colonizing mode of operation by powerful families for whom extensive control of land is more important than its productivity—since intensification of land use through control of labor was not possible except for brief periods of time. Iberians, whether Spanish or Portuguese, have rarely, if ever, invested their capital gains in the inten-sification and modernization of agriculture. Iberian capital, instead, has always gone into mercantile enterprises, military expenses to protect the mercantile operations, or conspicuous consumption.

In short, it is both inappropriate and inaccurate to lump the characteristics of the lowland tropics and its exploiters and exploited. To develop ways to reduce the risk of fertility degradation in the lowland tropics, one will need very precise descriptions of how contemporary cultivators, whether owners, renters or hirelings, use the land; whether they recognize when the land is not responding well and adjust their management accordingly; or whether they mine the soil to the point where it can no longer sustain cultivation or regenerate forest vegetation.

The Choice of Land Clearing Method

Choosing the method of land clearing is the first, and possibly the most critical, management step in coping with the risk of fertility degradation in the lowland tropics. One of the obvious risks in land clearing is compaction of the soil and loss of the nutrients in the top layer. The now well-known research of Seubert et al. (1977) in the Peruvian Amazon showed that bulldozer clearing seriously damaged soil chemical and physical properties. During the two years following clearing, crop yields on the bulldozed areas were only 33 percent of those on soils manually cleared (Alegre 1985). This significant difference results from the loss of the fertilizer value of the ash, soil compaction caused by bulldozing, and the loss of topsoil through scraping. Figure 4.3 illustrates the difference between slash-and-burn and bulldozer clearing on topsoil chemical properties, and Table 4.6 shows the effects on yields. After two years the bulldozed areas had to be abandoned and no secondary forest reestablished itself for six years following abandonment. Later research showed that the use of a KG blade (a blade that cuts trees at ground level rather than disturbing the soil by pushing the vegetation over) gave better results than a common straight blade.

Furthermore, the operator has as much to do with the damage that might be caused as the machine itself. In other words, erosion can occur once land is cleared, but it need not. If the operator minimizes the amount of disturbance of the soil surface, and the whole area cleared is subsequently covered with crops that provide good soil cover, the danger of erosion and compaction can be virtually eliminated. It is not uncommon, however, for people to clear more land than they can plant, and for bulldozer operators to be road construction crews more familiar with scraping and complete clearing and leveling than with minimizing disturbance. Thus, much of the erosion hazard and destruction of agricultural potential that has been noted by many observers of the settlement of lowland tropical areas is a result of the wrong kinds of land clearing procedures and equipment. In Indonesia, for example, the government promised a cleared hectare to transmigrants and employed bulldozer clearing. As a result of recent research, however, it has begun to substitute the KG blade for the straight blade. Although it would be better if the area were cleared manually by cutting and burning, the farmers appear to want a clean field, rather than one strewn with unburnt vegetation (Yost, personal communication, 1985). This preference for mechanical clearing by new settlers from areas long under cultivation was also observed by the author in the Amazon in 1984. The settlers chose to spend most of their capital paying road builders to clear their fields of all vegetation at a price ten times that of manual clearing rather than undertake the slow but more productive cutting and burning of vegetation.

Effects of Cultivation

The contribution of plant biomass to the total nutrient pool drastically declines when forests are brought under cultivation. Crop residues can contribute only a fraction of the 5 tons/ha of dry matter previously contributed by tropical forests (Sánchez 1976:172). Cultivation also accelerates organic carbon decomposition, although the rate will vary depending on the tillage practices and on whether annual crops, pastures, or permanent crops are planted. In areas intensively cultivated and having substantial animal populations, as in Asia, it is possible, by putting in 5.6 tons/ha of animal manures, to provide the needed levels of nitrogen and phosphorus

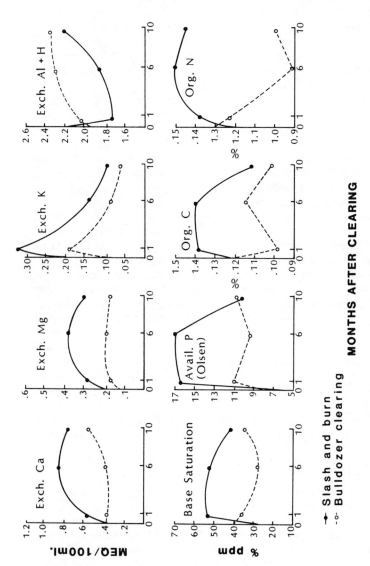

MONTHS AFTER CLEARING

→ Slash and burn
-o- Bulldozer clearing

Fig. 4.3 Effects of Two Land Clearing Methods on Change in Topsoil (0–10) Properties in a Typic Paleudult of Yurimaguas, Peru.

Source: Reproduced from Seubert, C. E., Sanchez, P., and Valverde, C. Tropical Agriculture, 1977, 54:314, by permission of the publishers, Butterworth & Co. (Publishers) Ltd. ©.

TABLE 4.6 Effects of Land Clearing Methods on Yields

Crops	Fertility Level*	Slash & Burn (in tons per hectare)	Bulldozed (in tons per hectare)	Bulldozed & burned (percent)
Upland rice	0	1.3	0.7	53
(3 crops)	NPK	3.0	1.5	49
	NPKL	2.9	2.3	80
Corn (one crop)	0	0.1	0.0	0
	NPK	0.4	0.04	10
	NPKL	3.1	2.4	76
Soybeans (2 crops)	0	0.7	0.2	24
	NPK	1.0	0.3	34
	NPKL	2.7	1.8	67
Cassava (2 crops)	0	15.4	6.4	42
	NPK	18.9	14.9	78
	NPKL	25.6	24.9	97
Panicum maximum	0	12.3	8.3	68
(6 cuts/yr)	NPK	25.2	17.2	68
	NPKL	32.2	24.2	75
Mean relative	0			37
yields	NPK			47
	NPKL			48

* 0 = no fertilizer; NPK = 50 kg N/ha, 172 P/ha, 40 kg K/ha; L = 4 ton/ha of lime.

to maintain yields at the high levels expected from contemporary paddy systems. Long-term manure application tends to improve water retention, and to increase pore space and bulk density.

Mulching is an important component of stable agriculture in the lowland tropics through its role in decreasing the rate at which organic carbon is decomposed and in reducing possible erosion. The role of agroforestry remains largely unexplored in the Amazon, although its productivity has been demonstrated in several parts of the Asian tropics. Certainly from a nutrient cycling point of view, this is likely to be the best strategy. How it may be integrated with the production demands of the local population and those of urban areas remains unknown.

An Example of Variation

In field research conducted last year in a newly colonized area of the Amazon, I found a region characterized by above-average soils, although with significant variations within the area. Table 4.7 includes the soil analyses from the samples taken. Of particular note is the column labeled FCC. This column uses the Fertility-Capability Soil Classification (FCC) System developed by Buol et al. (1975) and further modified in Sánchez et al. (1982). Note that some of the soils have no significant constraints in the plow layer (labeled as letters representative of "conditioner modifiers"). Only 7 percent of the Amazon is estimated by Cochrane and Sánchez (1982) to lack any major constraints. The FCC is the first attempt to group soils with similar fertility limitations using quantitative limits. Soils are grouped at the highest categorical levels according to topsoil and subsoil texture. Thirteen modifiers are defined to delimit specific fertility-related parameters. The quantitative parameters serve as critical levels following Leibig's Concept of the Minimum.

In the soils sampled in Carajas, Brazil, one finds several soils with no significant constraints among the list of modifiers, although clearly phosphorus appears to be likely to become one with cultivation. Those with constraints noted are low in ECEC (which defines the *e* modifier), medium aluminum base saturation (in the 10 to 60 percent range, which defines the *h* modifier), and potassium deficiency (under 0.20 meq/100g, which defines the *k* modifier). Only one sample had aluminum base saturation above 60 percent, which defines the *a* modifier—the threshold defined earlier as critical to most cultivation of domesticated plants.

Perusal of Table 4.7 should lay to rest the idea that an area that appears on a soils map at a scale of 1:100,000, as was made available to me by the colonization company, is an adequate representation of the soils being cultivated by farmers. Most farmers in the area that opened up in the first two years had already found two or three contrasting soils within their holdings (holdings varying in size from 17 to 400 hectares). As they acquire more familiarity with their land, they can be expected to make further identifications. However, they varied in their ability to identify a soil that was chemically different from the others.

Cultivation followed the plan common in newly settled areas. First, the area is cleared and planted in cereal staples such as rice, corn, and beans. Then, it is planted in manioc and bananas or in permanent crops such as cocoa, coffee, or rubber. This plan tended to be followed regardless of whether the farmer was on an Alfisol of medium to high fertility or on a very acid Oxisol with low base saturation. When the farmers' soils were ranked in quality from poor (i.e., #1) to very good (#4) and their soil type matched against their yields (see Figure 4.4), interesting but not altogether unexpected results emerged: farmers with poor soils experienced yields ranging between 432 kg/ha and 1,002 kg/ha, whereas yields of farmers

TABLE 4.7 Soils at Carajas

ID	PH	AL	CA	MG	K	N	P	CU	FE	MN	ZN	OC	OM	ECEC	BSAT	FCC	SAND	SILT	CLAY	TEXTURAL CLASS	FCC
			MEQ/100CC			MG/G			PPM			%		MEQ/100CC			%				
1	5.5	0.01	2.51	0.50	.11	1.02	4	2	71	11	2	0.86	1.48	3.13	1.00	ehk	83.44	11.67	4.89	Sandy Loam	L
2	5.0	0.08	1.28	0.63	.18	1.01	2	2	145	11	3	0.87	1.50	2.18	0.96	ehk	66.33	22.59	11.07	Sandy Loam	L
3	6.2	0.01	1.94	0.67	.23	.91	9	2	218	10	1	0.64	1.10	2.86	1.00	e	76.76	16.66	6.57	Sandy Loam	L
4	6.1	0.01	6.57	1.34	.25	2.17	3	10	166	3	2	1.92	3.30	8.17	1.00		49.37	26.97	23.66	Sandy Clay Loam	L
5	6.1	0.00	12.72	2.60	.16	3.28	2	6	75	1	3	2.54	4.37	15.49	1.00	k	30.94	41.03	28.03	Clay Loam	L
6	6.2	0.01	6.83	1.30	.23	2.12	2	27	97	1	2	1.82	3.13	8.38	1.00		44.77	35.08	20.15	Loam	L
7	5.1	0.07	1.67	0.52	.16	1.11	5	2	294	19	2	1.08	1.86	2.42	0.97	ehk	71.67	18.10	10.23	Sandy Loam	L
8	6.4	0.05	1.78	0.50	.10	.62	8	1	73	7	1	0.59	1.01	2.44	0.98	e k	85.12	11.19	3.69	Loamy Sand	S
9	5.0	0.52	0.75	0.46	.12	.25	2	3	90	3	2	0.16	0.28	1.86	0.72	ehk	68.22	10.66	21.12	Sandy Clay Loam	S
10	5.0	0.24	4.69	0.63	.26	2.17	9	9	1424	62	2	2.49	4.28	5.82	0.96	h	39.43	36.01	24.56	Loam	L
11	4.9	0.46	2.59	0.75	.08	1.36	2	8	145	3	0	1.15	1.98	3.88	0.88	ehk	31.99	29.76	38.25	Clay Loam	C
12	6.9	0.02	7.67	1.77	.32	2.86	10	4	159	4	1	2.48	4.27	9.78	1.00	hk	22.59	49.50	27.91	Clay Loam	L
13	5.6	0.00	3.45	0.81	.15	1.23	2	3	173	10	2	1.24	2.13	4.42	1.00		70.39	21.48	8.12	Sandy Loam	L
14	6.2	0.01	5.41	1.22	.32	2.14	4	6	92	2	1	2.11	3.63	6.97	1.00		55.17	25.73	19.10	Sandy Loam	L
15	7.3	0.01	5.43	1.18	.31	1.44	7	5	43	2	2	1.31	2.25	6.93	1.00		68.28	20.71	11.01	Sandy Loam	L
16	4.2	1.41	0.49	0.25	.12	1.04	5	2	60	1	1	1.00	1.72	2.27	0.38	eak	58.77	23.20	18.02	Sandy Loam	L
17	4.8	0.79	0.97	0.62	.12	.98	3	2	201	9	1	0.83	1.43	2.50	0.68	ehk	47.88	25.12	27.00	Sandy Clay Loam	L
18	6.8	0.00	7.88	1.13	.46	2.09	4	20	60	2	12	1.56	2.68	9.47	1.00		29.32	32.37	38.31	Clay Loam	C
19	6.9	0.02	7.13	1.68	.37	2.49	6	4	86	8	2	1.95	3.35	9.21	1.00		42.19	40.15	17.65	Loam	L
20	5.6	0.02	3.99	1.36	.27	1.61	2	3	211	3	1	1.38	2.37	5.64	1.00	h	53.54	25.13	21.33	Sandy Clay Loam	L
21	4.3	4.43	0.81	0.30	.08	1.67	4	8	970	60	1	1.54	2.65	5.62	0.21	ak	13.43	43.38	43.18	Silty Clay	C
22	5.2	0.12	1.66	0.36	.10	.91	5	1	166	6	1	0.79	1.36	2.24	0.95	ehk	80.67	12.65	6.68	Sandy Loam	L
23	7.3	0.01	6.94	1.23	.32	1.85	4	6	50	1	3	1.43	2.46	8.50	1.00		33.44	39.28	27.27	Clay Loam	L

Source: Moran, Soil Samples, 1984.

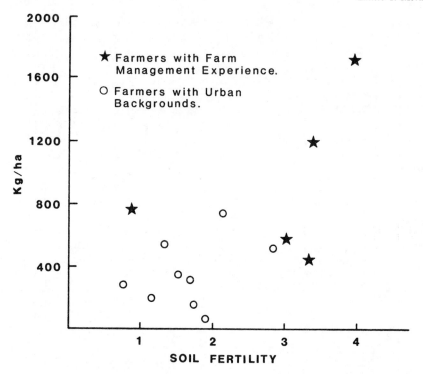

Fig. 4.4   Soil Fertility Level and Yields in Carajás.

Source: Moran, Soil Samples 1984.

on the best soils ranged between 570 and 1,880 kg/ha. Admittedly, the sample size per category is small, but in examining the life histories of the respective farmers one notices that the farmers with the highest yields in both categories of soil quality had more experience in farm management (they are marked with a star on Figure 4.4) than those with the lowest yields in both categories, who were characterized by urban, business experience (they are marked with a plain dot in Figure 4.4). Perhaps even more telling are the majority, who fall into the intermediate soil quality category but whose yields were all clustered between 0 and 800 kg/ha and whose main common characteristic was urban residence and wage labor experience before coming to the frontier (see Figure 4.4 for the distribution of yields).

Thus, the soil quality of these farmers was presumed by preexisting maps to be above average, and this assessment was generally correct. Very few major environmental constraints were present to these farmers, and the company that laid out the project built good quality roads—usually a major constraint in the early years of settlement. Despite the presence of generally good soils and all-weather roads, the yields in the first two years were very low. Why this might have been the case deserves some attention. These were presumed to be mostly intensive, experienced, mechanized small farmers from Rio Grande do Sul and Santa Catarina, to whom the company appealed as potential buyers. However, these mechanized farmers had never worked with primary vegetation before and were disinclined to undertake under-clearing and forest cutting on their own. As a result, they hired road builders to bulldoze the trees on their land despite the ten times higher cost of mechanical over manual clearing. Earlier studies had shown that bulldozed areas had yields only 30 percent of those cleared by hand (Seubert et al. 1977). The 46 percent who had no previous title to land to their name before coming, and only limited farming experience, invested most of their labor in wage-earning activities and only worked the land as time permitted. In other words, the most experienced farmers became decapitalized at the start of their operations and were constrained by the effects of bulldozer scraping on yields (see Figure 4.3 and Table 4.6), while those who came with less experience sought to maximize their capital gains by earning the high wages available in a labor-poor area and provided minimal management to their land. In either case, the results were disappointing from a farming point of view. Those who spent money on mechanical clearing found it difficult to recover their capital through production.

The strategies of these farmers were as diverse as they were themselves. Some were farmers of 28 years experience, with grown children who came to help maintain a family-farm operation. Others were single or newly married and hoping to get a start as agriculturalists. Among the more urbanized settlers were draftsmen, lawyers, physicians, accountants, grocers, carpenters, taxi drivers, mechanics, tavern keepers, pilots, and policemen. Each of these divided his time differently, depending on the demand for his particular skills in the frontier, and his interest in farming per se or in its economic returns through increased land value. Thus, each farmer's impact on his agricultural land is highly particular rather than easily generalized. Some were able to give a clear philosophy of the nurturing role of farmers and of their place in the balance of nature, whereas others were only concerned with how they might achieve a level of wealth that might permit them to live in comfort in cities in southern Brazil. These highly variable priorities played an important role in the management practices applied upon these lands and upon their fertility conservation or degradation.

Determining Risk of Fertility Degradation

In this chapter I have specified the constraints to sustained production that are most commonly found in the lowland tropics in general, and in the Amazon in particular. In addition, I have given to these constraints, initially at least, some critical quantitative value that might be useful in determining when an area is likely to be "at risk."

Clearly, the process of fertility degradation is not simply a physical one. The actions of the human population are affected by international investment and demand for raw materials, by national development policies, by regional priorities within national economic policy, and by the highly variable goals of different households. The main problem, however, is that very little attention has been paid by individual farming households, particularly pioneering populations, to the consequences of their management and the sustainability of their farming strategies. Pioneer households are not yet committed to the area of land they occupy, and frontier land becomes for them a source of potential wealth to do something else. From the point of view of how frontiers evolve, this choice is rational, given that the early agricultural frontier in capitalized economies tends to be primarily a land market rather than a commodities market, and that failure rates are very high in these frontier zones during the early stages. The unpredictability of this process makes it all the more important to be able to predict which areas are likely to be "at risk" and to protect such areas from deforestation, or implement from the outset controls over the ways to manage their constraints.

Less than 2 ppm of available P seems rather arbitrary, given that crop requirements vary so much, that much of P can become fixed and thus unavailable, and that crops vary in how much P they remove from the soil. Nevertheless, this figure seems to be a safe minimum—I expect that others working to refine this parameter will raise the amount of P that might be seen as a threshold for sustainable agricultural production.

Aluminum saturation above 60 percent is less likely to meet with any critique as this level is better established, although a higher level (75 percent) may be more critical for crops that are highly tolerant of aluminum because of their evolutionary history. Correction through burning or through liming can bring the level of aluminum saturation to non-constraining levels. Many experts advise not liming to a pH any higher than 5.5 for most crops. At this level 80 percent of maximum yield can be achieved through selection of varieties resistant to aluminum toxicity.

Effective cation exchange capacity lower than 4 meq/100g is also widely recognized as a realistic threshold figure, although a higher figure of 7 ppm might be used for early monitoring of soils before they reach too low a level of cation exchange capacity.

Areas with slopes above 30 percent should normally be kept under forest cover, given their high potential for erosion. Of course, in some countries, such as Costa Rica, over 40 percent of the steep lands have already been cleared of forest, and this trend continues there and elsewhere. These areas could be protected by terracing as is done in Ifugao, Philippines (Conklin 1980) and many of the other lowland tropics of Asia. However, the pioneering activities in most of the areas being opened up lack a population with a long-standing stewardship of steep valleys as characterizes some traditional Asian mountain populations. Whether such stewardship presumes very high population densities with a long time-depth of occupation is an intriguing research and policy question.

Land clearing methods should favor clearing using manual swidden techniques as both more economical and more ecologically appropriate. When that is not possible, clearance using a KG blade that avoids disturbing the topsoil should help. Local knowledge of the timing and control of burns should be sought.

Management and cultivation should emphasize soil cover and the planting of crops that make fewer nutrient demands from the soil. Crop rotations, mulching, manuring, and other forms of maintaining soil fertility will help extend the period before yields decline. Unless fertilizers can be provided, it is questionable whether development policy should encourage the clearing of forest to establish farmland. The costs to society ought to be explored and careful assessment made of the consequences to local inhabitants, migrants, and social order.

An important implication of this analysis is that if a land area is known— in planning documents or other available sources—to be at or below any of the critical parameters defined in this chapter, and if the planning entities are not capable of guaranteeing that the necessary correctives will be available to farmers at an economical cost and in a timely manner, then such areas should not be cleared for farmland, since the outcome will be uneconomic yields, fertility degradation, and possible non-regeneration of forest vegetation. In addition, provision for such correctives should be planned for, even in initially fertile areas, given the inevitable decline in nutrient levels with cropping. Thus, these constraints can serve to determine which areas should be opened up for "development" in the humid tropics and which ones ought to be protected due to their initial physical and chemical conditions. Policy-makers who open up areas with inadequate initial levels of fertility should take full responsibility for the degradation they have caused and reimburse farmers attracted to such areas.

It is the hope of the author that readers will be critical of the approach and the quantification of critical levels in this chapter, and that they will propose better threshold or critical points based on new research. The lowland tropics indeed risk losing much of their agricultural productive potential for future generations. We must strive to specify that risk for specific soils and to identify favorable types of management in order to understand the transformations taking place and the seriousness of the risk.

Notes

1. The author wishes to acknowledge the support of the Tinker Foundation, which provided a Post-Doctoral Fellowship during 1984, and Indiana University, which provided sabbatical year support. Without their assistance this research would not have been possible. I want to acknowledge the help of the Soil Science faculty at North Carolina State University, which served as a superb sounding board for the development of these ideas, especially Drs. Buol, Nicholaides, Miller, and Sánchez. I am also indebted to Susanna Hecht, Norman Schwartz, Pedro Sánchez, Michael Painter, and others who took time to give me the benefit of their expertise on the

earlier version of this chapter. The responsibility for the views presented is entirely mine.

References

Abruña, F., R. Pearson, and R. Perez-Escolar
  1975   Lime Responses of Corn and Beans Grown on Typical Ultisols and Oxisols of Puerto Rico. *In* Soil Management in Tropical America. E. Bornemisza and A. Alvarado, eds. Pp. 261–281, Raleigh, NC: North Carolina State University.
Abruña, F., J. Rodríguez, Jose Badillo-Feliciano, S. Silva, and J. Vicente-Chandler
  1978   Crop Response to Soil Acidity Factors in Ultisols and Oxisols in Puerto Rico; Soybeans. J. Agric. Univ. P.R. 62:90–112.
Abruña, F., and J. Vincente-Chandler
  1967   Sugarcane Yields as Related to Acidity of a Humid Tropic Ultisol. Agron. J. 59:330–331.
Alegre, Julio
  1985   Effects of Land Clearing and Preparation Methods on Soil Physical and Chemical Properties and Crop Performance on an Ultisol in the Amazon Basin. Ph.D. thesis, Department of Soil Science, North Carolina State University.
Buol, Stanley, and Pedro Sánchez
  1984   Quantity and Quality of World Soils and Their Responsiveness to Fertilizers in Relation to Future Food Production. Paper presented at the Annual Meeting of the American Association for the Advancement of Science. New York.
Buol, Stanley, Pedro Sánchez, R. B. Cate, and M. A. Granger
  1975   Soil Fertility Capability Classification. *In* Manejo de Suelos en la América Tropical. E. Bornemisza and A. Alvarado, eds. Raleigh, NC: North Carolina State University.
Cochrane, T. T., and Pedro Sánchez
  1982   Land Resources, Soils and Their Management in the Amazon Region: A State of Knowledge Report. *In* Amazonia: Agriculture and Land Use Research. S. Hecht, ed. Cali, Colombia: CIAT.
Conklin, Harold C.
  1980   Ethnographic Atlas of Ifugao. New Haven, CT: Yale University Press.
Farnworth, Edward, and Frank Golley
  1974   Fragile Ecosystems: Evaluation of Research and Applications in the Neotropics. New York, NY: Springer-Verlag.
Foweraker, Joe
  1981   The Struggle for Land. Cambridge: Cambridge University Press.
Kamprath, E. J.
  1970   Exchangeable Aluminum as a Criterion for Liming Leached Mineral Soils. Soil Sci. Soc. Am., Proc. 24:252–254.
  1980   Soil Acidity in Well-drained Soils of the Tropics as a Constraint to Food Production. *In* IRRI/Cornell, Soil Related Constraints to Food Production in the Tropics. Los Banos, Philippines: International Rice Research Institute.
Meggers, Betty
  1971   Amazonia. New York, NY: Aldine.

Moran, Emilio F.
1977 Estratégias de Sobrevivência: O Uso de Resursos ao Longo da Rodovia Transamazônica. Acta Amazônica (Manaus) 7:363–379.
1981 Developing the Amazon. Bloomington, IN: Indiana University Press.
1984 Colonization in the Amazon Basin. Interciencia 9:377–385.
1985 Socio-economic Considerations in Acid Tropical Soils Research. Paper presented at the IBSRAM Acid Tropical Soils Network Inaugural Workshop, 2 May 1985. Brasilia, Brazil.
National Research Council
1982 Ecological Aspects of Development in the Humid Tropics. Washington, DC: National Academy Press.
Salinas, Jose, and Pedro Sánchez
1976 Soil-Plant Relationships Affecting Varietal and Species Differences in Tolerance to Low Available Soil Phosphorus. Ciencia e Cultura 28(2): 156–168.
Samonte, H. P., and A. M. Ocampo
1977 Liming and Its Residual Effect on Corn-planted Soils. Philipp. Agric. 60:420–430.
Sánchez, Pedro
1976 Properties and Management of Soils in the Tropics. New York, NY: Wiley-Interscience.
1987 Management of Acid Soils in the Humid Tropics of Latin America. Paper presented at the IBSRAM Acid Tropical Soils Network Inaugural Workshop, 1 May 1985. Brasilia, Brazil. Mimeo.
Sánchez, Pedro, and T. T. Cochrane
1980 Soil Constraints in Relation to Major Farming Systems in Tropical America. *In* Priorities for Alleviating Soil-Related Constraints to Food Production in the Tropics. Los Banos, Philippines: International Rice Research Institute.
Sánchez, Pedro, Walter Couto, and Stanley W. Buol
1982 The Fertility Capability Classification System: Interpretation, Applicability and Modification. Geoderma 27:283–309.
Seubert, C. E., P. Sánchez, and C. Valverde
1977 Effects of Land Clearing Methods on Soil Properties and Crop Performance in an Ultisol of the Amazon Jungle of Peru. Tropical Agriculture 54:307–321.
Soares, W. V., E. Lobato, E. González, and G. C. Naderman
1975 Liming Soils of the Brazilian Cerrado. *In* Soil Management in Tropical America. E. Bornemisza and A. Alvarado, eds. Pp. 283–299. Raleigh, NC: North Carolina State University.
Tropsoils
1985 Tropsoils: The First Three Years. Raleigh, NC: North Carolina State University.
Uhl, Christopher
1980 Studies of Forest, Agricultural and Successional Environments in the Upper Rio Negro Region of the Amazon Basin. Ph.D. dissertation, Department of Biology, Michigan State University.
1983 You Can Keep a Good Forest Down. Natural History 92(4):69–79.

PART TWO

The Role of the State

5

The Political Economy
of Desertification
in White Nile Province, Sudan[1]

Michael M Horowitz and Muneera Salem-Murdock

As a techno-environmental event, desertification has been much discussed since the sudano-sahelian drought of 1968–1974. Desertification has been attributed by many to the abuse, through overgrazing and overcultivation, of nutrient-poor soils in an unfavorable hot and arid climate. In this view, overuse without adequate fallowing causes erosion of the soil and the invasion of sands, as well as changes in the species composition of rangeland vegetation, with less nutritious annual species increasing in proportion to more nutritious perennials. The situation is thought to provoke a vicious cycle, as the progressively declining fertility of the soils leads to declining production and the need to work the soil ever more intensively. In the space of a few years, soil degradation reaches the point of permanently impaired capacity to recover and to produce useful crops (for example, Lamprey 1983). Since vast reaches of the Democratic Republic of the Sudan fall in the seriously affected zone, actions have been sought to retard, stop, and reverse the impoverishment of the habitat. One "retardation" measure explored in the Sudan is the introduction of forestry in grazing systems.

In an effort to attract donor assistance to combat desertification, the Director of the Sudan Forestry Department submitted a proposal to the United Nations Food and Agriculture Organization (FAO) in which he wrote:

> The Government and the people of the Sudan, aware of the dangers of desertification and sand encroachment on valuable agricultural lands and the threat of desertification to the future of agricultural and animal production and the country's food security, have embarked on ambitious development programmes for which external assistance is welcome . . . (Badi 1981).

The objective of this Forestry-in-Grazing-Lands project proposed for White Nile Province was to complement other desert encroachment programs in the country with afforestation projects designed to halt soil erosion and sand dune encroachment, to increase dry season fodder for livestock, and to provide fuelwood and building timber (ibid. 1981). In this chapter we argue that without an adequate understanding of the social factors underlying behaviors that lead to overuse of the rural landscape, the proposed interventions are unlikely to achieve their desired effects.

The social factors leading to resource abuse in the northern Sudan are largely of recent origin. The affected areas have previously sustained human populations for long periods of time without degradation seriously diminishing production, despite deficient rainfall every few years and sustained drought at least several times each century (Kerr 1985).

Of these relatively recent changes in White Nile Province two are of prime importance: a rapid increase in the human population, leading to greater competition for fixed or declining resources; and the completion of the Jebel al-Awliya Dam in 1937 resulting in the massive intrusion of external demands on the local economy, which in turn increased social differentiation and the development of a class structure, and rendered most of the rural population impoverished and powerless. External demands on the rural economy led to an appropriation of regional production to urban centers within the country and to consumption centers overseas. This has created a paradoxical situation of recurrent shortages of foodstuffs within food-producing areas, and to the pricing of basic subsistence commodities beyond the reach of many local consumers. In short, desertification, which contributes to the impoverishment of the people who live in the affected area, is also caused by that impoverishment. Poverty is the primary causal event in the chain. And poverty is itself a political as well as an economic condition. Interventions that aim at improving the physical situation in northern Sudan must be based on a solid understanding of the nature and causes of rural poverty. These causes are not self-evident, because much poverty—and much affluence—is masked, leading to the superficial appearance of generalized poverty in the region. But appearances are misleading. Although all men may wear the same *jellabia* (a plain white gown), and all villagers may live in the same kind of house, local communities are highly differentiated. Some individuals have more land, more animals, and larger granaries than others.

Thus a purely environmental approach to understanding and solving the problem of desertification is inherently inadequate because the causes of "mismanagement" are social, economic, and above all political.

The Project Area

From a socioeconomic point of view, the western section of White Nile Province (the area west of the river) may be divided into two distinct zones, which correspond to broad environmental features: (1) the Riverine Clay Plains, adjacent to the White Nile River and extending for some distance inland; and (2) the Sandy Uplands, which link the western reaches of the province with Kordofan. Although the two zones appear to be economically quite separate—the one dominated by commercially oriented agricultural production on capital-intensive irrigated schemes, and the other dominated by subsistence-oriented herding and rainfed cultivation—they are intimately intertwined. The apparent dualism of the economy obscures the fact that the irrigated or pump schemes attempt to satisfy their periodic needs for additional labor by recruiting from the upland villages, while the latter attempt to satisfy their recurrent need for cash by laboring in the irrigated fields. The sandy uplands constitute a crucial labor reserve for the cotton farms on the riverine clay plains.

Prior to the 1937 completion of the Jebel al-Awliya Dam, the majority of White Nile Arabs productively utilized both zones. During the summer rainy season the people and their animals moved westward from the river banks to the sandy uplands, where there were both adequate grazing and land suitable for rainfed grain cultivation. The upland harvest was completed several months after the rains ended, around November-December, a time that also saw a diminution in surface water and nutritious herbage. As the dry season progressed, the people moved back toward the river, where the retreat of flood water offered recession lands for sorghum cultivation and fresh, rich riverine pastures for the animals. The cycle was concluded at the end of the dry season, with the sorghum harvest and the exhaustion of alluvial pastures. As the rains began anew, and the recession areas were again flooded, the herders trekked once more back to their upland fields and grazing lands.

The dam and its reservoir, along with human and livestock population growth, abruptly altered the ecology of the region. We do not mean to overstate the pre-dam situation as one of optimum exploitation of resources, but simply to indicate that a rough balance had been struck in the exploitation of the two zones, a balance radically altered by the construction of the Jebel al-Awliya Dam.[2] Where flood waters had previously retreated, making riverine land available for recession cultivation and pasture, the waters now remain at high levels until the drawdown starting in April. The changed environment has also encouraged colonization by the river fluke, which caused animal losses numbering in the thousands until herders learned to avoid the reservoir margins. Thus the later dry season, following the completion of the cereals harvest in November/December, has become an extremely difficult time. Large numbers of people and animals have had to congregate in the narrow belt between the two principal zones, and a number of villages have been established there. Both the labor demands of the irrigated farms and the scarcity of water further upland tend to lock the people into this area. According to the Sudanese geographer Anwar Abdu (personal communication), it is this mixed dune and clay belt that has experienced the most pronounced environmental degradation, evidenced by the recent mobility of formerly stabilized longitudinal dunes.

The establishment of modern large-scale hydraulic agriculture on the riverine clay plains has increased the demographic pressure—both human and animal—on the adjacent areas. Focused on cotton, wheat, and other irrigated crops, the system of production is controlled by a parastatal corporation that provides most of the inputs (seed, traction, fertilizer, pesticide, herbicide, credit), makes most of the managerial decisions (crop sequences, rotations), and serves as a monopsonist purchaser of the principal crop, cotton. The farm lands are divided into tenancies of from 5 to as much as 18 feddans each.[3] The major managerial decision that remains for the tenants themselves is the allocation of labor: labor may be provided from household resources (especially where there are children of the appropriate age), it may be exchanged among neighboring tenancies (*nafir* or exchange labor is also practiced in rainfed cultivation), and it may be hired from outside. At certain peak points during the annual cycle, and especially during weeding and the cotton harvest, labor requirements are high and few tenant households are able to satisfy them from internal resources. Transient labor is therefore sought, especially from nearby settlements. Lorries and labor recruiters leave the plains for the sandy upland villages, offering partial payment in advance as an incentive to tempt persons to leave their homes and herds and to pick cotton on the schemes. Although agricultural wage labor is denigrated in these villages and the wages offered are very low, poorer people need the cash and often accept the offers to spend one to several months laboring along the river.

On the sandy uplands of White Nile Province, dryland cultivation is the major consumer of labor during the rainy season (or *kharif*), from June to September/October. The demand for field labor during this period is very intense, especially for weeding, and also just before and during the harvest when birds attack the maturing grain. Following the millet harvest, labor requirements are reduced on the sandy *goz*. Herding also requires little labor during this period because pasture is rich and surface water remains adequate for livestock. As the dry season progresses, however, herding becomes more labor intensive: animals must be watered from dug wells, involving the arduous task of pulling up the water bag and pouring the water in a trough. Animals must also be walked greater distances from pasture to the watering points, and very young stock must often be carried the entire distance. The demand for labor on the irrigated schemes is also at its peak during the later dry season.

The geographic region that can be exploited by the local population is thus limited by the people's need to remain in close proximity to the scheme. This increases the pressure of both agriculture and pastoralism on the local landscape.

The very expansion of irrigated schemes contributes to the situation affecting labor availability. This expansion has served to contract the grazing area, especially the critical dry-season grazing in proximity to the river where water was readily available, and has thereby rendered the herding enterprise more vulnerable. Deprived of much of their customary dry season pasture, the animals remain on the semiarid sandy range for the entire year, and suffer from the decline of both nutritious herbage and easily available water as the long dry season progresses. Scheme managers view animals fundamentally as pests, as unwelcome competitors for land and for the attention of tenants, and have discouraged mixed farming and the integration of animals on the tenancies.[4] The herders themselves are welcome, indeed they are strongly encouraged to provide their labor for the benefit of the farms, but their animals are viewed with hostility, and the hapless cow or sheep that ventures on to a cultivated field may be seized and its owner fined. Yet without their animals, the herders could not survive the long periods when their labor is not required on the schemes. For the herders, their animals are the means both of production and reproduction; they make possible the reproduction of herder households and communities over time. Since labor has been identified as a major constraint on herd size in the Sudan (Cunnison 1966:68–69; Ahmed 1972:182; Asad 1964:45–58), as each herder can cope with only a limited number of animals, and since much labor is drawn away from the herds to the pump schemes during the dry season when it is needed for the arduous task of watering, herd growth and therefore herder income is also limited by the shift of personnel from the pastures to the irrigated fields.

Deprived of riverine lands by the dam and by the pump schemes, the people and their animals are compressed throughout the year in the sandy uplands. Parts of these areas are suitable for millet cultivation during the brief rainy season, although precipitation is frequently insufficient to permit a good yield. Most of the wadi and interdunal lands that can be sown in millet are divided, and some are formally registered with the government; newcomers to these villages obtain access to such lands with difficulty. Even some of the dunal or goz lands are divided and registered. The stock of unclaimed cultivable land is thus in extremely short supply. This had obvious implications for the Sudan Forestry-in-Grazing-Lands project as originally proposed, for if a substantial amount of land must be removed from current use—either from farming, wood-cutting, or pasture—and guarded for several years to permit the establishment of the new trees, increased pressure would be felt on the remaining land, already reduced by the irrigation scheme. We shall return to this point in discussing land tenure.

Ethnicity

The population of the sandy uplands is entirely native Sudanese, divided among a number of Arabic-speaking "tribal" groups, among the most prominent being the Hassaaniyya, Hisseinaat, and Ja'alyeen. These are segmented into sub-tribal units, such as the Kawaahla (Hassaaniyya) and Shiweihaat (Ja'alyeen), and further segmented into lineal descent groups or *khashm beit*, like the Beni Gerrar of the Shiweihaat in the village of Umm Deseis and the Awlaad 'Iteiq, also of the Shiweihaat, in the village of Uqeidat at-Teir. The boundaries among these ethnic groupings are not impervious, and there is a certain degree of situationality in the ethnic ascription of self and others.[5]

There is little functional distinction or specialization among these groups, although there is some stereotyping, such as an admiration of the Kawaahla, who are reputed to be the most devoted and skillful animal husbandmen, spending less time in the villages and more in the bush to care for their herds and guide them to good pasture. The Ja'alyeen have the reputation of being clever traders. Small villages tend to ethnic group homogeneity, with almost all residents members of a single descent group, while the larger villages like Helba and Shgeig include representatives of a number of ethnic and descent groups.

Economic Activities

A major objective of the proposed FAO project was to increase income levels of small herders in the sandy uplands areas by providing them with an improved arboreal browse. In order to assess the economic implications of the project, we outline the kinds of economic decisions that the people must make, for a successful economic performance in the sandy upland villages calls for the skillful management of a number of activities and the effective allocation of land, labor, animals, and cash. As indicated above, most persons are not able to provide for themselves and their households entirely from resources within the area, and are obliged instead to move seasonally to the irrigated schemes, where they find intermittent work as wage laborers. The fact that the more successful or affluent villagers and herders avoid this movement implies that a general rise in income levels would enable at least some others to remain in the uplands throughout the year. It is also likely that increased investment in animals by the affluent will result in opportunities for those without animals to work as hired shepherds. The ability of shepherds to secure favorable terms for employment will depend, of course, on the relative number of persons available for such employment.[6] If the number of persons who decided against a periodic shift into wage labor were to increase substantially, the scheme might have to respond either by raising wages to the point where the move became attractive again or by recruiting the additional labor required from more distant areas. Within the sandy upland villages, the following are the principal components of economic action:

Pastoral Herding

The people maintain camels, cattle, sheep, goats, and donkeys. While little fully migratory nomadism exists in the region—although the area is crossed by Kababish descending from the west and includes several established Kabbashi villages—pastoral herding tends to be carried out on a semi-sedentary basis.[7] The major determinants of pastoral movement are the availability of water (surface water, especially during and immediately following the rains; constructed entrapments or *hafirs*; shallow dug wells; and diesel-powered bore holes), graze and browse, and labor. The last is a critical determinant both of movement and of herd size, despite the broadly held—and, as noted above, in our opinion flawed—notion that pastoral herding is labor extensive. The number of animals that can be effectively managed is limited by the labor available for their watering during the dry season, especially where the shallow wells have a very limited output. The number is also constrained by the need to move animals ever-increasing distances from the wells to pasture, as the forage contiguous to the watering points declines precipitously with the advancing dry season. As the grass is consumed, the animals depend increasingly on the arboreal pasture, browsing the various acacias, leptadineas, balanites and other plants adapted to conditions of low rainfall and sandy soil. Camels and adult goats browse the taller plants without assistance, but cattle, sheep, and young kids often require the herders' help in shaking down nutritious seed pods and occasionally, though illegally, lopping whole branches.

Animals contribute directly to the subsistence of the herders, through the provision of meat and milk, cheese, and other dairy products. Indirectly they contribute, through sale via specialist brokers,[8] to urban consumers. Hides are sold, and the fuel and fertilizer capacity of dung is appreciated although unsystematically exploited. Animals are clearly the major repository of wealth in the region, and a very active market allows for their ready conversion to cash. While the people often complain about inadequate water resources, the graze and browse, they feel, is mostly good. Some have very large herds, and "were known as *ummar gabila*, literally, 'wealthy men of their tribes'" (Abbas 1980:23). Because many people, however, have very few animals, and some have none, a total reliance on herding for subsistence and cash needs is restricted to a still substantial though not dominant segment of the population.

Rainfed Cereals Cultivation

Almost all persons on the west bank of the White Nile, including those with tenancies on the schemes, attempt to grow dryland cereals during the short rainy season. Sorghum is cultivated on small clay patches immediately west of the irrigated lands, and scheme managers complain of absenteeism from work in the irrigated fields. Millet is cultivated on the sand dunes. Thus both tenants and upland villagers have claims to rainfed cereal fields, which are cleared during the late dry season and sown when the rains begin. Since western White Nile Province is characterized by exceptionally low rainfall as compared to neighboring areas at the same latitude, it often happens that precipitation is insufficient for the plants to mature. The markedly wide spacing between individual millet plants in the sandy areas is evidence of the marginality of the operation. Because of the low rainfall, and consequently low yields, a very large area must be devoted to the crop. As millet survives better than other crops under these conditions, it is the principal cultigen, while sesame has declined in importance because of the greater uncertainty in obtaining a satisfactory harvest.

When the rains are adequate, both in quantity and in distribution, the harvest is sufficient for domestic needs, and a few households may have small surpluses for sale. When the yields are insufficient, the shortfall must be made up in the market. There is a good deal of speculation in cereals, with prominent traders buying heavily in the good years at low prices, and selling off in deficit years at very high prices. Farmers in need of either cash or grain may borrow from traders under the *sheil* system, securing the loans by mortgaging their subsequent harvest(s). Sorghum also enters the area from higher production zones, and is sold in local markets. A peasant who must buy grain will sell animals to raise the necessary cash if he has animals to sell. Those without animals, or with herds so small that sales might threaten their reproductive capacities, must earn the money for cereals in the wage-labor market, migrating to the irrigated fields on the schemes. Other farmers try to increase production in the only way they can: by horizontal extension of cultivation into the pastoral areas, areas where herders are at a comparative disadvantage in defending their claims before the authorities. Soils in the arid and semiarid regions of the Sudan, for example, where annual rainfall is less than 400mm, are terribly vulnerable to the assault of cultivation. The low yields from degraded soils force the farmers to expand into ever more marginal lands, creating a vicious cycle of debt, environmental degradation, and poverty.

Since cereals constitute the basis of the diet, yields are low, shortfalls costly, and there is constant pressure to *expand* the amount of land under cultivation, such land can be found only at the expense of grazing. Given these shortages and competitions, it is unduly optimistic to suggest, as the Sudan Forestry-in-Grazing-Lands project implies, broad community willingness to reserve substantial amounts of land for tree culture, even for a few years.

Trade, Crafts, and Local Employment

Occupational complexity is characteristic of the larger towns, like Helba and Shugeig, which have important weekly markets. The small villages have much simpler occupational arrays, being limited largely to farming, herding, and wage labor migration. In the large markets, professional traders set up stalls and sell imported commodities like cloth, tea, soap, salt, sugar, spice, and perfume; vegetable produce from the irrigated areas, including onions, tomatoes, okra, cucumbers, and citrus fruits; and millet and sorghum. Some of the grain is from local surpluses, but most is brought into the area by truck. The major traders purchase grain at the moment of harvest, when prices are low, for resale during the remainder of the year when prices rise. Although some peasant farmers try to settle most of their debts in millet and sorghum, others purchase cereal grains in the market from time to time, when their own granaries prove insufficient.

The market also attracts local craftspeople, such as blacksmiths and weavers of straw mats. Itinerant medicinal/magical specialists and fortune tellers frequent the market. On the periphery of the market places are permanent tea shop/hostelries and temporary "coffee" shops established by women. Licensed charcoal merchants sell their goods, and, on a more clandestine basis, unlicensed charcoal makers[9] and beer brewers have operated, the latter at least prior to the general imposition of Sharia law in the Sudan in 1984.

One area of the market is devoted to animal transactions, where professional animal brokers link buyers and sellers and assure the legitimacy of the exchange. At large markets in Shgeig, animals are purchased for transport and resale in Khartoum.

The government sector is well established in the larger market towns: persons are employed as teachers, forest guards, health workers, policemen, and bore-hole operators. The private service sector includes tea-shop assistants; occasional truck drivers and their apprentices; and water carriers who draw water from shallow wells, load it on donkeys, and hawk it through the village. There are a number of small cheese factories and several diesel-powered grain mills in the region, as well as government-licensed fabricators and sellers of charcoal.

Wage Labor on the Schemes

Most local people hope that they can provide themselves with a reasonably satisfactory life by skillful management of animal husbandry, rainfed grain cultivation, and trade and crafts. But the contraction of the pastoral zone caused by the dam and the expansion of irrigated farming, the unpredictibility of the weather, periodic infestations of locusts and other pests, and epidemic diseases among the animals render the local economy vulnerable, and force all but the wealthier traders and those with substantial animal resources to make up their shortfall in earnings by laboring on the schemes.

The major result of the insatiable though intermittent requirements of the schemes for additional labor has been the partial transformation of these formerly subsistence-level agropastoralists and their households into an agrarian proletariat. The need to buy grain and other commodities from the market and to pay taxes creates cash flow problems from which few are exempt. For shorter or longer periods people respond to labor recruiters from the schemes and work for wages during the long cotton harvest. These wages—or rather the fraction that remains after deducting the expenses of food and housing away from home—are used to pay taxes and buy food. The people do not look forward to wage labor with enthusiasm.[10] They resent the hard work for low pay, and they complain about the poor conditions of health on the schemes. Their own areas, they say, which are less humid (and which are relatively free from schistosomiasis and malaria) are better for their health. But their economic fragility leaves them with little choice; although reliable figures are not available, it is clear that each year more of them meet their shortfalls with scheme labor. The inadequate yields from the rainfed cereals and livestock economy generate a labor surplus that is consumed by the lusher yields from the commercial and export irrigation economy. The two zones—one "commercial" and the other "subsistence"—in fact form parts of a single economy, with the so-called subsistence sector dependent on the commercial one for cash and the commercial sector on the traditional or subsistence one for labor.

Land Tenure

In the Sudan, as in other parts of the developing world, there are often gross discrepancies between formal and effective land tenure systems in rural areas. In law, all otherwise unregistered land belongs to the State. In practice, access to most grazing land and rainfed agricultural land (other than on the mechanized schemes) is regulated by local principles of tenure. In the region west of the White Nile, cultivable lands, particularly those in close proximity to the villages (and to sources of water) are divided and customary ownership recognized although not often formally registered. Permanent grazing land is held in common and is broadly available to all village herders. More precisely, the land is grazed by those who have firm rights of access to local wells. Because the output from these dug wells is low and considerable energy is expended in drawing water, the charge on surrounding pastures is moderated.[11] This does not mean that strangers are denied occasional access to water, but regular access is allocated only to those who habitually graze the area. (Certain grazing areas have become effectively privatized, including the peripheral greenbelts around important towns in Kordofan Province.) As has been pointed out above, low millet yields have led to an extension of cultivation and a consequent contraction of available pasture. The expansion of the cultivation of cereals in low rainfall areas has been identified as a prime factor in environmental degradation.[12]

While shallow dug wells have served to limit the animal load on the pasture, diesel-powered bore holes are another story. Their high output and ease of watering attract large numbers of herders and their flocks. Local overgrazing occurs as a result of this concentration around bore holes, and a considerable distance exists between the holes and adequate grazing. The concentration around permanent watering points varies with the seasons, being most intense in the late dry season. It will be recalled that prior to the construction of the Jebel al-Awliya Dam and the development of the pump schemes on the West Bank, animals were able to graze the rich recession pastures along the river during the dry season. Without that access today, the deep wells take on greater importance and are the principal points of animal congregation. During the rains, when surface water supplies are adequate, animals are widely dispersed across the terrain and the rain-induced flush is sufficient for its charge. The arboreal browse becomes increasingly important as the dry season progresses with the exhaustion of the terrestrial pasture. The natural regeneration of such important fodder sources as *Acacia tortilis* is impeded because the seed pods are ingested before they are ripe. Although such grazing is potentially beneficial for the spread of the plant, because the seeds are transported in a rich manured environment, their prematurity when they are ingested reduces the chance of germination.

Herders are cognizant of their seasonal dependence on the arboreal browse, and in general respond favorably to the possibility of its expansion.[13] Information provided by Anwar Abdu (personal communication) confirms our own observations. Abdu conducted a rural energy survey in White Nile Province, and asked villagers why they thought tree planting was beneficial to them. The villagers offered the following responses, in order of preference:

1. Trees are an important source of fodder.
2. Trees provide shade from the summer's heat.
3. Trees are the principal source of domestic fuel.
4. Trees provide building poles and tool handles.

Grazing land is vulnerable to the expansion of cultivation. We have no evidence, however, to indicate that elite groups or individuals have privileged access to open pasture as they have to the peri-urban greenbelts. A program of fodder-tree planting would obviously benefit in the first instance persons who own animals, especially those with large herds. Small herd owners would also probably have access to this resource. On the other hand, trees that sprout on millet fields, for example, during their fallow phase, might be reserved for the benefit of the title holder. Since such land is in short supply, and it is difficult for those without title to cultivate a millet field, they would not be likely to profit from the arboreal browse on registered fields. On communal grazing lands, access would be more widespread, but there the potential problem of proper management presents itself, since it is difficult to assign specific responsibilities for the protection of seedlings; hired guards may prove necessary. Some local villages have assumed responsibility for the protection of forest reserve areas, and unlicensed tree cutting and charcoal manufacture have been thereby constrained. It may be useful to explore the relationships between the fuel trade and the important, wealthy men of the villages, since the affluent may further consolidate their positions by monopolizing the trade and by discouraging others from having access to independent fuelwood sources.

Community Fuelwood Needs

The manifest interests of the state and the rural villagers are often opposed, and this is nowhere more evident than in the cutting of wood for fuel. The Forestry Department is interested in the establishment of mesquite (*Prosopis chilensis*) in the sandy upland region, with the dual objectives of improving the arboreal pasture and contributing to soil stabilization. The nitrogen-fixing qualities of this representative of the family *Leguminosae* are also recognized. The problem that must be faced, however, is that to large numbers of area people, despite their verbal appreciation of arboreal fodder, trees are exploited primarily as the basic source of domestic fuel, and this use stands in potential conflict with the above objectives.

Large areas in proximity to human settlements in White Nile Province have been denuded of their tree cover as the people extend their search for fuelwood further and further from their villages. Young trees of modest diameter are especially vulnerable because they are easier to cut with simple tools. The Sudan Forestry Department has attempted to confront this problem by banning the indiscriminate cutting of wood and by licensing the manufacture and sale of charcoal. Forest officers are vested with police authority in enforcing these regulations, and can arrest persons caught violating them. Forest guards are appointed in villages with substantial forest reserves, but in the smaller villages there is only informal pressure to control unlicensed cutting of wood.[14] The problem is compounded by the marked differences in income levels between larger villages, like Helba and Shgeig, and those smaller, some of which include just a handful of households. In the larger villages, market-related activities provide opportunities for increased earnings, and many persons there can afford to purchase wood and charcoal from licensed sellers. In the smaller villages, income-earning opportunities other than from animal husbandry and cereal cultivation are very limited, and the people are forced to satisfy their fuelwood needs from local resources. Such fuelwood gathering is very largely the responsibility of village women, and some of the poorest people earn meager incomes by selling gathered wood to their neighbors.

In discussions with persons from both small and large villages, it was clear that people appreciate the advantage to be gained from the expansion of arboreal fodder. The need for this resource, however, will be found mainly in the latter months of the dry season, when terrestrial pasture either has been consumed or has lost most of its nutrient value. The need for fuelwood is constant throughout the year. Thus, the temptation to cut young mesquite, in the absence of strong control mechanisms, will be very powerful.

Conclusions and Recommendations

The behaviors leading to desertification are often labeled "traditional"; the thrust of development, therefore, is perceived by many as requiring a break with tradition. Most projects envisage not only a technical package but also an extension capacity to convey that package to people. Frequently, however, affected people, especially poor people, resist those changes. Rather than demonstrating that such resistance is attributable to "the force of tradition, established over millennia," field research has often found that resistance is a rational outcome of the assessment poor people make of the likely consequences of those changes. Yet tradition is a good point at which to begin the analysis, for the area that is now threatened had in fact sustained production and population over a very long period of time.

Throughout the region, shifting cultivation and mobile forms of livestock raising existed in a symbiotic relationship for hundreds of years. In general, farming and herding peoples were ethnically as well as occupationally distinct, constituting a "cultural mosaic" in which separate ethnic groups maintained their distinctiveness in most social areas but came together in the marketplace and through the multiple use of land. In the market, pastoral produce (milk and milk products, live animals, meat, and hides) was exchanged for cereal grains; on the cultivated fields, crop stubble was exchanged for manure, as the harvested farms constituted an important source of dry season fodder.

The herders practiced other strategies facilitating survival in the difficult environment. The most critical of these was mobility. Because of the unpredictability of rainfall, herders had to shift locale rapidly as the quality and quantity of the graze and browse declined to the point where milk yields, on which their subsistence largely depended, declined. Herd numbers were regulated by controlled reproduction, by fluctuating off-take rates, and by the availability of labor, especially the ability to find dry-season pasture with adequate supplies of water. Although in principle much of the range was broadly available to the herders, access to water was more rigidly constrained. A de facto range management, therefore, resulted from the rotation implicit in mobility, from the control over access to water, and from the labor demands of herding itself. The other striking adaptive strategy of the herders was the mixed composition of the herd. Throughout the bulk of western Sudan pastures, people keep mixed herds of cattle, sheep, goats, and camels, as well as donkeys and some horses, although the preponderance of camels increases greatly in the north. Since the different species make different demands on the environment, some preferring graze and some browse, some consuming plants that are unpalatable to others (such as camels eating *Leptadenia pyrotechnica* not favored by other livestock), overall pressure was kept to a minimum and the environment was able to reproduce itself year after year, responding with resiliency to temporary declines in production due to low rainfall.

Despite the symbiosis between herders and farmers, occasional conflicts arose, engendered mainly by incursions of animals in the cultivated fields before the harvests or by the extension of cultivation into areas normally used for herding. These conflicts were few and localized, because sufficient land existed for both forms of exploitation, and all productive land was devoted to subsistence production for local use. There was only a small urban population that consumed rural produce. In most years, that urban population did not make excessive demands that threatened the producers' abilities to feed themselves.

With the completion of the Jebel al-Awliya Dam and the introduction of labor-intensive, mechanized, irrigated schemes along the river, the situation changed dramatically. This has led to profound changes in local social, economic, and political organization, most prominently a marked increase in rural social differentiation and the partial proletarianization of rural producers. The situation is exacerbated by the rapid increase in population due to a decline in mortality without a corresponding reduction in fertility. This is clearly the case with the human population. It may also be the case with the animal population (although reliable census data prior to the great rinderpest campaign of the 1960s are lacking). More people and possibly more animals are competing for an inelastic resource: land. Under these conditions—dramatic increases in social differentiation and population— access to land, especially access to *good* land, has become more problematic. The intensity of the problem is evidenced by two immediately apparent consequences: the movement of population from rural villages and pastoral camps to towns and cities and to the irrigated schemes along the river; and land overuse. Another consequence is a rapid escalation of food prices, which, in the abstract, would seem to benefit rural producers, small as well as large. But a paradox was noted above: small producers, having often mortgaged their crops before the harvest, are forced to buy back from the market the very grains that they grew and earlier "sold" at very low prices to settle their debts with the merchants. The inflated price for grains, as the traders withhold stocks until the dry season progresses, thereby further impoverishes rather than enriches the producers. With a rising population and the reduction in the size of cultivable area because of the expansion of irrigated schemes, small farmers cannot afford the luxury of fallow periods. The same field is cultivated continuously, leading inevitably to permanent degradation. Even this is insufficient, and there is great pressure to expand agriculture into more-and-more marginal areas, with a marked transgression of what Fouad Ibrahim (1978, 1984:112–118) calls "the agronomic dry boundary." Millet cultivation has migrated steadily northward, with tragic results. The farther north, the lower the available rainfall, the lower the yields, and the greater the need to find new lands even farther north. This scenario can result only in desertification. And as the area in cultivation expands, the area left to herding can only contract. An increasing number of animals is left to graze a diminishing amount of pasture. The "overgrazing" of which herdsmen are accused is a consequence not of an irrational desire for more animals, as is commonly claimed in development documents for the "livestock sector," but of constraints on access to lands that were once pasture.

The above analysis of the socioeconomic situation of the area points to a number of potential issues that will have to be resolved in order to implement socially and environmentally effective development interventions:

- competition between the need for fuelwood and the need for fodder;
- current shortages of farm and pasture lands, which would be aggravated in the short run by the removal of additional lands for tree planting; and
- differential benefits to the local population.

There are, unfortunately, no simple solutions. Persons with large herds and with sufficient cash to satisfy their fuelwood needs on the market would benefit most from improved arboreal browse. Those peasant farmers with few if any animals but with a continuous need for cheap fuelwood would have little incentive to participate. It is conceivable that an extension program aimed at persuading poor people as to the long-term benefits of the project, especially if associated with credit and appropriate technology components, might help. The credit component—which would require the cooperation of government offices external to the Forestry Department— would allow some of the poor to obtain animals and to participate thereby in the benefits of improved fodder. The appropriate technology component would advise villagers, again through extension officers, on more fuel-efficient means of cooking.[15] Finally, a compromise position with the villagers might be reached permitting some fuelwood harvesting. While each of these is potentially helpful, and a general cooperation might be obtained from the villagers, great optimism about project success is not warranted.

A better approach might well be to confront the entire set of problems in a single package rather than focus exclusively or almost exclusively on the potential contributions of *Prosopis chilensis* to the improvement of the environment through sand stabilization and expansion of the arboreal pasture. Such a package would be far more complex than the one initially proposed to FAO, and would minimally call for village woodlots, to respond to the fuelwood problem as well as to improve browse. Such a package would seem to require the participation of government agencies other than the Forestry Department alone, and of specialists from a variety of social and biological sciences. In this manner, the proposed interventions would be based on an intimate understanding of the entire system—animal, human, and environmental—and would, therefore, more likely obtain the willing participation of the people. Such a multi-disciplinary involvement should not disappear following the design phase of the project but should continue— as a built-in monitoring and evaluation capacity—through its implementation and evaluation phases. The monitoring and evaluation staff should be separate from the extension and implementation staff in order to assure objectivity, and should include members of the local community (especially from the poorer segments of that community). It would provide periodic guidance to project management relating to the receptivity of the people to project objectives and activities.

Without these changes, who would benefit from the proposed interventions? It is clear that the direct beneficiaries of fodder-producing trees will be livestock owners, particularly those with large herds. These persons are already among the more affluent members of the upland village communities, among those, that is, who are best able to avoid having to labor for wages on the pump schemes. The project would also directly benefit the large livestock brokers who regulate the animal trade, and, somewhat less directly, urban consumers of meat. Would it also benefit small herd owners and those without any animals at all?

The answer depends a good deal on the social relationships among the several economic strata in the rural areas. Available information does not permit a firm conclusion. If relationships between large and small herd owners are not exploitative, the project might benefit both, since improved grazing land has not yet been monopolized by the elite (as have the wooded greenbelts around larger towns). But the process of range privatization has been documented for other parts of pastoral Africa (Horowitz and Little 1986), and similar preconditions, including marked social differentiation, are present in White Nile Province. Able livestock management is a means to success in the region, and residual earnings (if any) from wage labor may be reinvested in animals. Improved range should therefore be generally beneficial. But the substantial internal differentiation that does exist in the area, and the access to political power enjoyed by the affluent, imply that such benefits as the proposed project may bring will accrue primarily to the already advantaged.

Notes

1. This chapter is based on fieldwork carried out by the authors in White Nile Province in 1981 in association with a United Nations Food and Agriculture Organization mission on the introduction of forestry in grazing lands. The chapter also draws upon research undertaken by Horowitz in a 1981 mission in Kordofan and Darfur on behalf of United Nations Sudano-Sahelian Office, and by Salem-Murdock in 1978 and 1980–1981 in Eastern Sudan with support from the Social Science Research Council, the Wenner-Gren Foundation for Anthropological Research, and the Institute for Development Anthropology. The authors acknowledge this support with gratitude. We especially wish to thank Kamal Hassan Badi for his collegiality and friendship in the field, and David Brokensha, Vivian Carlip, Tom Catterson, Peter Little, Endre Nyerges, and Joseph Whitney for their very helpful critical readings of draft versions of this paper.

2. The displacement of herds from the riverine plains to the sandy goz per se is not the prime cause of desertification. Here we must look to the extension of cereal cultivation (*Sorghum vulagre* and *Pennisetum typhoideum*, respectively *dura* and *dukhun* in Arabic) into the low rainfall areas. The migration of millet cultivation into formerly pastoral areas is striking throughout the northern Sudan. The causes of this expansion are political and economic. Small farmers often find it difficult to satisfy their consumption needs without credit. Since the state does not readily provide such credit, the small farmers turn to the traders and secure their loans by selling in advance the next harvest (the sheil system, discussed below).

3. According to Abbas (1980:129), tenancies or *hawashat* in units of 18 feddans (1 feddan = 1.04 acres = 0.42 hectare) were allocated on the Sufi-Wad Nimir Scheme in exchange for 60 feddans of previously owned rainfed land.

4. As Salem-Murdock notes elsewhere in this volume, management of the New Halfa Agricultural Scheme, which previously shared the hostility toward livestock, now sees their integration on the scheme as a solution to the problem of extremely reduced water availability due to siltation of the Khashm el-Girba reservoir.

5. Ethnic ascription is not invariable. In the context of the Sudan as a whole, "Northerner" means Arab and "Southerner" means non-Arab; further discrimination may not be made, despite the inclusion among Northerners of non-Arabic speaking Nubians, Hadendawa, Fur, and persons of Hausa and FulBe origins, and despite the division of Southerners among Dinka, Nuer, and others. Further, speakers of Arabic are segmented into Kababish, Baggara, etc. Tribal, sub-tribal, lineal, and household identifications are made where they are relevant. An individual identifying himself vis-à-vis another person may elect to communicate difference by choosing

the level of term most remote from the other or may elect to undercommunicate that difference by selecting a more inclusive term.

6. The socioeconomic research unit of the Niger Range and Livestock Project (Swift 1984), working in an area ecologically comparable to the sandy uplands of White Nile Province, has reported intense poverty among large numbers of pastoralists who lost their animals during the 1968–1974 drought and have been unable to reestablish demographically viable herds. Having few or no animals means having no milk for domestic consumption and no money with which to purchase grain. An index of the extent of this poverty is the large number of persons who work as herders and shepherds for urban-based traders and civil servants and for the more affluent farmers who invest in cattle. These shepherds have access only to the milk and not to any offspring as may be produced. Such labor does not serve, therefore, as an interim means of herd reconstitution but merely as a survival stopgap. We do not know the extent of such poverty in the Sudan, but the recurrence of drought in the 1980s, and especially 1984, has necessarily resulted in substantial further reductions in the national herd.

7. "Unlike the Kababish and the Baggara, for instance, the seasonal movements of the Hassaniya were of an intensive type. They moved within a limited range of the river and as far as possible within reasonable distance of their river and rain cultivation. Their urge to cultivate constrained the degree of mobility with the animals, while their urge to move as far as they actually did had already set a limit to what might be said to be a roughly optimal agricultural production" (Abbas 1980:22).

As the range becomes more and more constrained, competition for its use can lead to conflict and violence. The issue then becomes which group can better press its claim. Competition leading to conflict appears to be increasing in the Western Sudan, with reports of fights between herders and farmers and between different groups of herders. In the Eastern Sudan also, Salem-Murdock has observed farmers, mostly Nubian, protesting the Beja use of swords and knives in combat. On the basis of evidence from other parts of Northern Sudan then, we can predict similar cases in White Nile Province as pressure on the land intensifies.

8. Throughout sudano-sahelian Africa, there are traders intermediary between herd owners and consumers. Part of their task is to guarantee the legitimacy of the sale (e.g., assuring a potential buyer that the animal is not stolen). Livestock traders, particularly those who operate remote from the main market of Omdurman (and Port Sudan, the animal export market), buy in small lots during the dry season and hold the animals in proximity to good watering points (near a bore hole, for example) until the rain, when grass and groundwater allow for the trek to market—a trek that may last several months. One of the problems of environmental rehabilitation projects is the tendency for these traders, who were powerfully linked to the deposed Nimeiry regime, to monopolize improved grazing. This is seen in the old town perimeters in Kordofan, such as El Obeid and An-Nahoud.

9. By its very nature, reliable information on charcoal produced extralegally is not easily obtained. According to some reports, a good deal of the charcoal sold in Helba is illegally produced, but security is quite tight, and the risks are high. For example, during our field mission, a man was caught transporting two sacks of unlicensed charcoal. The charcoal was immediately confiscated by the Forestry Agent, and a summons issued for an appearance before a magistrate, where a fine may be assessed and even the camel used for transportation may be confiscated.

Legal, licensed charcoal in White Nile Province is produced mainly from trees cleared from the mechanized schemes southwest of Kosti and in Ed Dueim. Licenses are issued by the provincial head of the Forestry Department. These are obtained by businessmen who are allocated blocks for clearance and conversion to charcoal. They pay royalties on the amount produced. In 1975 there were severe shortages of charcoal in Ed Dueim, and for three years licensed cutting was permitted in the Helba region to satisfy demands in the provincial capital.

From time to time the Forestry Department announces opportunities for cutting *sunt (Acacia nilotica)* along the river. Since this wood has many uses other than charcoal manufacture—making railroad ties, for example—it is difficult to estimate the amount converted to fuel (see chapter by Whitney in this volume).

10. According to Abbas (1980:141), wage-labor in the pre-dam period was disdained by free men: "Only the very poor lineage fellows were forced to work for money, an activity which was much despised." The derogation of wage labor is seen in the reluctance to hire laborers from within the *khashm beit*, the lineal descent group, although it is acceptable to employ more genealogically remote lineage mates (ibid.:147).

11. The water table is about 9 meters in much of the area. Sheep, camels, and cattle are watered in troughs near the wells, while water for goats is often transported to them in skin bags.

12. As Ibrahim states (1978:10–11):

Field study in West Sudan has convinced us that the transgression over the agronomic dry boundaries is the main cause of desertification there. For the preparation of the fields for millet cultivation means the felling of all the trees and the extraction of all the fields. The soil is then loosened and made exposed to strong deflation. The repetition of this process leads finally to an irreversible destruction of the natural vegetation cover and enhances the erosion of fertile topsoil. Soil degradation leads to the diminution of productivity. The land cultivator is thus obliged to shorten the rotation of cultivation and fallow, and ultimately plants the land continuously. The soil becomes gradually exhausted, because all plant nourishment is used up.

(See also Ibrahim's chapter in this volume.)

13. See, however, the caveat relating to fuelwood use in the next section.

14. Wooded areas fall into one of three classes, each of which is differently managed:

- The Forest Reserves. These are the wooded tracts under direct Forestry Department management. Although grazing is permitted in the Reserves, cultivation is not. Individuals from the villages within the area are entitled to collect dead wood and fallen branches, but cutting of live wood and manufacture of charcoal are restricted to licensed specialists.
- Communal or Open Forest Areas. These are the areas that are diminishing in size, as unregulated exploitation—for grazing, firewood, and pole cutting—reduces them more quickly than they can regenerate.
- Village-Controlled Forest Areas. In close proximity to villages, these small areas are closely supervised by the villagers themselves. Wood collection and grazing is limited to actual members of the village. According to Anwar Abdu, these village-managed tracts are well maintained by local communities concerned

with environmental protection. The only privately owned wooded areas result from trees colonizing cultivated fields during fallow periods. Such trees belong to the title-holder of the field.

15. Domestic cooking accounts for most of the fuelwood use, and there has been a good deal of interest in reducing the amount of wood consumed in cooking: "Improved stoves can probably achieve an overall efficiency of between 20 and 30 percent and they have the potential for reducing wood requirements by five to ten fold" (NAS 1980:164). According to David Brokensha (personal communication), this 1980 estimate is now regarded as unduly optimistic, and savings from improved stoves have rarely exceeded 10–20 percent.

References

Abbas, Ahmed Mohamed
   1980   White Nile Arabs: Political Leadership and Economic Change. London School of Economics Monographs on Social Anthropology No. 53. Atlantic Highlands, NJ: Humanities Press, Inc.
Ahmed, Abdel-Ghaffar Mohamed
   1972   The Rufa'a al-Hoj Economy. *In* Essays in Sudan Ethnology. Ian Cunnison and Wendy James, eds. Pp. 173–188. New York, NY: Humanities Press.
Asad, Talal
   1964   Seasonal Movements of the Kababish Arabs of Northern Kordofan. Sudan Notes and Records 45:45–58.
Badi, Kamal Hassan
   1981   Technical Proposal to the Food and Agriculture Organisation Regarding the Planting of *Prosopis* spp. in Block Plots for Regeneration through Seed Spread in White Nile Province, Sudan. Khartoum: Forest Department.
Cunnison, Ian
   1966   Baggara Arabs. London: Oxford University Press.
Horowitz, Michael M and Peter D. Little
   1986   African Pastoralism and Poverty: Some Implications for Drought and Famine. *In* Drought and Hunger in Africa. Michael H. Glantz, ed. Cambridge: Cambridge University Press, forthcoming.
Ibrahim, Fouad N.
   1978   The Problem of Desertification in the Republic of the Sudan with Special Reference to Northern Darfur Province. Development Studies and Research Centre Monograph Series No. 8. Khartoum: Khartoum University Press.
   1984   Ecological Imbalance in the Republic of the Sudan—with Reference to Desertification in Darfur. Vol. 6. Bayreuth: Druckhaus Bayreuth Verlagsgesellschaft mbH.
Kerr, Richard A.
   1985   Fifteen Years of African Drought. Science 227:1453–1454.
Lamprey, H. F.
   1983   Pastoralism Yesterday and Today: the Over-grazing Problem. *In* Tropical Savannas. Ecosystems of the World 13. F. Bourlière, ed. Pp. 643–666. Amsterdam: Elsevier Scientific Publishing Company.

NAS (National Academy of Sciences)
   1980   Firewood Crops: Shrub and Tree Species for Energy Production. Washington,
           DC: National Academy of Sciences.
Swift, Jeremy, ed.
   1984   Pastoral Development in Central Niger: Report of the Niger Range and
           Livestock Project. Niamey: Ministère du Développement Rural and United
           States Agency for International Development.

6

Impact of Fuelwood Use on Environmental Degradation in the Sudan[1]

J. B. R. Whitney

Introduction

From one point of view, it makes good economic sense for a poor country like the Sudan to mine its forest resources for fuel rather than spend its meager hard currency earnings importing fossil energy. In the early 1980s the Sudan used 291 petajoules (PJ) of energy[2] (1 PJ $= 10^{15}$ joules) of which 2.7 PJ were derived from hydro-electricity, 41.5 PJ from imported fossil fuels, and 246.7 PJ from biomass fuels (firewood, charcoal and crop residues) (Sudan National Energy Administration [SNEA] 1983b). It would, therefore, be necessary to import an additional 247 PJ of fossil fuels to replace the biomass sources and to prevent further deforestation. This would require a six-fold increase of the present fossil fuel imports, a purchase that would far exceed the hard currency earnings of the country.

This simple economic justification for the continued mining of forest resources, however, ignores the social and environmental costs incurred. Declining environmental quality, caused by the overexploitation of biomass resources (forests, grasslands, and crop residues), has its greatest initial impact on nomads, poor farmers, and the women and children of rural communities who have to travel ever greater distances to obtain fuel and water. Although the social costs of deforestation will not be the focus of this chapter, it is my contention that degradation of the environment leads to what Baxter (1981) calls "degradation of people." Lands at risk put people at risk and the latter are usually those with the least influence on government policy and the least ability to ameliorate the situation.

The aims of this chapter are:

1. to indicate the current national and regional trends of fuelwood-energy availability and consumption in the Sudan;[3]
2. to assess the impact of the use of fuelwood (which includes both firewood and charcoal) on deforestation;

3. to examine local patterns of fuelwood exploitation;
4. to assess the environmental impact of deforestation in a semiarid region;
5. to estimate the ecological-economic costs and benefits of the present pattern of energy use; and
6. to review a number of policies to ameliorate the situation.

The Energy System of the Sudan

The Sudan is the largest country in Africa, with an area of nearly 2.5 million square kilometers and a 1983 population of slightly over 20 million (SNEA 1983a). As indicated in Figure 6.1, the average density of 8 persons per square kilometer conceals wide variations in density, with over 100 persons/km^2 along the Nile Valley, the Gezira plain, and in parts of the Southern Region. The desert and semidesert areas outside of the Nile Valley exhibit population densities much lower than the average. Figure 6.1 also reveals that there is little coincidence between the areas of dense population and the areas that have high rates of "allowable cuts." This term refers to the amount of wood that can be removed on a sustained-yield basis each year and is approximately equal to the net annual productivity of the forest.

Of a total of 292 PJ of energy consumed by the Sudanese economy, biomass sources contribute 248 PJ, or 85 percent of the energy consumed (UNDP and World Bank 1983; SNEA 1983). Fuelwood, defined as any wood used for energy purposes, provides the greatest portion (92 percent) of this amount. Households consume 80 percent of the national energy supply and rely heavily (98 percent) on biomass sources. Hence, household energy use is a major cause of deforestation.

As rainfall increases toward the south, the allowable cut varies from about 10 kg per ha in the desert region to one ton per ha in the humid southwest. The north, consisting of six regions (Figure 6.2 and Table 6.1), has 84 percent of the population but only 34 percent of the national allowable cut (Table 6.1); the Southern Region has 16 percent of the population and 66 percent of the allowable cut. Because of the poorly developed transportation network and the high cost of transferring fuelwood from one region to another, each region has to supply the greater part of its own household energy needs.

Figure 6.2 and Table 6.1 indicate that all areas but the south are experiencing overcutting, in which the annual rate of wood removal exceeds the allowable cut. These imbalances, which imply serious deforestation, are most severe in the Central Region, followed, in descending order of severity, by Kordofan, the Eastern Region, Khartoum, Darfur, and the Northern Region. In areas of intense fuelwood scarcity (Eastern, Central and Northern regions), crop and animal residues supply a small but important portion of the region's fuel supply (Table 6.1). In the Southern Region, where there is a fuelwood surplus, agricultural residues also make significant contributions to household energy sources. Fossil fuels (including electricity) are significant

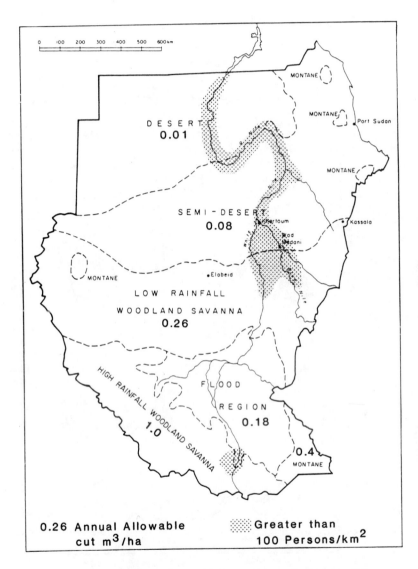

Fig. 6.1 Sudan: Vegetation, Annual Allowable Cut, and Densely Populated Areas.

118

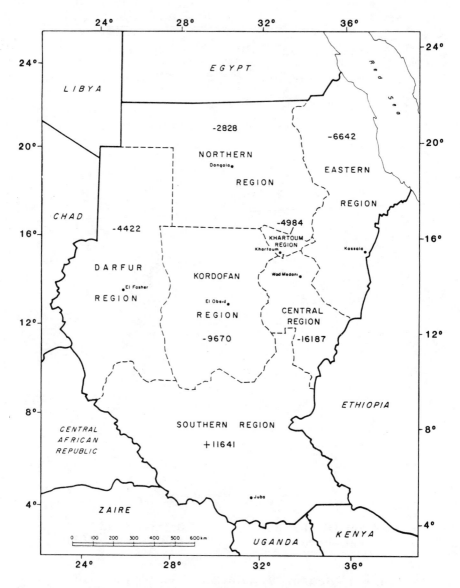

Fig. 6.2 Sudan: Administrative Regions and Annual Volume
of Wood Cut in Excess of Replacement Rate ($10^3 m^3$).

TABLE 6.1 Sudan: Regional Availability of Household Biomass and Fossil Fuels c. 1980

Region	Population ('000s)[a] Total	Allowable Cut[b] (10^3 m^3)	Consumption[c] (10^3 m^3)	Balance (10^3 m^3)	Source of Fuel Used (Tonnes of Oil Equivalent%)[d] Wood	Residues	Fossil[e]
Eastern	2409	457	7099	-6642	92.2	5.2	2.6
Central	5502	1109	17295	-16187	85.9	12.3	1.8
Khartoum	2029	252	5236	-4948	89.8	0	10.1
Kordofan	2704	3208	12878	-9670	99.2	0	0.8
Darfur	3020	9809	14231	-4422	99.5	0	0.5
Northern	1077	222	3050	-2828	86.1	11.5	2.4
SUBTOTAL:							
Northern Region	16741	15056	59789	-44733	92.7	5.1	2.2
Southern Region	3306	29300	17659	+11641	87.9	11.9	0.2
TOTAL	20047	44356	77448	-33092	91.3	7.1	1.5

a SNEA (1983a:123).

b SNEA (1983a:96).

c UNDP and World Bank (1983).

d SNEA (1983a:12).

e Includes electricity.

only in the Khartoum region, where they provide 10 percent of household energy needs.

During the last twenty years, there has been little variation in the pattern of per capita urban fuelwood consumption (Table 6.2). The ratio of firewood to charcoal use (in "growing stock wood equivalents" [GSWE]—which is the volume of timber that was used to produce the charcoal or firewood) has remained at about 1:4.7. There has, however, been an overall decline of 16.5 percent in per capita urban fuelwood consumption due to its greater scarcity and to the availability of other energy sources.

By contrast, there have been significant per capita changes in the pattern of wood consumption in the countryside. In 1960, the ratio of firewood to charcoal consumption (in GSWE) was 1:0.5 (Table 6.2); in 1980, the ratio was 1:1.4. The expansion of per capita consumption of charcoal by 127 percent (GSWE) during the twenty-year period has had serious environmental consequences and is seen as a response to the increasing scarcity of firewood, the per capita rural consumption of which has *declined* 12.5 percent during the period (Table 6.2).

Overall, the differential wood consumption of urban and rural dwellers has been reduced during the last twenty years. In 1960, the per capita annual consumption of fuelwood (GSWE) was 2.46 m^3 for rural and 4.1 m^3 for urban inhabitants, giving a rural/urban ratio of 1:1.7; in 1980, per capita use in both urban and rural centers was 3.4 m^3.

The Impact of Fuelwood Use on Deforestation

In the period between 1960 and 1980, the amount of deforestation attributable to household fuelwood consumption rose from nearly 7,500 km^2/yr to 28,000 km^2/yr. The major factors contributing to this rapid increase of 20,500 km^2 in the annual rate of deforestation due to household consumption include: (1) an overall increase in population; (2) growth of urban areas; (3) increases in per capita consumption of fuelwood, particularly of charcoal in rural areas; and (4) decreases in the volume of GSWE in the remaining accessible forested areas. Table 6.3 indicates the contribution of each of these factors to the increase of deforestation.

During the twenty-year period 1960–1980, the average annual increase in deforestation was 1,033 km^2, of which 61.8 percent can be attributed to overall population growth, 27 percent to changes in per capita demand for fuelwood, and 11 percent to the declining volume of the woodland stock in accessible areas, requiring larger areas to provide the same volume of fuelwood. Clearly, increase of population rather than increased per capita demand has been the primary factor in accelerating the rate of deforestation. The contributing factors to deforestation must be examined more closely, however, before appropriate policies can be designed to cope with the deforestation problem.

Table 6.3 indicates that 936 km^2, or 90.6 percent of the average annual increase in deforested area can be attributed to the increasing use of charcoal

TABLE 6.2   Total and Per Capita Growing Stock Wood Equivalent (GSWE)
Removals, Deforestation Area and Rates of Growth.   Sudan:
1960-1980

| REMOVALS | 1960 | | | |
	Total GSWE $(106m^3)^a$	Total deforestation $(103km^2)^b$	Per Capita GSWE $(m^3)c$	Per Capita deforestation $(m^2)d$
CHARCOAL:	(1)	(2)	(3)	(4)
Rural Households	8.7	4.3	0.9	423
Urban Households	3.8	1.9	3.4	1650
Industry/Commerce[i]	1.3	0.6	NA	NA
Households: Sub-total	12.5	6.16	1.1	547
All charcoal use: Sub-total	13.8	6.8	NA	NA
FIREWOOD:				
Rural Households	16.2	0.8*	1.6	78
Urban Households	0.8	0.4	0.7	349
Industry/Commerce[j]	0.8	0.4	NA	NA
Households: Sub-total	17.0	1.2	1.5	106
All firewood use: Sub-total	17.8	1.6	NA	NA
OTHER:				
Mechanized agriculture[k]	--	--	--	--
Lumber[l]	0.3	0.2	NA	NA
Overgrazing Fire/pests[m]	1.8	0.1*	NA	NA
TOTAL REMOVALS				
All rural households	24.9	5.1	2.5	501
All urban households	4.6	2.3	4.1	2000
All households: Total	29.5	7.3	2.62	651
All uses: Total	33.7	8.6	NA	NA

* Assumes that only 10% of volume cut results in deforestation.
  N.B.   Totals may differ from sub-totals due to rounding.
[a] GSWE data from SNEA (1983a:18B).
[b] Data in (1) divided by 20.27 cubic meters ha^{-1} (SNEA 1983a:17).
[c] Data in (1) divided by the respective populations for 1960: rural-
  10.13 million; urban-1.13 million; total 11.26 million (SNEA 1983a).
[d] Data in (2) divided by population in (c) above.

(continued)

TABLE 6.2 (Continued)

REMOVALS	1980 Total GSWE $(106m^3)$ [e]	Total deforestation $(103km^2)$ [f]	Per Capita GSWE (m^3) [g]	Per Capita deforestation (m^2) [h]
CHARCOAL:	(5)	(6)	(7)	(8)
Rural Households	27.4	15.5	2.0	1106
Urban Households	16.7	9.4	2.8	1574
Industry/Commerce[i]	2.4	1.4	NA	NA
Households: Sub-total	44.1	24.9	2.2	1246
All charcoal use: Sub-total	46.5	26.3	NA	NA
FIREWOOD:				
Rural Households	20.0	1.1	1.4	81
Urban Households	3.5	2.0	0.6	332
Industry/Commerce[j]	1.4	0.8	NA	NA
Households: Sub-total	23.5	3.1*	1.2	156
All firewood use: Sub-total	24.9	4.3	NA	NA
OTHER				
Mechanized agriculture[k]	1.1	3.0	NA	NA
Lumber[l]	0.5	0.3	NA	NA
Overgrazing/ Fire/pests[m]	1.6	0.1*	NA	NA
TOTAL REMOVALS				
All rural households	47.4	16.6	3.4	1187
All urban households	20.2	11.4	3.4	1906
All households: Total	67.6	28.0	3.4	1401
All uses: Total	74.6	34.0	NA	NA

[e] GSWE data from SNEA (1983a:18).
[f] Data in (5) divided by 17.65 cubic meters ha^{-1} (SNEA 1983a:95).
[g] Data in (5) divided by the respective populations for 1980: rural-14.01 million; urban-5.97 million; total-19.98 million (SNEA 1983a:123).
[h] Data in (6) divided by population in (g) above.
[i] Same proportions as found in 1980 (SNEA 1983a:92).
[j] As for (i) above.
[k] SNEA (1983a:92).
[l] SNEA (1983a:92).
[m] SNEA (1983a:92).

TABLE 6.3 The Average Annual Contribution to Deforestation of Urban and Rural Population Change, Per Capita Fuelwood Demand and the Declining GSWE Yield of Accessible Areas (km^2)[a]

	From Population				From Changes in Per Capita Demand				From Changes in Declining GSWE Yield				Total Sectors				Total Fuels	
	Rural	(%)	Urban	(%)	Rural	(%)	Urban	(%)	Rural	(%)	Urban	(%)	Rural (%)		Urban	(%)		(%)
Firewood	15.4	1.5	83.9	8.1	-6.3	-0.6	-10.3	-1.0	6.5	0.6	8.3	0.8	15.6 1.5		81.9	7.9	97.5	9.4
Charcoal	144.4	14.0	395.0	38.2	348.6	33.7	-52.6	-5.1	61.0	5.9	39.3	3.8	554.0 53.6		381.7	36.9	935.7	90.6
Total from each contributing factor	159.8	15.5	478.9	46.3	342.3	33.1	-62.9	-6.1	67.5	6.5	47.6	4.6	569.6 55.4		463.6	44.8	1033.2	100
Grand Totals	638.7	(61.8)			279.4	(27.0)			115.1	(11.1)								

Source: Table 6.2.

[a] The average annual contribution to deforestation of the different sectors has been calculated as follows:

$$\frac{dF/dt/1980 - dF/dt/1960}{20} = 1/2 \ (Y_{1980} + Y_{1960}) * 1/2 \ (P_{1980} + P_{1960}) * (D_{1980} - D_{1960})/20$$

$$+ \ 1/2 \ (D_{1980} + D_{1960}) * 1/2 \ (P_{1980} + P_{1960}) * (Y_{1980} - Y_{1960})/20$$

$$+ \ 1/2 \ (D_{1980} + D_{1960}) * 1/2 \ (Y_{1980} + Y_{1960}) * (P_{1980} - P_{1960})/20$$

where: F = annual deforestation in km^2
D = per capita wood demand m^3 (GSWE) cap^{-1} yr^{-1}
Y = area required to produce a given unit of wood km^2 m^{-3} (GSWE)
P = population

TABLE 6.4   Per Capita and Total Annual Deforestation Rates due to
             Rural and Urban Household Fuelwood Use: 1960-1980

Rates of Deforestation	Urban	Rural	All Sudan
Per Capita Annual Rate of Deforestation (m^2 cap^{-1} yr^{-1}) from:			
Firewood			
1960	349	78	106
1980	332	81	156
Percentage change	−4.9	+3.8	+47.2
Charcoal			
1960	1650	423	547
1980	1574	1106	1246
Percentage change	−4.6	+161.5	+127.8
All Fuelwood			
1960	2000	501	651
1980	1906	1187	1401
Percentage chage	−4.7	+137.0	+115.2
Total Annual Rate of Deforestation (km^2 yr^{-1})			
1960	2260	5080	7340
1980	11400	16600	28000
Percentage change	+504.4	+326.7	+381.5

Source: Table 6.2.

and that the rural population causes 54 percent of the deforestation, mainly because of charcoal use. In contrast, the provision of firewood is responsible for only 98 km², or 9.4 percent, of the annual increase of deforestation (Table 6.3). While rural and urban households, in 1980, consumed 1.4 and 0.6 m³ per capita GSWE of firewood (Table 6.2), respectively, the per capita impact of urban firewood cutting on deforestation (332 m², Table 6.2) was more severe than in rural areas (81 m²). This is because the commercial firewood and charcoal used in urban centers is obtained by clear-cutting of the woodlands, whereas in rural areas most of the firewood comes from dead branches, and I estimate that only 10 percent of the rural firewood used involves the destruction of entire trees (Whitney 1981a).

   The per capita deforestation attributable to the use of charcoal in rural areas increased by 161 percent from 1960–1980 (Table 6.4), while population in those areas rose by only 38 percent during the same period. In contrast, the urban population increased by 428 percent but per capita deforestation due to charcoal use *declined* by nearly 5 percent. These changing patterns of deforestation result from alterations in the types and quantities of biomass fuels consumed by urban and rural populations, respectively. As incomes rise (or fuelwood becomes more scarce) in urban areas, household energy consumption relies more on bottled gas and electricity (Whitney et al. 1985) and per capita use of both charcoal and firewood declines (Table 6.2). In rural areas, firewood scarcity leads to a greater reliance on charcoal (and accelerated deforestation), since electricity and kerosene are unavailable and bottled gas is too expensive and involves a large capital expenditure on suitable cooking appliances.

The net result of these changing fuel patterns is a reduction in the differential per capita impact on deforestation caused by the urban and rural sector respectively. In 1960 (Table 6.4), each rural dweller's total fuelwood use caused 501 m^2 of deforestation; each urban inhabitant 2000 m^2, or a rural/urban ratio of 1:4. In 1980, the corresponding ratio was 1:1.6.

The above examination, though cursory, indicates that the following factors must be considered when designing appropriate fuelwood policies for the Sudan:

1. the decline in per capita firewood use (GSWE) is likely to continue in both rural and urban sectors (Table 6.2);
2. per capita charcoal use will decline in urban centers but increase rapidly in rural areas, thereby exacerbating the per capita impact of the latter on deforestation;
3. the total, as opposed to the per capita, impact on deforestation of cities will continue to be higher for some time to come, despite declining per capita consumption of fuelwood, because of the more rapid growth of the urban population;
4. in the future, as fossil fuels replace fuelwood in urban areas, the countryside will make the predominant contribution to deforestation.

Patterns of Energy Use at the Local Level

The broad regional and sectoral data presented above mask the wide range of strategies available to energy users under conditions of increasing local fuel scarcity (Howes 1985). Three basic groups of fuel-coping approaches are available:

1. changing the method of fuel collection—spending more time for collection or traveling greater distances to more productive sources of fuel; changing the mode of transportation from human carriers to donkeys, for example;
2. using different types of fuel—changing from dead to green parts of the tree or from more to less preferred species or to species that have

other end uses, such as crop residues that can be used for fodder or thatching; changing to non-biomass fuel sources;
3. applying fuel-conserving strategies in the home—purchasing or constructing more efficient stoves or consuming foods that require less fuel in their preparation.

Although further research is required, the little evidence available indicates (Babiker and Abdu 1981; Hamer 1983; F. Ibrahim 1978; S. A. Ibrahim 1981) that where the opportunity costs of labor are low, the most common strategy is that of applying greater effort (distance and time) to fuel collection and of using younger trees and less preferred species. These practices have implications for woodland deterioration that will be examined below.

Deforestation does not, of course, occur in a uniform way in all parts of the country. There are distinct spatial patterns whose form and occurrence are based on economic principles first described by Thünen (1875) and Lösch (1954), and refined by writers such as Dunn (1954). The basic premise of these writers is that the type and intensity of economic activity is dependent on its location in respect to the market. As distance from a market center increases, the profitability of producing that product declines until it reaches zero, and it is no longer produced. Because products differ in their market price, production costs, and transportion costs, each will have a different location utility curve (i.e., the curve relating distance from the market and the profitability of producing a particular product at that distance) (Figure 6.3). At the point of intersection of the two curves, the product with the most favorable location utility will replace the competitive product. In this example, charcoal will replace firewood as distance from an urban center increases.

In a perfectly homogeneous environment, with equal access to all points, a concentric pattern of economic activity will arise. This theoretical pattern is modified by the lack of homogeneity of resource distribution and variations in accessibility to the market of different parts of the area exploited.

In subsistence fuel gathering, exemplified by much of the rural Sudan, location utility is expressed not in monetary terms but in terms of the effort and time expended to collect and transport the wood. If the opportunity cost of labor is zero, or the demand for wood is inelastic, a much greater effort will be expended on fuel collection, with resultant deforestation, than in a situation where the opportunity costs of labor are rising or where the demand for fuelwood is elastic (Adams 1979). In the former situation, fuel gatherers will continue to exploit one area until the perceived marginal effort (collection and transport) of producing the next unit of fuel exceeds the effort of moving to a more distant area where wood is more plentiful. This means that the zone of intense fuel-gathering will gradually move outward from a center leaving behind an area where most of the vegetation that can be used for fuel has been destroyed. In a situation where the opportunity costs of labor are rising or where the price elasticity of demand is high, there will be less destruction of local woodlands, since subsistence

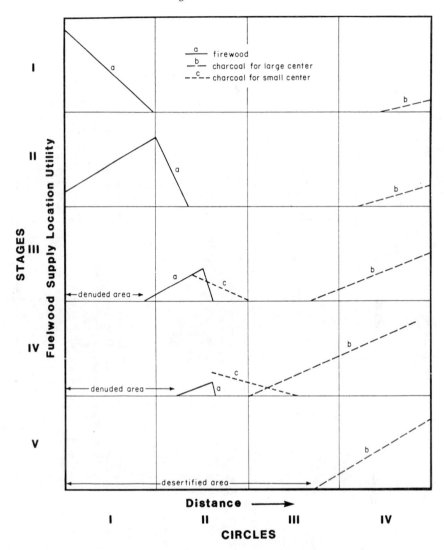

Fig. 6.3 A Model of Deforestation Around Urban Centers.

fuel production will be replaced by commercial firewood or charcoal produced at greater distances and utilized with greater economy because of rising prices.

Table 6.5 and Figure 6.3 represent a descriptive model of the sequence of fuel gathering activities and their environmental consequences, as they occur during the growth of a population center. The "stages" and the "circles" are used for descriptive purposes only. In reality they do not

TABLE 6.5 The Impact of Urbanization on Deforestation

Growth and Time	Circles:	I	II	III
Stage 1		Preferred species of dead wood collected by women and children Acacia tortilis ("sammar") Acacia seyal ("talih") Acacia albida ("haraz") Acacia senegal. Long fallow (20 yrs) with Acacia senegal replenishing fertility and providing wood. More time available for other activities. Minimal effort expended.	Little or no fuel gathering activity.	
Stage 2		Less favored species Balanites aegyptiacum ("heglieg") Ziziphus cambretum and parts of trees removed. Shorter fallow and declining soil fertility. Insufficient wood to provide all settlement needs. Continued exploitation of wood on return journey from circle 2. Whole trees destroyed. Off-take greater than natural growth and "tree cycle" declines.	Same as 1.I except greater distance and more effort expended and less time for other activities.	Little or no fuel production activity.
Stage 3		Standing trees destroyed. Stumps and roots removed. Crop residues and dung used for fuel leads to break in nutrient cycle, declining soil quality and interference with hydrologic cycle: floods and drought.	Same as 2.II but greater effort because of declining quality and quantity of wood stock. Women and children main collectors.	Preferred species of wood collected by men and/or girls and women and transported by donkey or camel to settlement. Charcoal produced Acacia senegal in inner part of circle by women: in outer part of circle charcoal produced and sold by men.

Stage 4	Soil erosion and fertility losses cause declining crop yields. All vegetation removed, desertification proceeds; nutrient cycling destroyed; soil moisture storage capacity diminished.	Same as 3.II.	Dwindling wood stock converted into charcoal. Higher order centers compete for declining supplies of favored species.
Stage 5		Same as 4.II.	Little woodland remains exploited by large urban market. Animal grazing further damages vegetation.

DESERTIFIED AREA

Hunger in rural areas, peasants abandon land.

possess discrete temporal or spatial boundaries but grade into each other. The stages represent increasing size and concomitant demand of urban centers; the circles, varying intensities of fuel-gathering activities located at different distances from an urban center. Although both circles and stages are impressionistic, they are based on fieldwork evidence from the Sudan and elsewhere (Hamer 1983; El Tayeb 1981; Babiker and Abdu 1981; Howes 1985).

In stage 1, the wood in the immediate vicinity of the settlement is exploited and the stock rapidly depleted not only for fuel use but because of overgrazing and clearance of land for agriculture (Figure 6.3, curve "a"). In the second stage, all the favored species have been removed from the first area and the total effort of collection and transportation will now be minimized (i.e., the location utility maximized) by concentrating fuel-gathering efforts in the next circle. Because distance, at the limits of circle 2, constrains the ability of women and children on foot to supply the necessary wood, animals (donkeys and camels) will be used increasingly. In an attempt to minimize effort, wood at the inner margin of circle 2 will be cropped more rapidly than the natural replacement rate and, eventually, whole trees will be destroyed. In the third stage, the first circle has been totally denuded and there is serious soil erosion. Fuel gathering is now forced to the next circle—a new zone of maximum location utility obtained by greater reliance on donkey and camel carriers and the replacement of wood by charcoal (Figure 6.3, curve "c"). Neighboring centers may also be competing for the dwindling wood supplies in this zone (curve "b").

To maintain the supply of energy, fossil fuels or charcoal from distant sources may be purchased, necessitating further involvement in the cash economy, or crop residues and animal dung may be used more, further impoverishing the soil.

In the fourth and fifth stages, the process of vegetational denudation has progressed to the second circle and the cycle of destruction is commencing in the third and more distant circles.

In a semiarid region such as Southern Kordofan, where woodland is sparse, it is difficult to provide the fuelwood needs of an urban center without causing deforestation. In this area, regrowth rates are low, averaging 0.26 m^3/ha/yr and per capita fuelwood use (GSWE) is approximately 4.6 m^3/yr for rural dwellers (settlements under 5,000) and 7.0 m^3/yr for urban inhabitants (SNEA 1983a). This means that to maintain a stable-state fuel collecting area, where annual harvest is equal to the natural growth rate of the woodland, you need 17.4 ha per capita for rural and 27.0 ha per capita for urban dwellers, respectively (see Table 6.6 for details of these approximate estimates). Thus, an urban center of 10,000 requires a fuel collecting area of 2,700 km^2 and would involve collecting wood from distances of up to 28 km in all directions from the center. Because land is used for purposes other than fuel collection (lumber, agriculture, etc.), and much of the land close to the center has become desertified, I estimate the radius for a self-sustained fuel collecting area (based on Hamer 1983) would amount

TABLE 6.6   A Comparison of Stable State and Actual Fuelsheds Required
to Support Settlements of Different Sizes Per Annum in
South Kordofan, Sudan

Settlement Size	Area of Stable State Fuelshed[a]	Maximum Travel Distance to Periphery of Area (km)	Actual Fuelshed Area[b]	Maximum Distance to Periphery (km)
250	47	4	12	2.2[c]
1,000	187	8	9	2.6[c]
2,500	466	12	19	3.9[c]
5,000	1,408	21	96	7.0[d]
10,000	2,816	30	687	13.0[e]
50,000	18,400	76	3,944	38.0[d]
100,000	28,160	95	16,460	75.0[d]

Source: Based on data from SNEA (1983a).

[a] The assumptions used in this calculation are: S. Kordofan allowable
cut (B) = 0.26 m^3 ha^{-1} yr^{-1}.   Per capita annual fuel consumption
(GSWE) (A) = 4.55 m^3 yr^{-1} for centers under 5,000 inhabitants; for
centers 5,000 and over the annual fuel consumption = 7.03 m^3 yr^{-1}.
Fuelshed required to support one person per annum F = B/A ha = 17.4
ha cap^{-1} for centers under 5,000 and 27.0 ha cap^{-1} for centers
5,000 and over, 1.16 ha per capita added to each area to account for
farm land and other uses (Hamer 1983).

[b] 1.16 ha cap^{-1} deducted from these areas nearest to center to account
for farm land and land used for other purposes, including desertified
areas (Hamer 1983).

[c] El Tayeb (1981).

[d] Based on FRIDA (1980) recalculated in Howes (1985:61).

[e] Hamer (1983).

to 30 km or an area of 2,816 km² (Table 6.6). To collect wood at the
sustained yield rate from such a large area, and at such great distances
from the settlement, would require more effort and time than is available.
One field study in the Sudan (Hamer 1983) indicated that, for a settlement
of 10,000, wood is collected at about 8 km from the center and charcoal
produced up to 16 km. The area actually exploited (687 km²) (inclusive of
non-fuelwood use lands), compared to 2,816 km² for sustained yield, indicates
an off-take rate far in excess of natural regeneration (Table 6.6).

Table 6.6 shows the stable-state and predicted actual areas required to
support settlements of different size in Southern Kordofan. In the small
settlements, less than 500, all household fuel needs can be supplied within

a radius of just over 2 km, a distance easily covered on foot. The energy supplies for settlements of 5,000 or more will require increasing animal or vehicular transportation. Because of high location utility, the fuel gathering area closest to the center will be deforested first and will eventually be added to the existing desertified zone around the settlement. As the distance to the fuel collecting area increases, a point is reached where its location utility, even for unpriced labor, is zero. Further energy must either be obtained from crop residues closer to the settlement or from the purchase of charcoal from greater distances. Production of the latter also results in more intense deforestation.

Two deforested zones will be created, one close to the center, the other at a greater distance, where charcoal is produced. Thus, centers with a population of 10,000 or more begin to deforest areas beyond the traditional fuel collecting area. A city of a million persons, such as Khartoum, is surrounded by a deforested area some 70 km wide; most of the city's wood and charcoal supplies are now derived from areas 450 km to the south (SNEA 1983b). The intervening area is covered with sparse vegetation barely able to satisfy the fuel needs of smaller centers located there.

The Environmental Impact of Deforestation

Three great interacting systems—involving the flow of energy, nutrients, and water—each having its own inputs, storage, and outputs, form the basis of all physical and biological processes on earth (Odum 1983). Vegetation, soils, and animals play a vital role in these systems, and any impact on one will have repercussions on all.

As the annual fuelwood off-take rate begins to exceed natural regeneration, energy and nutrient cycles are first affected (Anderson and Fishwick 1984). Removal of branches lowers the net photosynthesis rate, slows down the accumulation of biomass, and reduces the growth rate of the standing stock (Newcombe 1983). As more live branches are removed for fuel, less is available for wild and domestic animals. The natural food chain of predators, browsers, and grazers is affected and biological control mechanisms deteriorate, giving rise to insect and bird infestations damaging to crops. Removal of living branches reduces an important source of food for domestic animals in the form of leaves and pods (Bennett and Schork 1979). This is especially true of the *Acacia* species which are favored both by animals and as a fuel. As available woodland vegetation is removed, animals are forced to graze surface vegetation and eventually to migrate to remoter areas that often have lower carrying capacities.

Drastic environmental impacts follow the complete removal of woodland vegetation. In addition to the effects noted above, complete disruption of the energy, nutrient and hydrologic cycles occur. Since the dominant *Acacia* species are leguminous, and fix nitrogen in the soil, their destruction removes an important source of nutrients (Bennett and Schork 1979; Moss 1980). Studies in West Africa indicate that the presence of *Acacia* greatly enhances crop yields in semiarid regions (Felker 1978). The use of crop residues and dung fuels, particularly common in regions of severe deforestation where fuelwood is not available, further aggravates nutrient and moisture imbalances.

Soils unprotected by vegetation experience changes in their water and nutrient balances. Because the surface organic layer, which retains moisture after rain and allows it to infiltrate deeply into the subsoil, dries rapidly when exposed to the sun, it can easily be removed by wind and flood, thereby reducing the field capacity of the soil (Kirkby and Morgan 1980; Dunne et al. 1981).

The loss of the organic soil layer also removes many of the bacteria necessary to break down nitrogen into forms assimilable by plants and hinders revegetation. Moreover, when the underlying subsoil, particularly clays, is exposed to rain, crusting appears, further limiting the infiltration of water and causing more runoff (Kirkby and Morgan 1980). Crusting also reduces the circulation of oxygen and carbon dioxide between soil and atmosphere and inhibits a number of important biological and chemical processes within the soil. Moreover, as soil is removed by wind and rain, the effective root depth is decreased, limiting the volume of all growth materials available to plants. These processes lead eventually to total impoverishment of the soil and desertification.

In much of the Sudan, where slope gradients are low (less than 1 percent) and sheet, rather than gully, erosion is the principal form, the eroded material is distributed downslope and trapped in depressions so that little of it is transported to water bodies. This redeposited material, however, is often harmful, since it clogs pore spaces in the soil, reducing moisture and gaseous circulation and degrading its condition (Dunne et al. 1981).

The Costs and Benefits of Deforestation

It is the contention of this chapter that there are both beneficial and adverse consequences of the present deforestation practices in the Sudan. The adverse, mainly environmental in nature, must eventually be borne by society as a whole in one form or another and may be termed the *environmental costs*. These costs, or benefits forgone due to society's mismanagement of the environment, involve what Westman (1977) calls "the free services of nature" (such as groundwater supplies, nutrient replenishment, pest control). These environmental costs incurred must be weighed against the *benefits* of continuing the present practice of "mining" the forests for fuel. If the environmental costs *outweigh* the benefits, society will have to bear the damage and a *social cost* will be incurred.

The principal environmental costs of deforestation were discussed in the previous section and include: the loss of the excess nitrogen produced by *Acacia*, available to promote the production of palatable grasses and crops grown on traditional agroforestry farm plots; the loss of animal feed from the foliage of the destroyed trees and the subsequent overgrazing of the ground cover; the nutrients lost from the soil through erosion after the ground cover has been destroyed; the removal of nutrients stored in the wood and lost to recycling when transported to the market or burned in charcoal kilns, and loss of moisture storage due to the removal of surface and soil organic material through overgrazing and erosion. Before this removal, the moisture in the soil would have enhanced the growth of palatable grasses and crops grown in the traditional farming system, and maintained water levels in wells.

There are two major benefits of continuing deforestation: it eliminates the necessity of importing more fossil fuels, and it permits the production of domestic and export crops on large mechanized farms established on the cleared lands. In addition to the 28,000 km² deforested in 1980–1981 due to household consumption, some 3,000 km² were clearcut for mechanized farms (SNEA 1983a:92). Since the fertility of these cleared soils is exhausted in about five years (O'Brien 1978), the land is abandoned and the mechanized farmer acquires new land and repeats the clearing process elsewhere (Berry and Geistfeld 1983:42–44).

Table 6.7 summarizes in monetary terms the costs and benefits of deforestation in the Sudan. The assumptions used in the preparation of this balance sheet are fully described in the footnotes to Table 6.7 and must be borne in mind when interpreting the results. The replacement cost method of benefit-cost analysis (Hufschmidt 1983: 266–267) has been used to estimate the value of the environmental costs. This method equates these costs with the costs of replacing "the free services of nature" lost. I have applied the replacement cost approach very conservatively in that it includes only the market cost of replacing the "free services" lost and not the costs of their transportation to the site and their distribution over the area deforested.

In contrast, the *benefits* of deforestation are *gross* benefits calculated at the market prices of the commodities concerned and excluding production and transportation costs. Hence, the environmental costs have been *underestimated* and the benefits of deforestation *overestimated*, so that, even under these conservative assumptions, the seriousness of the social costs incurred will be apparent.

The streams of environmental costs and benefits, respectively, arise from the deforestation of a total of about 31,000 km² per year for the provision of fuelwood (28,000 km²) and to expand the agricultural area (3,000 km²). Since the environmental costs and benefits occur at different times and extend over different periods, all streams are represented by their present value (pv) in 1982 US dollars, using a discount rate of 10 percent per annum. To evaluate the significance of different policies over time, the streams of costs and benefits have been calculated for 20, 10, and 5 year terms, respectively. Because most of the environmental costs occur in the future, the use of a discount rate lower than that employed above would further have inflated the environmental losses (Hufschmidt 1983:39). Values have also been calculated on a per hectare basis for the total area annually deforested, and for the cumulative total of the area deforested over 5, 10, and 20 years, respectively.

TABLE 6.7   Economic and Environmental Costs, Benefits, and Social Costs
of Deforestation to Supply Household Energy

Item	$ ha^{-1} (present value in 1982 U.S. dollars)		
	20 years	10 years	5 years
Replacement Costs:			
Nitrogen produced by acacia[a]	51.5	37.2	22.9
Loss of animal feed from green part of tree[b]	55.0	39.7	24.5
Nutrients eroded from soil[c]	111.4	111.4	111.4
Nutrients stored in wood and removed when transported to market or burned[d]	74.0	74.0	74.0
Loss of soil water storage[e]	18.5	13.4	8.2
TOTAL COSTS	310.4	275.7	241.0
Benefits:			
Crops grown in cleared[f] area	127.0	127.0	127.0
Fuelwood (TOE)[g]	109.0	109.0	109.0
TOTAL BENEFITS	236.0	236.0	236.0
Social Costs (Benefits - Costs)	-74.4	-40.0	- 5.0
Social Costs of total annual deforested area (31,000 km^2) $x10^6$	-229.0	-124.0	-15.5
Social costs of continuing to deforest 31,000 km^2 for different numbers of years $10^6$$	-1946.0	-761.0	-59.0

The following assumptions have been used in these calculations:

[a] Refers to the annual production of nitrogen from leguminous nodules
on the acacia roots. 21 kg/ha/yr (Bennett and Schork 1979, Appendix
11). Average proportion of acacia to non-leguminous species 0.29
(fieldwork in S. Kordofan and Central Region: 21 x .29 - 6 kg/ha/yr.).
Assuming 20%N content of fertilizers, cost per ton nitrogen = $981.

[b] Edible part of trees assumed to equal annual net production rate of
0.26 m^3/ha (SNEA 1983b). Conversion from m^3 dry weight vegetation to
tons @ 0.33. Price of animal feed $74.6/ton (Sudan Department of
Statistics 1982:Table 1.3).

(continued)

TABLE 6.7 (Continued)

c Assumptions: 0.11% N (El Tayeb 1981) 20 cm soil depth. Bulk density
  1gm/cm^3; soil erosion loss rate of: year 1: 60%; year 2: 30%;
  year 3: 9%; year 4: 1%.

d Assume all nitrogen in wood unavailable for crops. Nitrogen stored
  in 20 year old savanna - 75 kg/ha (Moss 1980). Price of elemental
  Nitrogen - $981/ton.

e Assume top 20 cm of soil have 10mm moisture storage capacity, which
  will be lost as soil erodes (Kirkby and Morgan 1980). Gallons of
  fuel oil to pump water-head (40 m) x m^3 water pumped x 0.355 x 10^{-3}
  (Fawz and Karim 1983). Oil costs at $337/ton.

f Assume crop in dura @ 712 kg/ha and $45/ton (Sudan Ministry of
  Economic Planning 1983). Assume (O'Brien 1978) that yields on
  mechanized rain-fed area will be: year 1 = 1; year 2 = 0.84; year
  3 = 0.72; year 4 = 0.30; year 5 = 0.26; and, thereafter, 0.

g Assume clearcutting of 15.77 m^3/ha; TOE equivalent of wood 0.43 and
  oil price of $337/ton. Relative efficiency of wood = 14% oil
  (SNEA 1983b).

Because of data inadequacies, only *on-site* replacement costs of the "free services" have been included. If *off-site* environmental costs were added, the total costs would be much higher. Examples of off-site environmental costs caused by deforestation include: the replacement of crops damaged by pests; crop losses through the silting of irrigation canals and reservoirs and loss of hydro-electric power generation from sedimentation; increased costs of purifying silt-laden waters for drinking purposes and added health risks of increased dissolved and suspended solids (Jahn 1981); increased health costs and damage to equipment resulting from higher levels of dust in the atmosphere.

A number of interesting points emerge from Table 6.7. The net present value (npv) of the social costs (npv environmental costs > npv benefits to the economy) is $74 per hectare discounted over 20 years; $40 per hectare over 10 years, and $5 over 5 years. For every hectare deforested for fuel and crop production, the environmental costs *exceed* the benefits to the economy, and social costs are incurred.

The social costs are more dramatic when the entire annual deforested area is considered (31,000 km²). These amount to $229 million for the twenty-year period, $124 million for the ten-year period, and $15 million for the five-year period. If the present rate of annual deforestation continues (i.e., another 31,000 km² cleared per year), the cumulative social cost would be $1.9 billion over the next 20 years, $761 million for the next ten years, and $59 million for the next five years.

Unfortunately, even though these social costs are high, they are unlikely to affect present policy. The economic benefits of fuelwood mining flow primarily to the urban population, the locus of political power and decision-making. The environmental costs are largely invisible to the latter and are borne by local populations who have little political clout. Moreover, the off-site environmental damage affecting large urban centers is not readily perceived as being linked to deforestation, because the latter is taking place in areas remote from cities and the cause-effect links are complex and little understood. A further reason why these large social costs may not be considered (even if known) is that the time horizon of political decision-makers is notoriously short—probably the five-year scenario used in this analysis. It might, indeed, be considered that the five-year social costs incurred, although quite large, are a price worth paying, especially as large government revenues and private profits are derived from the clearance of land for crops and fuel (O'Brien 1978) and there appear to be no alternative sources of energy available to replace wood.

The discrepancy between political-economic and ecological time scales is not peculiar to the Sudan, but is also the cause of much environmental degradation in other parts of the world. Although present deforestation practices may be irrational from the perspective presented in this chapter, the argument can be made that they are rational so long as no alternative energy sources are available.

Alternatives

Elsewhere, Whitney et al. (1985) have argued that, in the absence of large-scale importation of fossil fuels and a national reforestation scheme (both unlikely in the present situation), there are a number of alternatives to the present exploitative practices:

1. improving the use of the present supply of fuelwood through the introduction of more efficient charcoal and wood-burning stoves;
2. improving the use of the present supply of fuelwood through a more efficient charcoal-producing process;
3. displacing fuelwood and charcoal by increasing the supply of kerosene;
4. reducing the demand for fuelwood through appropriate pricing policies;
5. increasing the supply of renewable energy resources, other than wood, at competitive prices.

For the purpose of examining the impact of these policies on the economy and environmental system, an input-output table incorporating ecologic and economic components was constructed for the Sudan (Dufournaud and Whitney 1983; Murck and Dufournaud 1983; Murck et al. 1985). The analysis derived from this table indicated that the alternative of introducing more efficient charcoal-burning stoves, a policy strongly espoused by the World Bank and a number of other agencies (Anderson and Fishwick 1984; Sudan National Council for Research 1984), produces economic benefits in the form of monetary savings to households. However, the redistribution of

TABLE 6.8   Total Ecological Impact of the Sudanese Economy Before and
             After the Introduction of More Efficient Charcoal Stoves
             into Urban Households

		Before	After
1.	Particulates (tons)	3.838×10^3	3.820×10^3
2.	Sulfur oxides (tons)	76.663	77.649
3.	5 day B.O.D. (tons)	1.711×10^2	1.707×10^2
4.	Suspended solids (tons)	2.495×10^4	2.485×10^4
5.	Phosphates (tons)	62.306	62.348
6.	Total energy used (gigajoules)	2.477×10^6	2.501×10^6
7.	Total wood used (tons)	16.432×10^6	16.344×10^6

Source: Murck and Dufournaud (1983).

Assumptions used in the input-output modelling for the above table:

   (i)   improvement of efficiency of charcoal stoves from 16% to 25%;

   (ii)   monetary savings from the use of less charcoal reallocated
          to other sectors of the economy in proportion to current
          patterns of consumption;

   (iii) input-output table run using entropy maximizing technique.

these savings generates environmental problems through increased consumption of energy-intensive commodities, leading to greater consumption
of fossil fuels and fuelwood and resulting in higher levels of other kinds
of pollution, such as sulfur dioxide (Table 6.8). The study indicates that the
introduction of more efficient charcoal-burning stoves would bring about
only a minimal reduction in wood use (Table 6.8).

Manipulating fuelwood demand levels by raising prices may cause social
and political unrest and involve hidden environmental costs such as a return
to more intensive pressure on "free" sources of wood in environmentally
sensitive areas near to urban centers (e.g., the "Green Belt" around Khartoum).

Improving the efficiency of charcoal production methods appears to be
an attractive alternative because it might result in substantial savings in
terms of wood use, reducing the net annual forest stock depletion rate by
50 percent or 14,000 km² (Whitney et al. 1985; SNEA 1982). The capital
cost of the technology required to produce these results, however, would
approach half a billion dollars, a sum vastly in excess of the annual hard
currency earnings of the country (Whitney et al. 1985). Moreover, because
of the sparseness of the woodland resource of the Sudan (and hence greater
distance required to transport wood to the kiln site) and the relative immobility
of modern charcoal kilns compared to traditional ones, it is by no means

certain that the former could be operated more profitably than the earthen kilns currently used (Macdonald 1986).

A return to the levels of kerosene consumption of the pre-oil-crisis years would reduce deforestation rates by only 2.3 percent and would be strongly resisted by all sectors of the economy using higher fraction gasoline fuels. Even if the entire fossil fuel imports of the Sudan were converted to kerosene, it would result in a saving of only 17 percent of the annual deforested area. Large-scale conversion to bottled gas is not feasible for reasons mentioned earlier.

Our previous study (Murck et al. 1985) suggested two practical alternatives to the present energy situation in the Sudan: the utilization of improved efficiency woodstoves (as opposed to charcoal-burning stoves) and the introduction of aquatic weed briquettes as a fuel source (Whitney 1981b). We advocated the former alternative because we believed that rural firewood use was a substantial cause of deforestation. The evidence presented in this study, however, suggests that such use is a declining cause of deforestation (Tables 6.1 and 6.3) and that increasing per capita charcoal use in rural areas and greater total urban demand for charcoal is a more serious influence on deforestation. However, social benefits, mainly accruing to women and children, may be derived from the introduction of more efficient wood-burning stoves: reduced time spent in gathering wood. The utilization of this saved time for more careful food preparation may lead to a further reduction in energy use (Parikh 1985), and to more healthy and productive lives (Baxter 1981:3–4). The second, and more desirable, alternative is the utilization of aquatic weeds, notably the water hyacinth (*Eichornia crassipes*) (SNEA 1982). These currently clog many sections of the White Nile and its tributaries and are removed at considerable expense and environmental cost due to the extensive use of herbicides (Philipp et al. 1983). Unlike the production of biogas, the briquetting of weeds involves no complex technology or change in cooking equipment or habits. Preliminary tests with briquettes produced by a very simple device indicate that the fuel could be burned in traditional stoves and utilized for cooking in ways similar to charcoal (Whitney 1981b).

The annual dry-weight production of aquatic weeds in the Sudan has been conservatively estimated at nine million tons (Whitney 1981b; SNEA 1982), an amount exceeding the total firewood consumed in a year. Because of their riverine habitat, aquatic weeds, particularly water hyacinth, can best be used by communities located close to the White Nile and in areas south of the Jebel al Aulia dam (45 km south of Khartoum), which provides a barrier to their northward movement.

While a detailed environmental assessment would have to be made, preliminary considerations suggest that use of this source of fuel would be doubly advantageous in that it would also remove an environmental pressure from waterways. Since the water hyacinth is an exotic plant introduced into the Sudan in the 19th century (Philipp et al. 1983), its partial removal for fuel use is considered unlikely, pending more detailed studies, to have any adverse effects on the environment. However, a major governmental concern with the introduction of water hyacinth briquettes as a fuel is the fear that, if moistened, they may re-germinate and infest the waterways of the most productive irrigated areas of the country around Khartoum, currently free of the weed. Further research is obviously required to demonstrate the economic and environmental feasibility of introducing this new type of fuel. If the briquettes could be produced and marketed at a price that was competitive with charcoal or at a labor cost lower than that required to collect firewood, they might substitute for fuelwood in many riverine areas of the country, thereby reducing the rate of deforestation. The two recommended alternatives, aquatic weed briquettes and improved wood-burning stoves, are desirable because they do not, as with the more efficient charcoal stoves, involve trade-offs between per capita economic gain and environmental improvement and are especially directed toward assisting poorer households to meet their energy needs in an ecologically beneficial and cost-effective manner.

In terms of short- to medium-range planning, the above alternatives may broaden options and provide replacement for fuelwood with no hidden social or environmental costs. For the longer term, a national policy of reforestation must be implemented to provide a constant and easily accessible source of energy for rural people and to repair the environmental damage done to vast areas of the country by deforestation.

Notes

1. Assistance for research in the Sudan is gratefully acknowledged to Project Ecoville, University of Toronto, and the International Federation of Institutes of Advanced Studies, Stockholm. Thanks are also due to Meric Gertler, Department of Geography, the University of Toronto, for suggesting the term "location utility" used in this chapter. Appreciation is also expressed to Dr. M. E. Mukhtar, Under-Secretary, Ministry of Energy and Mining, Sudan, for making available many of the documents upon which this study is based. Thanks are also due to Virginia Maclaren, Department of Geography, University of Toronto, Jack Donan, Ontario Ministry of the Environment, and Endre Nyerges, Institute for Development Anthropology, for helpful comments on the first draft of this chapter.

2. The values given in petajoules are all based on tons of oil equivalent of the respective fuels concerned (1 ton of oil equivalent [TOE] = 41.9 gigajoules).

3. The data for the present paper are derived primarily from two documents published by the National Energy Administration (NEA), Sudan Ministry of Energy and Mining (SNEA 1983a and 1983b), supplemented by information obtained by the author, who served on the Households and Services Sector Committee of the NEA study. This study, financed by USAID, involved field surveys covering all branches of the economy. The Household Energy Survey, the primary source of information for the NEA reports, involved administering a detailed energy-use questionnaire to a total of 1,143 urban and 1,300 rural households in every region of the country.

References

Adams, P. A.
   1979   Deforestation in Kenya: A Case of Over-exploitation of the Common Property Resource? Unpublished Master's thesis, University of Sussex.

Anderson, D., and R. Fishwick
   1984   Fuelwood Consumption and Deforestation in African Countries. Staff Working Paper No. 704. Washington, DC: World Bank.

Babiker, A. B., and A. S. Abdu
   1981   Rural Energy and the Environment. *In* Women and the Environment in the Sudan. D. Baxter, ed. Pp. 86–91. Environmental Research Paper No. 2. Khartoum: Institute of Environmental Studies, University of Khartoum.

Baxter, D.
   1981   Women and the Environment: A Downward Spiral. *In* Women and the Environment in the Sudan. D. Baxter, ed. Pp. 1–7. Environmental Research Paper No. 2. Khartoum: Institute of Environmental Studies, University of Khartoum.

Bennett, A., and W. Schork
   1979   Studies Toward a Sustainable Agriculture in Ghana. Heidelberg: Research Centre for International Agrarian Development.

Berry, L., and S. Geistfeld
   1983   Environment, Natural Systems, and Development. Baltimore, MD: The Johns Hopkins University Press.

Dufournaud, C. M., and J. B. R. Whitney
   1983   An Indirect Method for Estimating Technical Coefficients of Rectangular Input-Output Tables. Project Ecoville Working Paper No. 4. Toronto: Institute for Environmental Studies, University of Toronto.

Dunn, E. S.
   1954   The Location of Agricultural Production. Gainesville, FL: University of Florida Press.

Dunne, T., B. Aubey, and E. K. Wahome
   1981   Effect of Fuelwood Harvest on Soil Erosion in Kenya. Stockholm: Beijer Institute.

El Tayeb, S. A.
   1981   The Impact of Water Points on Environmental Degradation: A Case Study of Eastern Kordofan, Sudan. Environmental Monograph No. 2. Khartoum: Institute of Environmental Studies, University of Khartoum.

Fawz, M., and A. A. Karim
   1983   Energy Consumption in the Agricultural Sector. Khartoum: Ministry of Energy and Mining; National Energy Administration.

Felker, P.
   1978   State of the Art: Acacia Albida as a Complementary Permanent Intercrop with Annual Crops. Riverside, CA: Department of Soil and Environmental Sciences.

FRIDA
   1980   Domestic Energy in Sub-Saharan Africa: The Impending Crisis, Its Measurement and the Framework for Practical Solutions. London: FRIDA.

Hamer, T.
   1983   Wood for Fuel: Energy Crisis Implying Desertification—the Case of Bara, Sudan. Bergen: Chr. Michelsen Institute.

Howes, M.
   1985   Rural Energy Surveys in the Third World: A Critical Review of Issues and
           Methods. Ottawa: International Development Research Centre.
Hufschmidt, M. M.
   1983   Environment, Natural Systems, and Development: An Economic Evaluation.
           Baltimore, MD: Johns Hopkins University Press.
Ibrahim, F. N.
   1978   The Problem of Desertification in the Republic of the Sudan with Special
           Reference to Northern Darfur Province. Khartoum: University of Khartoum,
           Development Studies and Research Centre, Monograph Series No. 8.
Ibrahim, S. A.
   1981   Women's Role in Deforestation. *In* Women and the Environment in the
           Sudan. D. Baxter, ed. Pp. 80–85. Environmental Research Paper No. 2;
           Khartoum: Institute of Environmental Studies, University of Khartoum.
Jahn, S. A.
   1981   Water Decade Projects for the Tropics Based on Traditional Purification
           Methods of Sudanese Women. *In* Women and the Environment in the
           Sudan. D. Baxter, ed. Pp. 49–57. Environmental Research Paper No. 2.
           Khartoum: Institute of Environmental Studies, University of Khartoum.
Kirkby, M. J., and R. P. C. Morgan
   1980   Soil Erosion. Toronto: Wiley.
Lösch, A.
   1954   The Economics of Location. New Haven, CT: Yale University Press.
Macdonald, M.
   1986   Technology Transfer of Improved Charcoal Production in the Sudan: Impact
           on the Environment. University of Toronto: Project Ecoville Working Paper
           No. 29.
Moss, R. P.
   1980   The Ecological and Agricultural Aspects of Rural Energy Resources. *In*
           Rural Energy Systems in the Humid Tropics. W. B. Morgan, R. P. Moss
           and G. J. A. Ojo, eds. Pp.14–20. Tokyo: United Nations University.
Murck, B. and C. D. Dufournaud
   1983   Perspectives on the Interrelationship of Economic and Environmental
           Processes in the Sudan. Project Ecoville Working Paper No. 6. Toronto:
           Institute for Environmental Studies, University of Toronto.
Murck, B., C. D. Dufournaud, and J. B. R. Whitney
   1985   Simulation of a Policy Aimed at the Reduction of Wood Use in the Sudan.
           Environment and Planning (A) 17:1231–1242.
Newcombe, K.
   1983   An Economic Justification for Rural Afforestation: The Case of Ethiopia.
           Unpublished World Bank staff working paper, quoted in D. Anderson and
           R. Fishwick, Fuelwood Consumption and Deforestation in African Coun-
           tries. Staff Working Paper No. 704. Pp. 21–22. Washington, DC: World
           Bank.
O'Brien, J.
   1978   How Traditional is "Traditional" Agriculture? Bulletin 62. Khartoum, Eco-
           nomic and Social Research Council.
Odum, H. T.
   1983   Systems Ecology. New York, NY: Wiley.
Parikh, J. K.
   1985   Household Energy Assessment: Integration of Approaches and Additional
           Factors. Biomass 7(1):73–84.

Philipp, O., W. Koch, and H. Koser
   1983   Utilization and Control of Water Hyacinth in the Sudan. Eschborn: Deutsche
          Gesellschaft für Technische Zusammenarbeit.
Sudan, Department of Statistics
   1982   Internal Trade Statistics and Price Indices, 1978–79. Khartoum: Ministry
          of National Planning.
Sudan, Ministry of Finance and Economic Planning, Department of Statistics
   1983   Statistical Abstract. Khartoum (mimeo).
Sudan, National Council for Research
   1984   Canun El Duga: Improved Charcoal Stoves for the Sudan. Khartoum:
          Sudan Renewable Energy Project (mimeo).
Sudan, National Energy Administration (SNEA)
   1982   Renewable Energy Asssessment for the Sudan. Khartoum: Ministry of
          Energy and Mining.
   1983a Sudan: National Energy Assessment. Khartoum: Ministry of Energy and
          Mining.
   1983b Sudan: National Energy Assessment—Executive Summary. Khartoum: Min-
          istry of Energy and Mining.
Thünen, J. H. von
   1875   Der Isolierte Staat in Beziehung auf Landwirtschaft und Nationalöconomie.
          Hamburg.
United Nations Development Programme (UNDP) and World Bank
   1983   Sudan's Issues and Options in the Energy Sector. Khartoum, Report No.
          4511-SU.
Westman, W. E.
   1977   How Much are Nature's Services Worth? Science 197:960–964.
Whitney, J. B. R.
   1981a Urban Energy, Food and Water Use in Arid Regions and Their Impact on
          Hinterlands: A Conceptual Framework. Environmental Research Report
          No. 1; Khartoum: Institute of Environmental Studies, University of Khar-
          toum.
   1981b Turning Aquatic Weeds into Energy Resources. Sudan Environment 1(3):
          9–11.
Whitney, J. B. R., C. M. Dufournaud, and B. W. Murck
   1985   Energy Use and the Environment in the Sudan. Project Ecoville Working
          Paper No. 22. Toronto: Institute for Environmental Studies, University of
          Toronto.

7

Bringing Land Back In:
Changing Strategies
to Improve Agricultural Production
in the West African Sahel[1]

Thomas M. Painter

Introduction

This chapter concerns the difficulties encountered by programs of the Niger government and development assistance organizations to increase agricultural productivity among the country's peasant smallholders, when such endeavors lack a satisfactory understanding of the context and conditions of agricultural production. The chapter begins with an overview of the harsh yet varied physical conditions of rainfed production in Niger. It then describes the strategy of the Niger government to effect improvements in rainfed agriculture, particularly after a serious drought that lasted from 1968 to 1974. Concretely, this strategy took the form of large regional rural development projects, referred to as productivity projects because of their goal of increasing land productivity in agriculture. The productivity project strategy is critically assessed and a specific project in western Niger is examined in some detail. The project's lack of positive impact on agricultural productivity is considered, and possible reasons are given. The chapter closes with a discussion of current endeavors by the Niger government to devise new, more effective strategies to improve agriculture in the country. A major argument of the chapter is that whatever the specific nature of technological innovations introduced to improve agriculture, the chances of success will depend a great deal on careful attention to the physical and socioeconomic characteristics of the production setting. Such attention has not been given in the past. It is particularly important in Niger to recognize the poor quality of much of the country's arable land, to understand the reasons for its past and continuing degradation by a combination of climate and resident populations, to develop measures to stop its destruction as a productive resource, and finally, to restore its fertility. Land must no longer be considered a "given," but rather a precious resource in need of protection, management, and improvement.

The Context of Agricultural Production
in Niger

An estimated 76 percent of the Niger Republic, located in the West African Sahel, receives less than 350 mm of rainfall each average year. The remaining 24 percent of the country, where annual rainfall exceeds 350 mm on the average, is considered potentially useful for rainfed agriculture. This arable land is located in a band 200 to 250 kilometers wide in the extreme south of the country (Ferguson 1979:1). It is this narrow strip, sometimes referred to as the sudano-sahelian zone of Niger, that contains 80 percent of the country's population and, excepting the important contribution of pastoralists, accounts for most of Niger's agricultural production. Much of this area is accurately described as "land at risk" (Horowitz et al. 1983, Vol. 1, "Introduction," pp. 17–18).

The composition and types of soils vary greatly in Niger, but in large part soil quality in the agriculturally useful areas is considered to be poor (Ferguson 1979:5; cf. World Bank 1985:2–4).[2] Most of the soils are composed of fine or loamy sands, with sand accounting for 80 to 90 percent of total soil mass (Ferguson 1979:5). The capacity of these medium to highly acidic soils to retain water is limited, and leaching of soluble nutrients is pronounced. Niger's dunal soils contain little organic matter because of their texture and the effects of climate. Vegetation in these areas is a bushy steppe type. Principal naturally occurring species are *Anona senegalensis, Balanites aegyptiaca, Detarium microcarpum, Guiera senegalensis, Parinari macrophylla, Piliostigma reticulatum, Prosopis africana,* and *Ziziphus mauritania.* There occur scattered winterthorn (*Acacia albida*) and small populations of the doum palm, *Hyphaene thebaica.* Predominant grass species include *Aristida longiflora, Andropogon gayanus,* and *A. pallida* (Painter 1985:57).

Areas of sandy soils are broken up by dry river valleys and depressions where finer textured, loamy, or siltier soils predominate. These have a greater water retention capacity and are more fertile. In the dry river valleys, former tributaries of the Niger River, the water table may be very close to the surface, at a depth of five meters or less. Depressions where topsoil and silt accumulate during the rainy months may contain standing water for several months following the rains. Vegetation in these areas, particularly in the river valleys, is of a bush-arboreal savanna type. The dry valleys are often populated with large numbers of winterthorn and doum palm, (*Hyphaene thebaica*). Additional species often found include *Parinari macrophylla, Prosopis africana, Bauhinia reticulata, B. rufescens,* and scatterings of baobab trees (*Adonsonia digitata*). Further to the south, below 13° N, these heavier soils are populated with increasing numbers of baobabs, shea (*Butyrospermum parkii*), kapok (*Bombax costatum*), and tamarind (*Tamarindus indica*) (ibid.:60). Finally, the agriculturally useful zone of Niger also contains large areas of crusty lateritic soils characterized by low fertility and very subject to erosion. Where the crust is near the surface, these areas are practically useless for agriculture (Ferguson 1979:5).

As suggested above, climate greatly affects the subsistence base of Niger's peasant smallholders. Rainfall in Niger is scanty overall, exceeding 800 mm per year only in a very small section of the country in the extreme southwest (Gaya region, where the 1932–1974 average was 846 mm; Donaint and Lancrenon 1976:31). Thus for most of the agricultural population, the risk of partial or complete crop failure due to poor rainfall is a fact of life. The limited precipitation in Niger is concentrated during the months of June, July, and August, and averages between 30 and 50 days of rain per year (Ferguson 1979:4; cf. Painter 1985:40–49). Rainfall during this period can be very heavy, and resultant runoff often causes severe gully erosion in more sloped areas, as well as considerable sheet erosion on even the mildest slopes (Heermans 1984, 1986; SRD/ISAID 1978). What little topsoil exists suffers badly with each rainy season. Despite the difficulties, however, this is the time of year when plant life is most active. The explosive verdancy produced throughout the country by the rains makes it difficult to believe that these vast areas could remain barren, dry, dusty, and seemingly inert for so many months.

The situation of fragile soils and a very harsh climate is further complicated by the impact of the cultivation techniques used by peasant smallholders throughout Niger. The rainy season is the period of greatest activity among Niger's cultivators. During these months, agronomic techniques that range from hoe cultivation on ridges to weeding done upright with long-handled cultivating tools, (*ilers*), are used for the cultivation of millet, sorghum, cowpeas, Bambara groundnuts, sesame, and groundnuts (peanuts) (Raulin 1963). These crops are cultivated extensively on ever larger areas of land cleared by cutting and burning. During the period from 1961 to 1982, extensive agriculture resulted in an increase of 87 percent in surface areas planted in millet alone, from an estimated 1,640,000 hectares to more than 3,000,000 hectares (Borsdorf 1979:81; République du Niger 1984:40). This increase is shown graphically by line A in Figure 7.1.

Once the harvest is over, in September to October, these cultivated areas remain barren for up to eight months, stripped of all cultivated plant cover as well as that naturally provided by grass, low trees, and shrubs. In particular, the light sandy soils are exposed to the harmattan winds from November to January, Niger's cool season. The result is wind erosion of topsoil each year and, in some regions of the country, invasion of cultivated zones by sand dunes. To the erosive effect of wind is added the impact of high temperatures during the months of February through May, prior to the next rainy season. During this period, daily maxima may fluctuate from 35° C to 46° C in the shade (Donaint and Lancrenon 1976:35–37; cf. Painter 1985:52–53). During this period the soils of the agricultural zones and any organic matter therein are subject to severe transevaporation and desiccation (Ferguson 1979:6). Such is the setting for survival, that is, production, subsistence, and "development" in much of Niger's agricultural zone.

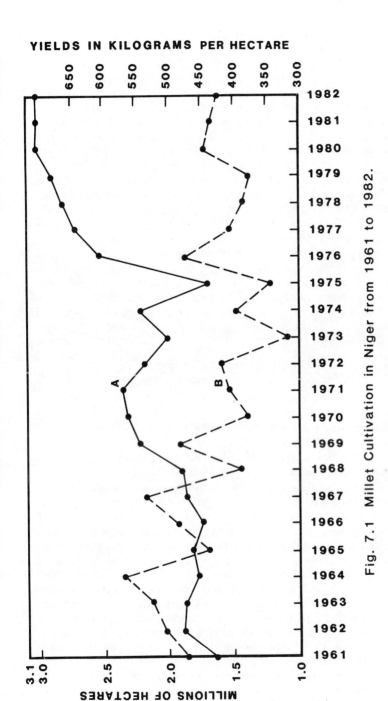

YIELDS IN KILOGRAMS PER HECTARE

MILLIONS OF HECTARES

Fig. 7.1 Millet Cultivation in Niger from 1961 to 1982.

Surface areas under cultivation and yields per hectare.

A ——— Millions of hectares under cultivation
B – – – Yields in kilograms per hectare

Source: Borsdorf (1979:81); République du Niger (1984:40).

The success of peasant productive strategies in this harsh setting is debated, but available evidence gives little ground for optimism. Data from studies of Niger's agricultural sector (Borsdorf 1979:81; République du Niger 1984:40; Sève and Tabor 1985; USAID 1977b:2), and from case study material (Painter 1985:375–377; Raynaut 1980; Sutter 1982) all suggest that in at least the case of millet, the country's principal staple grain, yields in kilograms per hectare have declined as areas planted have increased. Estimates vary widely, but for the period from 1961 to 1982 they place the overall decline in yields at between 11 and 25 percent (Borsdorf 1979, Vol. 2:81; cf. République du Niger 1984:40). The possibility of a gradual decline in yields is suggested by data from a variety of sources, which are plotted as line B in Figure 7.1.[3] Scattered evidence from archival sources dating from the 1920s reinforces this interpretation of a downward trend in millet yields (Painter 1985:375–377; cf. De Miranda 1979; Sutter 1979:24ff.). Clearly one important factor in this overall decline is the *nature* of new lands being cleared for rainfed agriculture. As agriculturalists expand cultivated areas, more and more marginal land (increasing portions of which are in pastoral areas) is brought into production. These areas are doubly marginal: they consistently receive less rainfall than "normal," and soil quality is even poorer than that (already poor) found in much of the country's agricultural zones (Thomson 1985:231f.).

A National Strategy to Improve Rainfed Agricultural Production in Niger

From 1968 to 1974, the usually difficult situation of peasant smallholders and herders in Niger became catastrophic. A severe drought and famine catapulted the country (and its sahelian neighbors) into the international limelight, and transformed it into an important recipient of emergency food aid from many countries. In the wake of the drought, the Niger government set self-sufficiency in staple food grains as a national goal (Kountché 1979:11–32). To achieve this goal, a policy of promoting more intensive rainfed agriculture was introduced in an effort to break with longstanding agrarian practices based on a combination of extensive cultivation and shifting bush fallows. This national policy was supported by large amounts of bilateral and multilateral development assistance. In part, these new orientations had their origins in earlier "integrated action zones" introduced by national planners during the mid-1960s. This term has its origin in early rural development strategies in Niger that called for coordination by government rural development services—agriculture, rural animation, the credit and cooperative union, the agricultural credit bank, and the livestock service—in relation to program objectives set for specific areas or zones of the country (République du Niger 1978; Enger 1979:53). These earlier orientations were subsequently influenced by the post-drought reconstruction thinking among members of a new interstate coordination body created in 1973, the CILSS, or Interstate Committee to Combat Drought in the Sahel (Franke and Chasin 1980:134; République du Niger 1982b:8).

Those areas of the country that were considered to have potential for improved rainfed agriculture (where annual rainfall generally exceeds 350 mm) were selected for attention. In six of Niger's seven major administrative divisions (*départements*, henceforth departments) located in the agriculturally useful areas, project zones were delimited. Together, these zones include more than half of the country's peasant smallholders (Enger 1979:53). Agricultural development projects were organized in each department by the government with financial assistance from the Common Market, France, the World Bank, Canada, the United States, and the Federal Republic of Germany. The first of these projects began in 1972; the latest, in 1982.

Each project had a specific character, in part a reflection of the intervention style of its foreign financer, but all of these "productivity projects," as they came to be known, had a common focus. They all sought to introduce new or modified agricultural techniques in the form of a technical package among peasant producers, and thereby to increase rainfed agricultural productivity in yields per hectare. By so doing, the scenario went, aggregate production would increase, and Niger would move toward self-sufficiency in food.

The core elements of this technical package were proposed by the Nigerien National Agronomic Research Institute (INRAN), having been developed earlier by its colonial predecessor, the French Institute for Research on Tropical Agriculture (IRAT). Thus, extension content and methods varied only slightly from project to project (Ithaca International 1983:10–11). The new practices included: the use of selected seed varieties and seed treatments; the use of chemical fertilizers (urea and phosphates); reduced, more regular spacing of plants (with a recommended spacing of no greater than 1 m x 1 m for millet, and 1 m x 0.5 m for sorghum) through use of a tracing tool;[4] thinning of plants in pure stands; timely weeding; the use of insecticides if needed; and the use of two oxen (and to a lesser extent, single-donkey) traction with plows and multicultivators to break up the soil before sowing, and for weeding.

The extension themes were the result of IRAT/INRAN research station trials, and rarely reflected on-farm conditions, but more importantly, they were unproven (Enger 1979:54; Painter et al. 1985:6, 11, 13; Poulin et al. 1985:15–16). What became the "standard agricultural extension package," then, was really an article of faith. The profitability of the combined production techniques promoted throughout Niger's agriculture zones by the productivity projects was based on an assumed farm-holding size of six hectares. This figure can be arrived at, according to Derriennic (1977:166), by dividing the total estimated cultivated area of the country during the mid-1970s (2,720,000 hectares) by the number of production units or farms (450,000; Derrienic 1977:166; cf. USAID 1977a:4; USAID 1980a:2), and takes no account of the distribution of farm size among Niger's agrarian populations.

No doubt the six hectare figure was a handy minimum for project planners and development assistance agencies in calculating rates of return and project impact, but judging from the actual rate at which the extension themes have been adopted by Nigerien producers, it was off the mark in many project zones. In fact, very little national data exists on farm size in Niger, but sample evidence from the Niamey Department in the west of the country strongly suggests that the "average holding" may be well under six hectares (see below; cf. Painter 1980a:13; Stier 1980). More was involved, however, than an extension package with a very doubtful cost effectiveness for the peasants who were invited to use it (Enger 1979:59; Ithaca International 1983:19; Poulin et al. 1985:15–22). The specific configuration of the techniques promoted by the projects also reflected a model that allowed for no variation in the physical conditions of production. This homogeneity does not and probably never has existed within single fields, much less a "project zone" or the whole of agricultural Niger (cf. Ferguson 1979:23). In reality, soil texture and quality, rainfall, depth of static water tables, and slope, all vary a good deal within the world of Niger's smallholder agriculturalists. Development planners have rarely taken this variation into account (Poulin et al. 1985:18–22).

As of 1982, expenditures for Niger's productivity projects amounted to more than $50.3 million, and the results were considered mediocre as well as costly (République du Niger 1984:31, 42). After as many as ten years of productivity project operations in some cases, the Ministry of Plan was obliged to conclude in 1984 that increased aggregate production of rainfed crops in the country continued to result from larger and larger areas being cultivated and not from greater yields per hectare. Moreover, during much of the period for the Five Year Plan from 1979 to 1983, yields are reported to have dropped, and with them, the government claims, soil fertility (République du Niger 1980:138–166, 1984:39; cf. République du Niger 1982a:7).

While diachronic data are not available on declining soil fertility, peasant cultivators throughout Niger's agricultural zones are keenly aware of a deteriorating situation. For more than two decades Hausaphone peasants in southern central Niger have been telling experts that "the land is tired" (*Kasar mu, ta gaji*). Perceptions among Zarmaphone peoples in parts of western Niger suggest a more serious situation: *Laabu, y bu,* "The land is dead." In conformity with a tradition of empiricism in peasant praxis, Niger's smallholders repeatedly cite two indicators of what they consider to be a change for the worse. The first is directly related to production. Whenever harvests and production are discussed, a predictable response is heard: fields do not produce as many bundles of grain as they used to. When peasants are pressed for details, recall may be limited to five years or so, but they can easily recall total harvests for these periods because they quantify their production each year. Before the harvest is carried to household granaries for storage, it must be bundled, and the bundles are counted. Not given to a fixation on statistics, peasants in Niger nonetheless interpret these global figures, together with less detailed information recalled from their youth, and knowledge passed from generation to generation, as pointing to a decline in production. The second indicator is less direct, but is more readily seen by even the casual observer who bothers to wander about village millet fields during the cultivation and early harvest seasons. The *Striga hermonthica* plant announces itself to the delight of the uninformed passerby with its clumps of bright red flowers. To Niger's rural inhabitants, however, this colorful display amidst their millet plants is a sure sign that the land is tired—or worse, "dead" (Painter 1985:377).

So troublesome had the combination of poor results and high costs of Niger's productivity projects become by 1982 that the government's Development Council held a national seminar in the city of Zinder on "Intervention Strategies in Rural Areas" (République du Niger 1982a). According to the major seminar report,

> A poor understanding of the rural settings in which development projects operate results in the organization of agricultural extension programs without satisfactory knowledge about obstacles to the adoption of extension themes by peasant producers (République du Niger 1982b:9).

The seminar recommended that agricultural extension be better adapted to the natural and social settings of peasant production in Niger (République du Niger 1982a:1, 8, 13, 15).

Since the Zinder seminar, the Niger government and development assistance organizations have been attempting to shift their rural development strategies, but effective changes are slow in coming since more is required than appropriate techniques. For effective changes to occur in strategies of rural development in Niger and throughout the Sahel, fundamental alterations are needed in the very conceptual and analytical apparatus, the manner of thinking, and the behavior of planners (expatriate and national alike) and extension agents, not to mention agrarian populations (Painter 1984, Part IV).

Productivity Projects:
A Case Study from Western Niger

During 1977, USAID and the Niger government began to operate an eight-year productivity project in the Niamey department, located in the west of the country. The purpose of the Niamey Department Development Project was ambitious:

> To institutionalize a process of rural development through the establishment of self-managed village organizations capable of assisting farm families with the achievement of increased food production on a self-sustaining basis (USAID 1980c, Vol. I:13).

The project purpose suggests, and USAID personnel repeatedly state, that the Niamey Department project is an "institution-building" project. Considerable effort has been invested by the project to form new operational links among government rural development services in the project zone and to reinforce existing linkages (Painter et al. 1985). Institution building is a slow and unsure process, however, and in the meantime the project has been promoting the standard agricultural package as the major component of its operations. This occurs during training programs at subregional and village-level training centers for peasant married couples. The extension themes taught at the centers closely resemble those promoted by all productivity projects in Niger (USAID 1977a:10; USAID 1980c, Vol. II), and like those taught elsewhere, have benefited from little on-farm testing (Enger 1980:14, n.2). Project workers expect that after nine months at the training centers, peasant couples will (a) use the extension themes on their own fields as directed, (b) produce more, and (c) actively promote the new techniques among their village neighbors.

Since its inception the Niamey project has promoted a wide variety of activities, which, in addition to the core of new production techniques, have included cooperative organizations, programs in adult literacy, radio clubs, village woodlots, the promotion of diesel-powered grinding mills, and small-scale irrigation. The effectiveness of these measures has been discussed elsewhere and need not be repeated here (Aboubacar et al. 1985; CFCA 1982; Keita 1982; Painter 1980b, 1984). Here I will limit my attention to the project's improved techniques for rainfed agriculture and the relation of these techniques to peasant production on lands at risk.

The Niamey project has been studied and evaluated numerous times, with major evaluations conducted in 1979, 1980, 1983, and 1984. Each evaluation produced additional evidence that many of the project's production techniques were poorly adapted to the needs and limitations of peasant producers in the project zone, were not being used, or at best were being used only partially (Ithaca International 1983; Poulin et al. 1985; Roberts et al. 1983; USAID 1980c, Vol. II). A study in 1984 of all persons who completed training in the project's centers since 1977 indicates that very few (ranging from 3 to 19 percent of former trainees contacted) had attempted to use all of the recommended techniques (Poulin et al. 1985:19). Most used only a few of the techniques. Not surprisingly, those used were the simplest and least expensive, hence least risky from the producers' points of view (e.g., seed treatments, thinning of young plants). Among those who use the new techniques, few use them as directed, and the number of neighboring villagers who adopted the methods due to promotional efforts by the project's trainees is negligible. So much for the "spread effect" (Ithaca International 1983:24–25).[5] In general, the techniques promoted by the project appear to have had a very limited impact in the project zone.

Peasant Resistance to Improved Productivity
or Project Resistance to Reality?

How do we explain the lack of response by peasant producers in the project zone after almost seven years of extension efforts? Not easily to be sure, but two factors, closely interlinked, are important.

First, for most trainees, all of whom operate during their real lives in a context where anything more than minimal investment in rainfed agriculture is *avoided,* some of the techniques, and certainly the package taken as a whole, are considered too costly (Poulin et al 1985:15f). Even at subsidized prices (and these are being withdrawn) they are too expensive, too risky, and their payoff too small (Mullenax 1979; Poulin et al. 1985:15–22; Roberts et al. 1983:5ff.; USAID 1977a:2; Wybo 1983:18–19). The lack of enthusiasm among thousands of producers in the project zone suggests that much of the technical package is simply not worth the investment.

The second factor, which is also a cause of the first, is the homogeneity and inflexibility of the extension package in relation to the considerable variation within the Niamey Department in rainfall, soil characteristics, size of land holdings, and even social organization.

Average annual rainfall varies from about 350 mm in the north of the project zone (Ouallam) to more than 550 mm in the south (near Say) (cf. Painter 1980a:5), and within the project zone itself there occurs a transition from one climatic zone, southern sahelian, to another, northern sudanian (Morel 1980:16–17). But as anyone familiar with "average" rainfall figures for sahelian areas will be quick to realize, year-to-year variations may be substantial, and, more importantly for producers in the project zone, the distribution of rainfall during a given rainy season may be far from optimal for successful germination, growth, and maturation of rainfed crops. Thus an above-average rainfall, poorly distributed, can be more damaging to crop growth than a total rainfall that is somewhat below average but well-distributed during the rainy season months.

Soil characteristics in the project zone reflect the variations described in the first part of this chapter. They range from light sandy dune soils in the north to ferruginous, crusty soils in the central region, to heavy clayey soils in the south.

The size of land holdings also varies widely (Painter 1980a; Stier 1980; USAID 1977a:4). Sample data on farm holding size in three *arrondissements* of the Niamey Project zone suggest that as much as 83 to 90 percent of all holdings are smaller than six hectares, the threshold used by planners to determine the profitability of extension techniques. In all of the cases studied, more than half, and in one arrondissement, up to 70 percent of the holdings were smaller than three hectares, that is, less than half the size considered the minimum for the technical package to cover investment costs by producers (Stier 1980:9–10).[6]

Finally, there is considerable variation in the social organization of production among the various ethnic groups that have been lumped together within the project zone. This is particularly so for the roles of women at different times of the year. In some areas, women commonly labor during the rainy season in the cultivation of major staple grains (millet, sorghum), in addition to crops (e.g., sesame, Bambara groundnuts) grown on their own, smaller plots. Elsewhere in the project zone they do not. In the latter cases, where women's participation in the cultivation of staple grain crops is negatively, not positively sanctioned, considerable ridicule may be suffered by wives who, conforming to project recommendations, attempt to help their husbands with the use of ox-drawn multicultivators (Painter 1984:46–47). In areas where women are actively involved in all stages of staple crop production, the additional labor demands created by the use of ox-drawn equipment may result in neglect of the women's own fields. The extra labor requirements of "labor saving" animal traction are, after all, simply added to a long list of tasks for which women are routinely responsible (Diarra 1971:98–108; Painter 1985:80–82; Samna 1980:17–18). Dry-season irrigated gardening is almost exclusively done by men in some areas, while in others, women participate a great deal more (Stier 1980, cf. Painter 1979:55–59). The implications of these differences for a global promotion of dry-season gardening among women in the project zone are significant, but variations of this kind in the social organization of labor have not been taken into account (Painter 1984:41–50).

Despite these important variations at all levels of what we might call "subsistence production reality," the project has, until very recently, promoted the same set of production techniques throughout its operational zones.

Problems of the Productivity Project Approach to Life on Lands at Risk in Niger

The specific weaknesses of the Niamey Project's "problem-solving" strategy reflect problems long suffered by all productivity projects in Niger. They have attempted to promote a de facto "standard" extension package for widespread application under conditions of agricultural production that are far from standard. For lack of something better, and lacking the capacity to innovate for its own purposes, the project has used the package developed by government research institutes. Further, the productivity projects in Niger have had no effective feedback mechanism to permit systematic use of information gathered by their own follow-up divisions (which information is mushrooming due to the recent introduction of microcomputers), in order better to adapt training and extension content according to local possibilities and limitations (Painter et al. 1985:11f.; cf. Enger 1979:14–15). The Niamey project, also like its counterparts in Niger, has been preoccupied from a planning standpoint with an oversimplified conception of the production process: one in which more and better inputs (should) yield greater production. The black box between agricultural inputs and production—the land—has, like the elements of the extension package itself, remained poorly understood and subject to little critical consideration. The techniques promoted have ignored the main fact of productive life throughout the region: agricultural production is based on poor, eroded, and badly treated land (Heermans 1984, 1986).

Unless these essential problems are recognized and measures taken to address them, the future of dryland agricultural production in Niger, the use of extension themes by peasants notwithstanding, will remain problematic indeed. What is more, the practice of continuous cultivation at the expense of fallows, as the use of project extension themes implies, may aggravate rather than alleviate the already serious problems of soil erosion and loss of fertility. The project has devoted considerable expense and planning to providing a more effective organization of input storage and delivery (warehouses and vehicles) in the project zone, but it has given little attention to long-standing processes of ecological change—often degradation—of the Niamey peasants' habitat, or to means of arresting or improving the situation. Only this year, during the project's eighth year, has some attention been given to the land in the project zone, the soils that make it up, and the land's naturally occurring and increasingly depleted vegetative cover (Thomson 1985:230, passim).

Ironically, USAID has been supporting, also in the Niamey Department, an extremely innovative but low-key forestry project. Under the auspices of this project (the Forestry and Land-Use Planning Project; cf. USAID 1979), precisely the kinds of antierosive, restorative techniques that should have long been an integral part of the Niamey project's training and extension programs are being experimented with and evaluated in the national forest near Guesselbodi, just south of the capital, Niamey (Heermans 1984, 1986). Elsewhere in Niger, USAID money has been partially financing programs administered by CARE and other nongovernmental organizations which have been experimenting with and promoting successful erosion-control programs through the use of windbreaks and simple techniques for slowing movement of sand dunes (SRD/ISAID 1978). Evidence from the work at Guesselbodi on the effectiveness of simple, relatively inexpensive techniques to slow or stop erosion, reduce soil degradation, and even enhance soil quality is encouraging (Dumont 1984; Heermans 1986; Sève and Tabor 1985). Finally, in the Majiya valley of central Niger, researchers have shown that demonstrable increases in millet yields can be obtained due to the microclimatic improvements caused by lines of windbreaks being promoted by CARE (Bognetteau-Verlinden 1980). Both programs provide examples of relatively successful endeavors to engage local interest and participation in programs for more effective resource management (cf. Thomson 1983, 1985:250; World Bank 1985:19–20, 28–31).

These activities suggest not that USAID is ignoring conservation and restoration issues, but that its heavy emphasis on productivity gives only meager attention to understanding the ecological basis of production. Conservation and restoration, then, are given little importance in practice. At one time, the Niamey project had a soil conservation element, but it appears to have been abandoned due to lack of success, caused in large part by the approach used and by organizational problems (USAID 1977b:5, 29, 50; USAID 1980b:2; USAID 1980c, Vol. I:39). More interestingly, it also seems that there have been few links (this is true of the government as well as USAID) between programs in the "forestry sector" and those in the "agricultural sector" and that there is a great need for these links to be created and reinforced.

If viable options are to be developed for making life in a harsh environment more livable for Niger's peasants, some important changes will be necessary in national and bilateral conceptions of production and productivity. The concept of land as a problem to be addressed and understood must replace the current practice of taking it as a given to be ignored, or simply dosed with fertilizer. Increasing attention must be given to mitigating the combined negative effects of climate and of agrarian practices where rural populations see no choice but to continue extensification (cf. Raynaut 1980). Land must be brought back in.

Prospects for Change in Approaches to Increased Productivity on Niger Lands at Risk

The Niger government and the organizations that are helping to finance its rural development programs are searching for new and effective strategies for improving agricultural production, and there is evidence of a change in official thinking about the issues discussed above. The beginnings of new orientations were outlined in 1982 as a result of the Zinder rural development seminar described earlier: the productivity project option was judged largely ineffective and far too expensive.

During 1983 and 1984, preliminary efforts were made in some productivity projects to introduce extension themes that are better adapted to local conditions. After almost ten years of operation in the Maradi department, a World Bank project is taking noteworthy steps toward reorienting some of its programs. This is being done on the basis of socioeconomic and agronomic research done earlier in the project zone by an independent group from the University of Bordeaux (De Miranda 1979; Grégoire 1980; Grégoire and Raynaut 1980; Raynaut 1980). Concretely, a social geographer, recently hired by the project, has the task of following up and supplementing the research of the Bordeaux group. On the basis of continued fieldwork in the area, he will help the project adapt extension strategies to local conditions. Some combinations of animal traction techniques, for example, are appropriate on heavier soils while they are not as effective on lighter, sandier soils. The impact of chemical fertilizers also varies greatly depending on existing soil chemistry and rainfall. This effort to situate and carefully design interventions in relation to specific variations in the context of production may be the most useful innovation in almost 20 years of rural development in Niger. In western Niger, the Niamey project is also beginning to introduce greater flexibility in its extension package. In 1985 the project began to ask basic questions about the long-ignored ecological, edaphic, and social variability of the project zone.[7] A preliminary study is currently under way to delineate naturally occurring zones within the department, but it is far too soon to predict how the research findings will affect the project's extension themes. Clearly the time is ripe to "unpack" as it were, the so-called "standard" agricultural package.

Is it possible that the era of Niger's productivity projects, now on the wane, was also a period of unpreparedness and technological smugness on the part of national planners, agronomists and development assistance organizations? Perhaps. It is also worthwhile to reflect on the significance of crisis, or *"la conjoncture"* as it is referred to in Niger, as the basis for changes in rural development strategies. In large part, the expensive, marginally effective productivity projects were born of the disastrous 1968–1974 drought. Something had to be done. For Niger and its neighbors, the drought years were years of crisis at all levels—agronomic, economic, and political. This was a *conjoncture* of sorts, based on climatic changes, and aggravated by blatant mismanagement of resources, as elements within Niger's ruling classes sought to maximize the gains made possible by access to the state. The crisis precipitated the downfall of the Diori Hamani regime in 1974. Now, more than ten years later, the search for more responsive, less expensive rural development strategies is to a large extent the result of another crisis, another *conjoncture*. This time, however, it is grounded less in the impact of drought than in the recession of the world market for Niger's principal export—uranium, and the stagnation and retrenchment this has imposed on the country's national development plans (Kountché 1984:7; République du Niger 1984:11–21; cf. Painter 1986 and Charlick 1985). Who knows what innovations will be born of this latest adversity? But this much is clear: critical reflection and sharp questions about the realities of agricultural production in Niger are long overdue. Questions about the nature of land, and how to protect and improve it, can no longer be ignored by endeavors to improve agricultural production.

Notes

1. I would like to thank A. Endre Nyerges and Peter D. Little for their helpful comments on an earlier draft of this chapter, delivered at the IDA workshop on Lands at Risk in the Third World, October 10–12, 1985. I bear sole responsibility for any shortcomings in the present version.

2. On the basis of a classification developed by the Inter-African Committee for Hydraulic Studies, soils in Niger's agriculturally useful areas have been described as "generally poor to moderate" to "generally poor" (Arizona 1980:18–22). The former category refers to tropical ferruginous and desaturated ferallitic soils, while the latter includes light textured sandy soils and heavy textured vertisoils (Horowitz et al. 1983, Vol. I, "Introduction," p. 16).

3. The inverse relation between total surface areas under cultivation and yields suggested by data on millet in Figure 7.1 is reinforced by a recent estimation of overall changes in agricultural production in Niger from the early 1960s to 1984. On the basis of materials from CILSS (CILSS/MHE 1985), Sève and Tabor provide comparative data, which are summarized in Table 7.1.

4. As a rule, planting densities used in rainfed agriculture in Niger are low, occasionally with a mild decline in already low densities as one moves from village in-fields (fields nearest to village settlements, often cultivated year after year, and benefiting from regular applications of compound sweepings, cooking fire ashes, and periodic manuring) to out-fields (located from two to as many as ten kilometers from the village, and cultivated for several years, followed by a fallow). Average planting densities for millet (plants per square meter) observed in 40 plots in areas of the Dosso department roughly comparable to areas of the Niamey project zone,

Table 7.1   Food Crop Production in Niger,
             1960-1967 to 1979-1984

	Period	
	1960-67	1979-84
Average surface area cultivated in food crops (millions of ha)	3.1	5.5
Average yields of grain (unspecified) in kilograms per hectare	475	350

Source: Sève and Tabor (1985:1).

Table 7.2 Comparative Data on Farm Holding Size in
          Three Arrondissements (Niamey Department)

Arrondissement	Average Cultivated Area (ha) per Exploitation	
	1979 (Stier 1980:10)	1980 (Wagner 1980:3-6)
Niamey (Kollo)	3.69	7.9
Ouallam	2.56	4.98
Filingue	3.45	7.7

ranged from 0.36 to 0.73 in in-fields, with most being closer to the lower figure (Painter 1985:84).

5. The following analysis of the dominant technical package in Niger is equally applicable to the situation described by numerous studies and evaluations of the Niamey project:

The fact that the inputs of this package are costly to the farmer, must be heavily subsidized by the government, and are often unobtainable by the extension services and farmers means that the application of the package is incomplete even where the techniques have been accepted by cultivators. When only some of the themes are applied, yields may be less than those found [with traditional] techniques, and other deleterious effects on the harvest and soils may ensue (Enger 1979:54).

6. A survey of trainees who had attended the project's centers in 1980 (Wagner 1980) revealed an average farm holding size greater than values measured by the

Nigerien Section Statistiques Agricoles during 1979 on the basis of randomly sampled holdings in the project zone (Stier 1980:10). One possible explanation given for this difference is the bias which may result from the manner in which trainees are selected by their co-villagers for participation in the project's training program. Comparative figures for the three arrondissements are shown in Table 7.2.

7. For the first time since the beginning of the project, basic questions are being asked about the existing forms of local social organization in areas affected by the project's operations, and their implications for project methods and objectives (Sidikou and Charlick 1985). Compare this approach with that described by Bradley, Raynaut and Torrealba (1977).

References

Aboubacar, Saibou, Moussa Abdou, Eric Arnould, and Idrissa Hamzata
1985   Evaluation comparative de la formation et des retombées au sein des projets productivité de Maradi, Niamey, et Zinder. Résultats provisoires et non-opposables. Niamey: République du Niger, Ministère du Développement Rural, Direction de l'Evaluation et de la Programmation des Projets, Service de l'Appui à l'évaluation des Projets. Juin.

Arizona
1980   Draft Environmental Report on Niger. Tucson, AZ: Office of Arid Lands Studies, University of Arizona.

Bognetteau-Verlinden, Els
1980   Study on the Impact of Windbreaks in Majiya Valley, Niger. Bouza/ Wageningen, Holland: CARE/Agricultural University, Department of Sylviculture. February.

Borsdorf, Roe
1979   Marketing Profile: Cereals and Cash Crops. Part F. *In* Niger Agricultural Sector Assessment, Vol. II. Niamey: USAID/Niger.

Bradley, Phillip, Claude Raynaut, and Jorge Torrealba
1977   The Guidimaka Region of Mauritania: A Critical Analysis Leading to a Development Project. London: War on Want (U.K.). May.

CFCA
1982   La formation au sein des centres de perfectionnement technique du Projet Productivité Niamey. CFCA Document du Travail No. 1. Niamey: République du Niger, Ministère de l'Education Nationale, Centre de Formation des Cadres de l'Alphabétisation. 23 novembre.

Charlick, Robert B.
1985   Small Farmer Production in Western Niger: Lessons and Opportunities of Crisis and "*conjoncture*." Paper presented at the Annual Meetings of the African Studies Association, New Orleans, LA, November 22–26.

CILSS/MHE
1985   Plan directeur de lutte contre la désertification. Document I: Etat de la situation actuelle. Niamey: Comité Inter-état pour la lutte contre la Sécheresse.

De Miranda, E.
1979   Etude des déséquilibres écologiques et agricoles d'une région tropicale semi-aride du Niger. Programme de Recherches sur la Région de Maradi, Université de Bordeaux II. Paris: DGRST/ACC Lutte contre l'Aridité en Milieu Tropical. Avril.

Derriennic, Hérvé
  1977   Famines et dominations en Afrique noire. Paysans et éleveurs sous le joug.
          Paris: l'Harmattan.
Diarra, Fatouma-Agnès
  1971   Femmes africaines en devenir: Les femmes Zarma du Niger. Paris: Editions
          Anthropos/Centre Nigérien de Recherches en Sciences Sociales.
Donaint, Pierre, and François Lancrenon
  1976   Le Niger. Paris: Presses Universitaires de France, «Que sais-je?»
Dumont, Réné
  1984   Forêt naturelle ameliorée ou plantations artificielles? Niamey: USAID/
          Niger. Typewritten draft document.
Enger, Warren J.
  1979   The Government of Niger's Agricultural Strategy and the Potential for
          Meeting Long-Term Goals. Part B. *In* Niger Agricultural Sector Assessment,
          Vol. II. Niamey: USAID/Niger.
  1980   Economic Analysis. Annexe B. *In* Niger: Niamey Department Development
          Project, Phase II, 683-0204. Vol. II, Project Paper Annexes. Niamey: USAID/
          Niger.
Ferguson, Carl E.
  1979   Agronomy and Agricultural Research. Part C. *In* Niger Agricultural Sector
          Assessment, Vol. II. Niamey: USAID/Niger.
Franke, Richard W., and Barbara H. Chasin
  1980   Seeds of Famine: Ecological Destruction and the Development Dilemma
          in the West African Sahel. Totowa, NJ: Rowman and Allanheld.
Grégoire, Emmanuel
  1980   Etude socio-économique du village de Gourjae (Département de Maradi,
          Niger). Programme de Recherches sur la Région de Maradi, Université de
          Bordeaux II. Paris: DGRST/ACC Lutte contre l'Aridité en Milieu Tropical.
          Octobre.
Grégoire, Emmanuel, and Claude Raynaut
  1980   Présentation générale du département de Maradi. Programme de Recherches
          sur la Région de Maradi, Université de Bordeaux II. Paris: DGRST/ACC
          Lutte contre l'Aridité en Milieu Tropical.
Heermans, John G.
  1984   The Guesselbodi Experiment: Case Study of Brushland Management in
          Niger. Niamey. Typewritten document.
  1986   The Guesselbodi Experiment with Improved Management of Brushland in
          Niger. IDA Development Anthropology Network 4 (1):11–15, Binghamton,
          NY: Institute for Development Anthropology.
Horowitz, Michael M, with E. J. Arnould, R. B. Charlick, J. H. Eriksen, R. H.
          Faulkingham, C. D. Grimm, P. D. Little, M. D. Painter, T. M. Painter, C.
          Saenz, M. Salem-Murdock, and M. O. Saunders
  1983   Niger: A Social and Institutional Profile. Binghamton, NY: Institute for
          Development Anthropology.
Ithaca International
  1983   An Evaluation of the Agricultural Packages for the Republic of Niger.
          Ithaca, NY: Ithaca International, Ltd.
Keita, Thérèse
  1982   Evaluation de l'implantation des moulins à grains dans le Département
          de Niamey. Niamey: USAID/Projet Productivité Niamey. Mai.

Kountché, Seyni
    1979   Discours et messages, 15 avril 1974–15 avril 1979. Niamey: Imprimerie
            Nationale du Niger.
    1984   Préface du Chef de l'Etat. *In* Programme Interimaire de Consolidation,
            1984–1985, p. 7. Niamey: République du Niger, Ministère du Plan. Juillet.
Morel, Alain
    1980   Climat. *In* Atlas du Niger. Edmond Bernus and Sidikou A. Hamidou, eds.
            Pp. 14–17. Paris: Editions Jeune Afrique.
Mullenax, John H.
    1979   Are the Technical Packages that are Currently the Basis for Attempts at
            Improving Nigerien Agricultural Production Profitable? Niamey: Niamey
            Department Development Project. 19 June.
Painter, Thomas M.
    1979   Dosso Agricultural Development Project: Sociology Working Paper. Prepared
            for the World Bank. Binghamton, NY: Institute for Development Anthro-
            pology. January.
    1980a   Social Soundness of the Niamey Department Development Project (Niger
            Republic): Evaluation of Phase I; Recommendations for Phase II, Part 1.
            Overview of the Area and Populations within Project Zones; Analysis.
            Annexe C. *In* Niger: Niamey Department Development Project, Phase II,
            683-0204. Vol. 2, Project Paper Annexes. Niamey: USAID/Niger.
    1980b   Adult Literacy and Cooperative Training Programs in the Niamey De-
            partment Development Project (Niger Republic): Evaluation of Phase I
            Activities and Recommendations for Phase II. Annexe C. *In* Niger: Niamey
            Department Development Project, Phase II, 683-0204. Vol. 2, Project Paper
            Annexes. Niamey: USAID/Niger.
    1984   Training, Extension, and Support for Local Organizations in the Niamey
            Department Development Project (Niger): An Evaluation, with Additional
            Notes on the Impact of Project Training for Women. Binghamton, NY:
            Institute for Development Anthropology.
    1985   Peasant Migrations and Rural Transformations in Niger: A Study of
            Incorporation within a West African Capitalist Regional Economy, c. 1875
            to c. 1982. Ph.D. dissertation. Sociology Department, State University of
            New York at Binghamton.
    1986   *La conjoncture* and Changing Development Strategies in Niger. *In* IDA
            Development Anthropology Network 4(1):1–2. Binghamton, NY: Institute
            for Development Anthropology.
Painter, Thomas M., Roger J. Poulin, David Harmon, and Douglas Barnett
    1985   Development Management in Africa: The Case of the Niamey Department
            Development Project in Niger. AID Evaluation Special Study No. 36.
            Washington, DC: US Agency for International Development. December.
Poulin, Roger J., David Harmon, Thomas Painter, and Douglas Barnett
    1985   Niamey Department Development Project: Second Interim Evaluation.
            Washington, DC: Development Alternatives, Inc. February.
Raulin, Henri
    1963   Techniques et bases socio-économiques des sociétés rurales nigériennes.
            Etudes Nigériennes No. 12. Niamey: Institut Fondamental de l'Afrique
            Noire–Centre Nigérien de Recherche en Sciences Humaines.
Raynaut, Claude
    1980   Recherches multidisciplinaires sur la région de Maradi: Rapport de synthèse.
            Programme de Recherches sur la Région de Maradi, Université de Bordeaux.
            Paris: DGRST/ACC Lutte contre l'Aridité en Milieu Tropical. Octobre.

République du Niger
   1978   Structures Agraires et Développement Rural au Niger. Niamey: Ministère
            du Développement Rural, Direction de l'Agriculture. Juillet.
   1980   Plan Quinquennal de Développement Economique et Social, 1979–1983.
            Niamey: Ministère du Plan. Avril.
   1982a   Recommandations. Séminaire National sur la Stratégie d'Intervention en
            Milieu Rural, Zinder, du 15 au 22 Novembre 1982. Niamey: Conseil
            National de Développement.
   1982b   Rapport de la Commission I. Thème: Structures et Méthodes d'Intervention
            en Milieu Rural. Séminaire National sur la Stratégie d'Intervention en
            Milieu Rural, Zinder, du 15 au 22 Novembre 1982. Niamey: Conseil
            National de Développement.
   1984   Programme Interimaire de Consolidation, 1984–1985. Niamey: Ministère
            du Plan. Juillet.
Roberts, Richard, Theresa Ware, and Douglas Barnett
   1983   Niamey Department Development (NDD II): First Interim Evaluation.
            Niamey: République du Niger, Ministère du Développement Rural, Projet
            Productivité Niamey. 12 February.
Samna, Hadizatou
   1980   La contribution de la femme rurale à la vie économique: Exemple de la
            région de Dogondoutchi, République du Niger. Mémoire pour l'obtention
            de la Maîtrise, Sciences Economiques, Ecole Supérieure des Techniques et
            de Gestion. Université de Benin, Lomé, Togo. Juin.
Sève, J. E., and J. A. Tabor
   1985   Land Degradation and Simple Conservation Practices. A Case Study of
            Niger. Draft document No. 2. USAID. (Mimeo.) 4 October.
Sidikou, Hamidou A., and Robert B. Charlick
   1985   Etude sur les organisations locales dans le Département de Niamey. Rapport
            Préliminaire. Niamey: République du Niger, Ministère du Développement
            Rural, Projet Productivité Niamey. Juillet.
SRD/ISAID
   1978   Projet Tapis Vert. Project Outline. Dayton, Ohio/Toronto, Canada: Strategies
            for Responsible Development/Institute for the Study and Application of
            Integrated Development. May.
Stier, Francis
   1980   Social Soundness of the Niamey Department Development Project (Niger
            Republic): Evaluation of Phase I; Recommendations for Phase II, Part 2.
            Ethnographic Background, Technical Package, and the Use of Animal
            Traction. Annexe C. *In* Niger: Niamey Department Development Project,
            Phase II, 683-0204. Vol. II, Project Paper. Niamey: USAID/Niger.
Sutter, John W.
   1979   Social Analysis of the Nigerien Rural Producer. Part D. *In* Niger Agricultural
            Sector Assessment, Vol. II. Niamey: USAID/Niger.
   1982   Peasants, Merchant Capital and Rural Differentiation: A Nigerian Hausa
            Case Study. Ph.D. dissertation. Department of Anthropology, Cornell
            University.
Thomson, James T.
   1983   La participation, l'organisation locale, la politique d'utilisation des terres
            et du secteur forestier: orientations futures de la foresterie sahélienne.
            CILSS.

1985   The Politics of Desertification in Marginal Environments: The Sahelian Case. *In* Divesting Nature's Capital: The Political Economy of Environmental Abuse in the Third World. H. Jeffry Leonard, ed. Pp. 227–262. New York, NY: Homes and Meier.

USAID
  1977a   Brief Description of Animal Traction Activities, Niamey Productivity Project, 1st Phase. Niamey: USAID/Niger.
  1977b   Niger: Niamey Department Development Project (No. 683-0205). Project Paper. Niamey/Washington, DC: USAID/Niger/AID. May.
  1979   Niger: Forestry and Land-Use Planning Project (No. 683-0230). Niamey/Washington, DC: USAID/Niger/AID.
  1980a   USAID/Niger. Country Development Strategy Statement, Fiscal Year 1982. Niamey: USAID/Niger. January.
  1980b   Avant-projet: Projet de Développement Rural du Département de Niamey, Phase II (AID 683-0240). Niamey: USAID/Niger. 15 Mars.
  1980c   Niger: Niamey Department Development Project, Phase II, 683-0240. Vol. I, Project Paper; Vol. II, Project Paper Annexes; Vol. III, Environmental Annex. Niamey/Washington, DC: USAID/Niger/AID.

Wagner, Deborah K.
  1980   Rapport sur les Stagiaires de la Promotion 1980 des CPT dans le Cadre du Projet Productivité Niamey. Niamey: Projet Productivité Niamey. 22 Décembre.

World Bank
  1985   Desertification in the Sahelian and Sudanian Zones of West Africa. Washington, DC: World Bank.

Wybo, Michael D.
  1983   Crop Enterprise Budgets for Three Project-Trained and Two Traditional Farmers in the Area Surrounding the CPT Chiwil. Niamey: Niamey Department Development Project.

8

Unequal Exchange: The Dynamics of Settler Impoverishment and Environmental Destruction in Lowland Bolivia[1]

Michael Painter

Introduction

The San Julian settlement project is located in the eastern lowlands of Bolivia, some 150 kilometers northeast of the city of Santa Cruz. Since its beginning, in 1972, the project has become the home of approximately 5,436 people residing in 1,661 family units. In addition, there are some 7,730 people living in 2,518 family units in the immediate vicinity who are not part of the San Julian project, but who were drawn to the area by road construction and other activities associated with San Julian.

The San Julian project was conducted under the general direction of Bolivia's National Colonization Institute (Instituto Nacional de Colonización—INC), and it received some $9 million in support from the U.S. Agency for International Development in Bolivia (USAID/Bolivia).[2] The project has received a great deal of attention from evaluators and academic researchers because of the central role that a private voluntary organization, the Integral Development Foundation (Fundación Integral de Desarrollo—FIDES), played in planning and executing settlement activities. Due to the work of FIDES, many problems associated with Amazon settlement were overcome, and San Julian has assumed importance as a possible model for future settlement.

Based upon research conducted in San Julian in 1984 (Painter et al. 1984), the present chapter seeks to emphasize the following points. First, while many criticisms can and should be made of it, the San Julian project has made a number of important advances over previous efforts to settle people in the Amazon. Second, in spite of these advances, the minimal conditions for settlement success have not been met. This suggests that settlement success is not determined at the project level. Third, while San Julian has not yet experienced impoverishment and environmental destruction on the scale observed in settlement areas elsewhere in the Amazon, these processes are at work. Because they are at an earlier stage, we have the opportunity to examine in detail how the relationship between these two processes is established. Finally, the chapter argues that impoverishment and environmental destruction are the products of relations of unequal exchange that are established between a settlement area and the larger society.

Unequal exchange in the present context is understood to be the extraction of surplus from producers through unfavorable terms of trade, whereby producers receive low prices for commodities they sell in relation to the costs they must pay for commodities they purchase. This condition may arise from a number of causes, including competition with capitalist agriculture, monopolistic merchants, cheap food policies, and the international transmission of prices (Deere and de Janvry 1979:608).

In the case of San Julian and the smallholder settlement areas of Santa Cruz department generally, conditions of unequal exchange were created by agricultural policies that solidified preexisting inequalities in wealth distribution and created barriers to participation by settlers in the capitalist development being promoted in the region. Settlers received only lands that were located outside of transportation networks and physically distant from the market centers that were beginning to develop in the region.

In addition, development planners focused on rice and corn as the basis for smallholder production systems. This emphasis has helped insure that families control the basic elements of their own food supply, but smallholders' attempts to market corn and rice for cash have created chronic overproduction problems. As a result, the prices of rice and corn have steadily lost ground to the price of agricultural labor power. This, combined with the physical isolation that characterizes most smallholder settlement areas, has made it increasingly difficult for settlers to earn a living through agriculture.[3] Maxwell (1980:165) indicates that the income-earning possibilities of small farmers in Santa Cruz are not appreciably better than those of seasonal agricultural wage laborers.

Furthermore, opportunities for earning off-farm income are extremely limited. Because their incomes are low, settlers have few resources to invest in agroprocessing enterprises, and efforts to establish businesses that provide goods and services to fellow settlers tend to stagnate for lack of demand. While the large numbers of small shops and stores found in some settlement areas have frequently been cited as signs of economic dynamism on the part of settlers (cf. Solem et al. 1985; Ward 1984), interviews conducted in the San Julian project indicated that such enterprises were symptomatic of impoverished households trying to find a way to make ends meet rather than prosperous farm families investing revenues earned through agriculture (Painter et al. 1984; Painter and Partridge 1986).

Settlers seeking to increase their cash incomes are thus left with two alternatives. On the one hand, they can seek wage-earning opportunities off their own farms; on the other, they can pursue a more extensive on-farm land-use strategy. Unfortunately, opportunities for off-farm employment are very limited, as most are tied to the regional agricultural economy. As a result, the periods when the greatest amount of off-farm employment is available are also the periods when smallholders face the greatest labor demands from their own farms.[4] This creates pressure to reduce the amount of labor required on the farm, either through the introduction of labor-saving technology, or by seeking to "shortcut" labor-intensive activities.

Turning to more extensive land use involves trying to take advantage of the high level of soil productivity that is usually characteristic of the years immediately following forest clearing to raise the absolute quantity of agricultural production to a level that will provide a satisfactory income. Unfortunately, it takes more labor to keep land cleared for agriculture than it did to clear it in the first place, and necessary cash expenditures for fertilizer tend to increase as the initially high level of organic matter in the soil is exhausted. This exerts pressure on smallholders continually to clear new areas rather than maintain those they have already cleared. When such a strategy is pursued by large numbers of people, considerable forest areas are lost very quickly, with little in the way of improved living standards for the farmers. Maxwell (1980) has described this dynamic as the "*barbecho* crisis."

The relationship between settler impoverishment and destructive land use underscores the importance of insuring that settlers enjoy access to the resources necessary not simply to subsist, but to accumulate capital, as a central element of any settlement effort. Furthermore, the experience of the San Julian project suggests that access to critical productive resources is not an issue that can be addressed at the level of individual projects. The problems faced by settlers in San Julian are a function of the unfavorable exchange relationship that exists between them and the rest of the regional capitalist economy, which is in turn a function of their exclusion from the political power necessary to command a share of the resources that have been invested in the development of capitalist agriculture in Santa Cruz.

Previous Studies

Scholars and development practitioners have accorded considerable attention to the San Julian project. The early years of San Julian were the object of doctoral research by Hess (1978, 1980), and it has been discussed at length in published work by Blanes et al. (1984), Fifer (1982), Maxwell (1980), and Stearman (1980, 1983, 1985b). As a result of the financial support it received from USAID/Bolivia, San Julian was evaluated by agency employees and outside consultants (cf. Castro 1978; Curtis 1978; Locatelli 1978; Nelson 1978; Solem et al. 1985; Stearman 1978; Ward 1984). In general, these works have been favorable in their assessments of the project, leading observers to conclude that San Julian is a bright spot in the generally dark history of Amazon settlement (Scudder 1981). Solem et al. (1985:19), for example, are enthusiastic in their praise: "The confidence in prospects for growth cannot be overstated." The feeling seemed to be one of inevitability—that time and energy were sure to be rewarded.

The judgment of San Julian as an example of successful lowland settlement was based upon favorable assessments of several innovations in project design. These innovations include:

1. A three-month orientation program for new settlers that provided training in lowland cultivation techniques and survival skills along with rustic communal shelter and food assistance until settlers could build their own houses and realize an initial harvest;
2. A *núcleo* settlement pattern (Figure 8.1), which encourages community organization by facilitating face-to-face contact among settlers, provides equitable access to schools, health posts, wells, and other facilities; and is supposed to concentrate a sufficient number of people in a single area to permit the growth of off-farm businesses; and
3. A selection procedure that permitted people in the highland and valley regions of Bolivia to decide for themselves whether they wanted to settle in San Julian, but which tended to discourage those aspirants who were less likely to be successful.

Reports frequently give considerable credit to these project design features when they describe San Julian as an established agricultural area that provides itself with food, and enjoys good prospects for continuing economic growth.

In spite of these features, praise for San Julian has not been unconditional. Nelson (1978) and Fifer (1982) have warned that the successes enjoyed by the project during its early years could be reversed if its isolation from urban markets is not overcome sufficiently for agriculture to become an income-producing venture rather than simply a means of satisfying household needs. Blanes et al. (1984) argue that reliance on corn and rice as cash crops, and physical isolation from markets have caused settlers to become progressively poorer. Noting that declining yields, weed control, and falling incomes have become problems in areas where high forest has been exhausted and settlers have begun to cultivate areas of secondary growth, Maxwell (1980) predicted that high rates of abandonment might result once San Julian settlers have cleared the original forest cover from their parcels.

Stearman (1983) has also expressed concern about the economic prospects of San Julian settlers. She argues that despite innovations in planning and execution, settlement projects eventually become caught up in larger processes of social and economic change. These processes are beyond the control of smallholding settlers and project officials alike. In Amazon frontier areas, smallholder settlement has often been only an intermediate step in development, opening the area to use by large agricultural and cattle-raising enterprises.

Many evaluations of the San Julian project imply, but do not explicitly discuss, problems in the sustainability of settler production systems in the lowland environment. It has frequently been assumed that the inability of settler populations to establish sustainable production systems is a function

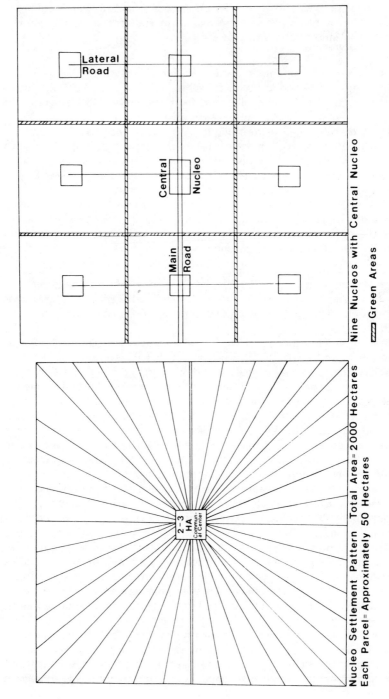

Nucleo Settlement Pattern Total Area=2000 Hectares
Each Parcel=Approximately 50 Hectares

Nine Nucleos with Central Nucleo

▨▨▨ Green Areas

Fig. 8.1 The Settlement Pattern of San Julian.

of poor management. Poor management, in turn, derives from their unfamiliarity with the lowland environment. Teaching them how to manage the lowland environment is complicated by the low level of education generally associated with smallholding settlers. The policy implication generally drawn from this line of reasoning is that settlers need greater technical support than they customarily receive, while the inadequacy of technical support has been attributed to a lack of attentiveness on the part of state and private sponsoring institutions.

The planners of the San Julian project had faith in the ability of smallholders to be successful lowland settlers if they were provided access to information necessary to make resource management decisions. To this end, they included lowland peasants already living in the area as beneficiaries of the food aid, training in cooperative management, and other support provided by the project. This was partly in order to avoid creating antagonisms between them and settlers from the highlands and valleys, and partly also to recruit lowland peasants to teach settlers from other parts of Bolivia techniques of tree felling, forest clearing, cultivating lowland crops, and utilizing lowland flora and fauna resources as part of their production systems.

Nevertheless, the doubts expressed by observers such as Fifer, Maxwell, Nelson, and Stearman about the long-term prospects of San Julian do not really have much to do with whether settlers are able to manage lowland resources rationally. Rather, they all imply that settlers are constrained in their resource management decisions by the kind of access that they actually have to the resources in question. Fifer and Maxwell see physical isolation and poor market access as a limiting factor; Maxwell is concerned about settlers' apparent lack of economic resources needed to gain access to techniques and technologies that would permit them to manage secondary forest growth; and Stearman points to the lack of access to the political and economic resources necessary to direct the process of frontier expansion once it has been set in motion.

While the critiques made by the authors noted above are perceptive in their identification of problems and their causes and consequences, they do not explore the dynamics underlying the phenomena they observe. In this regard, Collins' recent article (1986) is suggestive. In an examination of the processes of environmental destruction associated with settlement projects in Brazil, Ecuador, and Peru, she finds that all arise out of prior processes of settler impoverishment:

> . . . unfavorable market integration, high levels of surplus extraction, and policies that engender indebtedness have double consequences. Not only do they perpetuate poverty and underdevelopment, but the strategies that smallholders adopt to insure their survival under such circumstances are frequently incompatible with sustained, environmentally appropriate land use and lead to deterioration of soils and other natural resources (1986:1–2).

The question that remains to be answered, however, is why settlers become impoverished in so many settlement projects located in environmentally diverse Amazonian regions. The San Julian case provides an instructive example. Despite the fact that the project has received more support and less interference from outside agencies than virtually any other settlement area in the Amazon, there are indications that processes of settler impoverishment have been set in motion. Maxwell (1980), for example, reports that settlers have been unable to break out of the straitjacket imposed by the combination of a lack of financial resources, declining productivity in the years following forest clearing, and inadequate labor to manage a sustainable production system in the absence of expensive technical improvements. Settlers interviewed as part of our research stated that they found themselves increasingly unable to earn a living through agriculture, and faced having to choose between going elsewhere and seeking off-farm employment in order to earn additional income. The support given settlers under the San Julian project has facilitated the establishment of a production regimen that enables families to satisfy most of their basic food needs, but it has not created conditions whereby agriculture can become a revenue-generating activity.

Background to Settlement in San Julian

Lowland settlement in Bolivia has traditionally been seen by nationals and foreigners as one of the principal means of solving the many social and economic ills associated with life in the highland and valley regions of the country (see Figure 8.2). One of the earliest efforts to translate this perception into practice was made by the Ballivián administration (1841–1847), which established military colonies in Santa Cruz department in order to dismantle an army that had grown beyond the capacity of the state to support it during the constant fighting leading up to and following political independence (Klein 1982:121).

In 1886 Bolivia established a Ministry of Colonization in response to the realization that its sparsely populated lowlands were vulnerable to encroachment by predatory neighbors. It then attempted, unsuccessfully, to recruit North Americans and Europeans to settle in the lowlands with offers of large land grants and easy credit for development. When Brazil annexed large tracts of Amazonian territory in the early part of the century, worries about maintaining control over the region increased. In 1905 the state designated eight areas encircling the eastern lowlands as a "frontier ring," where vulnerable points along international boundaries were to be fortified and settlement was to be encouraged. Because these pronouncements did nothing to link the areas of the frontier ring to the rest of the nation, settlement activity did not follow. In fact the first settlement effort to be undertaken by Bolivia occurred in 1937, when the Busch administration created a colony for Chaco War veterans near the Yapacaní River. By 1940 the project had attracted only about 200 residents and state support ended soon after (Fifer 1982:411; Hess 1980:56).

Serious efforts to settle Bolivia's eastern lowlands did not begin until the Movimiento Nacionalista Revolucionario (Nationalist Revolutionary

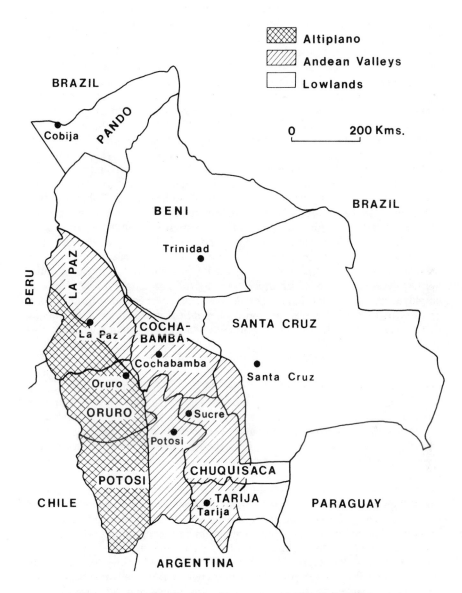

Fig. 8.2   Bolivia: Geographical Regions.

Source: Adapted from Ortiz Lema (1981), Map No. 1.

Movement, or MNR) government assumed power, in 1952. The MNR undertook two initiatives that radically altered the social relations organizing the national economy and stimulated rapid expansion of capitalist agriculture and industry in the eastern lowlands. The first was the Bolivian agrarian reform. Prior to this time, the agricultural economies of the highland and valley regions of the country had been dominated by large manorial estates, which extracted rents in the form of agricultural labor and personal service from resident peasant populations. Under the reform, the estate lands were expropriated and divided among the populations residing on them. Peasants were also relieved of the labor and personal service obligations that had previously restricted their freedom to seek economic opportunities off the estates.

The new freedom of movement and the fact that many families could not meet their minimum subsistence requirements on the lands they had been allotted led many people to seek permanent jobs in Bolivia's cities. Others sought seasonal employment on commercial agricultural enterprises, sometimes outside of the country and increasingly in Bolivia's own eastern lowlands. Greater incorporation into the national economy was accompanied by greater participation in the nation's political life. The populations released from the estates took the lead in organizing peasant trade unions, popular militias, and, in the case of those who found permanent nonagricultural employment, industrial labor movements. All of these institutions have played an important role in shaping the political and economic life of the nation since 1952 (Albó and Barnadas 1984; Carter 1964; Kay 1981; Paz 1983).

The second initiative concerned the eastern lowlands more directly. The MNR government gave high priority to the promotion of capitalist development in this region, particularly in the department of Santa Cruz. It hoped that development of the lowland region would expand economic opportunities for the large numbers of people in the highland and valley regions who continued to live in poverty despite the agrarian reform. Drawing on recommendations for the economic development of Santa Cruz made ten years earlier by a North American delegation (Bohan 1942), President Víctor Paz Estenssoro requested aid from the United States for a variety of projects. The sums received were substantial, and as a result of the aid given for lowland development Bolivia became the world's single largest recipient of economic assistance under the US-sponsored Point Four program. The threat that their property would be expropriated under agrarian reform, combined with the investment opportunities provided by the Point Four program, encouraged large landowners to modernize production on their estates.[5] Point Four provided landowners with access to cheap credit and helped finance the establishment of a machinery pool for land clearing. It also financed the paving of the Santa Cruz–Cochabamba highway, improving access to markets in other regions of Bolivia and facilitating the migration of seasonal wage labor from the highlands and valleys. The program also provided funds for the construction of a sugar mill and alcohol distillery, stimulating sugarcane production.

Coffee, cotton, sugarcane, and rice production expanded rapidly. By the early 1960s Santa Cruz was producing more rice and sugarcane than could be absorbed by the national market. Efforts to export rice proved unsuccessful, so that those with the financial resources to do so concentrated on more profitable crops, such as soybeans and peanuts. Rice became increasingly identified as a smallholders' crop, and those who continued to grow it struggled among themselves for a share of the limited market. Santa Cruz also had become one of South America's important centers of cotton production (Heath 1969:289–299; Hiraoka 1980), although enthusiasm for this crop has tended to wane since 1975, when a precipitous drop in prices exacted a heavy toll on those enterprises involved in its production. This dramatic expansion of capitalist agriculture depended heavily upon seasonal wage labor from the highland and valley regions. While landowners invested in mechanized land clearing and in such inputs as chemical fertilizers and pesticides, they did not experience many pressures to replace labor with capital inputs, due to the low cost of employing seasonal workers in comparison with the costs of importing and maintaining farm machinery. In 1976, agricultural employment fluctuated between 18,000 people in February and 95,000 people in August, the month when the greatest amount of land clearing is done (Rivière d'Arc 1980:158).

Many of the people who originally went to Santa Cruz as seasonal wage laborers remained there as settlers. Census figures show a population increase from 286,145 in the department in 1950 to 715,072 in 1976 (Klein 1982:297). García-Tornell and Querejazú (1984) estimate that since 1950, 135,000 people have migrated permanently to Santa Cruz department from other areas of Bolivia. Such permanent migration was encouraged by a succession of national governments, beginning with the MNR, who on the one hand were concerned about relieving social and economic pressures resulting from the inadequacy of the agrarian reform, and on the other hoped that the infusion of highlanders would undermine strong regionalist and separatist movements found in Santa Cruz (see Heath 1969; Painter 1985; Stearman 1976, 1985a).

The state attempted to encourage both spontaneous and directed settlement of highland and valley peasants in the lowlands. These efforts included radio and leaflet campaigns and visits to peasant communities by government officials, urging people to consider moving to the lowlands as a way of improving their economic situations. Directed settlement projects received support from a number of organizations, including the United Nations, the Inter-American Development Bank, and various private voluntary organizations and church-related agencies. International donor agencies also assisted the government in fostering spontaneous settlement through the construction of roads and bridges, which encouraged continuing penetration of the forest by new settlers and improved the market linkages of those who had already settled. In 1965, Bolivia established the National Colonization Institute (INC), which was charged with formulating general settlement policy and guidelines, administering land allotments, and awarding land titles (see Stearman 1985b:234–239).

The bulk of settlement in Santa Cruz department has been spontaneous. In 1980, the INC reported that 28,712 settlers had arrived in Santa Cruz during the preceding year. Of these, 20,810 were spontaneous settlers, while 6,058 had arrived under the auspices of a directed project. The remaining 1,844 who arrived that year were classified as private settlers, most of them belonging to one of the Japanese or Mennonite colonies, or to other small foreign enclaves that have established themselves in Santa Cruz (Fifer 1982:420, 430–431).

While the state was successful in promoting population movement into the eastern lowlands, both spontaneous and directed settlements brought new kinds of problems. In areas of spontaneous settlement, families tended to disperse along roadways if these had already been built or in the forest if they had not. This complicated the process of economically and equitably providing potable water, schools, and access to markets; and it inhibited the formation of communities that could serve as loci for establishing agroprocessing facilities and off-farm employment opportunities that would add value to settler production and diversify the economic base.

Environmental destruction was widespread in some areas of Santa Cruz. Settlers frequently lack the capital and/or the knowledge to maintain their holdings, and plots cleared at the expense of considerable labor are often overrun with weeds and secondary forest growth. As a result, many plots have been sold to wealthier individuals who had the resources either to bring them under permanent cultivation or to convert them to pasture for cattle raising. As rumors spread about possible future infrastructure-building projects likely to increase land values, speculation has become rampant in some areas. Since, for a number of years after settlement began, there was no mechanism for claiming a legal title, and since, when established, the INC-supervised titling procedure proved slow and unreliable,[6] smallholders who found themselves on land coveted by someone more powerful enjoyed little protection (Stearman 1976:298–301; 1985b:242–245). Lacking labor and capital and faced with an uncertain title situation, many settlers arrived with no intention of establishing permanent cultivation systems. Instead, they "mined" their plots in order to accumulate capital for some other venture, or they established patterns of extensive land use characterized by constant movement into new areas of primary forest (Maxwell 1980:166).

While large areas of land were converted to permanent cattle pasture, the haphazard process of land clearing and consolidation caused other areas to be abandoned from all agricultural use. This, combined with the damage done by large landowners whose heavy equipment compacted the soil in some areas and whose bulldozers scraped away topsoil as part of the clearing process in others, resulted in large tracts of land being transformed from forest into uncultivated scrub brush and shifting sand dune areas in less than 20 years (Crossley 1985:182; Rivière d'Arc 1980:156).

The experience with directed settlement also proved disappointing. While land speculation on the scale associated with some spontaneous settlement areas has not been reported for directed projects, they have been characterized by high rates of settler turnover and parcel abandonment.[7] Directed settlers also were frequently unprepared to deal with weed and secondary forest growth. In addition, project planners did not often consider soil geomorphology, and many areas proved uninhabitable because of flooding during every rainy season (see Pereira and Salinas 1982). Directed projects also found it difficult to organize settler communities to manage their own affairs and defend their interests, and sponsoring institutions were frequently criticized for excessive paternalism that fostered dependency relationships. At the same time, many of the support services they attempted to provide were either inadequate or inappropriate because of poor knowledge of local conditions (Fifer 1982:413–417; Hess 1980:102–116).

Directed projects thus share many of the negative features of spontaneous settlement. In addition, because of the high costs frequently associated with directed projects, spontaneous settlement frequently appears to perform better when subjected to a formal benefit/cost analysis (Nelson 1973). As a result, observers such as Wennergren and Whitaker (1976) have recommended that Bolivian policy should encourage spontaneous settlement and channel state funds into constructing and maintaining access roads that would improve settlers' linkages to regional markets. The reasoning behind such a recommendation is that if settlers are provided with access to markets and kept free of bureaucratic entanglements they will pursue their own interest more effectively than a sponsoring agency can pursue it for them. This assumes, however, that the problems encountered by settlers stem essentially from inadequate project management by sponsoring agencies. It overlooks the fact that settlers are not alone on the frontier, but are competing for access to markets and other development resources with loggers, ranchers, and other interest groups. If all do not enjoy relatively equal access to the institutions that are charged with formulating development policy and allocating resources, then the market relations that develop will reflect and reinforce existing inequities. In Santa Cruz, smallholders have been excluded from regional political power. The issue is not the presence or absence of market and other relations with the regional economy, but the quality of those relations as determined by access to political power. Spontaneous settlement schemes cannot support settlers in representing their interests, and to date sponsored settlement projects have not.

The San Julian Project

The San Julian project attempted to overcome many of the difficulties experienced in previous efforts at both spontaneous and directed settlement.[8] First, it was usually able to insure that potable water, temporary shelter, and some form of access road were in place before settlers arrived. This initial provision of facilities and subsequent efforts by settlers to improve the area have been made easier by the núcleo settlement pattern diagramed in Figure 8.1, which insured relatively equal access by everyone.

Second, the San Julian project provided settlers with a structured orientation program, which taught them how to clear and cultivate the tropical forest. The orientation program was unique in that it relied heavily upon the expertise of local peasants (and migrants from other areas of the country who had substantial experience living in the area) to teach the new arrivals. The orientation program also included a number of measures to encourage settlers to form strong community organizations and begin managing their own day-to-day affairs as quickly as possible. These included providing settlers with reliable and useful information, and bringing locals and immigrants into face-to-face contact, diffusing much of the hostility that frequently characterizes the interactions between the two groups in lowland Bolivia. The orientation was also successful in stimulating the formation of strong community organizations capable of defining and representing settler interests before state institutions such as the INC.[9]

Finally, because much of the San Julian project has been conducted under the direction of a private voluntary organization, it has received economic support over a longer period of time than have most directed settlement efforts in Amazonia. Scudder (1981) has argued that a key problem with many settlement projects has been that they are planned, executed, and evaluated before the patterns of development that will ultimately determine their success or failure emerge. When the project began, in 1972, it was sponsored by the INC, which made a contract with the United Church Committee (CIU) to conduct a settler-orientation program. The CIU was an informal organization composed of representatives from various churches active in supporting settlers in Santa Cruz department. Based upon its experience, it had developed an orientation program intended to help ease the transition to life in the lowlands for migrants from the highlands and valleys.

In 1975, USAID/Bolivia, the INC, and the CIU agreed to coordinate the settlement of San Julian. USAID/Bolivia provided the INC with funds to build roads and wells, to clear land in each community center, and to contract the CIU to provide settlers with guidance and support in establishing a viable production system and strong community organization. In 1979, USAID/Bolivia agreed to support a project to consolidate the gains made by settlers in San Julian. Unhappy with how the INC had managed funds in the previous phase of the project, USAID/Bolivia sought an alternative institution through which it could channel its support. This came in the form of the Integral Development Foundation (FIDES), which was formed by CIU members to give what had been an informal organization legal standing under Bolivian law.

After the consolidation program ended in 1984, FIDES maintained its work center in San Julian, continued to provide support for the improvement of agricultural production, and conducted a program funded by the Inter-American Foundation to attempt to secure legal titles to their lands on behalf of San Julian settlers. FIDES also became involved in a USAID-sponsored project to establish cooperatively organized health clinics in several settlements, including San Julian, and it is a participant in a USAID/Bolivia project to improve the availability of potable water in San Julian

TABLE 8.1   Land Allocation among Major Cash Crops in Santa Cruz
            Department (hectares)

	1979-80	1980-81	1981-82	1982-83
Rice	38,020	39,095	40,000	27,273
Corn	64,392	80,800	56,000	56,908
Sugarcane	55,742	56,129	58,704	55,449
Cotton	24,917	14,371	8,000	3,700
Soybeans	35,000	25,000	40,000	25,997

Source: Adapted from Zambrana and Farrington 1984:31.

and the surrounding area. The interaction between FIDES and donor agencies
has provided San Julian settlers with support over a longer period than
frequently has been the case for planned settlement, while allowing donor
agencies to define discrete projects within the settlement process that could
be carried out within the three-to-five-year time frame they tend to prefer
(see Scudder 1981:92–126, 278).

Production in San Julian

In San Julian, as in much of Santa Cruz department, smallholder agriculture
is based on the cultivation of rice and corn, crops that fill a major portion
of family subsistence requirements and are the principal crops sold by
smallholders with any regularity. Of 58 producers interviewed in the San
Julian project, 94 percent responded that rice was the cultivar to which
they dedicated the largest amount of land, while 73 percent said that corn
is the cultivar on the second largest amount of land. Yucca was rated as
the third most important crop by San Julian settlers.[10]

Rice and corn are also widely grown in Santa Cruz department as a
whole. More hectares are ordinarily dedicated to corn production than to
any other crop, while rice ranks third in area under cultivation, after corn
and sugarcane (Table 8.1).[11] However, while the other major crops listed
are grown by the commercial enterprises whose development has already
been discussed, rice and corn are intimately linked to smallholder production.

These two crops offer smallholders several distinct advantages over
alternatives. First, they have a double utility for settlers, serving as both
cash crops and food crops. Second, although rice is labor intensive, neither
rice nor corn requires technical knowledge or inputs unavailable to house-

holds. Settlers commonly grow both without the benefit of fertilizers, simply clearing an area, planting for two or three years until yields begin to decline, and moving on to newly cleared lands. Finally, because they are relatively nonperishable, both crops are well-suited for cultivation in areas such as San Julian, which are characterized by geographic isolation, scarce transport facilities, and frequent shipping delays.

The disadvantages associated with rice and corn production, however, make them very poor choices as crops upon which to base an agricultural system for settlers. Since the early 1960s, Santa Cruz has produced more rice than the national market could absorb (Heath 1969:289–299; Hiraoka 1980). The problem has been particularly acute since the mid-1970s, as rice production in the department met or exceeded the national demand in seven of the ten years preceding 1984. In 1984, the state rice marketing authority, the Empresa Nacional de Arroz (ENA) estimated production in Santa Cruz to be about 150,000 tons, of which Bolivia's national demand was expected to absorb about 70 percent. Prospects for increasing the size of the market for rice through exports are poor, due to the relatively low quality of Bolivian rice, logistical problems in shipping it to potential buyers, and a saturated international market (Corporación Regional de Desarrollo de Santa Cruz—CORDECRUZ 1984a).

Corn production has similar disadvantages. In 1984, Santa Cruz department produced an estimated 150,000 metric tons, of which national demand was expected to absorb about 100,000. While the departmental development corporation found a theoretical possibility of increasing the demand for corn through export, no institution can be found that is willing to pay producers immediately, without forcing them to wait until the corn is finally sold on the international market (CORDECRUZ 1984b; Farrington 1984:18–19).

Any strategy for increasing the market for agricultural products through export is unlikely to benefit smallholding settlers because of overpricing of the peso on the official market as compared to the unoffical market since the late 1970s (Table 8.2). By law, hard currency obtained through export must be exchanged for pesos at the official rate. However, since production costs reflect the unofficial price of the currency, a producer could easily lose money by attempting to export. In practice, large producers of high-value crops are able to turn this situation to their advantage through strategies such as buying hard currency at the official rate to pay their production costs, reselling it at the unofficial rate, and then borrowing again at the official rate. They also are able to underrepresent the amount of money they have earned through international sales, since they—or orga-nizations representing them—usually control the means to transport and commercialize what they produce. Smallholders, on the other hand, must sell any hard currency they earn at the official rate, but are rarely able to buy at that rate because they do not enjoy the access to officials of Bolivia's Central Bank necessary to secure exemptions from currency regulations. Since they must rely on others to transport and sell what they produce,

TABLE 8.2   Official and Parallel Market Prices of Bolivian
Peso(a)   (Bolivian Pesos = 1 US Dollar)

	Dec. 81(b)	Mar. 82	Aug. 82	Dec. 82	Mar. 83	Aug. 83	Dec. 83	Mar. 84	Aug. 84
Parallel	44	60	174	283	485	800	1,150	2,500	10,000
Official	25	44	44	200	200	200	500	500	2,000

(a) Figures provided for parallel exchange rates are indicative rather than exact values. Due to the extremely rapid devaluation of the currency, the price of the peso changed dramatically within very short periods. For example, in August 1984, the peso began the month at slightly more than 3,000 to the dollar. By mid-month, it was fluctuating between 3,500 and 3,600 to the dollar, when, within a three-day period, its price dropped to more than 10,000 to the dollar.

(b) The official rate of the peso was 25 to the dollar from November 1979 through February 22, 1982.

they also find it more difficult to underreport sales than do large farmers. As shall be discussed presently, these obstacles to export by settlers are symptomatic of more general problems of unequal exchange between markets where production is organized according to different social relations (Griffin 1974).

The problems faced by settlers trying to earn a living through corn and rice production have been growing over a number of years. During the last decade, for example, the prices of these crops have declined in relation to the costs of some agricultural inputs. Table 8.3 indicates changes in the prices of rice and corn, the cost of a day of agricultural labor power, and the cost of hiring a tractor for the period 1972–1982.

Drawing upon these figures, Table 8.4 indicates changes in the number of kilograms of rice and corn that had to be sold in order to pay for a day of agricultural labor power and for an hour of tractor use during 1972–1982. As may be seen, the prices of corn and rice have declined in relation to the cost of a day of agricultural labor power. In seven of the ten years recorded, the amount of rice required to finance the purchase of a day of agricultural labor power increased. Over the course of the decade as a whole, this increase has occurred at a mean annual rate of 6.4 percent. The amount of corn required to purchase a day of agricultural labor power increased in six of the ten years recorded, with a mean annual increase of 4.4 percent during the overall period.

The amounts of both corn and rice required to purchase the use of a tractor for an hour increased in five of the ten years recorded and declined

TABLE 8.3   Prices of Rice and Corn and Costs of Key Inputs, 1972-1982

Year	Rice pesos/qq(a)	Corn pesos/qq	Ag. Labor pesos/day	Tractor pesos/hr.
1972	134	23	17.5	65.0
1973	164	47	30.0	79.0
1974	453	79	40.0	96.5
1975	439	79	45.0	113.0
1976	394	82	55.0	115.0
1977	358	88	55.5	150.0
1978	415	87	60.5	160.0
1979	506	74	85.5	160.0
1980	880	190	113.5	300.0
1981	1,030	160	150.0	250.0
1982	2,050	433	500.0	760.0

(a) qq=quintal.   One quintal = 100 pounds.

Source: Adapted from Lawrence-Jones 1984:7.

in the remaining five. Overall, the price of rice increased at a mean annual rate of 2.6 percent in relation to the costs a producer would have to pay to use a tractor, while the price of corn increased at a mean annual rate of 4.5 percent in relation to the cost of using a tractor. That rice and corn prices fared better in relation to the costs of using a tractor than they did in relation to the costs of hiring a day of labor power should not, however, be interpreted as suggesting that substituting capital for labor power offers a solution for smallholding corn and rice producers. Our research in San Julian indicated that whatever the relationship between corn and rice prices and tractor costs, the absolute expenditure required to purchase the use of a tractor remains well beyond the means of virtually all settlers. There is also evidence to suggest that reported tractor costs are artificially low. Since the 1950s, organizations ranging from international donor agencies to locally based cooperatives have subsidized the operation and maintenance costs of tractors in order to make them more accessible to producers. In fact, FIDES has been the only organization providing tractors for use by farmers that has consistently attempted to charge prices that reflected their true operating and maintenance costs. As a result of these subsidies, the costs of tractor use reported by many organizations are low.

As a result of the overproduction of corn and rice, prices that San Julian settlers receive for their crops are low in absolute terms. During June–August 1984, for example, the mean price received for hulled rice was 38,875 Bolivian pesos per *quintal* (100 pounds), while unhulled rice brought

TABLE 8.4   Changing Value of Rice and Corn in Relation to Key
            Inputs,   1972-1982

Year	Kgs Rice/		Kgs Corn/	
	day labor	hour tractor	day labor	hour tractor
1972	6.0	22.3	34.3	127.5
1973	8.4	22.2	29.1	76.6
1974	4.1	9.8	23.3	56.2
1975	4.7	11.8	26.2	65.8
1976	6.4	13.4	30.8	64.5
1977	7.1	19.3	28.9	78.1
1978	6.7	17.7	32.1	84.9
1979	7.8	14.5	53.0	99.1
1980	5.9	15.7	27.4	72.5
1981	6.7	11.2	43.1	71.9
1982	11.2	17.1	53.1	80.7
Yrs. of increasing value of crop(a)	3	5	4	5
Yrs. of decreasing value of crop(b)	7	5	6	5
Mean % change in value of crop per unit of input per yr.(c)	-6.4	2.6	-4.5	4.5

(a) Value of rice (or corn) increases when number of kilograms
per day's labor cost (or per tractor hour) decreases.

(b) Value of rice (or corn) decreases when number of kilograms
per day's labor cost (or per tractor hour) increases.

(c) Logarithmic rate of change.   Negative result indicates
decline in crop value (input costs increasing more rapidly
than price of crop); positive result indicates increase in
crop value.

Source: Based on Lawrence-Jones 1984:8.

an average price of 66,231 pesos per *fanega* (1 fanega = 177 kilograms). The mean price received by producers in San Julian for corn was 12,000 pesos per quintal.[12] These prices are put into perspective when compared to the cost of transporting corn and rice to market. The fee officially recommended by the truck drivers' union for transporting goods over dirt roads such as those linking San Julian with the nearest market center, the city of Montero, 54 kilometers from the entrance to the project, was 39.37 pesos per quintal per kilometer. This meant that settlers at the project entrance were paying 18 percent of the selling price of their corn and between 5 and 11 percent of the selling price of their rice in transport costs alone. Producers located in the interior of the project were paying 41 percent of the selling price of their corn and between 13 and 26 percent of the selling price of their rice, if they were in fact able to locate a driver who would haul their grain at the recommended price. The settlers we interviewed reported that drivers take advantage of producers' anxieties to sell their grain by charging prices well in excess of those recommended. All settlers who reported selling rice also reported paying between 35 and 50 percent of the selling price of their harvest in transport charges.

Settler Responses to Unfavorable Prices

Settlers have responded to the unfavorable market conditions in several ways. With the support of FIDES, the Food and Agriculture Organization of the United Nations (FAO), and other institutions, some settlers have experimented with alternative crops. While they have identified a number of fruits and vegetables that can be cultivated successfully, these efforts have not had a positive economic impact. Generally either the goods do not survive the long, rough trip out of the settlement area, or, once out of the area, the processing and marketing facilities needed for successful commercialization are not available.

Other settlers have attempted to supplement agricultural production by establishing small businesses. Our research team surveyed 39 of the 44 settlement communities established under the San Julian project and found that ten (26 percent) contain shops where skilled or semi-skilled trades are practiced. These included rice hulling businesses, brickyards, and mechanic shops. Small retail stores were found in 23 (59 percent) of the communities surveyed; most of them sold general merchandise, such as processed foods, beer and soft drinks, hardware, and household goods.[13] Some observers have commented upon the growth of small businesses as a sign of commercial vitality in San Julian (cf. Solem et al. 1985; Ward 1984). To the extent that this growth results from the investment of revenues earned through the sale of agricultural products in off-farm employment, such assessments are accurate, but interviews with settlers indicated that many of them established businesses because they had been unable to support themselves through agriculture.

All of the families who started businesses had financed them from their own resources, and a few had supplemented these with small loans obtained from the San Julian Multipurpose Cooperative. Nearly all respondents reported that they had been forced to go into business as a result of inadequate incomes from agriculture. The only exceptions were among the owners of rice-hulling businesses, who had seen providing this service as an opportunity to make money shortly after their arrival in the project. However, because there are few income-earning activities for settlers, the population upon which these businesses depend exerts a very weak demand for even basic goods and services. As a result, with the exception of the rice hullers, who have something of a captive clientele, respondents report that their efforts to improve their living standards through business ventures have been largely a failure.

Third, some settlers have responded to the lack of economic opportunity in agriculture by declining to sell their produce and withdrawing into subsistence production. While this approach may spare settlers the frustration and financial losses associated with attempting to sell in a hostile market environment, it solves no problems and creates some new ones. In the first place, even basic subsistence requirements must be met through a relatively large number of cash expenditures. For example, the wells provided by the San Julian project require frequent servicing to continue functioning. This involves fairly regular expenditures to have parts repaired and replaced, and occasional expenditures to bring a technician to the community to effect major repairs. All plans to improve the region's potable water supply contemplate financial contributions from settlers. Similarly, a current plan to improve the low quality of health care in the region, which is sponsored by USAID/Bolivia and in which FIDES is a participating institution, calls for the establishment of a series of health posts and rural hospitals to be organized as self-financing cooperatives with the settlers as members. Settlers also find that they must pay for services that would be free elsewhere in the country. For example, because of the physical isolation and rustic living conditions, school teachers frequently do not stay in the area for very long. In several cases, settlers have attempted to respond to this problem by hiring a teacher and running their own community school.

Finally, the production system itself requires cash expenditures that settlers did not have to make in the highland and valley regions from which they came. For example, avian cholera is endemic to the region, and families must choose between systematic vaccination of all their fowl or accepting that they will be wiped out periodically by an epidemic. Families frequently find themselves obligated to buy pesticides or fungicides to save a harvest, or to rent a chain saw or a team of draft animals to clear and cultivate enough land to meet their subsistence needs. Thus, the level of technology required to satisfy basic household subsistence requires cash expenditures that preclude long-term withdrawal from marketing agricultural production. The fact that large numbers of settlers nevertheless attempt to follow this route, reducing the capacity of the population to exert a demand for goods and services, places a damper on the efforts of others to increase their incomes by establishing businesses.

A fourth response of settlers to the unprofitability of selling corn and rice is by attempting to increase the total amount of product they offer for sale. To accomplish this, they must intensify labor, giving rise to the self-exploitation described by Chayanov (1966). When this occurs, the marginal productivity of labor decreases as labor inputs are added, so that the average productivity of labor also declines. When large numbers of farmers adopt this strategy, the increased supply results in lower prices, causing producer revenues to drop (given relatively inelastic demand) and creating pressures for additional intensification of labor (cf. Geertz 1963; Barlett 1982).

In lowland Bolivia, as in much of Amazonia, it is relatively easy to acquire new lands simply by moving into an unused area and beginning to cultivate. In contrast, it is difficult to increase production by intensifying labor inputs, for while large amounts of labor power are required to clear an area for cultivation, even larger amounts are required to control weed and secondary forest growth if the land is to be kept cleared for permanent cultivation or conversion to pasture.

In San Julian, we found that in our sample of 58 settlers, forest land was being cleared at a mean rate of 3.48 hectares per household annually. Of the 58 settlers interviewed, 26 (45 percent) had kept some land cleared for conversion to pasture. Among the 26 who were establishing pasture areas, the amount of pasture land was increasing at a mean rate of 0.57 hectares per household annually.[14] Settlers unanimously reported that labor availability is the limiting factor on their ability to clear more land and convert larger areas into pasture, given the level of technology at which they must work.

Settlers find that their labor resources are taxed by the normal demands of agriculture in the tropical forest. Therefore, in order to increase the total volume of production they place on the market, they turn to more extensive land use. Settlers who adopt this strategy fell large areas of forest with no intention of keeping it in production, and as soon as yields begin to fall, they move into a new area and begin the process again.

In an area like San Julian, this extensive approach offers producers some short-term advantages over intensification. In the first place, it does permit a family to increase the total volume of grain that it can place on the market. Yields per hectare are lower than when smaller areas are cleared more carefully as part of a longer term land use strategy, but by farming extensively a family can increase its total production without additional labor resources. Second, in addition to creating higher gross cash income, having a larger quantity of a product to market makes a farmer more attractive as a customer for transporters looking to minimize the amount of driving they have to do on the poor roads of the project area in order to fill their trucks.

Over the long run, however, these apparent advantages prove to be illusory. In San Julian, as elsewhere, increasing production in response to falling prices is at best a short-term solution to a family's revenue problems. In addition, the practice leaves behind large areas of land with no ground cover to protect it from wind and water erosion and leaching of the soil by the sun. Even when declining soil quality is not a problem, the land remains essentially unusable until the forest reclaims the area from weeds and secondary growth, as the labor requirements for bringing this kind of land back into production make it very undesirable.

In San Julian, we found that 4 of the 58 settlers we interviewed (7 percent) were engaging in this pattern of extensive land use, with the areas each cleared annually ranging from 9 to 35.5 hectares. That the percentage is so low reflects the efforts of project officials to screen out people unlikely to become permanent settlers during the orientation program, and the emphasis placed on teaching appropriate cultivation techniques to new arrivals to the lowlands. Unless economic opportunities improve, however, the pressures on settlers to move toward this strategy can be expected to increase. Settlers interviewed reported that, as their economic situation worsens, they are beginning to consider some form of more extensive land use.

Discussion and Conclusions

Several factors have placed smallholding settlers in an unfavorable exchange relationship with the larger economy. When the MNR began to foster capitalist development in Santa Cruz, it used agrarian reform laws permitting the expropriation of landholdings as a means of discouraging political opposition rather than as a tool for insuring equitable access to infrastructural facilities such as roads and markets. This allowed large landowners to monopolize access to these facilities as part of the modernization of their estates. By permitting a continuing domination of the regional economy by elites—without taking specific steps to enfranchise settlers—state agricultural policy prevented settlers from representing their own interests in order to gain access to hard currency, credit, and inputs under conditions comparable to those available to large landowners.

San Julian settlers are becoming increasingly impoverished because they depend upon a production system based on the cultivation of low-value crops that are intended to satisfy family consumption requirements, and to be marketed as their major source of cash income. The unprofitability of the crops, which precludes settlers from investing in capital inputs on their own farms or in improved infrastructural facilities at the level of the San Julian area as a whole, also prevents them from breaking free of the constraints of the production system. The low level of revenues from agriculture also means that settler incomes exert insufficient demand for stores and shops to become profitable, or to attract investment in the area from elsewhere.

Given the lack of money to invest in labor-saving technology, settlers are also constrained from overcoming the limitations of the production system through intensifying the exploitation of their own labor power. Because more labor is required to maintain an area than to clear a new one, and because the productivity of an area tends to decline sharply in a cleared area after a few years unless fertilizers are applied, families attempting to establish permanent cropping systems or pasture for livestock frequently find that their labor resources are inadequate to accomplish this and to grow enough food for their consumption requirements at the same time. The combination of agriculture with off-farm employment is difficult because the limited employment opportunities are tied to the regional agricultural cycle, and compete directly with the labor requirements of the farm.

Underlying these dynamics is the unequal exchange relationship that characterizes the links between the settler production system and the rest of the regional economy. The defining condition of unequal exchange is the declining price of settler production in relation to the cost of labor power. What is significant about unequal exchange is not its presence or absence, although for some observers this in itself may be an issue, but the fact that as we attempt to explain the relationship we are forced to examine how San Julian fits into the larger economic system. This is a different approach from that of development project planners and evaluators who limit their considerations to questions of project-level design and implementation. It is also different from more regional approaches that reduce the question of linkages of settlers to the rest of the economy to whether roads, markets, and other empirical manifestations of such linkages are present, and that avoid such key issues as the nature of the linkages, and how they came to be.

Failure to look beyond the level of project design and implementation has caused evaluators to interpret the diversification strategies of households seeking to cope with impoverishment as evidence of the investment of agricultural revenues that exceed the levels needed to meet consumption requirements. Even observers who are fortunate enough to conduct long-term research may not recognize the difference between the two trajectories— one headed toward pauperization and environmental destruction, the other linked to capital accumulation—if they confine their analyses to the level of individual projects. It is the historical development of the qualitative relations between San Julian and the rest of the region that provides the basis for interpreting the empirical manifestations of economic change described here.

The class relations that characterize a region such as northeastern Santa Cruz are the result of continuing historical processes. Thinking explicitly about where smallholding settlers will fit into the structure that these relations delimit, and supporting settlers in competing on an equal footing with other class interests, is essential if settlement is to be a means of improving rural living standards, and if it is to be an environmentally sustainable approach to development.

Notes

1. The research upon which this chapter is based was sponsored by the Cooperative Agreement on Human Settlement and Natural Resource Systems Analysis of the

U.S. Agency for International Development, Clark University, and the Institute for Development Anthropology. The views expressed herein are those of the author and do not necessarily reflect the positions of any of the above-mentioned institutions. The author thanks Jane Collins, Peter Little, and Allyn MacLean Stearman for reading and commenting upon previous drafts of this chapter. Vivian Carlip reviewed and made important corrections on the accompanying tables.

2. Under its 1974 loan to Bolivia for Sub-Tropical Land Development (Project No. 511-T-050), USAID/Bolivia planned expenditures of $8,324,400.00 for the San Julian project. The funds were to be used for the construction of penetration roads, access trails, wells, health posts, credit for settlers, an information and orientation program, an agricultural service center, a resource survey, and administrative costs over the period 1975–1981. At the time the final evaluation of the project was published, in January 1985, actual expenditures in each of these areas still had not been determined. USAID/Bolivia also sponsored a Consolidation Project (Project No. 511-0514) to help insure that gains made by settlers under the original project would not be lost after it ended. Planned expenditures for the project over the period 1979–1984 were $1,480,936.00, of which $956,485.00 had been spent when the final evaluation was published (Solem et al. 1985: Appendix B, 1–4).

3. See Scudder (1981:142–151) for a discussion of how smallholders in settlement areas around the world frequently find themselves trapped in a production system that satisfies most family food needs, but generates no revenue.

4. For discussion of agriculture and off-farm employment competing for the limited labor resources of smallholders, see Collins' article in this volume.

5. In fact, little property was expropriated in lowland Bolivia as access to the abundant land resources never became a political issue. Because lowland estates claimed large extensions that could be shown to be unutilized or underutilized, and because these claims were recognized more often by custom than by any legally recognized titling procedure, the estates were subject to expropriation under the agrarian reform law. However, rather than actually expropriating estates, the MNR chose to use the threat of expropriation as a means of discouraging political opposition (see Heath 1969:291–295).

6. To date, the INC has not awarded any titles in the San Julian project, for example. Instead settlers receive a "certificate of possession," the value of which has not been challenged in a court of law by someone with a conflicting claim. Theoretically, settlers can trade the certificates in for a legal title, but none has yet successfully completed the complex bureaucratic process, which involves multiple trips to the cities of Santa Cruz and La Paz. FIDES has received support from the Inter-American Foundation to provide settlers with legal and logistical aid in securing titles. How successful they will be in this effort remains to be seen.

7. That land speculation has been less of a factor in directed projects may have to do with their being located in more remote, less desirable areas. It certainly does not have to do with a more secure tenure situation, as the INC-directed titling process is just as slow and unreliable in the directed areas as in the spontaneous ones.

8. The experiences that led to the innovations attempted at San Julian are described in detail by Hess (1980:102–116) and recounted in Painter et al. (1984:35–38). Taylor (1983) also describes how the San Julian project attempted to improve upon the experiences of previous settlement projects through the formation of the San Julian Multipurpose Cooperative. Run by the settlers themselves with a minimum of outside technical support, the cooperative sells agricultural inputs to settlers at wholesale prices, purchases rice from settlers, then processes and sells it on their behalf, and attempts to provide settlers with support in the areas of credit and supplies.

•

9. Perez-Crespo (1985:5–6) describes how settlers rely heavily upon their community organizations to define and defend their rights to land. Communities grant land rights to those people they have defined as members. Access to land is an expression of membership in a group of people as well as an economic relation to a productive resource. This indicates that the settlers regard the community as the true owner of the lands they have claimed. Thus, while land is officially viewed as individually owned private property, settler behavior frequently appears to be guided by notions of community ownership. The strength of the communities in San Julian derives from two factors. One is its orientation program's emphasis on participatory institutions. Another is that people who arrive from the highland and valley regions of the country, representing about 90 percent of settlers, come with considerable experience in the organization and administration of peasant and industrial unions. See also Blanes et al. (1984:170–178) for a discussion of this point.

10. All the settlers interviewed had farms of 50 hectares in size, in accordance with the policy of the INC.

11. While rice is the most widely grown crop among San Julian settlers, corn is the most widely grown in the department as a whole. Two factors may account for the greater relative importance of corn outside of San Julian. First, as one moves south from the settlement area, the climate becomes too dry for successful rice cultivation. Second, in addition to being marketed for human consumption, large quantities of corn are sold to enterprises that produce balanced feed mixes for livestock.

12. For sales of hulled rice, $n=8$ and the standard deviation is 10,426 pesos. For unhulled rice, $n=13$ with a standard deviation of 9,567 pesos. In the case of corn, which is sold dried and removed from the cob, $n=14$ and the standard deviation is 2,746 pesos.

13. For a detailed description of commercial activity and the growth of urban functions in San Julian, see Painter et al. 1984:14–18.

14. The standard deviation for the mean annual rate at which families are clearing forest for cultivation is 5.18, and the standard deviation for the mean rate at which pasture is being established is 0.8. These figures vary somewhat from those presented in Painter et al. (1984:14) because the sample discussed here contains additional cases, which had not been tabulated when the original report was written. The change does not affect our original interpretation, however.

References

Albó, Xavier, and Joseph Barnadas
   1984   La cara campesina de nuestra historia. La Paz: Unitas.
Barlett, Peggy F.
   1982   Agricultural Choice and Change: Decision Making in a Costa Rican Community. New Brunswick, NJ: Rutgers University Press.
Blanes J., José, Fernando Calderón G., Jorge Dandler H., Julio Prudencio H., and Luis Lanza G.
   1984   Migración rural-rural: el caso de las colonias. *In* Tras nuevas raices. Pp. 53–252. La Paz: Ministerio de Planeamiento y Coordinación.
Bohan, Merwin
   1942   Misión económica de los Estados Unidos en Bolivia. La Paz: U.S. Embassy.
Carter, William E.
   1964   Aymara Communities and the Bolivian Agrarian Reform. Social Sciences Monograph No. 24. Gainesville, FL: University of Florida Press.

Castro, Robert J.
1978   San Julian and Chane-Piray Colonization. Project Evaluation Report submitted to USAID/Bolivia.
Chayanov, A. V.
1966   The Theory of Peasant Economy. D. Thorner, R. E. F. Smith and B. Kerblay, eds. Homewood, IL: Irwin.
Collins, Jane L.
1986   Smallholder Settlement of Tropical South America: The Social Causes of Ecological Destruction. Human Organization 45(1):1–10.
CORDECRUZ
1984a   Arroz boliviano. Boletín Informativo Agropecuario, Departamento de Comercialización Agropecuaria, Corporación Regional de Desarrollo de Santa Cruz 1:3–4.
1984b   Maíz: enfrentando una sobreproducción. Boletín Informativo Agropecuario, Departamento de Comercialización, Agropecuaria, Corporación Regional de Desarrollo de Santa Cruz 1:3–4.
Crossley, J. Colin
1985   Innovations in Colonizing Bolivian Amazonia. *In* The Frontier After a Decade of Colonization. Change in the Amazon Basin. Vol. 2. John Hemming, ed. Manchester: University of Manchester Press.
Curtis, Ronald
1978   Overview of Project Evaluation Study: Sub-Tropical Lands Development Project. Report prepared for the U.S. Agency for International Development, Washington, DC.
Deere, Carmen Diana, and Alain de Janvry
1979   A Conceptual Framework for the Empirical Analysis of Peasants. American Journal of Agricultural Economics 61:601–611.
Farrington, John
1984   El desarrollo de los precios mayoristas de los principales productos agropecuarios en el departamento de Santa Cruz. Boletín Informativo Agropecuario, Departamento de Comercialización Agropecuaria, Corporación Regional de Desarrollo de Santa Cruz 1(7):18–27.
Fifer, J. Valerie
1982   The Search for a Series of Small Successes: Frontiers of Settlement in Eastern Bolivia. Journal of Latin American Studies 14:407–432.
García-Tornel, Carlos, and Maria Elena Querejazú
1984   Migraciones internas permanentes. *In* Tras nuevas raices. La Paz: Ministerio de Planeamiento y Coordinación.
Geertz, Clifford
1963   Agricultural Involution. Berkeley, CA: University of California Press.
Griffin, Keith
1974   The Political Economy of Agrarian Change: An Essay on the Green Revolution. London: McMillan.
Heath, Dwight B.
1969   Land Reform and Social Revolution in the Bolivian Oriente. *In* Land Reform and Social Revolution in Bolivia. Dwight B. Heath, Charles J. Erasmus, and Hans C. Beuchler, eds. Pp. 241–363. New York, NY: Praeger Publishers.
Hess, David
1978   Adaptation to a New Environment: Pioneer Migration in San Julian. Paper presented to the 77th Annual Meeting of the American Anthropological Association, Los Angeles, California.

1980   Pioneering in San Julian: A Study of Adaptive Strategy Formation by Migrant Farmers in Eastern Bolivia. Ph.D. dissertation, University of Pittsburgh.

Hiraoka, Mario
1980   Settlement and Development of the Upper Amazon: The East Bolivian Example. Journal of Developing Areas 14:327–347.

Kay, Cristobal
1981   América Latina: hacia la agricultura capitalista. Historia y Sociedad 24:71–88.

Klein, Herbert
1982   Bolivia: Evolution of a Multiethnic Society. New York, NY: Oxford University Press.

Lawrence-Jones, W.
1984   La carrera de los precios y la investigación agropecuaria. Boletín Informativo Agropecuario, Departamento de Comercialización Agropecuaria, Corporación Regional de Desarrollo de Santa Cruz 1(8):6–8.

Locatelli, Eduardo
1978   Evaluation of the Colonization Project in San Julian. Report prepared for the U.S. Agency for International Development, Washington, DC.

Maxwell, Simon
1980   Marginalized Colonists to the North of Santa Cruz: Avenues of Escape from the Barbecho Crisis. In Land, People, and Planning in Contemporary Amazonia. Françoise Barbira-Scazzocchio, ed. Pp. 162–170. Cambridge: Cambridge University Centre of Latin American Studies.

Nelson, Michael
1973   The Development of Tropical Lands. Baltimore, MD: Johns Hopkins University Press.
1978   Evaluation. Chane-Pirai and San Julian Colonization Projects. Report of the Regional Development Specialist submitted to USAID/Bolivia, La Paz.

Ortíz Lema, Edgar
1981   Macrozonificación y densidades poblacionales: migración y colonización en Bolivia. Tarija, Bolivia: Asociación Villamontes Sachapera, Corporación Regional de Desarrollo de Tarija.

Painter, Michael
1985   Ethnicity and Social Class Formation in the Bolivian Lowlands. Working Paper 16. Binghamton, NY: Institute for Development Anthropology.

Painter, Michael, and William Partridge
1986   Lowland Settlement in San Julian, Bolivia. In The Human Ecology of Tropical Land Settlement in Latin America. William Partridge and Debra Schumann, eds. Boulder, CO: Westview Press (forthcoming).

Painter, Michael, Carlos A. Perez-Crespo, Martha Llanos Albornóz, Susan Hamilton, and William Partridge
1984   New Lands Settlement and Regional Development: The Case of San Julian, Bolivia. Working Paper 15. Binghamton, NY: Institute for Development Anthropology.

Paz, Danilo
1983   Estructura agraria boliviana. La Paz: Librería Editorial Popular.

Pereira, Francisco, and Jose G. Salinas
1982   General Evaluation of the Agricultural Potential of the Bolivian Amazon. In Amazonia: Agricultural and Land Use Research. Susana Hecht, ed. Pp. 17–31. Cali, Colombia: Centro Internacional de Agricultura Tropical.

Perez-Crespo, Carlos
1985   Resource Competition and Human Settlement in the San Julian Project of Bolivia. Development Anthropology Network 3(1):3-8.
Rivière d'Arc, Helene
1980   Public and Private Agricultural Policies in Santa Cruz (Bolivia). *In* Land, People, and Planning in Contemporary Amazonia. Françoise Barbira-Scazzocchio, ed. Pp. 154–161. Cambridge: Cambridge University Centre of Latin American Studies.
Scudder, Thayer
1981   The Development Potential of New Lands Settlement in the Tropics and Subtropics: A Global State-of-the-Art Evaluation with Specific Emphasis on Policy Implications. Washington, DC: Agency for International Development.
Solem, Richard Ray, Richard J. Greene, David W. Hess, Carol Bradford Ward, and Peter Leigh Taylor
1985   Bolivia: Integrated Rural Development in a Colonization Setting. AID Project Impact Evaluation Report No. 57. Washington, DC: U.S. Agency for International Development.
Stearman, Allyn MacLean
1976   The Highland Migrant in Lowland Bolivia: Regional Migration and the Department of Santa Cruz. Ph.D. dissertation, University of Florida.
1978   San Julian Colonization Project Evaluation Study. Subtropical Lands Development Project. Report submitted to USAID/Bolivia, La Paz.
1980   San Julian—Bolivia's Newest Experiment in Colonization. El Dorado 4(1):28–54.
1983   Forest to Pasture: Frontier Settlement in the Bolivian Lowlands. *In* The Dilemma of Amazonian Development. Emilio F. Moran, ed. Pp. 51–63. Boulder, CO: Westview Press.
1985a   Camba and Kolla: Migration and Development in Santa Cruz, Bolivia. Gainesville, FL: University Presses of Florida.
1985b   Colonization in Santa Cruz, Bolivia: A Comparative Study of the Yapacaní and San Julian Projects. *In* Frontier Expansion in Amazonia. Marianne Schmink and Charles Wood, eds. Pp. 231–260. Gainesville, FL: University Presses of Florida.
Taylor, Peter Leigh
1983   The San Julian Multipurpose Cooperative: An Experience in Adaptation through Participation. Santa Cruz, Bolivia: Fundación Integral de Desarrollo.
Ward, Carol Bradford
1984   Settling Bolivia's Lowlands. Horizons (Summer):13–15.
Wennergren, E. Boyd, and Morris D. Whitaker
1976   Investment in Access Roads and Spontaneous Colonization: Additional Evidence from Bolivia. Land Economics 52(1):88–95.
Zambrana, Róger, and John Farrington
1984   Estudio del abastecimiento de insumos agropecuarios en el departamento de Santa Cruz. Santa Cruz: Departamento de Comercialización Agropecuaria, Unidad de Programas Rurales y Agropecuarios, Corporación Regional de Desarrollo.

PART THREE

Changing Rights to Land and Other Resources

9

Land Use Conflicts
in the Agricultural/Pastoral
Borderlands: The Case of Kenya

Peter D. Little

Introduction

Early studies of the interactions between pastoral and agricultural land use in Africa emphasized the symbiotic, rather than the competitive dimensions. Excellent analyses were made of the complementary linkages between herder and farming communities that, in some cases, were strong enough to suggest treating them as a single analytical unit (Scott 1984). The positive ties took the form of reciprocal labor arrangements, exchanges of agricultural products for livestock products, and exchanges of organic fertilizer (manure) for post-harvest fodder. While not discounting the importance of complementary relations today, recent studies document increased pastoralist/cultivator competition over land and other resources. This occurs especially when irrigation is developed in strategic pastoral zones, such as river basins, or when dryland farmers migrate onto prime dry season grazing reserves (Campbell 1986; Ibrahim 1984). Such changes constrict the pastoralists' territory, result in the overuse of certain range areas, and increase tensions between herders and farmers that can erupt at times into violence (Evangelou 1984; Shepherd 1984).

Although the focus of research has changed, studies of pastoral/agricultural relations remain couched in the same analytical framework. The model is based on a herder/farmer dichotomy drawn along ethnic lines and phrased, for example, in terms of Kikuyu farmer versus Maasai pastoralist (Kenya) (Campbell 1984), or Hausa cultivator versus FulBe herder (West Africa) (Schultz 1981). Differences and conflicts that are emphasized are inter-group, rather than intra-group. Thus, land tenure and land use problems in pastoral areas are seen as stemming from outside factors, such as farmer encroachment, rather than from processes within the pastoral community. Following this line of reasoning, one might suggest policies that further differentiate farmer and herder groups (in the Niger case, a zonal policy not permitting cultivation above a certain latitude [Swift 1982]) or that legitimize, vis-à-vis outsiders, pastoral claims to land—in the Kenya case, group registration of land by herders.

This chapter supplements the herder/farmer ("encroaching farmer") model of land use problems by looking at two other sources of conflict, the "cultivating herder" and the absentee herd owner. Unlike the encroaching farmer model, the latter two models, whose categories of actors may be ethnically similar to the herder (i.e., "insiders"), draw attention to local processes, including increased social differentiation, changes in land and water rights, and local competition and conflict among herders themselves. I examine these three sources of land use problems in Kenya, drawing on my own research in Baringo District (1980–1981, 1984, 1985)[1] and on other recent studies of pastoralism in Kenya. I argue that each of these sets of actors—the encroaching farmer, the cultivating herder, and the absentee herd owner—has implications for natural resource use. The chapter concludes with a discussion of the policy implications of the Kenya material and suggests that the complexity of land use problems requires policy changes at the local, regional, and national levels.

Historical Context of Pastoral Land-Use Problems

Several major historical experiences have contributed to the present situation in Kenya's pastoral regions.[2] The most important of these was colonialism, and its effects on herders were considerable:

> In the early years of colonialism, the predominant attitude of government toward the pastoralists was to pacify them and to maintain law and order. Fixed boundaries were therefore drawn with little regard to seasonal variation and the needs of the people for pasture. The establishment of native reserves with rigid boundaries undermined the intricate marketing networks that had previously existed between neighboring agriculturalists and pastoralists. Furthermore, alienation of land for European settlement and later the creation of game parks deprived some of the people of their pastures (Migot-Adholla and Little 1981:45).

Pastoral groups, like the Nandi and Maasai who inhabited the higher, better-watered areas, were particularly vulnerable. In the early twentieth century, the Maasai alone lost more than 5,000 square kilometers to European settlement, including the Laikipia plateau, Uasin Gishu, and large parts of the central Rift Valley. In the case of the Nandi, large-scale military expeditions were conducted against them to secure land for the Kenya-Uganda railroad.

The advent of colonialism altered the territorial boundaries of pastoral groups even where there was no appropriation of land for settlers. The Laikipiak Maasai, for example, were relocated from Isiolo, which allowed the Borana to occupy the area (Hjort 1979:20), and punitive efforts against the Turkana opened the way for the Pokot to claim most of north Baringo (Little 1984:46). Tugen and Il Chamus herders, in turn, benefited from the forced removal of the Maasai from central and south Baringo; while the

Samburu permanently settled large parts of the Leroghi plateau after the evacuation of Maasai from the area (Sobania 1979:44). The current map of herding groups in Kenya only remotely approximates their distribution prior to colonialism.

Following the pacification effort and the transfer of certain rich pastoral lands to Europeans, the colonial stance toward pastoral groups was one of "benign neglect" (cf. Migot-Adholla 1981). The remaining pastoral areas were generally isolated and far removed from European settlement. They were perceived to be of little value to either the Colony or European settlers because, among other factors, African labor for European farms came mainly from farming areas. Most pastoral lands were held in trust by the groups themselves,[3] and the government rarely intervened other than during times of famine and drought, or when conflicts arose between pastoralists and Europeans. The latter usually occurred when pastoralists moved their cattle to European-controlled grazing areas, or when stock diseases in the pastoral areas threatened settlers' ranches. The colonial state did maintain, however, strict market quarantines (due to animal disease) in pastoral areas, which restricted the selling of surplus animals. This accelerated the overstocking and overuse of rangelands.

The onset of independence in Kenya (1963) brought a new dimension to land use conflicts in the pastoral areas. African cultivators began increasingly to encroach on the better-watered grazing zones. The native reserve policy in the colonial period discouraged rural-to-rural migration (important exceptions are found in Kajiado District; see Campbell 1981), but with independence and the ensuing political dominance of agriculturalists, such as the Kikuyu, cultivators were permitted greater freedom of movement. With support from the state and, in some cases, from international finance organizations (see World Bank 1975), they began to settle in range areas. The lands often bordered existing agricultural areas and were usually an integral component of the overall grazing system. At present almost 30 percent of the population of Kajiado District, the largest Maasai district in Kenya, is Kikuyu, which is a good indicator of the extent of agricultural encroachment in the area. Further evidence of this trend comes from the population census of 1979, showing that pastoral districts including Narok, Tana River, West Pokot, and Kajiado Districts are among the most attractive for rural migrants (Dietz 1985).[4]

Land tenure reform, which had its origins in the colonial period (Swynnerton 1954), has been aggressively pursued by the Kenya government. The pastoral areas present a predicament to the policy of private landholdings, since they do not easily lend themselves to subdivision. Dry season pastures and water points are widely dispersed in range areas, making privatization impractical as well as disastrous to production systems that require mobility. The registration of land on a group basis ("group ranches") was seen as a compromise between the state's preference for private land ownership and the indigenous system of communal tenure (see Grandin, forthcoming). The group ranch became a mechanism by which herders acquired the legal means to defend their lands against migrant farmers (Galaty 1980:165).

The 1970s and 1980s have witnessed marked changes in pastoral areas, including prolonged droughts and famines and additional losses of grazing lands, that have left them impoverished and vulnerable to environmental assault. The differences between the past and present are so striking that some suggest a "new pastoralism" is emerging, characterized by the presence of large numbers of stockless or near-stockless pastoralists and a small minority of very wealthy herders (Baxter 1985; Hogg 1986). The data seem to support this. Up to 30 percent of stock owners in certain regions have herds (ten cattle or less) well below sustainability (cf. Hogg 1980), while a small proportion maintain cattle herds in excess of 100 head.[5]

Two current processes symptomatic of these changes are the investment in agriculture by herders, and the practice of absentee herd ownership, which is restricted to wealthy individuals either from within or, more commonly, from outside the area. In the latter case, absentee owners have been able to alienate pastures for their own private use. Analysis of these cases is less straightforward than the herder-versus-farmer example, since it requires an understanding of the process of economic differentiation taking place within pastoral regions and communities. Rich and poor herders are increasingly pursuing different production and investment strategies, resulting in contradictory and conflicting uses of land and water.

The Baringo Region

Baringo District provides an excellent setting to examine pastoral land use problems. Its livestock areas have experienced many of the problems noted above: loss of pasture to European settlers, market quarantines, encroachment by farmers, use of communal grazing by absentee herd owners, and expansion of cultivation by herders. The area, from at least the 1920s, has been depicted as in "crisis" and described, at different times, as "the agricultural slums of Kenya" (Maher 1937), "an overgrazing end point" (Brown 1963), "an ecological emergency area" (Kenya 1974), and "an embarrassment to Kenya" (Kenya 1966). While conditions are perhaps more extreme in Baringo than elsewhere in Kenya, the socioeconomic processes responsible for natural resource problems are strikingly similar to those of other pastoral areas (cf. Campbell 1986; Dahl 1979; Hogg, forthcoming).

Ecological Diversity

Baringo District is located on the southern fringe of Kenya's northern rangelands. It is bordered by important agricultural areas to the south (Nakuru District), to the east (Laikipia District) and, to a lesser extent, to the west (Elgeyo-Marakwet District). Situated in the Rift Valley, it is characterized by a diverse ecology, ranging from semiarid rangelands in the north to forested highlands in the west and southwest. Rainfall and land use vary along this gradient, with rainfed agriculture dominant in the highlands and pastoral and agropastoral production important in the lowlands. Changes in altitude of more than 1500 m over a distance of 10 km are not unusual. The region's varying vegetation reflects these changes in elevation, with drought resistant *Acacia* species being dominant at lower altitudes.

The Il Chamus (Njemps), among whom I conducted research, reside in the lowland zone, where altitude ranges from approximately 1000 to 1400 meters above sea level. Rainfall distribution is low (approximately 640 mm per annum) and very erratic, displaying considerable monthly and annual variation and lacking a well-defined wet season (Kenya 1983:282). The area is characterized by brush *Acacia* species, including *A. reficiens, A. mellifera, A. senegal,* and *A. tortilis* (FAO 1967), and by a large permanent swamp centered around Lake Baringo and the drainage basin of the Molo and Perkerra Rivers. Around the fringes of the swamp, severe gully erosion is evident and vegetation cover is sparse throughout most of the year. Common annual grasses are *Eragrostis* spp. and *Tetrapogon spathecus,* but weed-like vegetation (forbs), such as *Heliotropium* spp. (highly unpalatable) and *Portulaca* spp., are increasingly dominant. Perennial grasses, including *Cynodon dactylon, C. plectostachyus, Echinochloa haplocada,* and *Digitaria velutina* (FAO 1967), are found only in the swamp areas, which are under water one to two months of the year.

Agricultural Encroachment

Over the past 50 years, the Il Chamus have lost considerable land to neighboring agriculturalists, from the lower parts of the Tugen Hills.[6] Their emigration recently has been spurred by land registration and export crop programs at home that have left some farmers landless. Private titling of land in the Tugen Hills began in the 1960s, and by the early 1980s most prime agricultural land in the area was under individual ownership. As has been witnessed elsewhere in Kenya, land adjudication has created significant inequities in distribution, and the poor, who either did not have the political clout to enforce their rights or sold their land in order to meet immediate cash needs, suffered disproportionately (cf. O'Keefe et al. 1977). Landowners in the hills began to grow high-value export crops, such as coffee and pyrethrum, pushing up the price of land and forcing poorer farmers into more marginal lands that were not under private ownership. In these areas, which were often used seasonally by herders, migrants tried to grow food crops, such as maize and finger millet. Competition for land with herders ensued. In the Endao area along the Il Chamus western border, for example, Tugen farmers have steadily moved across the boundary and are presently settled one kilometer inside the range areas. In similar fashion, Tugen settlement has crossed borders near Eldume, Kampi ya Samaki, and Marigat. Although the migrants rarely are wealthy farmers—since most of this class remain in the highlands—their settlement nonetheless restricts herder mobility during the wet season when animals are moved westward toward the Tugen foothills.

Perhaps more alarming has been the loss of dry season grazing at Ol Arabel in southeastern Njemps. With the exception of the swamp, this is the most critical grazing resource in the area, and one that has been disputed by the Il Chamus and Tugen since the early part of the century. Following the report of the Kenya Land (Carter) Commission (1934), established to investigate African land rights and claims, the Ol Arabel area was legally turned over to the Il Chamus. The formal ruling did not completely stop encroachment, which, in at least one case, was supported by the colonial state. During the 1940s and 1950s, the administration made informal concessions to Tugen farmers in the Ol Arabel area, permitting them to settle there, although land was still to remain under Il Chamus ownership (Ott 1979:103). Most cultivators had come from south Baringo, where good grazing and agricultural land were particularly scarce. This area bordered European farms of Nakuru District, which controlled most of the good agricultural and grazing land and water points in the area; Tugen stock trespass onto these farms was quite common (Anderson 1982). Crowded into their native reserve, the southern Tugen badly degraded the land through excessive cultivation and animal grazing. When the degradation threatened neighboring estates, action was deemed necessary, and the easiest option was to encourage resettlement of Tugen elsewhere. In the case of Ol Arabel,[7] it could be argued, herders made only intermittent use of the area. Thus Tugen from south Baringo were allowed to settle spontaneously in Ol Arabel without fear of government reprisal.

What was thought to be a "temporary" arrangement has proven permanent. Agricultural encroachment in Ol Arabel has persisted to the present, with even more land being taken over by farmers since independence. Estimates are that Il Chamus herders have lost 75 percent of Ol Arabel since the 1940s, a reduction in dry season grazing in the area from 13,750 to 3,333 hectares (FAO 1967:1). This loss forces Il Chamus herders to keep their animals in the swamps throughout the dry season, or to compete for the land with Tugen farmers and herders, the latter of whom seasonally graze in the area. While heavy use of swamp grazing during the dry season is unlikely to damage the vegetation there (Homewood 1985), the concentration of large numbers of animals around the swamps devastates the surrounding soils and vegetation:

> One very striking feature of the vegetation in semi-arid Baringo is the complete lack of perennial ground cover away from the swamps. Although immediately after the rains there is often good growth of ephemeral herbs, they quickly die back. Reports from early travellers indicate that these areas were not always in this degraded state, and it is generally agreed that the main changes have taken place over the last 50 years. In virtually all areas, other than the swamps, productivity in the grass/herb layer is low (Kenya 1984:64).

The decline in productivity of the lowland range and the loss of dry season grazing at Ol Arabel occur at a time when annual human population growth in the area exceeds 2 percent. This creates even further demands on available land.

In the Ol Arabel and the Endao cases, the issue is complicated by the increasing practice of mixed farming/livestock-keeping (agropastoralism) among both the Tugen and Il Chamus. Tugen cultivators keep large numbers of cattle, goats, and, to a lesser extent, sheep, which graze near their homesteads throughout the year. These animals compete for available grazing with Il Chamus herds, with their owners having the added advantage of residing permanently in the area. The diversification of both the Tugen and Il Chamus economies makes it particularly inappropriate to distinguish land-use conflicts along a herder-versus-farmer model. With the recent deterioration of the pastoral economy, herders have looked to (1) increasing cultivation, especially irrigated cultivation, which is made difficult in some areas by Tugen competition for water, and (2) recovering lost lands for grazing and possible cultivation. The frequency of land and water disputes between Tugen and Il Chamus, which increased considerably during the 1970s and 1980s, is partially related to the growth of irrigated agriculture. Because they were little interested in irrigation 20 to 25 years ago, the Il Chamus allowed the Tugen to irrigate on their western and southern boundaries, areas that were later to become disputed.[8]

The security of their lands vis-à-vis the Tugen and Pokot is the main reason that the Il Chamus have overwhelmingly supported group ranches. These cooperative ventures reconfirm the colonial trustland boundaries, provide herders with a title deed to land, and allow a group of residents to apply for credit. In the group ranch concept, the Il Chamus see a legal means of defending their territory, keeping out non-Il Chamus cultivators and herders, and discouraging permanent settlement in Ol Arabel. The registration of land on a group basis has predictably been most controversial in the Ol Arabel area, the location in Njemps that was rated highest for ranching potential. Plans for group ranches began in the 1960s, at approximately the same time that group ranches were being formed in Maasai areas, but ranch committees were not organized until the late 1970s. At first, the Il Chamus and the Tugen of Ol Arabel each formed committees and separately petitioned the government for official recognition. After considerable debate and strong government intervention, a caretaker committee, with two-thirds Il Chamus and one-third Tugen representation, was formed. But this has not allayed the ill-feelings between the two, and the government has not yet gone ahead with defining ranch boundaries and registering members. The division of Njemps into three large ranching units would force the government to confront the encroaching farmer issue, not only in Ol Arabel but in Endao and other areas as well. It is highly unlikely that a solution similar to that in Maasai areas, where ranch membership was restricted to herders (Maasai), will be forthcoming for the Il Chamus.

Cultivating Herders

In recent years, many Il Chamus have themselves turned to farming as a supplement to livestock production, and have done so in some cases without the active encouragement of government.[9] The amount of land presently cultivated in Njemps (excluding Ol Arabel and the government-controlled Perkerra Irrigation Scheme) is approximately 375 ha (irrigated) and 125 ha (dryland), with the latter varying annually depending on rainfall. The growth in agriculture has meant that the Il Chamus, and to some extent the pastoral Pokot of northern Baringo, are developing economies strikingly similar to the neighboring Tugen. While the degree of involvement in different sectors varies, each group is involved with herding, farming, and wage employment. The greatest expansion of cultivation in Njemps since the late 1970s has come from investment by the herders themselves, rather than from neighboring agricultural groups.

The process of agricultural sedentarization among herders is very complex, requiring a thorough understanding of diversification strategies and how they vary according to class differences. In Baringo (and I suspect elsewhere), several factors are responsible for increased cultivation, including loss of stock through drought, devaluation of livestock relative to other commodities, and a desire to be food self-sufficient. While the Baringo data do not possess sufficient time depth to confirm the ecological effects of such increased agriculture, evidence from elsewhere in Kenya demonstrates that pastoral sedentarization can contribute to environmental degradation (Lusigi 1984; O'Leary 1984).[10]

In Il Chamus, two paths have led to cultivation: rich herders farming to support their livestock holdings, and poor herders cultivating from the necessity to eke a subsistence (Little 1985b). One is a question of investment, the other of survival. By having their own grain, rich herders are able to minimize livestock sales while poor pastoralists deplete their holdings to finance grain purchases. The distinction is further reflected in the differences between irrigated and dryland farming, particularly in respect to cost requirements. Rich families are able to mobilize the labor and capital required for irrigation more easily than poorer families. The poor tend to engage in less costly, but riskier, dryland farming. As the value and numbers of livestock have declined, rich herders have transferred some of their wealth from livestock into irrigated land, which allows them to have a dominant stake in both sectors.

The irrigation expansion has been around the fringes of the Molo-Perkerra swamps and near such seasonal rivers as the Mukutan, Arabel, and Endao. Irrigation is only practiced during the wet season, when graze is not particularly scarce; therefore its competition with livestock production is presently minimal. Dryland agriculture, on the other hand, which also is a wet season activity, has been concentrated in the non-swamp areas, where herds are grazed during the rains. The potential for conflict is greater here because the activities can be distinguished along class lines (rich herders versus poor dryland farmers) and because seasonal competition is involved. I witnessed two cases in 1980–1981, involving two of the wealthiest cattle owners in Njemps, whose herds during the wet season had grazed in a farmer's rainfed field; in both cases the local elders required the herders to pay compensation. Rather than risk further penalties, the livestock owners moved their animals to the swamps, which they would normally not have done until later in the year. Unlike transgressors in interethnic conflicts, the culprits in these cases are difficult to identify and, consequently, what usually happens is that the farmer seeks only minimal compensation, knowing that in the future the tables could be turned (i.e., his animals could be caught grazing in another's field). More than 10 percent of all farmers, both irrigated and dryland, experienced at least one occasion during 1980–1981 when either their animals grazed another's farm, or their animals consumed part of another's harvest.

Cultivation by herders can complement livestock production if animals are grazed on harvested fields. The practice was common during my fieldwork period (1980–1981), but since that time a number of irrigated farmers have begun to fence their fields with barbed wire and restrict post-harvest stubble to their own animals. To prepare for what they see as eventual subdivision on an individual basis, wealthier Il Chamus have carved out larger farms than they are able to cultivate, and have fenced these areas. These same individuals, who often have positions in government or in other nonfarm occupations, have most actively supported private subdivision. There are parallels in Maasailand, where influential herders have used traditional grazing concepts to make individual claims to land in anticipation of private titling (see Peacock et al. 1982; Grandin, forthcoming; The Standard 1985). In Maasailand, the privatization of rangelands by influential Maasai, which has been going on since colonial times, is one of the practices that the majority of herders hoped would cease with group adjudication (Grandin, forthcoming).

The involvement in cultivation, and the corresponding decline in herder mobility, has resulted in overuse of certain pastures around irrigation areas and settlements and underutilization of distant range areas. Traditional dry season transhumances, which require considerable hard work, have declined in recent years, as cultivation and wage-earning activities have increased. The loss of labor is especially prevalent among males between 15 and 30 years of age who, in the past, were responsible for most of the dry season herding and watering. Poorer herders are especially affected because often, if labor is scarce, they must herd their animals near settlements where vegetation is depleted. Wealthy herders, in contrast, have the family labor and/or resources to hire others to take advantage of distant grazing (cf. Kjaerby 1979). In times of drought the concentration of stock around settlements is even greater, as impoverished pastoralists send family members out to seek employment and then settle near centers to purchase grain or receive it as famine relief. What visible signs of environmental degradation exist in Njemps (gullying, overcutting of trees, and prevalence of unpalatable forbs), tend to be near the population concentrations (including the perimeters of the swamps), not out in the range.

Recent evidence from elsewhere in Kenya confirms that herder cultivation (sedentarization), whether spontaneous or state-sponsored, can be a major land use problem in range areas. What had originally been perceived as a problem of overgrazing by nomadic herders is now seen as a dilemma of combining agriculture with sedentary livestock rearing:

> At Kekarongole (Turkana District), a small irrigation and trade centre some 30 km south of Lodwar, in an area of 8 square km the population increased from about 1000 to 3000 in less than one year. As a result traditional controls on the cutting of trees for firewood/charcoal, garden clearing, fodder for animal and house building poles were insufficient to prevent widespread forest destruction. . . . Sedentarization has meant a declining resource base and increased insecurity, and desertification, as a result of population and livestock concentration, has continued unabated and largely unchecked. If this decline is to be halted then government and donors must make a positive commitment to the importance of pastoral nomadism. Every effort should be made to encourage mobility and maintain full utilization of the rangeland (Hogg, forthcoming:7, 14).

> The growth of towns and irrigated agriculture tends to cause further immobilization of livestock (Isiolo District). For when town dwellers come from a rural environment, they tend to bring some of their livestock with them, and strong urban demand for milk attracts livestock to concentrate in an area around the town whence people can walk in carrying fresh milk every day. The result is a zone of devastation around the town due to overgrazing, and demands by townspeople that an area around the town be "set aside" for the exclusive use of their animals. . . . Around irrigation schemes (e.g., Rapsu, Malka Daka) the same tendency due to concentration of the human population arises, indeed it is worse (Dahl and Sandford 1978:175–176).

These findings, based on long-term fieldwork among herders, point not only to potential environmental problems associated with cultivating herders, but also to the very different parameters under which contemporary pastoralism takes place. This is a context now marked with increasing economic differentiation, diversification, and impoverishment, each a process that has implications for land use and ecology.

The state has strongly encouraged cultivation among herders, and, surprisingly, in some pastoral districts of Kenya it has financed a larger number of agricultural than livestock development activities. The favoring of agriculture over livestock has been especially strong in Baringo, where government planning for agricultural schemes began in the 1920s. Already by the 1930s, there was concern among planners who were designing the Perkerra Irrigation Scheme that irrigation would create imbalances in the local grazing system: "Such a scheme (Perkerra) even if successfully carried out would only lead to a concentration of cattle at one point which would become more and more isolated as the surrounding grazing was destroyed by the over-grazing that would naturally occur" (Kenya National Archives 1932:1). This prediction has proven accurate for the Perkerra Scheme area, where massive land use problems are evident, and is likely to hold true for other large irrigated areas in Njemps.[11] The smaller irrigation projects, which have been planned by the communities themselves, have fewer problems with excessive concentration of animals and people.

Absentee Herd Owners

Among recent changes that make the Il Chamus land use system vulnerable to resource mismanagement is the prevalence of absentee herd ownership. This phenomenon has emerged mainly in the past fifteen years, and is associated with both "outsiders" (non-Il Chamus) and "insiders" (Il Chamus) (for this distinction, see Galaty 1980:160). Using the most basic definition, it is the practice whereby ownership of the animals is divorced from the management and care of the animals, the latter being left to hired herders or "contracted" families (see Little 1985a). Unlike indigenous patterns of stock loaning, this practice resembles an employer/employee relationship. It has become prevalent in areas of Kenya that were especially hard hit by the droughts of the 1970s and 1980s, when herders had difficulties in rebuilding herds, and settled farmers, townsmen, and other non-pastoralists were able to purchase animals inexpensively. The ownership of animals consequently became distinct from livestock herding. In Baringo, the two main categories of absentee herd owners are private ranchers and traders.

Ranchers are found south of Njemps, where private land ownership prevails and producers are organized into jointly owned company ranches. The ranches are greater than 15,000 ha, but Tugen herd owners usually restrict their animals to their privately owned parcels, which range from approximately 25 to 300 ha. Each landowner also produces crops on a portion of his or her parcel. Water points and dip facilities are owned by the companies and can be used equally by shareholders.

During the dry season, ranchers frequently send their cattle north to use communal grazing of the Loboi Tugen and of the Il Chamus. Private landowners note that without access to communal grazing their enterprises would not be viable. The first stop on the annual migration is Loboi; when the concentration of cattle is excessive there, animals are moved further north to Il Chamus. During the 1981 dry season, 700 cattle and an undetermined number of small stock from Loboi (many of them originating on ranches) were grazed in Kailerr swamp (Il Chamus). At the time, they comprised 40 percent of total cattle there (Little 1981). Most of the outsider cattle were herded by Il Chamus families, some of whom had marriage or other social ties to the owners, under contracts giving them milk and wage compensation.

A second form of absentee herd ownership is found among livestock traders and other businessmen. Il Chamus traders usually are in partnership with larger businessmen from outside of Njemps, serving them as suppliers. They buy cattle locally, hire herders to look after the animals, and organize stock movements to the markets of south Baringo and Nakuru District. The more affluent middlemen may invest in watering facilities (e.g., a shallow dam) for their enterprises, and may have entire families working for them.

Stock traders predominantly keep male animals (oxen and bulls) in their herds. These males have higher fodder requirements than female animals (with the exception of lactating females), and, therefore, they are more likely to overexploit the range than a pastoral herd of predominantly cows and heifers. Using local grazing, stock traders are able to feed and fatten animals at minimal cost (i.e., the wage of a hired herder). Concentration of their herds in range areas of Njemps recently has increased due to an unfavorable security situation in north Baringo and in south Turkana. Such herds were particularly evident around the Mukutan center during the 1981 dry season, where, combined with Pokot cattle, outsiders' animals outnumbered local herds. The concentration of stock was so great that transhumance patterns were altered: rather than undertake the usual dry season migration to highland areas east and south of Mukutan (within 20 km), some families moved their cattle more than 50 km to Ngambo swamp. Because traders often have local elite and political support, it is difficult for the Il Chamus to correct the situation.

In only one case have I witnessed direct expropriation and fencing of land by a businessman, but its location in the swamps made it significant. Approximately 100 hectares of prime lakeside grazing were recently fenced by an Il Chamus civil servant to raise dairy cattle for the markets of Marigat and Kampi ya Samaki. The owner lives and works outside of Njemps, but maintains family in the area and hires workers. I am not sure how the individual was able to acquire permission to fence communal grazing, nor am I clear from whom permission was sought.

These examples of absentee herd ownership highlight the importance of political variables in examining pastoral land-use systems. While the intensity and specifics of absentee herd ownership vary, I would argue that it is a trend that is growing in significance in Kenya,[12] and elsewhere in Africa (cf. Swift 1982). Its occurrence has important implications for local ecology, since this group of "part-time" pastoralists usually operates outside the indigenous management system, and is likely to be less concerned than local herders with long-term conservation and grazing control.

Concluding Remarks and Policy Scenarios

I have addressed, in this chapter, three sources of land use conflicts in pastoral areas: the encroaching farmer, the cultivating herder, and the absentee herd owner. In other areas of Kenya, conflicts arising from the expansion of wildlife parks assume more importance than in Baringo (cf. Campbell 1984, 1986). Each of my examples can be associated with a different level and form of social and political differentiation. For example, at the level of the state, herders are clearly differentiated, in terms of policy and investment, from farmers and urban dwellers. They are also vulnerable to the activities of a national class of elites who, in some cases, have strong commercial interests in the range areas (e.g., ranching and development of tourist facilities), interests that differ considerably from the priorities of local pastoralists.

At the level of the region, herders are losing out politically and economically to neighboring agriculturalists (the encroaching farmer model). This process of regional differentiation is partly responsible for the large gains in land-holding that cultivators have made at the expense of pastoralists. The Baringo case, discussed here, is a good illustration of this.

Finally, the cultivating herder and, to some extent, the absentee herd owner are symptoms of social differentiation at the community level, in which rich and poor producers pursue different land use strategies that are potentially competitive. In the Il Chamus case, the gap between rich and poor is growing, which makes it difficult for the community to mobilize collectively to correct land management problems. Thus, resource abuse in Njemps is increasingly associated with the activities of "insiders."

Kenya's land use policies and their social and environmental ramifications can be interpreted in terms of this three-level (state, region, and community) schema. The major land use innovation for the pastoral areas, the group ranch, deals predominantly with the state and regional levels. By formalizing land ownership on a group basis, the group ranch provides herders with a means of legally protecting lands against some absentee herd owners and neighboring farmers. This does not, however, address land use conflicts that are internally induced, such as those resulting from cultivation and fencing of rangelands by herders. The government's present emphasis on decentralized resource planning and management (the "district focus"), on the other hand, does confront land use issues at the local level by giving resource decision-making power to local institutions and groups (Makokha 1985). Yet this initiative does not give the community legal ownership of the land, nor does it rule out the strong possibility that the power associated with decentralization will be co-opted by local elites. Advocates of political decentralization rarely acknowledge this latter possibility.

Solutions to land-use conflicts in Kenya's pastoral areas are no less straightforward than are the causes of these conflicts. As I have indicated, they must be perceived in a historical context and should be evaluated at several different levels, where potentially conflicting interests in range areas exist. Because certain policy alternatives can be taken only at a national level—for example, the establishment of a state land use commission to mediate conflicts among pastoralists, farmers, tourist promoters, and businessmen[13]—giving greater autonomy to local communities over land and water use is only a partial solution. Under the present circumstances in Kenya, policy interventions must be combined so as to give local institutions (which have more than just elite representation) more autonomy, while at the same time protecting pastoral lands from further infringement by outsiders. In doing this, local producers, especially those without considerable outside interests and investments, might decide on appropriate forms of resource use, without suffering further losses of land.

Notes

1. Support for field research in Baringo District was provided by the Social Science Research Council, the American Council of Learned Societies, and the Graduate School, Indiana University. In Kenya, research affiliation was kindly provided by the Institute for Development Studies, University of Nairobi. The support of the above institutions is gratefully appreciated.

2. Much of this discussion is drawn from Migot-Adholla and Little (1981) and Little (1984).

3. Certain rangelands of northern Kenya are held by the state, rather than in trust by the people. This means that local herders have no legal access to the land, and that government can expropriate land for its own use, as witnessed in the cases of the Bura and Hola irrigation schemes, without compensation to displaced pastoralists.

4. While there is considerable immigration into pastoral districts, there is also pastoral outmigration from these areas for wage employment. Increasingly, the pastoral districts are serving as "labor reserves" for large commercial farms and the unskilled job sector of the urban centers. This was not the case prior to the 1970s.

5. Elsewhere I have explored the recent transitions in livestock distribution among pastoralists, and the reasons for these changes (1983, 1985b).

6. It should be noted that both the Il Chamus and Tugen kept few livestock and the groups were restricted to a relatively small area in the precolonial period (see Little 1985b). During this time, the control of the Baringo basin was contested by a number of powerful groups, including the Maasai. Thus, the early movement of Tugen from the hills was partly a result of pacification of the lowlands by the British, allowing them (Tugen) to settle on new lands.

7. For the sake of brevity, the discussion of land disputes in Ol Arabel has been greatly simplified. The historical dimensions of Tugen/Il Chamus disputes in Arabel are discussed in greater detail in Anderson (1982).

8. A parallel case can be found in Kajiado District, where in the past Maasai allowed non-Maasai to cultivate along border areas. However, recent agricultural expansion into critical grazing zones and the desire of certain Maasai to farm in areas where non-Maasai now are cultivating, have strained relations between Maasai herders/farmers and Kikuyu and Kamba farmers in the region (Campbell 1984:40–43).

9. In areas of Kenya where rainfed agriculture is only marginally feasible (e.g., Turkana District), the state, donors, and relief agencies have been the major sponsors of agricultural (irrigation) schemes. While in this sense agriculture was not locally initiated, herders were rarely ever forced to settle and cultivate.

10. Stronger comments on the environmental consequences of herder cultivation come from Tanzania:

> In terms of land-use, the two forms of production combined in agro-pastoralism compete both for available land and labor power (Hanang District, Tanzania). The conflicting requirements of sedentary agriculture and mobile pastoralism tend to impose mutual limitations upon each other with the result of lowering productivity in forms of production. In the long run, as population and stock pressure builds up, the likely result will be land degradation and further impoverishment. Agro-pastoralism does not appear to be a viable future agricultural system (Kjaerby 1979:141).

11. Irrigation schemes of more than 200 hectares currently are planned for the Lamelok and Ngambo areas.

12. In a 1985 field visit to Tana River District, I found large herds of cattle (in some cases in excess of 500 animals) being herded for absentee owners from Mombasa and Garsen towns.

13. In theory the Kenya government has an interministerial committee to mediate land disputes among herders, farmers, ranchers, and tourist interests, but in practice it is nonfunctional, having never convened.

References

Anderson, D.
1982   Herder, Settler, and Colonial Rule: A History of the Peoples of the Baringo Plains, Kenya, circa 1890–1940. Ph.D. Thesis, Department of History, Cambridge University.

Baxter, P. T. W.
1985   The "New" East African Pastoralism. The Monroe Lecture, Department of Anthropology, University of Edinburgh, December.

Brown, L.
1963   The Development of Semi-Arid Areas of Kenya. Nairobi: Ministry of Agriculture.

Campbell, D. J.
1981   Land-Use Competition at the Margins of the Rangelands: An Issue in Developing Strategies for Semi-Arid Areas. *In* Planning African Development. G. Norcliffe and T. Pinford, eds. Pp. 39–61. Boulder, CO: Westview Press.

1984   Response to Drought among Farmers and Herders in Southern Kajiado District, Kenya. Human Ecology 12:35–63.

1986   The Prospect for Desertification in Kajiado District, Kenya. The Geographical Journal 152(Part I):44–55.

Dahl, G.
1979   Suffering Grass: Subsistence and Society of Waso Borana. Stockholm Studies in Social Anthropology, University of Stockholm.

Dahl, G., and S. Sandford
1978   Which Way to Go: A Study of People and Pastoralism in the Isiolo District of Kenya. Unpublished report. Nairobi, Kenya.

Dietz, T.
1985   Migration To and From Dry Areas in Kenya. Paper presented at Anglo-Dutch Symposium on Regional Disparities and Migration in the Third World, Amsterdam, Netherlands, 12–13 April.

Evangelou, P.
1984   Livestock Development in Kenya's Maasailand. Boulder, CO: Westview Press.

FAO (Food and Agriculture Organization)
1967   Survey of Njemps Territory, Baringo District. Nairobi: FAO.

Galaty, J. G.
1980   The Maasai Group-Ranch: Politics and Development in an African Pastoral Society. *In* When Nomads Settle. P. Salzman, ed. Pp. 157–172. New York, NY: Praeger.

Grandin, B. E.
   1986   Land Tenure, Sub-Division, and Residential Change on a Maasai Group
           Ranch. Development Anthropology Network 4(2):9–13. Binghamton, NY:
           Institute for Development Anthropology.
Hjort, A.
   1979   Savanna Town: Rural Ties and Urban Opportunities in Northern Kenya.
           Stockholm Studies in Social Anthropology, University of Stockholm.
Hogg, R.
   1980   Pastoralism and Impoverishment: The Case of the Isiolo Boran of Northern
           Kenya. Disasters 4:299–310.
   1986   The New Pastoralism: Poverty and Dependency in Northern Kenya. Africa,
           forthcoming.
Forthcoming   Development in Northern Kenya: Drought, Desertification and Food
           Scarcity. African Affairs.
Homewood, K.
   1985   Pastoralism, Conservation and the Overgrazing Controversy. Paper pre-
           sented at the Conference on "The Scramble for Resources in Africa:
           Conservation Policies in Africa, 1884–1984." Cambridge University, 19–
           20 April.
Ibrahim, F. N.
   1984   Ecological Imbalance in the Republic of the Sudan—with Reference to
           Desertification in Darfur. Bayreuth: Druckhaus Verlagsgesellschaft mbH.
Kenya, Republic of
   1966   Agricultural Report. Marigat: Ministry of Agriculture.
   1974   National Development Plan: 1974–1978. Nairobi: Government Printer.
   1983   Central Kenya—Natural Conditions and Farm Management Information.
           Farm Management Handbook of Kenya. Nairobi: Ministry of Agriculture.
   1984   Baringo Pilot Semi Arid Area Project: Part I: Basic Resources of the Area.
           Marigat: Ministry of Agriculture.
Kenya Land (Carter) Commission
   1934   Evidence and Memoranda, Vol. II. Nairobi: Government Printer.
Kenya National Archives
   1932   Irrigation—Baringo District, Report on Perkerra River Irrigation Project.
           File KNA/PC/RVP, Nairobi, Kenya.
Kjaerby, F.
   1979   The Development of Agro-Pastoralism Among the Barabaig in Hanang
           District. BRALUP Research Paper No. 56, University of Dar es Salaam,
           Tanzania.
Little, P. D.
   1981   The Sociology of the Il Chamus. Marigat: Ministry of Agriculture.
   1983   The Livestock-Grain Connection in Northern Kenya: An Analysis of Pastoral
           Economics and Semi-Arid Land Development. Rural Africana 15/16:
           91–108.
   1984   Land and Pastoralists. Cultural Survival Quarterly 8:46–47.
   1985a   Absentee Herd Owners and Part-Time Pastoralists: The Political Economy
           of Resource Use in Northern Kenya. Human Ecology 13:131–151.
   1985b   Social Differentiation and Pastoralist Sedentarization in Northern Kenya.
           Africa 55:242–261.
Lusigi, W.
   1984   Integrated Project in Arid Lands. Technical Report A-6. Nairobi: UNESCO.

Maher, C.
  1937   Soil Erosion and Land Utilization in the Kamasia, Njemps, and East Suk
          Reserves. Nairobi: Ministry of Agriculture.

Makokha, J.
  1985   The District Focus: Conceptual and Management Problems. Nairobi: Africa
          Press Research Bureau.

Migot-Adholla, S. E.
  1981   Settlement Policy and Its Implications to the Development of Semi-Arid
          Areas. In D. Campbell and S. E. Migot-Adholla, eds. The Development
          of Kenya's Semi-Arid Lands. Pp. 40–52. Occasional Paper No. 36, Institute
          for Development Studies, University of Nairobi, Kenya.

Migot-Adholla, S. E., and P. D. Little
  1981   Evolution of Policy Toward the Development of Pastoral Areas in Kenya.
          In The Future of Pastoral Peoples. J. Galaty, D. Aronson, P. Salzman, and
          A. Chouinard, eds. Pp. 144–156. Ottawa: International Development Re-
          search Centre.

O'Keefe, P., B. Wisner, and A. Baird
  1977   Kenyan Underdevelopment: A Case Study of Proletarianisation. In Landuse
          and Development. P. O'Keefe and B. Wisner, eds. Pp. 216–228. London:
          International African Institute.

O'Leary, M.
  1984   Ecological Villains or Economic Victims: The Case of the Rendille of
          Northern Kenya. UNEP Desertification Control Bulletin 11:17–21.

Ott, R.
  1979   Decisions and Development: Lowland Tugen of Baringo District, Kenya.
          Ph.D. Dissertation, State University of New York at Stony Brook.

Peacock, C. P., P. de Leeuw, and J. M. King
  1982   Herd Movement in the Mbirikani Area. Nairobi: International Livestock
          Centre for Africa.

Scott, E.
  1984   Life Before Drought: A Human Ecological Perspective. In Life Before the
          Drought. E. P. Scott, ed. Pp. 49–76. Boston, MA: Allen and Unwin.

Schultz, E., ed.
  1981   Image and Reality in African Interethnic Relations: The Fulbe and their
          Neighbors. Studies in Third World Societies No. 11, College of William
          and Mary, Williamsburg, VA.

Shepherd, A. W.
  1984   Nomads, Farmers, and Merchants: Old Strategies in a Changing Sudan.
          In Life Before the Drought. E. P. Scott, ed. Pp. 77–100. Boston, MA: Allen
          and Unwin.

Sobania, N. W.
  1979   Background History of the Mt. Kulal Region of Kenya. Integrated Project
          in Arid Lands Technical Report Number A-2. Nairobi: UNESCO.

The Standard (Daily Newspaper)
  1985   Group Ranch to be Sub-Divided. Saturday, 9 November, p. 10. Nairobi,
          Kenya.

Swift, J.
  1982   The Future of African Hunter-Gatherer and Pastoral Peoples. Development
          and Change 13:159–181.

Swynnerton, R. J.
   1954   A Plan to Intensify the Development of African Agriculture in Kenya.
           Nairobi: Ministry of Agriculture.
World Bank
   1975   Kenya: Into the Second Decade. Baltimore, MD: Johns Hopkins University
           Press.

10

Ecology and Land Use Changes in the Semiarid Zone of the Sudan

Fouad N. Ibrahim

The Impact of the Drought Disaster in the Sudan in 1984–1985

Available data do not permit a proper estimation of the 1984–1985 drought disaster in the Sudan, although UN sources have estimated the numbers of those who are severely affected, and therefore susceptible to starvation, at 8.4 million persons. About 7 percent of the affected population (approximately 600,000 persons) were, as of 1985, gradually starving to death. During the 12 months from June 1984 to May 1985, starvation in the areas of northern Darfur, northern Kordofan and the Red Sea Hills reached the alarming rate of 36 percent.

This rough approximation of the starvation rate is based on findings of a social survey conducted in the Red Sea Hills in March 1985 by the research team of the University of Bayreuth (West Germany). This survey, including data collection from official sources, tribal chiefs, and sampling in some villages, found that most families had lost about 50 percent of their children and 90 percent of their livestock. In the relief camp of Derudeb, Red Sea Hills, the health authorities reported death rates ranging from 8 to 12 persons per day in February 1985. The total number of camp inhabitants was about 10,000 persons. Thus, the death rate was 3 percent per month.

My own fieldwork in the Jebel Abu Hadid area of northern Kordofan in September 1984, including interviews with Nuba and Arab former herders who now cultivate millet, points to similar findings. During the 1982–1984 period, 7 percent of the population had migrated to towns and to the southern zone, total rainfall had dropped to 100 mm (the annual mean is usually 200 mm), and the price of drinking water had reached 0.40 Sudanese pounds (£S) per gallon. Food aid in the drought-stricken area was distributed only twice and was very limited in quantity. In August 1984, 6.3 kg of sorghum per household (6 persons) were distributed at a subsidized price of 0.10 £S (US $0.08) per kg. A second ration did not come until October.

It amounted to 3.2 kg per household at a less subsidized price of 0.76 £S (US $0.60) per kg. By September 1984, 97 people from 17 villages had died in one month. Since the average village size is about 150 inhabitants, the monthly starvation rate for these villages can be calculated at 3.8 percent, mostly women and children who are left helpless in the villages when the men migrate away in search of a means of living.

In Table 10.1 I present estimates, based on these sources, of the dimensions of the current famine disaster in the most affected regions of the Sudan. But a legitimate and significant question not answered by these statistics is, what are the causes that underlie this disaster? In the first place, while the terms "famine" and "drought" are not synonymous, the most immediate cause of both the current famine and its forerunner of 1972–1973 is the prolonged drought that prevailed in the Sudan between 1966 and 1984. But, as agricultural experts often forget, other less direct causes of famine, such as land mismanagement, soil deterioration, and the destruction of the traditional socioeconomic system, are often far more significant in their effect than is drought alone. It is these social and ecological factors, which make the Sudan prone to the disaster of famine in the wake of a drought, that I will examine in the rest of this paper.

An Overview of the Affected Zone

The semiarid zone of the Democratic Republic of the Sudan encompasses about half of the surface area of the country. It extends roughly 800 km from 10 to 17 degrees North Latitude. An overview of this zone is given in Table 10.2, dividing the Sudan into four ecological subzones with varying climatic conditions and different land use systems. Seventy percent (15 million) of the Sudanese population live in this area with farming and livestock raising as the main source of livelihood. Despite the existence of large irrigation schemes (e.g., Gezira, New Halfa, Rahad, Gash Delta) and large mechanized rainfed farming (especially in El Gedaref, southern Kordofan, and the provinces of Blue Nile and White Nile), the majority of the rural population depends mainly on subsistence production, which has been exposed repeatedly to the hazards of drought during the last two decades. Compared with the preceding two decades, the precipitation deficit for this time period has amounted to 40 to 50 percent.

The problem of drought in this area is not a new one. The people of the Sudan remember at least four major droughts that have occurred in the last 100 years. The first, in 1886 during the Mahdi Revolution, was named "Sanat Setta," i.e., "the year six," referring to the Hidjra year 1306 of the Islamic calendar. "Golo" was the next drought disaster that struck the country between the years 1910 and 1930. The people of Malha informed me that during one of these early drought phases the Meidob nomads, faced with a total lack of green fodder, made charcoal out of the dead trees, crushed the charcoal, and gave it to their animals as food. The drought phase of the years 1940–1945 is known as "Malwa," referring to the smallest unit

TABLE 10.1   Estimations of the Hunger Disaster in Darfur,
Kordofan, and the Eastern Region in 1984   (Source:
Field Surveys in August-October 1984 by F. N.
Ibrahim and M. A. Ali.)

		Total affected population	Have already migrated to towns and wetter areas	Remaining affected population
Severely Under-nourished (Very thin)	Darfur	1,400,000	560,000a	840,000
	Kordofan	1,800,000	720,000	1,080,000
	E. Region	1,770,000	450,000b	1,320,000
	Total	4,970,000	1,730,000	3,240,000
Currently Starving (Unable to move because of long under-nourish-ment)	Darfur	112,000	28,000	84,000
	Kordofan	146,000	36,000	110,000
	E. Region	100,000	40,000	60,000
	Total	358,000	104,000	254,000
Starved in Aug-Oct 1984 (death cases due to lack of food)	Darfur	80,000	30,000	50,000
	Kordofan	96,000	36,000	60,000
	E. Region	76,000	40,000	36,000
	Total	252,000	106,000	146,000

a added to an estimated number of 20,000 migrants from Chad

b excluding 600,000 Ethiopian political refugees and 70,000
Ethiopians who migrated into the Sudan very recently because of
the severe drought disaster in Ethiopia. These migrants are
sharing the Eastern Region's meager resources.

TABLE 10.2 Climatic-Vegetational Zones of the Arid and Semiarid Sudan (Sudano-Sahelian Zone)

Type	Precipitation in mm	Mean Rainfall Variability %	Arid Months after Thornthwaite	Dominant Vegetation	Dominant Land Use (excluding irrigation)
I Hyper-arid to arid Saharan marginal zone	50-200	35-50	11-12	Sparse thorn-scrub grasslands in favorable areas. Acacia tortilis, A. mellifera.	Nomadic and semi-nomadic grazing, limited millet cultivation.
II Arid northern Sahel	200-400	27-35	10	Thorn-scrub savanna with a dominance of Acacia tortilis, A. mellifera, A. nubica, Balanites aegyptiaca, Commifora africana, A. senegal.	Grazing combined with millet cultivation for subsistence, gum arabic planting.
III Semi-arid southern Sahel	400-600	25	9	Degraded low-rainfall woodland savanna with a dominance of Acacia senegal, Adansonia digitala, Hyphaene thebaica, A. mellifera, A. tortilis, Balanites aegyptiaca, A. seyal, Guiera senegalensis, Combretum cordofanum.	Cultivation of millet and sorghum combined with ground-nuts and sesame as cash crops; pastoral and sedentary animal husbandry.
IV Semi-arid Sudan zone	600-900	20	6.5-8	Partly degraded low rainfall woodland savanna with a dominance of A. seyal, A. albida, Combretum cordofanum, Cordia gharat, Dalbergia melanoxylon, Anogeissus schimperi.	Intensive cultivation of millet, sorghum, maize and ground nuts; spread of large mechanized rain-fed farming in recent years, pastoral and sedentary animal husbandry.

Source: Ibrahim 1984:22. Reprinted by permission of Druckhaus Bayreuth Verlagsgesellschaft mbH.

of measure for millet, indicating its acute scarcity. The drought disaster of 1970–1973 was called "Ifza'una," i.e., "rescue us," referring to the severe hunger of that time. The latest famine, of 1984–1985, has not yet been named, but there are good prospects for "Eish Reagan," (Reagan's grain).

The perception of the desertification problem in the Sudan goes back to E. P. Stebbing in the 1930s who expressed it most clearly in *The Creeping Desert in the Sudan and Elsewhere in Africa* (Stebbing 1953). It took both scientists and policymakers a long time, however, to understand the real nature of desertification: that drought is only one factor among many others and that desertification is a series of interacting processes including, above all, land-use practices incompatible with the natural conditions, which are slowly destroying the regenerative capability of the environment. Soils, plants, the soil-water balance, and thereby also the local climate, are seriously affected by these practices, so that desert-like conditions are spreading.

How Fragile Is the Semiarid Ecosystem of the Sudan?

Fragility Versus Stability of Ecosystems

Most ecologists are inclined to consider the natural ecosystems of the arid and semiarid zones to be neither more fragile nor more stable than humid ecosystems. Some ecologists go even as far as to maintain that arid ecosystems are less vulnerable to perturbation than humid ones, for the former have managed, through long processes of adaptation and adjustment, to develop a significant degree of resiliency to disturbance. Specifically, the stabilizing mechanisms of the semiarid ecosystems are a function of the behavioral, morphological, and physiological adaptations of plant and animal populations to drought conditions and climatic irregularities. Stabilizing processes of another kind also occur in the equilibrium dynamics of climate, water balance, soil formation, and the geomorphological processes of erosion, transport, and accumulation (see Weischet 1980). Thus, when one speaks of the fragility of the semiarid ecosystems, one should not imply that the humid ecosystems are less fragile. Furthermore, the question of fragility versus stability should not be separated from the degree and quality of human impact, not only because humans are an integral part of the fauna, but also because virtually no ecosystem still exists that has not been more or less influenced by human activity.

During the most recent long drought phase in the Sudan, in which a chronic lack of food, fodder, and water prevailed, both humans and animals proved to what extent biological adaptation to sustain food and water deficits could go. Many men, women, and children were compelled to live for months on one small meal every two to three days plus a minimum amount of drinking water daily. Those who were not able to endure the harsh conditions starved, and a loss of weaker members of the population had already begun before relief measures were underway.

In addition to the capacity to sustain food deficits, however, one of the most important, but often overlooked, mechanisms of stabilization in the semiarid zone is migration. This is most apparent in the case of humans and animals, but plants also are known to recede and transgress in deserts through valleys and wind passes. Resilience through the mechanism of human and animal migration has, however, been extremely impaired during the last 100 years due to changes of land-use systems and processes of urbanization in the Sudan. The improvement of water supply and educational and health services in central villages and towns has tempted the people to settle. Thus, they lost their former mobility.

Ecological Fragility in the Semiarid Sudan

Fragility can only be assessed in relation to the mode of usage. Generally, land-use systems in the Sudan have changed from pastoralism combined with small-hold shifting cultivation to sedentary, non-rotational farming, partly for subsistence and partly for cash. More recently, large-scale mechanized farming and export-oriented commercial cropping has caused the clearing of about 5 million hectares of good savanna woodland. The vulnerable aspects of water balance, rainfall, vegetation, soils, and relief are discussed in this context.

Water Deficit. As in other arid zones, the main problem here is the deficit in water balance. Water deficit in itself is no reason to consider an ecosystem to be fragile, but it sets limits and rules for cultivation. These rules have not been kept for some decades now, and this change has resulted in severe ecological damage.

Concentration of Precipitation. The concentration of precipitation occurs at two levels: the concentration in the summer wet season (high seasonality) and the concentration in a limited number of strong rainfalls (high intensity). High seasonality of rainfall favors seasonal migration. Permanent settlement of rural population with livestock raising is detrimental to the land resources which are very poor during the long dry season from November to May. In the northern Sahel, the dry season is 10–11 months long. High intensity combined with high variability can lead to the occurrence of drought spans within the crop-growing period, resulting in crop failure. High intensity added to high variability of precipitation may also mean too early or too late rainfall for crop growth. Again this precipitation behavior favors nomadic pastoralism, which is more independent of set periods of plant growth.

Rainfall Variability in Place and Time. The hazards of spatial and temporal variability of rainfall in the Sudan are mainly connected with rainfed farming. Mobile livestock holders have no difficulty in coping with this climatic phenomenon. The wide range of local variability of precipitation in the semiarid Sudan within the same period and the same zone is clearly shown in Table 10.3.

The temporal variability of rainfall is more complex and manifests itself at various fluctuation levels:

- variability over long periods of more than a decade
- annual fluctuation

- fluctuation of the rainfall of the same month from year to year
- fluctuation of rainfall of the same pentad from year to year.

All these variability types are relevant to farming and increase the liability to crop failure. Table 10.4 shows four alternating wet and dry phases in El Fasher, Darfur, between 1919 and 1984. It becomes apparent that the long-term annual mean of 278.3 mm in El Fasher hardly ever occurs, and it therefore plays an insignificant role in the pattern of land use. During the long wet phases, the farmers and livestock holders become accustomed

TABLE 10.3   Rainfall from January 1 to August 31 Compared to the Mean (1951-1980) for Selected Stations in Semiarid Sudan

Station	Mean 1951-80	1981	1982	1983	1984	1985	1985 percent of mean
Kadugli	492	547	403	441	308	421	85
El Obeid	284	239	124	278	96	155	55
El Gedaref	470	591	629	417	248	605	129
Kassala	227	177	179	243	69	120	53
Port Sudan	17	Traces	1	Traces	0	24	141
Khartoum	131	122	63	78	1	58	44
Atbara	60	14	18	15	0	26	43
Ed Damazin	546	537	557	557	430	391	72
Abu Na'ama	424	505	284	271	294	407	95
Sennar	375	312	191	291	149	313	83
Kosti	323	124	239	238	71	292	90
Ed Duem	209	190	167	193	56	156	75
Wad Medani	280	225	152	148	83	387	138

Source: Meteorological Department, Khartoum 1985.

TABLE 10.4   Wet and Dry Phases in El Fasher between 1919 and 1984

Period	Duration (years)	Wet/ dry	Annual mean (mm)	Deviation from long-term mean (277mm) (percent)
1919 - 1939	21	wet	329.3	+ 18.9
1940 - 1949	10	dry	218.9	- 21.0
1950 - 1965	16	wet	329.2	+ 18.8
1966 - 1984	19	dry	196.0	- 29.2

Source: Ibrahim (1984:67). Reprinted by permission of Druckhaus Bayreuth Verlagsgesellschaft mbH.

to a precipitation whose mean lies at about 330 mm, considering it normal. With the transition into the dry phases, the pendulum abruptly swings back to the other side, so that a decrease of 133 mm (i.e., 40 percent) takes place.

For cultivators this means that farming would be practically impossible unless the rainfall distribution were particularly favorable (i.e., concentrated in July and August). Although such rainfall behavior is typical of the semiarid climate of the tropical marginal zone, farmers are rarely prepared to cope with it. It is almost always hazardous for their crops.

Limits of Regeneration Ability of the Degraded Savannas of the Sudan. Despite the well-developed resiliency of the vegetation of the arid and semiarid areas, one should not conclude that the original stock of the degraded vegetation cover is fully retrievable. By maladaptive methods of land use humans have so changed the original ecological balance that the natural ability of regeneration has been drastically weakened. Through overcultivation, overgrazing, excessive tree-felling, and savanna fires, a change in the density and species composition of the original, natural vegetation has taken place.

This process of vegetation degradation may in fact be reversible, but reversing it will require not only serious conservation and improvement measures, but also a cessation of the current "strip-mining" methods of land use. In the Sudan, under the present disastrous economic conditions and the ever-increasing human and livestock pressure on land, the imposition of adequate protective and remedial measures seems almost impossible.

The Vulnerability of Soils to the Processes of Desertification. Certain soils in the semiarid Sudan are especially susceptible to degradation. Three prevalent soil groups are discussed here as to their fragility.

The **Sandy Goz soils** form a zone in the fixed old-dune belt that extends from El Geneina in the west to Goz Reb'geb in Kassala Province in the east. Owing to excessive millet cultivation combined with long-term over-grazing, the "fixed" Goz soils have been reactivated, especially north of 12 degrees North Latitude. The loss of the more fertile topsoil and the loosening of the relatively compact soil structure have disturbed the original favorable soil/water balance and ultimately led to a drastic decrease in land productivity. Figure 10.1 shows the decrease of millet yields, and the concomitant increase in cultivated areas in the Sudan since 1960. As a crop grown mainly on Goz soils, millet production per hectare can be taken as a good indicator of Goz soil degradation. Precipitation in El Fasher (a main millet growing area) is given for a better interpretation of the changes taking place.

Goz areas that have not been taken intensively under the hoe still retain their soil stability and rich vegetation cover, regardless of the degree of aridity prevailing there. Examples occur in Um Gozein in northwest Kordofan, in the Babannusa-Ab Zabad area, and in Goz Dango in southwest Darfur. Lack of permanent water sources in these areas has rescued them from the devastating effect of cultivator settlements.

Large plains of **clayey soils** occur in southern Darfur, southern Kordofan, and in the Eastern Region. They are mostly cracking soils with clay contents ranging from 40 to 80 percent. Before the introduction of large mechanized farms, especially during the last two decades, the clay plains had a rich cover of savanna woodland mainly with *Acacia seyal, Balanites aegyptiaca, Acacia albida, A. nilotica* and *A. mellifera*. Mechanized farming rendered these vast areas completely treeless. Grasses and herbs have also been destroyed. Shallow disc-plowing led to the concretion of the subsoil, while lack of tree roots and the increasing compactness of the clayey soils enhanced runoff velocity and hindered water seepage and moistening of the soil. A remarkable drop of sorghum yields took place and gully erosion occurred in areas where it had been completely unknown before. In the dry season the denuded soil is exposed to intense wind erosion. Whirlwinds (*hoses*) and dust storms (*haboob*) have increased. Added to this, the sun-exposed soil dries up and develops a thin, surface layer with minute air pockets, which hinders water seepage when the first rains arrive.

Skeletic soils are shallow soils covering pediments and flat outcrops of Nubian sandstone. They are highly vulnerable to fluvial erosion once their thin vegetation cover is destroyed. Gradually, the bedrock is laid bare and further land use becomes most unfavorable. In the sudano-sahelian zone

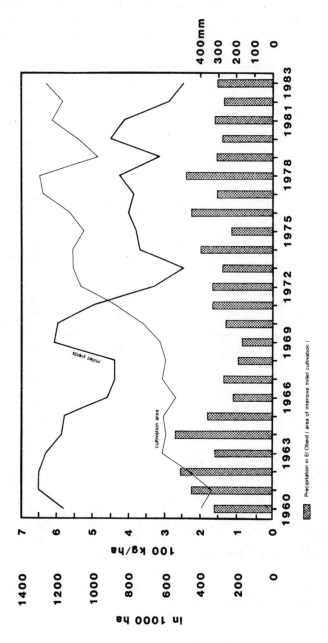

Fig. 10.1   Development of Millet Yields and Area of Millet Cultivation
in the Sudan 1960–1983.

of the Republic of the Sudan, these soils have been almost destroyed by excessive tree felling and overgrazing. Enhanced skeletization delays the restoration of the tree cover, while washed-out soil is practically irrecoverable. New soil formation takes centuries and would require conservation interventions that are impractical at present.

The Impact of Land-Use Changes

Land-use changes with far-reaching impacts on the environment can be divided into two main categories:

- intensification of traditional land use owing to population increase as well as population concentration in settlements with secure water resources and other services, and
- changes in the methods of land use and in the rural economy in general.

Intensification of Traditional Cultivation. Although there are large uncultivated areas in the Sudan, farming is concentrated in areas of drinking-water supply. Thus, the low figures for population density (9 inhabitants per square kilometer) are misleading. In the perimeters of most settlements land is cultivated annually without allowing for a fallow period for soil regeneration. After five or six years, the production decreases so much that the farmer is forced to give up cultivating the plot. Thus a compulsory and not a planned fallow is practiced.

This excessive cultivation of marginal areas clearly is the result of the enormous population increase during the last few decades. Soil erosion and the deterioration of the land's productivity is shown by the decrease in millet yields in the Sudan (see Figure 10.1). The decrease in millet yields per hectare by about half within 18 years and the increase in the population by about the same rate within the same time span was balanced by more than trebling the cultivated areas (from 392,000 hectares in 1960 to 1,300,000 hectares in 1978). It is especially hazardous for the environment that in just the very years in which dryness is most severe, farmers must cultivate larger areas to secure their own subsistence.

Millet yields tend to average between 200 kg and 650 kg per hectare. In the belt north of the 300 mm isohyet, however, the yields are much lower. In dry years, which are about 50 percent of all years, the peasants there harvest at most 100 kg per hectare, and sometimes nothing at all. The population suffers from a chronic crisis of undernourishment.

A six-member family in the western Sudan requires about 1,200 kg of millet yearly. The average area cultivated per family is 5 ha, mainly of millet. Accordingly, the family requirements of millet can be met only in particularly wet years. Peasants resort to a speculative sowing of land, and if they are lucky one of their plots may receive enough rain for millet to grow.

Research on the problem of desertification in western Sudan has strongly implicated millet cultivation as the main factor in the process of desertification,

224   *Fouad N. Ibrahim*

for it transgresses the climate limit of rainfed cultivation. The actual boundary of millet cultivation in the western Sudan has been extended by about 200 km too far to the north. While the agronomic limit of rainfed cultivation is at about the 500 mm isohyet, millet cultivation has reached the 200 mm isohyet in places. Sporadic farming is practiced even in drier areas, especially when the rains are particularly favorable (Figure 10.2).

Ignoring the agronomic dry limit has a far-reaching impact on the fragile ecosystem of sandy areas. To prepare the land for cultivation, farmers fell all trees. Before sowing, they clear all grasses and herbs and loosen the soil with the hoe. During the period of growth, the field is weeded twice to ensure the removal of all natural plants. The repetition of this process leads ultimately to the entire destruction of the natural vegetation cover, thus intensifying erosion of the fertile topsoil. Soil erosion takes place both by wind (deflation) and by water (deep fluvial erosion). Deflation occurs especially in the long dry season of eight to ten months.

The impact of this pattern of land clearing is further exacerbated by the concentration of farms around settlements, as revealed by aerial and satellite photographs. A desertification ring, caused by millet cultivation, extends out about 5 km from the center of these settlement zones.

Sedentarization and "Overgrazing"

Nomadic pastoralism is the best adapted form of land use in the Sahel because of its capacity to cope flexibly with the high rainfall variability. Unfortunately, this cultural adaptation, evolved by the sahelian tribes over past centuries, is not functioning today, after decades of rapid population growth. Sedentary animal husbandry, with a more limited mobility, together with rainfed cultivation, is intruding into the nomadic pastures. Thus nomads are being pushed into extremely marginal areas with poor pastures. These changes result in severe overgrazing of pastures, of which the nomads are unfairly accused.

The consequences of overgrazing are most severe where sedentary animal husbandry is practiced in areas also suffering from the consequences of concentrated millet cultivation. The areas surrounding settlements therefore suffer most from desertification, through overgrazing combined with over-cultivation. After surveying many settlement perimeters in Darfur, I have worked out a scheme of concentric rings that often recur around these settlements as a result of overuse (see Figure 10.3). In particular, both tree and grass species composition change considerably the closer one approaches the center from which livestock are brought out to graze and people walk out to farm and gather firewood. From about 10 km out, the palatable acacias are gradually replaced by unpalatable species, such as *Acacia nubica*, *Guiera senegalensis*, *Albizzia* species and *Leptadenia pyrotechnica*. In addition, *Aristida* grass species are usually replaced by *Cenchrus biflorus*.

To solve the problem of overgrazing the first step is to control the number of grazing animals to conform to the carrying capacity of the land. The problem would partly be solved if an even distribution of animals on all

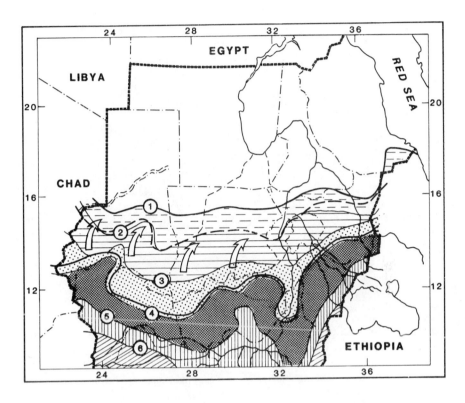

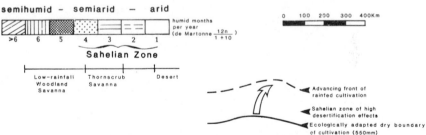

Fig. 10.2 The Sahelian Zone of the Republic of the Sudan.
The Extension of Rainfed Cultivation Beyond the
Ecologically Adapted Agronomic Dry Boundary.

Source: Adapted from Mensching and Ibrahim (1977).

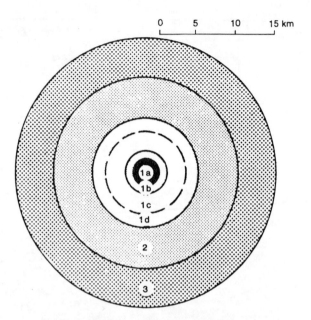

Fig. 10.3 Idealized Scheme of Desertification in the Perimeter of Settlements in the Sahelian Zone of Darfur, Sudan.

The nearer to the center, the higher the degree of degradation.

1) Inner ring of excessive cultivation combined with overgrazing
   a) Settlement with old, shade-giving trees (*Balanites aegyptiaca, Acacia raddiana, Ziziphus spina christi, Azadirachta indica*)
   b) Settlement fringes, with unpalatable herbs and shrubs *(Acacia* species, *Calotropis procera, Guiera senegalensis, Albizzia* species)
   c) Ring of excessive cultivation with no fallow
   d) Ring of cultivation interspersed with fallow. Also overgrazing damages
2) Ring of permanent overgrazing
3) Ring of excessive tree-felling and seasonal overgrazing

Source: Ibrahim (1979).

available pastures were achieved. This could be promoted by a more even distribution of watering points, encouragement of nomadism and trans-humance, and a rotational use of water pumps so as to control grazing activities.

Other necessary measures are improvement of pastures by reseeding degraded areas, establishing firelines to check uncontrolled savanna fires, hay making and storage in the rainy season, and buying fodder from favorable areas during the dry season. At the same time, laws must be issued to regulate the rights of certain segments of the population to use grazing areas, so as to encourage appropriate management and to protect the rights of local users. Where there is ambiguity over user rights, pastures are often recklessly exploited to the degree of complete destruction, i.e., a process of "strip mining."

The fact remains, however, that the areas affected by overgrazing are overpopulated and in need of comprehensive development measures. It is impractical to demand that hungry people reduce the size of their herds by half. Improving the animal stock and the marketing conditions, on the other hand, would enable better management.

Excessive Use of Timber and Firewood

In the areas where no other fuel than wood is available, and where the purchasing power of the population is insufficient to allow the use of imported fuel, tree felling is considerable. Observations in the Sudan show that much of this fuel energy is wasted. For cooking purposes women often keep a whole tree stem or a big branch glowing the whole day. Energy-saving ovens, such as those used in North Africa or in India, are all but unknown in the Sahel. Furthermore, nomads and travellers light big fires, partly to keep wild animals away and partly to show cattle thieves that the livestock are well guarded. Negligence in handling these fires often causes devastating savanna burns. In addition to the nomads and settled peasants, the town inhabitants use wood every day for cooking. Even the town bakeries seldom use other fuels for their ovens.

One of the most urgent measures for combating desertification should be to reduce the population's requirement for wood. Wood consumption can be reduced by about two thirds, if the "life" of homesteads and kraal fences is prolonged by better building methods. The best solution would be to do without fencing altogether. The problem of fuel supply, however, is much more difficult to solve. As long as the people can get their firewood "for nothing" from the valleys and highlands, they have no reason to buy fuel, however low its price might be. More efficient burning methods can, however, reduce the consumption of firewood to a considerable extent. While open fires allow the use of only 5 percent of the energy produced, traditional closed ovens have a 40 to 50 percent efficiency. Although the transformation of wood into charcoal involves a partial loss of energy, charcoal is more energy saving than fuelwood. Its smaller volume makes it easy to use in smaller ovens where less energy is lost because of the concentration of fire.

Sedentary farmers consume approximately 80 percent of the felled trees. Thus, the increasing sedentarization of the population of the semiarid Sudan in the last 100 years can be held largely responsible for the destruction of the savanna woodland. Mobile nomads are able to collect dead branches for fuel on their migrations. Since they are not compelled to cut down green trees for fuelwood, their contribution to deforestation is very limited.

Unplanned Expansion
of Large-Scale Mechanized Farming

In the Eastern Region alone, large mechanized farms have occupied 2.75 million hectares in the last 2 decades. More than half of this area is occupied by the "unplanned" farming that is illegally practiced by rich merchants. Both "legal" and "illegal" mechanized farmers, however, constantly disobey the law. They refuse to practice a cultivation-fallow rotation or to keep a certain portion of land as woodland to function as windbreaks, although these conditions are clearly stated in their leases. The serious hazards of the mismanagement of the clay plains have been discussed above. The old land-use methods—extensive (light) grazing, forestry, and small-scale shifting cultivation—were adapted to soil conditions and were more beneficial to the local inhabitants. The local peasants, driven away by big mechanized schemes, are now unable to produce enough for subsistence. At the same time, the price of the sorghum produced on the mechanized farms is beyond the range of their purchasing power. It is either sold in other regions or exported abroad both legally and illegally. This paradox of local people starving because they are unable to purchase locally-produced surplus grain has parallels in southern Kordofan and other areas of large-scale mechanized farming. Unfortunately, both Sudanese and foreign development experts defend mechanized farming as a method of improving the country's food security.

In areas of both traditional farming and modern agriculture, a class of merchant-farmers has appeared who lease land and exploit it in an ecologically inappropriate manner. These merchants also exploit seasonal laborers usually recruited from the groups who actually have local rights to use the land. Local farming systems have thus been replaced by export-crop farming in vast areas. Added to these drawbacks, to the poor peasants, of export orientation, monoculture, and market manipulation, this capital-intensive, mercantile farming has caused the ecological devastation of vast areas of the semiarid zone of the Sudan. In comparison, small-holder farming is much more limited in its environmental impact.

Conclusions

Natural conditions in the semiarid zone of the Sudan entail a certain degree of susceptibility to ecological hazards. Indigenous pastoralism and farming have proved to be essentially compatible with the natural resources and constraints of the semiarid zone. Recent changes of land rights and land management have led to the excessive use of these resources, on the one hand, and to the implementation of land-use methods that have caused the devastation of vast areas of the low-rainfall woodland savannas, on the other. Unless a drastic change of land management takes place soon, little hope for ecological rehabilitation can be expected. The major culprits are both the urban merchants who are practicing the "strip mining" of rural areas, and national and international decision makers. Solutions should begin at these levels, before hungry peasants are asked to reduce production further in order to conserve, protect, and improve their environment.

References

Ibrahim, F.
  1979   Desertification. A World-wide Problem. Series of Transparencies. Information Material. Düsseldorf: Hagemann.
  1984   Ecological Imbalance in The Republic of the Sudan. Bayreuth: Bayreuther Geowissenschaftliche Arbeiten, Vol. 6.
Mensching, H., and F. Ibrahim
  1977   The Problem of Desertification in and around Arid Lands, with Two Contributions on the Anthropogenic Destruction of Land Use Potential and a Discussion of Measures for Rehabilitation. Tübingen: Applied Sciences and Development 10:7–43.
Stebbing, E. P.
  1953   The Creeping Desert in the Sudan and Elsewhere in Africa, 15–30 Degrees Latitude. Khartoum.
Weischet, W.
  1980   Die Ökologische Benachteiligung der Tropen. Stuttgart.

11

The Politics of Lands at Risk in a Philippine Frontier[1]

Maria Elena Lopez

The politics of lands at risk involves competition between indigenous communities and migrant farmers in the course of frontier development. An examination of one case, the Palaw'an of the Philippines, indicates that given resource competition, long-term environmental management cannot be separated from problems of tenure. The negotiability of land allocation at the local level varies with the modes of political intervention by the state, which exercises control over ancestral lands.

Introduction

Anthropological research on Philippine swidden-based systems documents two different patterns of social and ecological change in the course of frontier development. In the first pattern of change, the penetration of migrant farmers and extractive industries has led to the displacement and fragmentation of indigenous communities. Some of these indigenous peoples have sought to maintain some autonomy by retreating to marginal environments where they face less competition. Others have remained in place as tenant farmers and laborers on what were formerly their own lands (Estioko Griffin and Griffin 1981:67; Schlegel 1981:111). As is generally acknowledged, those indigenous communities with a long history of swiddening have evolved what Olofson refers to as "harmonic" practices, that is, practices that conserve forest resources (1981:3). By contrast, Filipino farmers who have migrated from the lowlands to the uplands are new to shifting cultivation and their practices are "disharmonic," or conducive to the destruction of forest, watersheds and soils (ibid.; Fernandez 1972:180; Rice 1981:75–77).

These immigrants provide indigenous communities with "a poor model for agricultural modernization" (Warner 1981:27). The pattern of resource exploitation they practice is one of extensive forest clearing, which results in the depletion of the flora and fauna that are important food resources for indigenous communities. Extensive clearing accompanied by short fallowing also exposes the uplands to erosion and loss of soil fertility.

In the second pattern of change, indigenous swidden farmers are developing viable resource management strategies in response to the influence of the market economy. Such practices as arboriculture, agroforestry, and animal husbandry are expected to conserve rather than deplete the local ecology of the uplands (Eder 1981:91; Rice 1981:85). What is noteworthy in the recorded instances is the fact of secure land tenure. While the eventual success of these strategies involves other variables as well, such as the availability of capital, technical expertise, and price incentives, these factors appear to work best in conjunction with a secure land base.

The problem addressed by this paper is the difficulty of securing land in the context of frontier expansion. By "lands at risk" I refer to a situation in which lands within the so-called "public domain," inhabited by indigenous communities, are open to the competing claims of the wider society, and thus expose the former to the loss of land and the basis of their communal identification. In short, I take as the basic problem the control of land itself. Because the uplands are subject to national development policy, the state plays a crucial role in directly or indirectly influencing the displacement or entrenchment of indigenous communities. I hope to clarify the linkage between extralocal and local systems by focusing on one arena of competition, land, and the processes that generate specific forms of mobilization in this arena (Moore 1984:3). It is my argument that the process of mobilizing to control land involves both continuity and change in the local community and in the society at large.

Just as Philippine swidden-based communities have been flexible in "remodelling their economies in response to changing environmental conditions" (Olofson 1981:3), they are equally flexible in their political strategies and modes of social organization as they seek to defend their lands. This will become apparent in the following description of how one indigenous group, the Palaw'an, has sought to secure its ancestral lands in the face of displacement and uncertain tenure. The discussion is divided into four parts. The first section situates migration and dislocation within the national pattern of land tenure. The second describes national policies affecting the allocation of land among cultural minorities, which include the Palaw'an. The third examines local patterns of political mobilization around land as they are affected by extralocal factors. The last section concludes with an assessment of continuity and change in the dynamics of resource competition.

Migration and Dislocation

Palawan is the largest province of the Philippines. It is composed of a long, narrow main island and numerous outlying islands. The land area of the province is 1.48 million hectares. Its population reached 405,058 in 1983 (estimate of the Palawan Integrated Area Development Project or PIADP) (Philippine Government Documents 1981a), about 70 percent of whom live on the main island, concentrated south of Puerto Princesa, the provincial capital (see Figure 11.1). The main island's indigenous peoples constitute over 30 percent of the total population. Among the major groups, there are around 60,000 Palaw'an, 60,000 Tagbanua and 7,000 Batak (Philippine Government Documents 1981b:144).

Palawan is known as the last local frontier open to settlement by land-seeking colonists. In 1948, it had a population of 106,269. This figure has grown progressively from 162,669 in 1960 to 236,635 in 1970, for an annual growth rate of 3.8 percent, and to 300,065 in 1975, for an annual growth rate of 4.9 percent. The large increase is attributed primarily to immigration (Philippine Government Documents 1980:6). Palawan's population density is 0.5 person/hectare of agricultural land, which is far below the national average of 1.9 person/hectare. However, the bulk of Palawan's agricultural land is found in the foothills and not in the alluvial plains. About 70 percent of mainland Palawan's hilly terrain still retains its forest cover, though logging and shifting cultivation by increasing numbers of migrants threaten the island's long-term ecological stability.

The influx of migrants to Palawan can hardly be dissociated from land tenure inequalities in the Philippines. Behind the rhetoric of land redistribution, the real purpose of agrarian reform has been to reduce rural unrest through minimal concessions (Kerkvliet 1979:117). Palawan was opened for colonization in 1949, following a critical period of peasant unrest and armed rebellion in Central Luzon. Agrarian policy favored land resettlement rather than a redistribution of land controlled by elites. Through resettlement, landlords retained their holdings and landless peasants found the opportunity to secure land with government capitalization. The national government opened a 24,000 ha resettlement site in central Palawan, the largest plain on the main island. The site became known as Narra, the acronym of the National Resettlement and Rehabilitation Administration which is responsible for the project. Though 3000 families have been settled by the government, the bulk of migrants to Palawan have been self-financed settlers who sought new lands for cultivation with the opening of the island to settlement.

The main island of Palawan is bisected into eastern and western sections by a chain of mountains running through its entire length. From the central highland area, the landscape changes to lower foothills and inland valleys, then to a fairly narrow alluvial plain that gives way to the tidal flats. Generally, there are more plain areas in the southern and eastern parts of the mainland, and this coincides with the settlement preferences of migrants. When settlers first arrived in Palawan, most of the province was still covered with primary forest. Today, the areas they occupy have been converted to paddy fields, but there are also vast stretches of eroded hills.

Large-scale migration was not preceded by measures to protect the land rights of Palawan's indigenous ethnic minorities, and, as the settlers moved southward of Puerto Princesa, they displaced Tagbanua and Palaw'an from the alluvial plains, inland valleys and lower foothills. Deprived of access to the more productive lands of the province, the dislocated populations

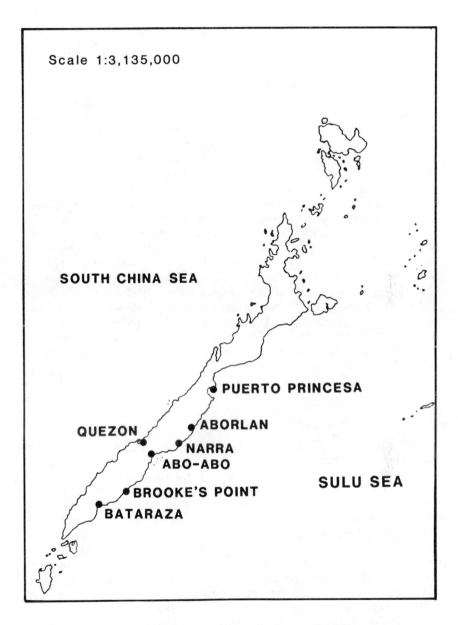

Fig. 11.1 Map of Palawan, Philippines.

moved toward the interior hills and mountains, and began cultivating much steeper slopes. Today, swiddening on steep slopes produces one-half the yield of lowland rainfed paddy rice. On less hilly terrain, the yield is three-fourths of rainfed paddy rice (Philippine Government Documents 1981a, Annex 5:6).

Land reform since 1972, when an authoritarian regime was established, has brought little improvement for the vast majority of Filipino tillers. Like the reform programs that preceded it, the purposes of the program under martial law are to keep rural unrest at a manageable level and to legitimate the government, rather than to redistribute political and economic power (Kerkvliet 1979:117–119; Wurfel 1981:192). On the whole, land reform has been characterized by slow implementation, procedural requirements favorable to landlords, and minimal peasant participation in decision making. Additionally, government activities are concentrated in Central Luzon, where peasant rebellion occurred thirty years ago. Through the manipulation of policy, state elites, who themselves have interests in land, have narrowed the scope of land reform to cover only eight percent of 5.28 million peasant farmers and landless agricultural laborers (Kerkvliet 1979:131). It is estimated that one out of every ten farms in the Philippines is smaller than a hectare, that one in 500 amounts to more than 50 hectares, and that four out of five farmers are landless or almost landless (Myers 1984:151). There is also a large and growing population of landless agricultural workers who find employment on plantations or provide seasonal labor for small landowners. It is within this broad context of land tenure inequalities that the push and pull of migration to a frontier province like Palawan operates, and, within local settings, generates competition over land between indigenous communities and migrant farmers.

The Legal Framework of Displacement

The land rights of Palawan's indigenous minorities have been affected by public land laws implemented to further goals of national integration, economic development, and environmental management.

When frontier areas were opened to migration and resettlement in the Philippines, the land rights of indigenous minorities were ignored. The common assumption was that their ancestral lands belonged in the public domain, which eventually led to competition from various groups in Philippine society. In Mindanao, land problems between resident Muslims and incoming Christian settlers and developers led to the breakdown of peace and order. The state responded to political instability and the threat of Muslim secession by promulgating a policy of "national integration." Its social and cultural goals were assimilative rather than pluralistic in character. For example, the land claims of Muslim and tribal Filipinos were to be formalized—i.e., registered and titled—on the basis of individual private property, the system prevailing among Christian Filipinos. The Commission on National Integration advocated the implementation of permanent settlement on individual homesteads. However, the system of tenure among cultural minorities has traditionally been one of "farm tenure," in which rights to farms rather than to particular parcels of land are recognized (Kiefer 1976:106). Where shifting cultivation is practiced, rights to farms are transient rather than permanent. The maintenance of tenure was often based on labor and the presence of cultigens (Yengoyan 1971:366). A system of common property prevailed whereby individuals, through their kinship ties and/or common residence, had rights to obtain farmland.

Land legislation under the policy of national integration was allegedly designed to give indigenous minorities the opportunity to secure their land claims legally. In 1963 the Philippine Congress amended the Public Land Act, which had previously recognized the legal efficacy of property rights in the absence of title only when land had been occupied and cultivated since 1945. The amendments specifically entitle Muslim and tribal Filipinos who have been in continuous occupation and cultivation of land since 1955 to free patents for plots of land not exceeding 24 hectares (Philippine Government Documents 1936). Lands open to free patent include even those within the forest zone, provided that they are agricultural. By virtue of actual possession of the land through continuous occupation and cultivation, the indigenous minorities are presumed "to have performed all the conditions essential to a government grant and shall be entitled to a certificate of title" (Philippine Government Documents 1936). The amendments have largely gone unimplemented (Lynch 1983:30). Under the martial law administration of Ferdinand E. Marcos, the Ancestral Lands decree was promulgated in 1974 (Philippine Government Documents 1974). Like earlier legislation, it professes to provide Muslim and tribal Filipinos with the means to secure land ownership. The decree states that ancestral lands shall be surveyed and subdivided into small plots not exceeding five hectares, and opened to titling. However, the opportunity to complete and to perfect titling shall exist for a period of ten years, after which untitled lands "shall be declared open for allocation to other deserving applicants" (Philippine Government Documents 1974). The decree has never been implemented. A decade after its promulgation, not one qualified citizen acquired a paper title before the deadline (Lynch 1984:18). Coincident with the non-implementation of the decree, amnesties have been declared to the effect that migrants within the forest zone cannot be evicted if they entered before certain cut-off dates, first May 19, 1975, and then December 31, 1981. Where migrants occupy areas inhabited by indigenous minorities, the amnesties only deprive the latter of their ancestral lands and make it difficult for them to seek reinstatement on lands from which they have been displaced.

Land titling entails lengthy and complicated procedures that institutionalize differential tenure security. Landed elites, with their strong political connections, wealth, and access to legal expertise, can more readily obtain titles than settlers or cultural minorities. But even settlers enjoy a competitive advantage over indigenous groups. They are more familiar with national land laws and more able to manipulate them. Kin and friendship networks link some settlers to provincial bureaucrats, who usually belong to the same dominant group of Christian Filipinos. One example will illustrate the problem. Land patents can be issued to occupants of agricultural lands if they have been there on or before June 12, 1945. One clerk at the Bureau of Lands in Palawan points out that, although most settlers do not qualify under this provision, if they have had their lands surveyed and have filled out the appropriate forms, the Bureau overlooks the date of occupation and issues the title to them.

To summarize, land policies falling within the framework of "national integration" have been formulated to help the politically powerful by decreasing pressure for land reform and present a public image that government was trying to minimize inter-ethnic conflict. They have not sought to provide indigenous minorities undisputed ownership of their lands. Consequently, implementation has been contrary to the interests of the minorities.

Leaving aside the problem of legal ownership, discussed above, indigenous minorities face difficulties even in maintaining the use of their lands. Most tribal Filipinos occupy forested and unclassified areas, and are therefore subject to the economic development policies affecting the utilization of forest and mineral resources. These policies favor commercial users rather than agricultural users (Makil 1983:272). An amendment to the Revised Forestry Code of 1975 explicitly states that members of the cultural minorities can be ejected and relocated "whenever the best land use of the area so demands" (Philippine Government Documents 1978:Sec. 53). What "best land use" usually means is commercial forestry. In Palawan, 45 percent of the total land area of the mainland, approximately 671,720 hectares, is classified as commercial timberland; nine logging companies possess aggregate holdings of 505,315 hectares. As of 1975 a number of mining companies also operated in the forest zones. At the municipal level, the preferential allocation of forest lands to elite interests is replicated. In Brooke's Point municipality, where my fieldwork was conducted, leases for pastures and minor forest products have been awarded to high-ranking local government officials and businessmen. An agro-forestry lease had been awarded to a Manila-based corporation.

Government policy on forest management regulates the activities of swidden farmers, among whom are indigenous minorities and rural migrants. Swiddening is illegal and subject to punitive measures. However, the Bureau of Forest Development has begun to implement measures to provide forest farmers with positive incentives for ecologically sound farming and reforestation. With the impetus of foreign funding, it has launched an Integrated Social Forestry Program, which seeks to promote tenure security through long-term forest leases. Significantly, through the lobbying of an American consultant, the program recognizes the existence of "forest communities" and allows for communal forest leases (Philippine Government Documents 1982). The provision for communal stewardship is based on two prototypes developed by private organizations working with tribal Filipinos. While it is too soon to evaluate the merits of the new provision, which became effective in 1982, it is significant that an ecological approach, rather than the more politically sensitive issues of national integration and ancestral land rights, provides the mechanism whereby cultural minorities can begin to assert their communal land claims. Admittedly though, the provision falls short of communal ownership and reinforces the notion that ancestral lands fall within the public domain.

The Politics of Lands at Risk

The fact that ancestral lands are defined as part of the public domain has fostered a competitive process in which indigenous groups confront migrant farmers and developers in search of land. The patterns of confrontation, accommodation, and resistance of the Palaw'an of Abo-abo to incoming settlers are discussed below. There have been three outcomes in the competition over land: (1) displacement without political recourse, (2) displacement with political recourse, and (3) collective entrenchment.

Displacement Without Recourse

Displacement without political recourse occurred in the 1950s. Unsupervised migration to Palawan was accompanied by the absence of government regulation to protect the land rights of indigenous occupants. Settlers made their own arrangements to acquire land and expanded throughout the province.

The movement of migrants to southern Palawan from the Narra resettlement area was influenced by ecological changes and the building of new roads. Fernandez has described the nature of such changes (1972:180). The earliest group of migrants came from parts of the Philippines where paddy cultivation was practiced. Because they lacked knowledge and skill in clearing virgin forest, they destroyed the delicate ecosystem of the resettlement area. They cleared forest improperly and exposed topsoil to an acute laterizing process; then they plowed and cropped for two or more years without irrigation. When farms were left to fallow they were invaded by weeds and grasses (*Chromolaena odorata* and *Imperata cylindrica*). Farmers abandoned their fields and extended their practices to the foothills, thereby destroying valuable watersheds and reducing the irrigation potential of the area.

National roads from Narra were built to Brooke's Point in the southeast (1957–1958) and to Quezon in the southwest (1962–1963). Migrants followed the contours of the roads in search of new land, especially flat land that could be converted to paddy fields, although the preference for flat land did not preclude entry into the foothills. Some settlers made extensive swiddens to produce surplus rice with which they could pay lowland labor to carve paddy fields. In Abo-abo, an important junction linking the two roads, Palaw'an have been displaced from plains and inland valleys adjacent to the roads. They presently occupy the interior foothills.

Settlers regard Palaw'an land as government land, that is, public space open to their private claims (see Stone 1973). Palaw'an private rights to cultigens are respected, but unless they plant permanent crops their land claims are considered temporary. When Palaw'an move from one clearing to another and leave their fields to fallow, settlers can occupy the vacated area. As the road network expanded, migrants moving into Abo-abo acquired lands by squatting on "vacant" forest. Some compensated Palaw'an for clearing forest and for fruit trees the Palaw'an had planted, a practice meant to avoid conflict. Others swindled Palaw'an by giving them "gifts" of tobacco, fish, sugar, and clothing. Palaw'an claim that they were then unaware of the consequences of accepting what settlers gave them. After some time, settlers demanded payment for the "gifts" and, lacking cash, Palaw'an were forced to cede their lands. Where Palaw'an refused to leave, settlers threatened violence.

Settlers have established land claims in Abo-abo through residence and cultivation. Few of them have acquired legal title, mainly because of lengthy and expensive procedures. Bureaucracies are urban-based and distant from the communities they are meant to serve. In the entire province of Palawan—main island and outer islands—less than 10 percent of all agricultural landholdings are titled. Settlers know through experience that squatting is condoned and, in fact, have little reason to pursue formal titling procedures.

In the absence of legal title, settlers in Abo-abo have capitalized on cultural differences to enforce an ethnic hierarchy that protects their land claims. As settlers began to acquire land, they ridiculed Palaw'an, by comparing adult men in G-strings to monkeys, for example. Settlers also asserted that Palaw'an were inferior because they lacked amenities associated with "civilization"—clothes, soap, literacy, "religion," and wet rice farm technology. Today, settlers assume a paternalistic attitude, treating Palaw'an as minors or as ignorant and lazy people who need constant supervision. They exercise social privilege by, for example, participating in Palaw'an rice wine feasting while an equivalent open invitation to their own gatherings, like weddings and dances, is withheld. The most vivid expression of dominance, however, has been violence or the threat of it. It has created a fear among Palaw'an that encourages them to maintain physical distance from settlers. To avoid or escape conflict, Palaw'an retreat to the interior foothills.

When Abo-abo was opened to large-scale migration, Palaw'an had no access to legal channels to seek redress for their grievances. Though they were politically powerless, there is evidence that their retreat was accompanied by resistance to settler usurpation. For example, one Palaw'an sold his land to a neutral lowland farmer as a means of getting back at another settler, who had threatened him with a crowbar when he refused to give up his land. Palaw'an have also resisted settler ethos in charters of ethnic differentiation. Settlers have acquired land through both voluntary sales and involuntary pressures. Palaw'an acknowledge legitimate land transactions, but the cases of usurpation stand out in oral history. The stereotype of the settler is one who is deceitful, prone to anger, and capable of violence. Among Palaw'an, the acquisition of land rights expresses and creates bonds of kinship. The cultural elaboration of the settler's use of coercive power to secure Palaw'an land, articulating strong sentiments of injustice, delineates the boundaries of mutual trust and of membership in a Palaw'an moral community.

Palaw'an attachment to the interior hills, where they have retreated, is explicit in mythology. They differentiate themselves from ethnic groups associated with the exterior lowlands. As relations with the exterior have deprived Palaw'an of territorial control and threaten their communal integrity, they have emphasized relations within the interior, where autonomy and self-esteem are preserved. Palaw'an identify with activities of the interior, like swiddening and shamanism, which involve them in bonds of solidarity with household and local groups.

The retreat of the Palaw'an is a product of both their marginality in the national political arena and their desire to maintain control over the social relationships and behavioral ethos they value. By retreating into an exclusive ethnic community, displaced Palaw'an have chosen to live and to act in ways that allow them to retain their autonomy. To continue to live among settlers who exercise ownership rights would reduce the Palaw'an to subservience and dependence as tenants or wage workers.

Displacement with Recourse

Displacement with political recourse, specifically through the intervention of the Commission on National Integration, began in the sixties and lasted until the abolition of the Commission in 1975. Unsupervised migration was accompanied by government supervised land transactions. The area covered continued to be lands along the national roads. Settlers also continued making temporary claims to the foothills. They made their swiddens in the uplands while maintaining permanent residence in the lowlands.

Despite its statutory mandate to protect cultural minorities from land loss, the Commission in fact legitimized settler claims to Palaw'an lands. I have come across records indicating that between 1967 and 1975 the Commission investigated interethnic land transactions, some of which had occurred a decade earlier. The documents filed under "Inspector's Report on National Cultural Minorities Conveyances and/or Encumbrances" illustrate the readiness with which the Commission approved land sales to settlers. It supervised land compensation rather than reinstatement. Forty-six Palaw'an transactions in the municipality of Brooke's Point have been recorded. Not one application to sell land was rejected. Palaw'an lands, amounting to 237 hectares, were nibbled away. Once they had been sold to settlers, further sales were made to other settlers. Land did not revert back to Palaw'an.

Why did Palaw'an sell their lands? Physical survival is a central concern of Palaw'an society. Palaw'an are swidden farmers whose subsistence production is insufficient to meet household needs. Drought, pests, and winds account for rice shortages. Oral tradition recounts that epidemics wiped out Palaw'an hamlets. Malaria and pulmonary and gastro-intestinal diseases result in high rates of morbidity and mortality. Ironically, the survival concerns of Palaw'an society have increased rather than limited the incidence of land loss.

Land sales occurred during the hunger season, that period in the agricultural cycle beginning at planting, or shortly before, when Palaw'an no longer have rice. Traditionally, Palaw'an turned to foraging in the forest. However, settlers destroyed this resource through indiscriminate and extensive clearing. Through paddy cultivation, settlers produced surplus rice that was available during hunger months and offered to Palaw'an in lowland stores. Because forest foods had been depleted, Palaw'an took the rice, either in exchange for land or on credit. When creditors pressed payment, Palaw'an were forced to sell their lands.

Other contingencies arose in crisis situations. Palaw'an sold their lands in emergencies such as sickness, when they had to pay for medicines, doctor's fees, and transportation to distant health centers. Traditionally, Palaw'an vacated a household when a death occurred. With the presence of settlers, they began to sell land to pay for food expenses incurred at various stages of the mourning cycle. As land acquired a monetary value, heirs who had alternative farm sites would jointly sell the deceased's clearings and trees and divide the cash, thereby preventing any single heir from selling land.

Likewise, the introduction of a cash economy stimulated new agricultural options for Palaw'an. Palaw'an told Commission inspectors that they would sell their lands to buy draft animals and farm implements. The inspectors favored such land sales and saw in them the fulfillment of their goals, namely, the adoption by Palaw'an of sedentary agriculture and a lowland way of life.

Not only did the Commission supervise land sales, but it also became involved in the settlement of land disputes, ostensibly to help indigenous minorities. Its presence became a vehicle through which individual Palaw'an sought redress for land grievances. Given the opportunity to protect their lands, Palaw'an adapted to the strategies open to them. They sought the Commission's assistance in evicting settlers who encroached on their lands. However, the success of these strategies was severely limited. Because the urban-based Commission operated through sporadic visits to local communities, Palaw'an had to accumulate financial resources to pay for transportation and other incidental costs, like the payment of real property taxes to obtain a certified document of occupancy and cultivation. With their meager funds, Palaw'an could not sustain the prolonged processing of their claims. Nor did the Commission possess adequate finances and personnel to support the judicial process. Instead, it chose out-of-court settlement. Compromise solutions meant that Palaw'an ceded a portion of their landholdings to settlers. Alternatively, the Commission allowed a case to drag on until Palaw'an were defeated by attrition. Palaw'an retreated to the interior hills, sometimes as entire displaced communities. The net effect of the Commission was to provide a public image that the problem of ancestral land usurpation was being alleviated. However, in the backstage region of the frontier, Abo-abo Palaw'an were dispossessed: there has been no successful eviction of settlers from lands that Palaw'an claim to be theirs. The work of the Commission was taken over by the Presidential Assistant on National Minorities (Panamin) in 1975. While the Commission made sporadic entries into Palaw'an hamlets, Panamin has had no comparable presence. Its program has been reduced to routine office work rather than field operations. In the absence of a specialized agency to handle land issues, the officials of the local administrative unit, the *barangay*, have filled the gap. In Abo-abo, barangay officials, who are settlers themselves, perceive Palaw'an lands as "public"—open to all residents of the barangay—and thus, make little effort to protect them. Newcomers seeking land are directed to the uplands inhabited by Palaw'an. When disputes arise, officials adopt a compromise solution that seeks to divide contestable land between Palaw'an and settlers. These actions maintain the steady encroachment on Palaw'an lands.

Collective Entrenchment

Beginning in 1982, Palaw'an in Abo-abo have organized two corporate foundations to secure their lands through government-issued communal leases of 25 years, renewable for another 25 years. The Pinagsurotan Foundation, the first to be established, became a precedent for another group of hamlets, who then followed the pattern. A number of factors catalyzed the organization of the Pinagsurotan Foundation.

First, Palaw'an remain vulnerable to continued encroachment by settlers. Settlers not only make temporary claims to the foothills but permanent ones as well; and they have penetrated even the interior hills. Unsupervised migration continues under changing economic circumstances. Palawan has become a corn-exporting province. Forty-two percent of grain producing lands in the province, or 16,000 hectares, are planted in corn (Philippine Government Documents 1981a, Annex 5:6). Ninety percent of the corn crop is exported to Manila for manufacture into feeds, oil, and starch. In Abo-abo, a random survey of 25 lowland farmers indicates that 48 ha are planted in paddy rice, 14 ha in swidden rice and 26.25 ha in corn.[2] Cash cropping creates new demands for lands among settlers and also among Palaw'an, who are beginning to follow suit. While settlers demand that upland areas be open to them for cultivation, Palaw'an realize that encroachment has reached a point where they have nowhere else to retreat.

Palaw'an have begun to grow corn as a cash crop to repay debts incurred during hunger. Corn sales also provide a source of income at harvest, when traders converge in makeshift markets to sell clothes, plastic containers, and other manufactured goods to the Palaw'an. Palaw'an prefer to sell corn and to keep rice, one reason being that corn is not a staple. Traditionally, and even today, corn is grown in small quantities around a swidden. Its earlier maturity supplies Palaw'an a food source while they wait for rice to ripen; thus, corn is a hunger food. Palaw'an also prefer to grow corn as a cash crop because it requires less labor. On plowed land, corn needs only one weeding, compared to rice which needs two to three rounds of weeding. Then, too, the market value of a sack of corn (60 kg) is comparable to a sack of unhusked rice (44 kg), which the Palaw'an value more highly. The factors of labor, dietary practices, and competitive pricing are inducements to corn production. A second factor in the organization of the Pinagsurotan Foundation was an acceleration of the tax collection campaign of the municipality of Brooke's Point. The municipal government announced that, unless Palaw'an paid their property taxes, their lands would be confiscated and sold at a public auction. The announcement was made in July (1982), a hunger month, when Palaw'an cash earnings were allocated for rice.

A third factor was the establishment in 1981 of a small, experimental agroforestry project in Ipilan hamlet, Abo-abo. The purpose of the project was to improve husbandry techniques in an area where long fallow cycles had been drastically reduced. The fallow period has been shortened from eight to two years, and consequently, soils are exhausted and rice productivity is low. The project was initiated by a government research and training institute with the help of foreign funding. It was staffed by an agronomist, an American Peace Corps volunteer, and one or two part-time students from an agricultural college in Palawan. The presence of the Peace Corps Volunteer, in particular, provided a middleman linkage in local land problems. Although the project was not primarily directed at tenure issues, Palaw'an used its presence to resolve continuing problems of settler encroachment. This, and the municipal government's announcement on real property taxation, prompted the volunteer to convince Palaw'an to form a corporate foundation to secure their lands. Palaw'an responded favorably and began organizational meetings. A communal forest lease, patterned after those obtained by two other tribal Filipino groups, rather than individual forest stewardship certificates, became the goal of the foundation. Given bureaucratic inefficiency, Palaw'an would stand a better chance of securing one survey and one document from the Bureau of Forest Development, rather than numerous membership applications. The foundation generated pan-hamlet unity. What began as a project of five hamlets grew to ten hamlets, with a membership of over 200 households. The role of the volunteer was to inform and to assist Palaw'an with the paperwork. Palaw'an headmen scheduled monthly meetings in each of the member hamlets and public participation was encouraged. Those who attended discussed land problems and their responsibility in implementing an agroforestry project, which was the rationale of their lease application. The meetings crystallized a sense of community beyond the hamlet level. The host hamlet for each meeting collected food contributions and fed the visiting headmen and local participants. Through the circulation of meetings, men, women, and children from all the member hamlets were given the opportunity to listen and to participate in the discussions. Food sharing and informational exchanges strengthened social cohesion.

Additionally, the name Pinagsurotan denotes linkages with a Palaw'an shaman and folk hero, Damar, who represents mystical power. That power is associated with the survival of children and the sick, and thus of Palaw'an society itself. Damar was arrested three times before the outbreak of World War II by Filipino authorities, who charged him with opening virgin forest with the assistance of his followers. Within Palaw'an tenure, clearing forest establishes occupancy rights. Prior to his final departure from Abo-abo, Damar told Palaw'an that when Americans had come to the locality, their presence would indicate that he had reached an agreement or *pinagsurotan* with them. In naming their foundation Pinagsurotan, Palaw'an reinforce cultural cohesion. They draw upon historical precedents to express indigenous power in securing the basis of their survival and cultural continuity today, namely, land. The formation of the Pinagsurotan Foundation generated opposition from the local administrative unit, the barangay. Unlike earlier land disputes involving individual contestants, competition has developed between two corporate entities. The barangay represents settler interests for free and open access to the uplands. The barangay council, dominated by lowland settlers, perceives the foundation as a threat to its autonomy. Local officials associate barangay power and continuity with the extent of territorial occupation. Abo-abo's control over its own boundaries is not guaranteed because most barangay lands are still classified as forest, and therefore fall within the jurisdiction of the Bureau of Forest Development. Additionally, Abo-abo's population, estimated at 1,609 in 1975, is about 80 percent Palaw'an. Palaw'an control over their own territory could lead to the formation of a separate barangay, which could legally be formed with a minimum of 100 households. If barangay Abo-abo were to be subdivided, local officials fear that settlers would be relegated to a narrow strip of land along both sides of the national highway, with little room for territorial expansion. Additionally, 67 ha of land adjacent to the highway already belong to an educational reservation administered by a provincial agricultural college.

Confronted with the potential loss of upland areas, at a time when growing corn for cash in the hills was becoming more lucrative, settlers organized their resistance formally as a corporate entity, and informally through individual action. The barangay filed a complaint with the Bureau of Forest Development. It petitioned for the opening of an upland agricultural settlement for all members of the barangay. The adjacent barangay of Isumbo, where three hamlets had joined the foundation, also sent a complaint to the Bureau in which it claimed that the foundation would be taking over "thousands of hectares" presumed to belong to the barangay rather than to the Palaw'an. Informally, settlers sought to intimidate Palaw'an by continuing to encroach on their lands. Rumors were also circulated to the effect that the foundation and the agroforestry project were a front for a large corporation to take over the area.

The Palaw'an have sought to protect their lands through interpersonal networks; this has led to new opportunities for political action beyond the local level. The regularity with which Palaw'an approached the volunteer to register their land problems was their way of creating linkages to sources of authority, like bureaucracies, where they are not represented. Interaction with the volunteer and his superior information eventually led to collective mobilization, a strategy that gave the Palaw'an the opportunity to press their land claims with minimal risk. They were spared the expense of traveling to distant towns to process the necessary papers. The volunteer and the connections he established with national organizations expedited the application process. Furthermore, the follow-up of the foundation's lease application has been facilitated by cooperation with the Manila-based Philippine Association for Inter-Cultural Development. Unfortunately, the agro-forestry project, which had provided the impetus for resource management, was terminated due to lack of funds. However, the continuity of its goals can be be secured through the communal lease which, after all, advocates improved upland farming practices. Resource management is linked to a perceived Palaw'an concern—land tenure—and thus acquires a significance beyond the technological and economic goals of the original agro-forestry project.

Conclusion

The politics of land in a frontier setting involves a complex pattern of linkages between delocalized and localized decision making. The concept of "delocalization" refers to "shifts in interdependencies and points of decision making . . . with the result that more and more decisions affecting a particular location are made . . . in distant capitals and trading centers" (Poggie and Lynch 1974:362). However, the outcomes of those decisions take different trajectories as local actors use, manipulate, or disregard the intervention of the larger system in order to accommodate their priorities.

The Palaw'an case points to "recurrent" and "emergent" change (Barth 1981:118) in the process of political negotiation. There is a continuing contradiction in the state's policy of land allocation. On the one hand, it promotes distribution by declaring lands within the public domain open to alienation and disposition for smallholding farmers, and by opening public forest to certified occupancy; but, on the other hand, it continues to retain control over these lands. The fragmentation of lands into individual parcels for titling or for forest permits, and the complex procedures the system entails, keeps land largely within state control. Similarly, ancestral lands that have not been surveyed, parcelled, and titled revert back to the state; and communal forms of landholding are recognized on the basis of leasehold rather than ownership. Its reluctance to forgo control allows the state to allocate the resources of the "public domain" to the sectors most likely to reinforce the class and ethnic structures upon which it is built, or to those that do not challenge control of the state apparatus.

Within this framework, changing patterns of political mobilization and negotiation emerge at the local level, partly through the opening of new social and communication networks. Among the Palaw'an, responses to land encroachment reflect the way power is exercised in a multi-ethnic locality. In the initial period of resettlement and government neglect, migrants displaced Palaw'an. Palaw'an, having no political power to protect themselves against settler encroachment, retreated into the interior hills. Government negligence of Palaw'an land rights was followed by active intervention in land transactions and disputes through the Commission on National Integration. However, the Commission was concerned with the reduction of political conflict rather than the protection of indigenous land rights. Palaw'an mobilized individually to avail themselves of the Commission's services, but they made no significant progress in securing their lands. In their impoverishment, they accommodated themselves to the Commission's strategy of compensation for lands secured by settlers.

The combination of public and private interest in upland resource management provided the conditions for renewed interest among the Palaw'an in securing their lands. Palaw'an collective mobilization was initiated by an outsider as a means of bringing to the forefront of bureaucratic attention the issue of tenure among cultural minorities. This, in turn, was brought about by Palaw'an insistence that an agro-forestry project planned for the district should also address tenure problems. Given a situation of inter-ethnic competition over land, it appears that environmental management could not be separated from the basic problem of security of tenure. In the absence of representation in bureaucratic offices, Palaw'an have relied on middlemen for information and access to the procedures whereby they can secure their interests. The outcome of Palaw'an activity, however, remains tied to the politics of the bureaucratic arena. The opportunities and setbacks in the course of getting their lease will be affected by their marginal position in Philippine society as well as by the flow of political events in a much more complex and diverse situation of national resource distribution.

The evolution of Palaw'an political activity likewise responds to changes in local economic-ecological realities. The initial period of displacement occurred when Palaw'an were still a relatively mobile population, with available interior land for retreat. As settler migration continued unabated, Palaw'an developed an interest in land retention to deflect settler intrusion into their communities; and thus, they sought to limit dispossession through political channels. Today, Palaw'an form a stabilized swidden population with little land available for the establishment of new settlements, much less for the retention of long fallowing cycles. As traditional forest foods are no longer readily available, Palaw'an rely on lowland stores for rice, and repayment is beginning to be made in terms of a cash crop, corn. Because corn cultivation requires land in addition to swidden plots, Palaw'an are strongly motivated to keep their lands. Additionally, through control of land, Palaw'an can keep themselves from becoming dependent on settlers for their source of livelihood. They can also maintain the sense of communal identity that they previously protected by retreating into the interior hills.

In summary, the politics of lands at risk involves a set of social mechanisms created by the state and the attempts of competing claimants to monopolize or to protect their resource interests. At critical junctures of state intervention, indigenous minorities experience setbacks and gains in terms of their ability to protect themselves against encroachment. The Palaw'an case suggests that the initial period of failure to avert dispossession reinforced a social and cultural cohesion that eventually fostered receptivity to collective mobilization. A unified political organization carries strong potential not only for securing long term tenure but also for endowing a communal meaning to the pursuit of sound ecological practices.

Notes

1. I would like to acknowledge Robert L. Franklin for his comments and editorial assistance in the preparation of this paper.

2. The average farm size in Palawan is 4.6 ha. In Brooke's Point municipality, to which Abo-abo belongs, the average is 5.4 ha. However, much land that is claimed is underutilized for reasons like shortage of farm labor and inadequate farming technology. Under these circumstances, corn production is carried out on relatively small-sized farms and marketing involves an elaborate arrangement. Farmers sell their corn to local dealers who resell the large quantities they accumulate to wholesalers from larger towns. The wholesalers truck the corn from various assembly points to a main warehouse, and then ship it to Manila wholesalers who, in turn, sell it to processors.

References

Barth, Frederick
    1981   On the Study of Social Change. *In* Process and Form in Social Life: Selected Essays of Frederick Barth. Vol. 1. Pp. 105–118. London: Routledge and Kegan Paul.
Eder, James
    1981   From Grain Crops to Tree Crops in a Palawan Swidden System. *In* Adaptive Strategies and Change in Philippine Swidden-based Societies. Harold Olofson, ed. Pp. 91–104. Laguna, Philippines: Forest Research Institute.
Estioko Griffin, Agnes, and P. Bion Griffin
    1981   The Beginnings of Cultivation among Agta Hunter-Gatherers in Northeast Luzon. *In* Adaptive Strategies and Change in Philippine Swidden-based Societies. Harold Olofson, ed. Pp. 55–72. Laguna, Philippines: Forest Research Institute.
Fernandez, Carlos
    1972   Blueprints, Realities and Success in a Frontier Resettlement Community. *In* View from the Paddy. Frank Lynch, ed. Pp. 176–185. Quezon City, Philippines: Institute of Philippine Culture.
Kerkvliet, Benedict J.
    1979   Land Reform: Emancipation or Counterinsurgency? *In* Marcos and Martial Law in the Philippines. David A. Rosenberg, ed. Pp. 113–144. Ithaca, NY: Cornell University Press.
Kiefer, Thomas
    1976   From Farm Tenure to Land Tenure in Jolo: Some Aspects of Change in Tausug Land Law. Studies in Third World Societies 1(1):97–100.

Lynch, Owen J.
   1983   A Survey of Research on Upland Tenure and Displacement. Paper presented at the National Conference on Research in the Uplands, Quezon City, Philippines, April 12.
   1984   The Invisible Filipinos: Indigenous and Migrant Citizens within the "Public Domain." Philippine Law Register, pp. 18–22.
Makil, Perla Q., Ruby E. Reyes, and Fadzillah M. Cooke
   1983   Toward a Social-Forestry Oriented Policy: The Philippine Experience. Reprinted in Human Rights and Ancestral Land: A Sourcebook. Pp. 272–280. Quezon City, Philippines: Ugnayang Pang-Agham Tao.
Moore, Sally F.
   1984   Legislated Transformation: Central Government and Rural Life on Kilimanjaro. Paper presented at the 83rd Annual Meeting of the American Anthropological Association, Denver, Colorado, Nov. 15–18.
Myers, Norman
   1984   The Primary Source: Tropical Forests and Our Future. New York, NY: W. N. Norton and Co.
Olofson, Harold
   1981   Introduction. *In* Adaptive Stràtegies and Change in Philippine Swidden-based Societies. Harold Olofson, ed. Pp.1–12. Laguna, Philippines: Forest Research Institute.
Philippine Government Documents
   1936   Public Land Act (Commonwealth Act No. 141, 1936, as amended).
   1974   Office of the President. Presidential Decree 410. Declaring Ancestral Lands Occupied and Cultivated by National Cultural Communities as Alienable and Disposable, and for Other Purposes. Manila: Central Book Supply Incorporated (CBSI).
   1978   Office of the President. Presidential Decree 1559. Revising Presidential Decree No. 705, otherwise known as the Revised Forestry Reform Code. Manila: CBSI.
   1980   Palawan Integrated Area Development Project. Project Feasibility Study, First Stage Report, June. Quezon City: National Center for Integrated Area Development.
   1981a   Palawan Integrated Area Development Project. Draft Final Report. Background to the Project. Quezon City, Philippines: National Center for Integrated Area Development.
   1981b   National Economic and Development Authority/National Census and Statistics Office. Philippine Yearbook. Manila.
   1982   Bureau of Forest Development. Administrative Order No. 48. Regulations and Guidelines Implementing LOI 1260, Otherwise Known as PROFEM II.
Poggie, John J., and Robert N. Lynch
   1974   Rethinking Modernization: Concluding Comments. *In* Rethinking Modernization: Anthropological Perspectives. John J. Poggie and Robert N. Lynch, eds. Pp. 353–375. Westport, CT: Greenwood Press.
Rice, Delbert
   1981   Upland Agricultural Development in the Philippines: An Analysis and a Report on the Ikalahan Programs. *In* Adaptive Strategies and Change in Philippine Swidden-based Societies. Harold Olofson, ed. Pp. 73–90. Laguna, Philippines: Forest Research Institute.

Schlegel, Stuart A.
  1981   Tiruray Traditional and Peasant Subsistence: A Comparison. *In* Adaptive
          Strategies and Change in Philippine Swidden-based Societies. Harold
          Olofson, ed. Pp. 105–116. Laguna, Philippines: Forest Research Institute.
Stone, Richard
  1973   Philippine Urbanization: The Politics of Public and Private Property in
          Greater Manila. Report No. 6. DeKalb, IL: Center for Southeast Asian
          Studies.
Warner, Katherine
  1981   Swidden Strategies for Stability in a Fluctuating Environment: The Tagbanwa
          of Palawan. *In* Adaptive Strategies and Change in Philippine Swidden-
          based Societies. Harold Olofson, ed. Pp. 13–28. Laguna, Philippines: Forest
          Research Institute.
Wurfel, David
  1981   Philippine Agrarian Policy Today: Implementation and Political Impact. *In*
          Peasantry and National Integration. Celma Aguero, ed. Pp. 171–198. Mexico:
          El Colegio de Mexico.
Yengoyan, Aram
  1971   The Effects of Cash Cropping on Mandaya Land Tenure. *In* Land Tenure
          in the Pacific. Ron Crocombe, ed. Pp. 362–374. Melbourne: Oxford Uni-
          versity Press.

12

Lands at Risk, People at Risk: Perspectives on Tropical Forest Transformations in the Philippines

James N. Anderson

Introduction

In two critical Philippine environments, the competition for resources in the drive to achieve rapid development of marginal resource areas has posed serious threats to the ecology and to the cultural survival of Filipino groups. This chapter discusses the process, paying particular attention to economic trends, national policies, population growth, internal migration, land tenure, and power relations, which conspired to alter local socioeconomic conditions and transform diverse ecosystems in the vast Philippine uplands and coastal zones. Fuller consideration is given to upland forests and resources than to coastal zones, because impacts are more dramatic there.

The Philippine case provides insights into the general problem of the incorporation of "marginal" resources and people into a national economy and polity. Following a brief sketch of the geographic and sociopolitical setting of these changes, the chapter describes the status of upland forests and coastal resources and the processes influencing them. It then examines interactions between certain particularly vulnerable populations and the ecosystems they occupy, as well as their responses to external forces.

A Landscape Dominated by Mountains and Coastlines

The Philippines is a mountainous island nation of 56 million people. Its more than 7,000 islands stretch 1,850 kilometers south to north and 965 kilometers east to west. Eleven major islands occupy 96 percent of the total land area. The land area, about the size of Arizona, exhibits extraordinary regional differences. On the larger islands high mountains and hilly lands are cut by narrow valleys that widen into small alluvial plains, major exceptions being the wide plains of central Luzon, southern Mindanao, western Negros, and southern Panay. Over 65 percent of the Philippine landscape is elevated "uplands" presently dominated by grassland and varying forest cover. The country's coastline is 18,417 kilometers long— twice that of the USA. Situated above and below the most economically productive lands (the lowland basins), the uplands and coastal zones are critically important environments where rapid changes are taking place.

The Sociopolitical Setting for Forest Degradation

Natural geological and hydrological processes at work in the typhoon-prone Western Pacific continuously agitate the uplands, basins, and coasts, but rates of runoff, erosion, and siltation are accelerated by certain human interventions, especially deforestation and intensive land uses (Sutlive et al. 1980a, 1980b; UNESCO 1978).

Deforestation has been occurring throughout the tropics at rapid rates but nowhere faster than in the Philippines (FAO 1981; Meyers 1980). Early in the Spanish period the impact of the population on Philippine forests was minor (see Hutterer 1982). The longstanding trade in forest and coastal zone products contributed little to resource deterioration (Anderson and Vorster 1983). Well over 90 percent of Philippine forests were essentially undisturbed, but forest exploitation and occupation began increasing after 1850 along with stepped-up commercial activity. In 1900, when the population numbered 7.6 million, the estimate of forest cover was about 70 percent. Commercial agricultural production expanded rapidly under American hegemony. Larger areas of forests were cleared for plantation agriculture, mining, homesteads, and log and lumber industries (Ofreneo 1980:14–27).

Meyers (1981:57) places the Philippines first in his highest category, "areas undergoing broadscale conversion at rapid rates." Official reports do not reflect actual circumstances. According to the FAO (1981) assessment, the total remaining "closed forest" area, including "undisturbed" (32 percent), "logged" (41 percent), "unproductive" (incapable of regeneration, 20 percent), and "parks" (7 percent), is just over 9.5 million ha. The same assessment, however, classifies 3.52 million ha of the total as "forest fallows" located within "closed" forest patches. Actually, in terms of remaining forest area per capita, the Philippines stands next to last among Southeast Asian countries, having less than one-fourth hectare for each Filipino. Moreover, the deforestation rate is 91,000 ha (or 1 percent) per year. Revilla et al. (1977) have projected that forest extinction will occur by the year 2000 even if reforestation takes place at optimistic rates.

Two processes are at work. One concerns the comparatively gradual impacts on natural resources by relatively stable human populations. The second concerns the more ecologically degrading, rapid exploitation that accompanies an aggressive competition for scarce resources by commercial enterprises and entrepreneurs during certain critical periods. It is this second process, begun in earnest in the mountainous upland and coastal regions of the Philippines in the 1960s, that most concerns us here. This period initiated a final opportunity to exploit forest, land, mineral, water, and human resources cheaply and profitably. With the population now numbering

56 million, forest cover stands at less than 30 percent, hardly any of it undisturbed.

The process is taking place elsewhere, especially in the humid tropics (see Brown et al. 1984:74–94; National Research Council 1982; Sutlive et al. 1980a), but the Philippine case assumed a unique form and velocity with Marcos' martial law regime (Anderson 1982; Bello et al. 1982). In his first term, Marcos had adopted a modernizing and reformist posture. After declaring martial law (in 1972), however, he accelerated direct and indirect involvement of the government in the economy to pursue resource exploitation, consolidation of political power, and the restructuring of the long-entrenched oligarchy. Aided principally by the World Bank, Marcos moved to reorganize economic and social development based on land reform and agricultural growth and on export-oriented industrialization, hoping to mimic the rapid development achieved by autocratic regimes in South Korea and Taiwan (Bello et al. 1982). Relying on foreign loans, encouraging foreign private investment, removing restrictions on trade and capital flows, and developing closer trade ties with Japan and the United States, Marcos opened the Philippine economy to rapid exploitation. The commercial orientation greatly accelerated the forest destruction apparent today (Ofreneo 1980). The policy, and the mismanagement and abuses that came to permeate its implementation, eventuated in shocking costs to the majority of Filipinos, to natural resources, and to national autonomy. Agriculture, which includes forestry and fisheries, paid the bills.

Having already established a corps of Western-trained "technocrats," Marcos used his new elite to implement his development plans. By the mid-1970s he had curtailed the power of the old elite and replaced them with a group of "cronies" who were granted monopolies in the coconut and sugar industries and in other strategic sectors of the economy (Doherty 1982). He created government-owned corporations to exercise controls over all basic sectors in what has been called "Marcos socialism." The government's role in financial markets also grew substantially. Thus a decade of rapid "development" was initiated which, after early gains, devolved into efforts to consolidate Marcos' own political and economic power. Abuses by Marcos supporters became the norm.

The peoples and the resources of the marginal upland and coastal regions were to be incorporated rapidly into the national economy and legal system, whatever the cost. Agricultural development policies for marginal areas essentially paralleled those pursued in the more resilient lowlands. They consisted of expansion and intensification of commercial crops that were expected to make the uplands and coastal zones contribute their share to the GNP. Thus, export-oriented, foreign-exchange-earning monocultures were developed mostly on large-scale enterprises with no apparent concern for local people or the tolerance of the ecosystems involved (Political Economy of Philippine Commodities 1983). Stepped-up mining, timber cutting, and intensive cropping resulted in damage from accelerated runoff of rains, erosion, and siltation, especially on steeper slopes affecting upland, lowland and coastal areas.

The struggle for control of upland and coastal resources has been waged by several interest groups. On the one hand there are the residents, some indigenous and others more recent. On the other hand, there are a variety of newcomers including Filipino peasants, private entrepreneurs (some of whom were favored Marcos' civilian and military clients), government agencies, domestic corporations, and multinationals.

The Destruction of Upland Resources

Rapid deforestation has resulted from the activities of all these groups. Government and media reports most often blame the indigenous *kaingineros* (hill farmers) for upland forest destruction. Because of their numbers and techniques, however, they cannot be the major culprits (Conklin 1957; Olafson 1981). By contrast, a large number of underemployed or displaced lowlanders have migrated to the uplands in recent decades in response to the dearth of economic opportunities and the failure of agrarian reform. They are responsible for much forest damage, but even more has been caused by small entrepreneurs, corporations, government agencies, and multinationals.

Logging, forest industries, livestock operations, cropping schemes, resettlement programs, and plantations have had massive impacts on ecosystems and resident populations. The millions of marginalized tribal and Muslim peoples and some established hill cultivators are the chief victims of such operations. The drastic transformations of these peoples and their natural resource systems and the usurpation of their land rights are justified by the Philippine government in the name of "development," but this accelerated exploitation has produced mainly personal and not national gains. Most development investments in the marginal areas have added relatively little to the gross domestic product and almost nothing to employment, but Philippine upland development has benefited existing elite groups in the economy and polity (Salgado 1985).

Despite new attention to the agricultural sector, government programs remained unbalanced in favor of industrial and urban development. Gains in food production achieved in the late 1960s and early 1970s could not be sustained. Effective efforts toward land reform on rice and corn lands slowed by 1975 (Kerkvliet 1979; Wurfel 1977). In the meantime a foreign debt burden ($26 billion in 1984) began to accumulate. The Philippines' balance of trade deteriorated by more than 40 percent. Energy and foreign exchange dependence made oil shocks and world recessions disastrous events for the Philippine economy. While the economy grew at respectable rates during the 1970s, it remained essentially unchanged structurally. Indeed, participation narrowed (Doherty 1982). Moreover, mismanagement of traditional exports and failures to diversify the economy exacerbated unresolved structural problems. In short, "development" during the Marcos era was seriously flawed. Rather than benefiting them, it devastated rural people (Carner 1982; Fegan 1985; May 1985).

Unsolved agrarian problems have led to deforestation. Until early in this century, unhappy tenants had the option of escaping to nearby lowland forest frontiers, which have long served as a safety valve for pressures on land resources (Anderson 1982; McLennan 1982). Many Filipinos were pushed into the uplands in the past two decades as population growth saturated the lowlands, and the failure of agrarian reform policies made landless tenants expendable (Kerkvliet 1979; Wurfel 1977). Those who were expelled had the choice of becoming rural or urban wage laborers, or becoming upland cultivators in nearby hill areas.

Once in the uplands, the former lowland tenants and agricultural laborers encountered ecosystems whose cultivation demanded skills that were unknown to them. Moreover, these new cultivators encountered soils more vulnerable to erosion and degradation. Some found relatively favorable soils for the establishment of short fallow perennial or annual cropping systems, what Olafson (1980) calls "fixed hillside farming." Others, finding less fertile soils, were forced to take up short fallow "partial system" swiddening, which is highly unstable and ecologically damaging (Conklin 1957). The latter migrant cultivators managed to harvest enough annual crops to feed their families, or, through part-time upland cultivation, to supplement their household income, but annual cropping on infertile soils ultimately requires the clearing of new fields and thus expands areas that cannot be restored to forest.

After 1972, logging was expanded to increase export (Salgado 1985:111–113). In 1973 log and lumber exports exceeded all other exports by a considerable margin (IBON Databank 1984:85–87). In 1975 the government, realizing the decline in forest resources, reduced concessions for legal cutting, but implementation proved problematic; illegal cutting continued unabated. In 1976 a ban on log exports was decreed in order to secure profits on value-added processing of lumber products for the Philippine economy. Today domestic demand for lumber and plywood, and years of rapid, often illegal, cutting have depleted forests of first-class timber, thus markedly reducing future export potential and domestic self-sufficiency.

Logging does not necessarily cause permanent deforestation. Selective logging can cause considerable damage, but even clear-cutting, except over wide areas, does not suppress forest recovery. The scale of cutting and subsequent uses of the land are the major determinants of recovery time, which ranges from decades to over a century.

National parks and biosphere reserves have been generally unprotected from loggers or swiddeners. Worse, most of the nation's critical watersheds are already degraded to grassland cover. Serious reforestation efforts, begun in 1977, have proven ineffective. The total area converted to monoculture forest plantations under commercial management is 300,000 ha, although 98 percent of this is classified "non-industrial," that is, casually managed (Salgado 1985:115). Marcos, finally concerned, increased budgets for reforestation beyond those for agrarian reform after 1978, but burgeoning deficits have blocked allocations.

The most obvious Philippine upland landscape today is grassland (over 2 million ha). Forest is converted not so much to agriculture as to relatively unprotective and unproductive grasslands covered mainly with cogon (*Imperata cylindrica*) or talahib (*Saccharum* spp.). Grasses can provide a vegetation cover that slows the runoff of heavy rains and the worst ravages of erosion, but they do not perform these protective functions as well as closed canopy forests do, especially on steep gradients.

Fire plays a crucial role in the maintenance of grass succession and in suppressing forest recovery. In forest management, fire is used for the burning of vegetation in long fallow shifting cultivation. Its role is increasing with the creation of grasslands for the expansion of cattle raising operations in the drier uplands of the western Philippines. Increasingly, beef is being exported to the expanding Japanese market, with the remainder going to domestic urban markets. In those areas where commercial beef-raising has developed, often on ranches owned by government and military officials, serious erosion and soil nutrient deficiencies are becoming evident. Although sometimes mistaken for burns in connection with hill farming, the fires rising in the mountains on the western side of the archipelago during the dry season are often connected with the renewal of upland pastures.

In 1976 just under one million ha of "forest" lands were allotted under pasture leases and permits. These were almost all in annually burned grasslands. Although the area of legal concessions had been reduced officially since then, it is probable that with the government policy of expanding meat production, the total Philippine area under pasture has actually been expanded. This is land that is effectively denied to small producers who lack the power and capital to obtain leases. Moreover, the soil is mined of nutrients and forest recovery species are set back. Efforts to reclaim these areas for forestry or agriculture have proven costly and lengthy.

While the building of dams has also caused the forced resettlement of thousands of mainly tribal people, considerably more Philippine resettlement resulted from private, self-motivated effort. Whether from push or pull incentives or from government sponsored (or forced) or voluntary efforts, many Filipinos were relocated in upland areas. Some, using intensive agricultural methods, sought refuge in areas adjacent to their former lowland residences. Others have followed the loggers and other commercial operators up the newly cut roads into previously unimpacted habitats. A significant number underwrote their own successful migration to the few remaining distant, but still-promising, frontier areas (Eder 1982).

Government land settlement and forced resettlement schemes are stopgap policies that sacrifice forest resources to avoid undertaking structurally significant agrarian reforms. The resettlement process, managed by the Ministry of Agrarian Reform, proved expensive in monetary and human terms, and not very successful. Kickbacks for infrastructure development and services were endemic, and planning and administration inadequate. The result is that some of those who were resettled lost or transferred their new lands to others and returned to their old homes or joined the flight to the cities. Even in the more successful settlements, the conditions from which settlers are trying to escape have been recreated. Tenancy is rife; economic insecurity and indebtedness are commonplace. The overall result is that conditions declined both in the areas sending migrants and in those receiving them. The opening up of new lands has simply extended old vices, all the while displacing and exploiting indigenous people. Inequalities and inter-ethnic conflicts have been seriously exacerbated (Anderson 1982).

Recent resettlement has had to put people on marginal lands, given the saturation of available arable land. Marginal lands with little potential for conventional intensification, except at great capital expense, have given most migrants little choice but to pursue swidden cultivation, often pushing it beyond the limits of ecological resilience. Whether employing it as their major or supplemental form of farming, this expansion of swidden results in further losses of forest and watershed. Organized resettlement, justified on grounds of landlessness, results in more landlessness; and resettlement intended to halt swiddening in one area instead expands it. Similarly, resettlement designed to improve urban quality by exporting people back to rural areas from the cities has both failed to improve urban conditions and contributed to new rural degradation. Forced resettlement required by the building of new hydroelectric dams has often inundated prime productive cropland and has resettled the affected people on marginal lands, which practice damages the critical watersheds of the dams, thus threatening substantially to shorten the lives of these expensive development projects. Resettlement intended to improve land tenure has also created new tenurial conflicts with people who previously occupied the area. In general, forced resettlement exacerbates problems rather than solving them.

Economic and social problems that were used to justify martial law festered, requiring increasingly repressive military action to maintain control. Military engagements were fought mainly in the uplands and the coastal zones of the Muslim south.

The guerilla war that has dragged on in the Philippines, especially since the declaration of martial law in 1972 (George 1980; Bello and Rivera 1977), has been fought principally in the uplands where New People's Army and Moro National Liberation Front forces take refuge. In this war of attrition the principal victims have been neither rebels nor Armed Forces of the Philippines but upland residents. In politically unstable areas of Mindanao, Samar, Leyte, Mindoro, Palawan, and Luzon, major road and bridge construction went forward rapidly in the 1970s in response to military needs. Together with heavy shelling and bombing of certain suspected insurgent areas and the clearing of trails and approach areas around military facilities, road construction has scarred the upland landscape. Less intensive damage to coastal resources and inland water resources also resulted from the new construction and expansion of provincial port facilities or from power development (Washburn 1981).

Meanwhile, export-oriented agricultural policies came to impinge further upon public lands. After 1972 there was an impressive increase in areas planted in export crops on newly reclassified lands (Salgado 1985:94–115). Banana export burgeoned after martial law, quadrupling between 1972 and 1976. Banana land expanded by an average of 4 percent per year for the decade, part of it coming from converted corn, abaca or rice lands and the rest from newly cultivated former public lands (Wurfel 1977:29). Large-scale corporate operations have dominated this expansion (Political Economy of Philippine Commodities 1983).

Corporate cultivation expanded in another direction after 1974 with the issuance of General Order 47 and Presidential Decree No. 472 (PD 472). The former required corporations with more than 500 employees to produce or import rice sufficient to feed them. Wurfel (1977:29) estimates that corporations bought up more than 15,000 ha of rice lands from small producers as a result of the order.

Presidential Decree 472 required all holders of timber licenses and pasture leases on public land to develop areas within these concessions for the production of food to feed their workers. Thus, land that was technically classified as forest was brought under cultivation. Abuses were quite general. In the Sampaloc, Quezon province, for instance, PD 472 was used by a logging firm to justify clearcutting forest areas, which were then planted with a few scattered bananas. Since the 1974 oil shock, areas of remaining forests on public lands in Negros and Panay have come under the axe for use as fuel in sugar milling. By 1976, 26,000 ha were being farmed under the provisions of PD 472. Many of these areas will revert to grasslands, further expanding the estimated five million ha that have already succeeded to grass after deforestation.

Conflicts in Indigenous and State Land Tenures

The incorporation of the uplands into the wider Philippine economy has given rise to many conflicts. The most profound are those over rights to land and other natural resources. The major structural cleavages in Philippine society have long related to the competition for rights to labor and land. Conflict between national and customary resource tenures sharpened as the government neglected to recognize the land rights of tribal and peasant peoples of the marginal resource areas.

Philippine public land policies understandably are directed toward promoting the exploitation of natural resources for agricultural development to serve national economic goals. They are only incidentally concerned with making improvements in people's lives, especially if the people are members of cultural minorities. Upland and forest tenure policy provides a telling illustration.

After decades of slow progress, Philippine land classification was stepped up in the 1970s, aided in part by the use of LANDSAT imagery. The broadest distinction used by the Bureau of Forest Development is that between forest lands and alienable and disposable lands. Lands in the latter category may be used for agricultural and commercial development and settlement. In the early 1970s the ratio of forest to alienable and disposable land was set at 40:60 (the forest ratio target was later raised to 46:54). But in 1976 only about 30 percent of the country's land area was still covered by old-growth, well-stocked and low-density forests or cutover forest lands. Of approximately nine million ha of "forest" lands, 1.5 million were earmarked for conversion to agricultural land. Legally, forest reserves include all lands that exceed 18 percent of slope, of which only about one-third constitutes commercially valuable forests. The remaining two-thirds are cutover or denuded "forest" lands and are already occupied by tribal or peasant cultivators. The decade of the 1970s thus witnessed a marked increase in the reallocation of forests to crop land, pasture land, fish ponds, and for resettlement, in efforts to increase agricultural production. It might be hoped that such changes in public land would be distributed in the interests of its traditional occupants or at least of the public at large. Instead, the reallocation benefited only a favored few.

Two Marcos decrees in particular threatened age-old tribal rights. Presidential Decree 410 (the "Ancestral Land Decree"), effective March 1984, affects all 4.3 million tribal Filipinos. It enables the government to alienate and dispose for development projects the land areas long occupied by "cultural minorities" unless these minorities apply for title to their ancestral land. For a number of reasons, however, most tribal groups are unwilling or unable to apply. (For an exception to this, see Lopez in this volume.) Most retain confidence in their customary tenure system which lies at the heart of their cultural integrity, and they have learned to be suspicious of any dealings with the government. Beyond this, what appears to be private property actually is shared by the tribal people (Lynch 1983). Tribal political organizations, decentralized authority, and diverse tenure systems are incompatible with concepts and codes of the state. Finally, the lack of sophistication in dealing with the national law, the difficulties of determining traditional boundaries and of conducting surveys, and the time and costs involved in making application for title (with no assurance of success) discourage tribal peoples. Often viewed as squatters on public lands, they find that their rights to their ancestral lands receive scant protection under national laws.

Presidential Decree 705 (the "Revised Forestry Code") established a new land classification for the uplands. It dictates that no land in the public domain (that is, over 17 percent of slope) is alienable and disposable for agricultural and settlement purposes. Because most tribal lands, especially on the island of Luzon, including the famous irrigated rice terraces of the Cordillera Central range, are in excess of 18 percent, they are disqualified for titling.

Presidential Decree 1559 (effective 1978) provides for ejection of tribal Filipinos from their ancestral land whenever the "best land use" of an area as defined by the director of the Bureau of Lands dictates. This decree legalized awarding of more than 200,000 ha of indigenous Baguio pine stands and the fragile watersheds that they protect, to Cellophil Resources Corporation, despite the fact that this land was declared forest reserve. The decree threatens Tinggian, Bontok, and Sagada tribesmen in three provinces (Dorral 1979).

Although the thrust of Marcos' public-land policies was on rapid utilization of resources, selected conservation measures were decreed after 1976. Ironically, these decrees affect most adversely tribal peoples and poor smallholders. For instance, *kaingin* management by the Bureau of Forest Development was long pursued through punitive policy until the number and distribution of swiddeners made this course impossible. Presidential Decree No. 705 attempts to stabilize swiddeners and squatters in place within forest lands, thus dictating intensive agricultural technologies. The settlement approach requires forest cultivators, who occupied areas before 1975, to remain in place without enlarging their clearings. Unfortunately, proven intensive agroforestry technologies, except for those long-evolved indigenously, have only recently begun to be researched, developed, and adequately tested. Resettlement is forced on those swiddeners who occupy lands where erosion, sedimentation, and watershed damage might result from their continued activities, but the resettlement conditions have forced many of those resettled to undertake illegal swiddening in order to survive, thus recreating the problem.

Meanwhile, other martial law policies gave incentives to plantation operations and agribusinesses, domestic and foreign (Kerkvliet 1979:131–132; Ofreneo 1980:97–164; Political Economy of Philippine Commodities 1983). Many of these operations are situated in the uplands (Anderson 1982:156–158). Marcos preempted previous laws to encourage such investments (Ofreneo 1980:149–153; Wurfel 1977:29). Attractive incentives were also provided to entrepreneurs willing to develop biofuel plantations in the uplands (Salgado 1985:114). Finally, dendro-thermal energy production was adopted by the National Electrification Administration as the means of rural power generation (Denton 1983). This policy leads to increased major competition for forest land by energy plantations. All of the foregoing policies exacerbate land use and tenure conflicts for tribal peoples.

Tribal peoples of the Philippines number about 4.3 million, or 8 percent of the total population. This does not include Muslim populations of Mindanao and Sulu, which number about 5.5 million (George 1980:226). Approximately 72 tribal ethnolinguistic groups still practice culturally integrated ways of life (34 in Luzon, 33 in Mindanao, and 5 in the Visayas). Minority uplanders are seriously disadvantaged in the face of the power of the government and the dominant population. They live mostly in small-scale social aggregates and are often isolated by space or by cultural differences from Christian populations. They are treated as peripheral to the affairs of the dominant society. The general attitude of the dominant lowlanders toward these upland minority peoples is essentially one of benign neglect; they harbor strong negative stereotypes toward them and consider them fair game in all economic and political dealings. Rights of the majority population for hydroelectric or geothermal power, irrigation water, tree plantations, and the like have routinely taken precedence. The destruction of habitats that support the ways of life of upland minorities has required them to make drastic changes just to survive.

In response to ultimate threats to their resources and to their survival as peoples, some minorities have organized resistance movements (Bennagen 1982). Leadership has emerged from within groups, from Church social action groups, from private voluntary organizations, from legal aid groups (Lynch 1984), and from the New People's Army. In Mindanao especially, but also in Northern Luzon, Samar, and Bicol, the Armed Forces of the Philippines' response to cultural minorities with force has spawned much wider conflict than had existed prior to martial law. This widening war itself has brought further ecological destruction to the uplands, especially to forested areas where rebels take refuge. Muslim Filipinos and their habitats have suffered the most and the longest (George 1980; Gowing 1979:183–251; Keifer 1984). The savagery of the fighting in the early 1970s led to the migration of over 40 thousand Muslims from southern Mindanao and Sulu, to take refuge in Sabah (George 1980).

The lack of protection of land rights has hurt Muslim and tribal populations alike. For all of the cultural minorities the loss of ancestral land presages the loss of ancestral culture (Keifer 1984; Lynch 1983). At greatest risk are the Philippine Negrito populations. Scattered in forest refuges on the main islands, the Negritos are generally considered to be the original inhabitants of the archipelago. Having long occupied forest and forest-fringe ecosystems, they are forest-dependent peoples. Numbering perhaps 15,000 today, the Negritos of Luzon and the Visayas, who are the most populous, live in forests that are accessible to adjacent lowlands. As a result they are subject to epidemic diseases, land expropriation, and habitat destruction. Most groups have experienced sedentarization, pronounced population decline, and cultural disintegration. Far from being subsistence-oriented, isolated forager/hunters, most Negrito groups have long been involved in collection and trade in forest products, responding to the demands of distant markets. Their economies are closely adjusted to external trade and labor relations with specific lowland Filipino groups. These dependent relations have dictated increasing sedentarism and more commitment to rice swiddening. Agta groups in Luzon, Palawan, and Negros are under great pressure.

Headland (1984), who has resided with Agta in the Casinguran area of Quezon for over 20 years, believes that "they may be on the verge of disappearing as a people." Both culturally and biologically threatened, their numbers have dropped by half in 40 years (Headland 1975) to 616 persons and presently decrease by 0.3 percent per year. Infant and child mortality is almost 50 percent. Morbidity and nutritional stress for adults and children is particularly high during the rainy season. Homicide rates and alcoholism among Agta males are high. Morbidity and mortality appear to have increased with sedentarism, which has resulted from dependence on lowlander patrons and on swidden gardens. Logging, mining, and a population growth in lowland migrants of 149 percent between 1965 and 1975 brought ecological and socioeconomic changes that have forced Agta into greater dependency on more remote forest refuges. A growing market for wild meat during the 1970s encouraged the Agta increasingly to use firearms in hunting. The consequent game depletion represented a loss of a good cash source with which to purchase rice and of protein for the Agta.

Similar reports of population decline, sedentarization, loss of autonomy, and deculturation exist for the Agta of the Palanan area in Quezon province (Peterson 1978), for the Aeta of Zambales (Brosius 1983), and for the Batak Negritos of Palawan (Cadelina 1985; Eder 1978).

Dependence of many tribal Filipinos on forms of shifting cultivation has left them vulnerable to deforestation and land grabbing by lowlanders (private, corporate, and government). Attempts to defend ancestral homelands have usually led to military intervention. May (1985) suggests that although encroachment on the lands of tribal Filipinos is not new (Schlegel 1979 on the Tiruray; Mansmann 1982 on the T'boli of Cotobato; and May 1985:127 and Salgado 1985:110–111 on the Manobo of Bukidnon) two recent forces have accelerated the process. First, the encroachment of lowland settlers on the lands of tribal Filipinos was reinforced "by the incursion of large-scale, regime-supported corporate enterprises and development projects" (May 1985:125). Second, government agencies (especially the Bureau of Lands, Bureau of Forest Development, Ministry of Local Government and Community Development, and Presidential Assistance on National Minorities), "far from protecting the interests of tribal Filipinos, have frequently provided the means for their repression" (May 1985:126).

Protection of the "cultural minorities" and their rights after 1975 was charged to the PANAMIN (Presidential Assistance on National Minorities), which was created by President Marcos in 1967. But according to some critics, PANAMIN's function "was to facilitate control over the resources on which the tribes sat: rich deposits of gold, uranium, manganese, copper, [timber] . . . and hydroelectric power" (Payne 1982; May 1985:126). In Mindanao, the policy toward certain cultural minorities was that of sedentarization or resettlement in an effort to deny insurgents possible assistance. This "model villages" program, likened by some to "Vietnam-era strategic hamlets" (Rocamora 1979), enhanced PANAMIN control but made it extremely difficult for people to carry out their livelihoods. PANAMIN complicity in efforts to force resettlement of thousands of Kalinga and Bontoc from their ancestral lands, so that 4 large dams could be constructed on the Chico River, is well documented (Carino et al. 1979; Winnacker 1979). The resistance of the Kalinga and Bontok peoples, at least temporarily, stopped the project. Almost as well known are the activities of PANAMIN with regard to the Lake Sebu T'boli and the Bukidnon Manobo (Rocamora 1979; May 1985). Dorral (1979) provides a detailed description of how the Marcos-supported Cellophil Resource Corporation acquired the ancestral lands of the Tinggian in Abra, Kalinga-Apayao, and Mountain provinces, involving once again PANAMIN's complicity.

The Destruction of Coastal Resources

The rich and fragile resources of the coastal zone, which have long provided nutrition to major settlements, have suffered serious deterioration as a result of upland deforestation, of new lowland agricultural technologies, and of urban and industrial pollution. Because upland, basin, and coastal zones are not discrete, but are coupled in various ways, no resource in one can be exploited without affecting the others. Upland deforestation permits rapid runoff of rain from heavy tropical storms to cause significant erosion and siltloads on the coastal plains. Flooding annually damages crops and property in the rich agricultural plains. As the floodwaters with their burden of suspended silt reach the estuaries, they inundate homes, kill aquatic life, scour riverbanks, destroy fish traps and pens, and deposit more silt. The turbid water hampers the penetration of sunlight, reducing productivity. In moderate amounts, the eroded soil nutrients would provide the materials and energy necessary to sustain mature estuarine, mangrove and coral communities, but heavy silt loads pour into these ecosystems, exceeding their environmental tolerances and causing serious deterioration. Add to this the adverse effects of fertilizer, pesticide, and herbicide runoff from croplands, and industrial pollutants, urban effluents, and oil spills, (Rau 1980; NEPC 1980), and these ecosystems are placed under great stress. Weakened mangrove or coral communities are then susceptible to damage from the high winds and seas caused by violent tropical storms (Gomez 1979).

Pressure on coastal zone resources has more than doubled with the doubling of population during the past 20 years, and with burgeoning economic development and urbanization. Increasing foreign and domestic demand for coastal and marine products led to huge capital inputs which transformed fisheries technology (Salgado 1985:115–118). In a 22-year period the catch of municipal fishermen quadrupled, before declining (Smith et al. 1980). Overexploitation has stressed the fisheries resources beyond their reproductive capacities. The choicest species and the richest stocks have already been overfished in many of the best-endowed areas. The future nutritional consequences of this decline in fish availability for Filipinos are truly alarming.

Few people appreciate just how rich (and how vulnerable) coastal ecosystems can be. The highest primary productivity of any world ecosystems are found in estuaries, coral reefs, mangrove, nipah, and other swamps and marshes, and tropical forests. While these ecosystems are not as obviously useful for human consumption as the closely adjacent alluvial basins, the enormous Philippine coastline, with its rich coral, mangrove, and strand resources, is the spawning and nursery area for many species of fish, shrimp, and shellfish.

As in the uplands, emphasis upon quick exploitation of specific resources has characterized coastal zone development, with devastating effects. Philippine marine fisheries are estimated to have a maximum sustainable annual yield of 1.95 million tons. Presently, about 1.3 million tons are landed. With the commercial exploitation of the past decade, industrial, agricultural, and urban pollution is taking a serious toll in estuaries, and economic exploitation is diminishing mangroves and coral.

The mangrove forests of the coastal zone (0.35 percent of total Philippine forests) are under the most intense pressure of all Philippine forests (Gabriel 1978; NEPC 1980). The groves are vital as seedling and nursery areas for mangrove species and for numerous fisheries, as coastal and coral reef protection, and as sources of valuable natural products. Yet they are rapidly being replaced by brackish water fishponds (which total over 178,000 ha), by real estate developments, and by salt pans, while the trees are being cut for wood chips, firewood, charcoal, tanbark, building materials, and furniture. Official estimates put the average annual rate of degradation of mangroves at more than 6 percent, but this figure must actually be higher. LANDSAT imagery in 1976 suggested that only about 106,133 ha of mangrove forest remained in the country. In the Eastern and Western Visayas, in Mindanao, and in Luzon, huge areas have been cleared illegally since then. Tremendous political pressure has been mounted by elite-dominated fishpond associations to release the remaining areas and to place mangroves exclusively under the Bureau of Forest Development. (Jurisdiction is presently shared with the Bureau of Lands and the more conservation-oriented Bureau of Fisheries and Aquatic Resources.)

If fishpond owners are the main beneficiaries of mangrove destruction, who are the principal losers? The process of rapid mangrove exploitation has been almost entirely at the expense of local fishermen and rural people who previously depended upon mangrove use as part of their subsistence. Like the expansion of brackish-water fishponds, the tremendous expansion of freshwater fishpens, such as those in Laguna de Bay, has also excluded small-scale, subsistence fishermen from participation, and deepened their plight.

Fishermen are the poorest and most desperate of the Filipino rural poor (Juliano et al. 1982; Carner 1982). The high costs of fishpond construction exclude the poor from these operations except for a few caretaker jobs. More generally, there are a few jobs in the exploitation of mangroves, corals, seaweed, shells, and minor intertidal products, and in handicraft manufacture, but most are undesirable and unremunerative. Whether in traditional municipal fisheries, in capital-intensive (and job-curtailing) trawler and other modern fisheries, or in aquaculture, there was no place for poor fishermen in President Marcos' "Blue Revolution."

Conclusions

The Marcos era, which exacerbated many of the processes of degradation reviewed here, is finally over. Surely things must improve under President Aquino's leadership. Sadly, there is little reason for optimism concerning the marginal resource areas and their longstanding inhabitants. The relationships underlying resource and minority welfare problems and the legacies of Marcos possess enormous inertia. The Aquino government is faced with monumental tasks and severely restricted options, and it must begin almost from scratch. The trends would be difficult to slow and perhaps impossible to reverse even under the best circumstances. Marcos left the country looted, indebted, divided, and the government dismantled.

I hope that Cory Aquino's leadership can keep the country afloat and begin the long and difficult journey back toward solvency and stability. She provides a moral force that has renewed the pride of Filipinos, but the task of reducing the destructive exploitation of the marginal resource areas and providing for the welfare of cultural minorities pales before the immediacies of finding funds to operate the government, alleviating the poverty of the Filipino masses, and dealing with the insurgency. In the longer term the threats to natural resources may be the most serious problem.

The enormous debt and the urgent need for foreign exchange leaves the new government little choice but to fall back on natural resource exploitation. The option is not between development and conservation, but between continued exploitative development and slower but sustainable development in which immediate benefits may be reduced but long term interests are better served.

A growing body of research suggests that along with reforestation, the most productive and protective use of "forest" land lies in indigenous and newly developed agroforestry management systems, which are among the best adapted land use systems in the tropics (Anderson 1986; Olafson 1983; Vergara 1981). Such ecologically and socially sound development strategies can help stabilize and reverse resource deterioration and socioeconomic decline, but they require adequate protection of communal and private land rights as well (Lynch 1983). Of course, these efforts will not substitute for those required to slow population growth, implement equitable and effective land tenure reforms for all Filipinos, and meet the needs for employment creation, but they will help.

References

Anderson, J. N.
    1982   Rapid Rural "Development": Performance and Consequences in the Philippines. *In* Too Rapid Rural Development. C. MacAndrews and L. S. Chia, eds. Pp. 122–171. Athens, OH: Ohio University Press.
    1986 (forthcoming) House Gardens: An Appropriate Village Technology. *In* Community Management. D. C. Korten, ed. Boston, MA: Kumarian Press.
Anderson, J. N., and W. T. Vorster
    1983   Diversity and Interdependence in the Trade Hinterlands of Melaka. *In* Melaka: The Transformation of a Malay Capital c. 1400–1978. 2 Vols. K. S. Sandhu and P. Wheatley, eds. Pp. 439–457. New York, NY: Oxford University Press.

Bello, W., and S. Rivera, eds.
  1977   The Logistics of Repression and Other Essays. Washington, DC: Friends
         of the Filipino People.
Bello, W., D. Kinley, and E. Elinson
  1982   Development Debacle: The World Bank in the Philippines. San Francisco,
         CA: Institute for Food and Development Policy.
Bennagen, P.
  1982   Philippine Cultural Minorities: Victims as Victors. *In* Mortgaging the Future.
         V. R. José, ed. Pp. 161–168. Quezon City: Foundation for Nationalist
         Studies.
Brosius, J. P.
  1983   The Zambales Negritos. Philippine Quarterly of Society and Culture 11:123–
         148.
Brown, L. R., et al.
  1984   State of the World 1974. New York, NY: W. W. Norton and Company.
Cadelina, R. V.
  1985   In Time of Want and Plenty. Dumaguete City: Silliman University Press.
Carino, Joanna, Jessica Carino, and G. Nettlethorn
  1979   The Chico River Basin Development Project: A Situation Report. Aghamtao
         2:37–103.
Carner, G.
  1982   Survival, Interdependence, and Competition Among the Philippine Rural
         Poor. Asian Studies 22:369–384.
Conklin, H. C.
  1957   Hanunoo Agriculture in the Philippines. FAO Development Paper No. 12.
         Rome: FAO.
Denton, F. H.
  1983   Wood for Energy and Rural Development. Manila: F. H. Denton.
Doherty, J. F.
  1982   Who Controls the Philippine Economy? *In* Cronies and Enemies. B. A.
         Aquino, ed. Pp. 6–35. Honolulu, HI: Philippine Studies Program, University
         of Hawaii.
Dorral, R.
  1979   The Tinggians of Abra and CELLOPHIL: A Situation Report. Aghamtao
         2:116–149.
Eder, J. F.
  1978   The Caloric Returns to Food Collecting. Human Ecology 6:55–71.
  1982   Who Shall Succeed? Agricultural Development and Social Inequality on a
         Philippine Frontier. Cambridge: Cambridge University Press.
FAO (Food and Agriculture Organization)
  1981   Tropical Forest Resources Assessment Project (GEMS). 4 vols. Rome: FAO/
         UNEP.
Fegan, B.
  1985   Rural Philippines: Central Luzon. *In* The Philippines After Marcos. R. J.
         May and F. Nemenzo, eds. Pp. 164–174. London: Croom Helm.
Gabriel, B. C.
  1978   Mangrove Forest—Problems and Management Strategies. Likas-Yaman
         (Journal of the National Resources Management Forum) 1(3):11–24.
George, T. J. S.
  1980   Revolt in Mindanao: The Rise of Islam in Philippine Politics. Kuala Lumpur:
         Oxford University Press.

Gomez, Edgardo
  1979   Philippine Corals: Issues on Conservation and Management. Likas-Yaman
          (Journal of the Natural Resources Management Forum) 1(9):10–15.
Gowing, P. G.
  1979   Muslim Filipinos—Heritage and Horizon. Quezon City: New Day Pub-
          lishers.
Headland, Thomas
  1975   The Casinguran Dumagats Today and in 1936. Philippine Quarterly of
          Culture and Society 3:247–256.
  1984   Agta Negritos of the Philippines. Cultural Survival Quarterly 8(3):29–31.
  1986   International Economics and Tribal Subsistence. Philippine Quarterly of
          Culture and Society 13:235–239.
Hutterer, K. L.
  1982   Interactions Between Tropical Ecosystems and Human Foragers. Working
          Paper. East-West Environment and Policy Institute, East-West Center,
          Honolulu, Hawaii.
IBON Databank
  1984   What Crisis: Highlights of the Philippine Economy 1983. Manila: IBON
          Databank Philippines, Inc.
Juliano, R. O., J. N. Anderson, and A. R. Librero
  1982   Philippines: Perceptions, Human Settlements and Resource Use in the
          Coastal Zone. *In* Man, Land and Sea. C. Soysa et al., eds. Pp. 218–240.
          Bangkok: Agricultural Development Council.
Kerkvliet, B. J.
  1979   Land Reform: Emancipation or Counterinsurgency? *In* Marcos and Martial
          Law in the Philippines. D. A. Rosenberg, ed. Pp. 113–144. Ithaca, NY:
          Cornell University Press.
Kiefer, T.
  1984   Martial Law and the Tausug. Cultural Survival Quarterly 8(4):39–40.
Lynch, O. J., Jr.
  1983   Native Title: Its Potential for Social Forestry. Quezon City: Thirty-Seventh
          Natural Resources Forum.
  1984   Ancestral Land and Cultural Survival. Cultural Survival Quarterly 8(4):38.
McLennan, M. S.
  1982   Changing Human Ecology on the Central Luzon Plain. *In* Philippine Social
          History. A. McCoy and E. de Jesus, eds. Pp. 57–90. Honolulu, HI: University
          Press of Hawaii.
Mansmann, R.
  1982   The Case for T'boli Rights to Their Ancestral Territory. Dansalan Quarterly
          3(4):204–216.
May, R. J.
  1985   Muslim and Tribal Filipinos. *In* The Philippines After Marcos. R. J. May
          and F. Nemenzo, eds. Pp. 110–129. London: Croom Helm.
Meyers, N.
  1980   Report of Survey of Conversion Rates in Tropical Moist Forests. Washington,
          DC: National Research Council.
  1981   Conversion Rates in Tropical Moist Forests. International Symposium on
          Tropical Forest. Pp. 48–66.
NEPC (National Environmental Protection Council)
  1980   The Philippine Coastal Zone. Vol. 1. Coastal Zone Resources. Quezon City:
          National Environmental Protection Council.

National Research Council
    1982   Ecological Aspects of Development in the Humid Tropics. Washington,
            DC: National Academy Press.
Ofreneo, René E.
    1980   Capitalism in Philippine Agriculture. Quezon City: Foundations for Na-
            tionalist Studies.
Olafson, H.
    1980   Swidden and Kaingin among the Southern Tagalog. Philippine Quarterly
            of Culture and Society 8:168–180.
    1981   Adaptive Strategies and Change in Philippine Swidden-Based Societies.
            Luguna, Philippines: Forest Research Institute.
    1983   Indigenous Agroforestry Systems. Philippine Journal of Society and Culture
            11:149–174.
Payne, K. W.
    1982   Human Rights, Genocide, and Ethnocide: The Case of the Philippines'
            National Minorities. *In* Toward a Human Rights Framework. Pp. 151–167.
            New York, NY: Praeger.
Peterson, J. T.
    1978   The Ecology of Social Boundaries: Agta Foragers in the Philippines. Urbana,
            IL: University of Illinois Press.
Political Economy of Philippine Commodities
    1983   Political Economy of Philippine Commodities. Quezon City: Third World
            Studies Center, University of the Philippines.
Rau, N.
    1980   Adverse Effects of Economic Development on Small-Scale Fishery and
            Aquaculture in Southeast Asia. Philippine Quarterly of Culture and Society
            8:181–190.
Revilla, A. V., Jr., M. L. Bonita, and M. Segura
    1977   An Evaluation of Certain Policies and Programs Affecting Forestry Pro-
            duction Through 2000 A.D. *In* Population, Resources and Environment in
            the Philippine Future. Manila: Development Academy of the Philippines.
Rocamora, J.
    1979   Agribusiness, Dams and Counter-Insurgency. Southeast Asia Chronicle.
            No 67: 2–10.
Salgado, P. V.
    1985   The Philippine Economy. Quezon City: R. P. Garcia Publishing.
Schlegel, S. A.
    1979   Muslim-Christian Conflict in the Philippine South. *In* Culture Change in
            the Philippines. M. Zamora, ed. Studies in Third World Societies. No. 1.
            Williamsburg, VA: College of William and Mary.
Sutlive, V. H., N. Altshuler, and M. D. Zamora
    1980a   Where Have All the Flowers Gone? Deforestation in the Third World.
            Studies in Third World Societies. No. 13. Williamsburg, VA: College of
            William and Mary.
    1980b   Blowing in the Wind: Deforestation and Long-Range Implications. Studies
            in Third World Societies. No. 14. Williamsburg, VA: College of William
            and Mary.
Smith, I. R., et al.
    1980   Philippine Municipal Fisheries. Manila: International Center for Living
            Aquatic Resources.

UNESCO
  1978   Tropical Forest Ecosystems: A State of Knowledge Report. Natural Resources Research 14. Paris: UNESCO.
Vergara, N. T.
  1981   Integral Agro Forestry. East-West Environment and Policy Institute, East-West Center, Honolulu, Hawaii.
Winnacker, M.
  1979   The Battle to Stop the Chico Dams. Southeast Asia Chronicle. No. 67: 22–29.
Washburn, L.
  1981   An Unequal Contest: the Philippine National Power Corporation versus Maranao Muslims. Dansalan Quarterly II (4):213–227.
Wurfel, D.
  1977   Philippine Agrarian Policy Today: Implementation and Political Impact. Occasional Paper No. 46, Institute of Southeast Asia Studies, Singapore.

PART FOUR

Local Management Strategies

13

Diversity and Change in Andean Agriculture[1]

Stephen B. Brush

Alarm has been raised that massive population increases and accelerating economic change occurring in high mountain areas are leading to an ecological breakdown that will destroy productivity and wreak havoc on large populations living downstream. The widely held view is that traditional cultures in areas such as the Andes and Himalayas, after having created successful land-use technologies to utilize the fragile mountain environment without destroying it, are now being undermined by factors such as population increase and capitalist penetration. Thus, it seems the descendants of successful mountain cultures are now desperately trying to improve their lot by overexploiting precious natural resources of highland watersheds.

In the Andean context of central Peru, this view of the ecological breakdown of high mountain agroecosystems is mistaken in several aspects. First, the pattern and rate of economic change is as uneven as the mountain landscape, making it impossible to generalize about the region as a whole. Although change is evident everywhere and large scale in some areas, there is also evidence of stagnation or very slow change. Second, although population increase in the Andean countries has been above 2.5 percent for the last three decades, many places have stable or declining populations due to emigration to urban centers or lowland areas. Third, although agricultural intensification is occurring, it does not inevitably lead to ecological simplification or degradation. In some areas intensification has clearly increased degradation, but in others it has led to greater complexity and without apparent degradation. Finally, the concept of traditional agriculture as existing in a harmonious and fixed relation to the mountain environment is logically flawed, as is the idea that this relation is somehow disrupted by forces beyond the control of farmers. Andean agriculture is complex and dynamic, and traditional practices continue not as cultural survivals but as rational choice.

These four points do not determine that ecological degradation is occurring, but they do indicate that our analytical tools to describe change need to be greatly improved. Our ability to measure change in key environmental components is severely limited. We lack baseline data against which to measure change, and we are unable to make a specific connection between general change in the environment and change in one component measured at one time and place. This lack of data and integrative research is true for deforestation, salinization, the loss of topsoil, and the loss of genetic variability—environmental costs frequently associated with development.

Research Issues in Andean Agriculture

Superimposed on the rugged Andean environment is a long history of occupation with such notable achievements as the invention of agriculture and domestication of world-class crops, the rise of autochthonous civilizations, and support of a dense population larger than that of any other high mountain area. Besides erosion, drought, frost and hypoxia—hazards posed by the mountain environment—the agricultural and cultural history of the Andes has created additional hazards. These include large communities of pests and pathogens that prey on Andean crops, and a predatory social class system that exploits rural people.

The success of Andean people in creating stable productive systems and building a great civilization has been the subject of anthropological and geographic research, which has described the general cultural history of the area and delineated the major responses to its physical, ecological and economic stresses. Cultural adaptations to the Andes include the domestication of plants and animals suited to a broad range of environments, the establishment of diverse production zones with different technologies and land-use practices, different levels and types of social control over these zones, demographic distribution across and exchange between different altitude zones, and the selection, maintenance and distribution of a tremendous genetic diversity of crops.

At the time of the European Conquest 450 years ago, the success of Andean cultural adaptation was evidenced by the population size and its organization into the Inca Empire. The shock of the Conquest produced a population collapse and social, political, and cultural disintegration. New crops, especially European cereals and legumes, made major inroads into Andean agriculture, and important elements of Andean technology, such as terracing, greatly declined. In spite of these shocks, major patterns of Andean land-use have survived into the twentieth century. The inventory of crops and animals found by the Spanish is still largely intact. Tools and tillage are similar, and elements of socioeconomic organization continue, such as communal control over land tenure and land-use.

Today, however, the Andean people face conditions and changes that seem revolutionary and traumatic: rapid population growth, urbanization, an accelerating penetration of capitalism, and changing consumption patterns. Economic change has been accelerated by political change and reforms, by the infusion of large amounts of international capital, and by persistent inflation. A sense of chronic crisis and instability now pervades the Andes. Can past solutions meet contemporary problems and demands for change?

Can theoretical models designed to describe historic conditions understand the present crisis and generate solutions for the future?

In the 1970s, anthropological research on Andean agriculture focused on two themes: "verticality" and political economy. Our current understanding of agriculture is derived from this work and elements from both are necessary in describing adaptation in the Andes. Both, however, are characterized by over-generalization and have only limited value in measuring agricultural and environmental change.

Verticality

The repetition of settlement, land-use, and economic patterns in the central Andes between southern Ecuador and Bolivia has been described frequently in terms of altitude belts or zonation (Troll 1968). A large literature on both the physical and human characteristics of mountain zonation was summarized by the term "verticality" to describe different patterns of land-use present at the time of the Conquest (Murra 1972). Verticality described the use of multiple altitude belts and the social means whereby access to different altitude zones was guaranteed to individual households and communities.

Verticality suggests that the Andean environment acts in two ways to structure Andean culture and behavior. First, it creates opportunities for a very diverse system of crop and animal production while constraining the area that can be devoted to any one activity. In an ecological sense, verticality emphasizes the opportunism of Andean people in using their environment. It acknowledges the hazards of the mountain environment, but does not define adaptation as in response to them. Second, the mountain landscape creates a template for the division of productive activities into different zones. Under verticality the definition of natural resources and the use of the environment should conform to regular patterns across different mountain landscapes. Especially important here is the "vertical archipelago" of dispersed island-like production zones that require migration and state management to permit individual use. The lasting contribution of research on verticality in the Andes is its recognition of both pattern and diversity in agriculture. Although the concept has been widely and successfully applied (Masuda et al. 1985), an important criticism of it is raised by Golte (1980) who argues that the use of multiple zones is a product more of need than of a cultural ideal or environmental template. Golte observes that environmental constraints on agriculture reduce productivity so that dependence on single crops or zones is impossible. Andean farmers are forced by a fragmented environment to maintain diverse production zones and cycles. This necessity leads to the creation of technologies to ensure that labor and land are used efficiently to overcome the inherent limits of the environment.

Golte's critique replaces the environmental opportunism of the original verticality concept with selective pressures in the environment. He shows the limits to productivity in a comparison between highland and coastal agriculture for maize and potatoes. In Peru, production of these crops on the coast requires half the labor than is needed in the highlands, and productivity by labor and land is far greater on the coast. He calculates, for instance, that 1,000 days in maize production on the coast is equivalent to 15,000 days in the highlands (Golte 1980:111). Although limiting factors are key determinants in Golte's analysis, they are never clearly defined and are treated only secondarily. The comparison of coastal and highland agriculture fails to account for the significant differences in the different farm systems that characterize each zone. This failure leaves open the question of the specific hazards in the region's agriculture and how such factors as population increase and market development affect adaptations to those hazards.

Political Economy

The second major approach to Andean agriculture is through the political economy of the agrarian structure. The contribution of these studies has been to demonstrate how important external markets, domination, and surplus extraction are to the behavior of local economies (Orlove 1977; Painter 1984; DeJanvry 1981). The prevailing consensus now is that the particular features of present-day agriculture must be understood in relation to Third World peripheral capitalism. Market penetration dates from colonial times and was drastically transformed through the wool, sugar, cotton, and coffee export economy. There is general consensus that the present day features of peasant agriculture are consequences of long-term capitalist penetration, not of market penetration into pristine precapitalist systems.

To what extent are the crops cultivated destined for consumption and for market? Is there a historic difference in peasant agriculture for these two ends? How does economic activity by peasants outside of the peasant sector influence practices within it? To date, the large number of community studies have not been very helpful in answering these questions. Nevertheless, there is evidence of the importance of surplus extraction and market penetration in such areas as demographic distribution and income (Deere 1978).

Risk and Response

The record of research outlined above has been successful in describing the major elements of the Andean physical and social environment along with the response of the region's people to environmental opportunities and risks. The Andean physical environment is characterized by great diversity that creates many opportunities but also frequent stresses. Risk is related to the naturally unstable Andean climate, to frequent frost and drought, to the narrowness of production zones and the proximity of effective crop limits, and to the high susceptibility to erosion. The agricultural and biological environment is shaped by this diversity but also by its history as a center of domestication. Millennia of crop evolution in the area have led to an abundance of pests, pathogens and competitors that share the

Andean agroecosystem. As limiting factors, these coevolved pests and pathogens are major elements in lowering the overall productivity of Andean agriculture (Jennings and Cock 1977). Finally, Andean history is characterized by domination and surplus extraction, and exploitation is facilitated by rigid class and racial systems.

Demographic, political, and technological responses by Andean people to these conditions have been dealt with by many authors, with emphasis on Andean agriculture. Three characteristics of this agriculture are especially significant adaptations to the physical and social environment of the area. First is diversity, both across the general system and within specific components. Second is the organization of the agroecosystem into specific production zones with different inventories of crops and animals, different levels of land-use intensity, and different types of control. Third is that various land tenure and land-use practices combine community and households as important actors in managing the agroecosystem.

These traditional agricultural adaptations are credited with limiting environmental degradation and contributing to stability in the agroecosystem of the Andes. The logic followed here is that traditional peasant agriculture, conducted without the benefit of external subsidies, uses resources in such a way as to keep them productive indefinitely. Agroecosystem stability is a prerequisite of the large populations that have inhabited the region for many centuries and of the creation of the advanced Inca civilization. Agricultural evolution has resulted in technologies that use the complex but risk-prone environment efficiently and without degradation. Second, it is assumed that traditional agriculture has only limited productive capacity and is unsuited to increased demands from larger populations, commercialization, and new consumption patterns. Finally, it is assumed that these demands require the replacement of traditional agriculture with modern and more intensive techniques that rely on capital and more active participation in the market economy and that these changes portend the demise of the Andean agroecosystem itself because they are shortsightedly insensitive to environmental degradation.

Unfortunately, this well known scenario and the widely held assumptions behind it have never been adequately tested. Our test of them is important not only for scientific progress but also for development planning. To build a research program to test them, we must shift our strategy from one that describes general processes to one that focuses on specific environmental components in agriculture. While we have a general outline of the Andean agroecosystem, we know little about the dynamics of its key components. Our measure of change and its impact on agriculture and the environment can best be accomplished by modeling specific components rather than attempting to discuss agriculture as a system. Key components may be thought of as proxies for the more general system. One component that may be useful in this endeavor is potato germplasm.

An Agroecological Model for the Andean Potato

The previous section discussed the general environment of the Andes and adaptive responses by its inhabitants. The environment is characterized by physical and biological diversity, by high risk to agriculture, by numerous pathogens and competitors to the indigenous staple crops, and by a socio-economic system of domination that extracts surplus from the majority of farmers. The response to this environment has been threefold: the main-tenance of diversity, the delineation of specific production zones, and the control over production by both households and communities. This envi-ronment/response model can be appreciated when applied to the Andes' most important crop, the potato (*Solanum* spp.).

Potato Diversity

Although the potato was not the earliest Andean domesticate, it has been its most important crop for several thousand years. There are over one hundred wild *Solanum* species in the Andes, and neolithic farmers in the region domesticated seven of them, representing four different ploidy levels, $2n=24$ to $2n=60$ (Hawkes 1978). Below the species level, however, diversity is even greater. The International Potato Center has a collection of over 12,000 named varieties, and geneticists there calculate that these may comprise 4,000 to 6,000 individual clones. The entire range of native potato varieties and clones has not been collected, and the genetic relation between varieties, clones, subspecies, species, and ploidy levels is not well understood. There are no ubiquitous varieties or clones, although one subspecies (*Solanum tuberosum* subsp. *andigenum,* $2n=48$) is found everywhere in the Andes. Several of the subspecies are grown only in certain geographic areas, an example being *S. ajanhuiri* of the altiplano around Lake Titicaca. *S. juzepczukii* and *S. curtilobum* are grown only in high altitude zones, while other species are grown between sea level and 4,000 m. Certain clones enjoy a very wide regional distribution and are grown by every household over thousands of square kilometers, while other clones have highly restricted distribution in specific valleys. Although the distribution of alleles and allele complexes is not well described, it is likely that some are highly cosmopolitan while others are much more narrowly distributed.

The genetic diversity of potatoes in the Andes relates to four factors: the physical diversity of the region; the long history of potato cultivation there; the large number of coevolved pests, pathogens and competitors; and cultural practices of selection, maintenance and distribution.

The core area of cultivation for the potato is located between central Peru and Bolivia along a transect crossing the Andes between roughly 2500 m on the dry western slopes, ascending to 4000 m, and ending at 2500 m on the humid eastern slopes. Numerous elements contribute to physical diversity within this transect; the primary ones are those related to altitude (temperature, humidity, evapotranspiration), to exposure (humidity, radia-tion), and to slope (soils). The distribution of potato varieties and diversity within the transect is most dependent on temperature and humidity regimes (frost and drought). Diversity is greatest at middle elevations (3000–3800 m) on the eastern slopes where rich organic soils predominate and where frost and drought are rare. In these areas, one hundred or more varieties are grown within single communities, and families may have as many as 50 varieties. Diversity is less in the dry intermontane valleys, on the dry western slopes, and above 3800 m where frost danger is greater. In high villages along the western rim, village inventories add up to less than twenty varieties, and that of a family may be only five or ten.

In addition to different patterns of resources and stresses that create niches, the physical diversity of the Andes stimulates potato diversity through isolation. Although exchange of varieties between local populations breaks down isolation, it is generally unable to overcome the barriers between intermontane valleys. The most important exchange is internal to these valleys, although recent commercial production has begun to change this.

The long history of potato cultivation in the Andes has contributed to its diversity that arises from natural crosses between cultivated potatoes and among cultivated, weedy, and wild varieties. This differentiation is abetted by the physical isolation between centers of cultivation. The long history of cultivation has also permitted the coevolution of a large system of pests, pathogens, and competitors that themselves create selective pressures for greater differentiation in the cultivated landraces.[2] Some of these pests are localized with local variants, and others are distributed widely. Theoretically, the genetic diversity in cultivated landraces should be understood as a response to this large and dynamic coevolutionary system (Dinoor and Eshed 1984; Vanderplank 1968). Both specific resistance to local variants of pests and horizontal resistance are attributed to genetic diversity. At this time, however, no empirical research on Andean potato cultivation corroborates this link between diversity and resistance.

Cultural practices of selection, maintenance, and distribution represent the fourth factor contributing to potato diversity in the Andes. A native taxonomy for classifying potatoes has been documented, and the major criteria for selection have been identified (Brush et al. 1981). These include both culinary and agricultural properties. Positive selection for diversity results from the desire for variety in a monotonous diet and from the link between mixed seed collections and seed viability. Andean farmers themselves do not recognize a connection between genetic diversity and crop stability or resistance to pests. Positive selection for diversity is evident in efforts to maintain diverse collections on some part of the family farm where commercialization and adoption of improved varieties has occurred, even though this may compete for scarce land and labor resources. Finally, diversity is enhanced by seed rotation practices that move seed between plots and between different altitudes. These practices are a universal way to keep seeds viable in the face of the accumulation of pests and pathogens, especially viruses.

The diversity of potato varieties maintained by Andean farmers can be explained by the four factors outlined above. As an environmental characteristic, this genetic diversity is a product of natural and cultural evolution. Diversity and complexity are often associated with ecosystem stability (Odum 1953), and this principle might be extended to agricultural systems (Clawson 1985). Although there is no connection between genetic diversity and other risks, such as soil erosion, there is a connection with the fragmented environment and the presence of numerous pests and pathogens. It is important to note in this regard that crop failure on the same scale as the one that caused the Irish potato famine has not been reported in Peru. The cause of the Irish catastrophe, *Phytophthora infestans,* is native to Mexico but had been present in the Andes for many years before chemical control was available.

Three elements now present in the farm system may potentially decrease genetic diversity: subsidies to control pests, modern varieties bred for specific resistance and commercial characteristics, and socioeconomic changes that impel higher production than usually attained in traditional agriculture. These changes will be discussed at the conclusion of the chapter.

Production Zones in Potato Agriculture

Four production zones characterize the general farm system of the Bolivian and Peruvian highlands:

1. a low altitude zone (below 1500 m) where fruits, tropical staples (e.g. *Manihot esculenta*), and coca (*Erythroxylon coca*) are cultivated;
2. a middle altitude cereal zone (2000–3000 m) where maize (*Zea mais*) is important;
3. a tuber zone (3000–4000 m) where potatoes and other Andean root crops predominate; and
4. a high altitude pasture zone (above 4000 m).

Specific communities and regions have local variants of these four and may add secondary zones. Boundaries between zones are flexible and overlapping. The concept of zonation derives from the replication of land-use patterns in many different Andean contexts. Local zonation is defined by a configuration of environmental and social factors relating primarily to altitude and land-use factors: crops, animals, land tenure, input levels, and degree of commercialization. Besides crop assemblages, important distinguishing characteristics include level of intensification in land use and the balance of commercial and community control over resources. Zonation has interested anthropologists for two decades, and the most ambitious current research is that of Enrique Mayer and Cesar Fonseca along a transect in central Peru (Mayer and Fonseca 1979). Mayer (1985:50–51) defines a production zone as "a communally managed set of specific productive resources in which crops are grown in distinctive ways." Communal management includes the control of land tenure, water, and the agricultural calendar. Systems for field rotation and irrigation are particularly notable aspects.

Production zones can be viewed as responses to the highland environment in several ways. Gade (1975) has shown that they represent the range of efficiency for crops. Zonation through community activity is essential for some crops, and it extends the range of others. The best example of this is irrigation in the lower tropical zone and middle cereal zone in intermontane valleys (Mitchell 1976). Zonation has also been viewed as a way to exercise community control so as to control degradation (Orlove 1976).

Potato cultivation occurs in the highest agricultural zone, and that zone is usually subdivided into two or three specific zones. The first subdivision in the tuber zone is between high altitude and frost-prone areas where bitter varieties (*S. juzepczukii, S. curtilobum* and *S. ajanhuiri*) are grown for freeze drying into *chuatno,* and lower areas where regular boiling potatoes are cultivated. In some areas, this second subzone is divided into a lower zone for the early crop (*maway*) and a higher zone for the regular crop (*hatun*). These subzones may have additional distinctions. The maway zone, for instance, is generally more intensively cultivated. In this zone fields are under cultivation more frequently and may be double cropped in a single year. Irrigation is often employed. In some regions, such as in the Tulumayo Valley of Peru's central highland Department of Junin, the maway zone is one of intensive commercial potato agriculture in which many modern inputs are employed. In the higher hatun zone, traditional potato agriculture predominates. Native varieties are more common than improved ones, and other external subsidies are less important. Land use is less intensive, and fallow periods are communally managed under a sectoral fallow system whereby individual plots are held within communally controlled sectors. The sector to be cultivated and the timing of cultivation and harvest are communally determined. Cooperative labor is prevalent in the initial field preparation. Other inputs and decisions are individually managed.

A connection between management practices derived from production zone organization and the stability of the potato agroecosystem has been posited but not sufficiently tested. Fallowing is clearly beneficial to limiting soil loss, to the recovery of soil nutrients, and to the control of pest populations. For instance, the seven year cycle that characterizes most communally managed sectoral fallow systems is the time necessary to kill cysts of the golden nematode, a principal potato pest (M. Scurrah, personal communication). Production zone organization also facilitates the scheduling of labor, a chronic problem in this complex farm system. Like genetic diversity, production zone organization can be explained as a result of the evolution of Andean agriculture, and it is an element in the stability of the Andean agroecosystem. Likewise, the same elements that confront diversity threaten production zone organization.

Individual and Community Control

In the organization of production zones, community and individual control of agricultural resources is important. Community control has been identified as a key component of highland agriculture in Peru and Bolivia (Mayer

1985; Guillet 1978; Harris 1982). It dates from pre-Conquest Andean economic organization (Murra 1972) and relates to the role of different levels of social integration above the household: to lineages (*ayllu*), ethnic groups, and the state. According to the verticality model, each of these levels played different roles in directing production in pre-Hispanic Andean culture. Although control above the local level was abolished by the Spanish Conquest, suprahousehold control continues as an important vestige of pre-Hispanic culture, having been formalized in Spanish policies on community organization during the Colonial period.

For the past 400 years, the peasant community was the principal social unit controlling the land and agricultural population not directly under the *hacienda* system. The community competed for land and population since the Colonial *reducciones* that initially organized most communities. Since the land reforms of the mid-twentieth century, the community has emerged as the predominant unit in the rural Andean social system, especially in Peru and Bolivia. Individual access to land depends on membership in a community. Communities exercise control over the production process in numerous ways: by determining who has rights to cultivate, by setting the agricultural calendar, by constructing and operating irrigation systems, by managing common grazing lands, and by building and maintaining trails, roads and bridges.

Individual management is complementary to communal management in that the diversity of the farming system involves many different decisions that cannot be generalized across an entire community or production zone. Community control defines the general parameters of production while individual decisions manage its content. Thus community control may set the beginning and end of the production cycle, while individuals decide when the many secondary tasks, such as weeding, are to be carried out. Individual management may, however, conflict with community control under current conditions of commercialization and intensification. This complementarity and conflict is evident in potato production, and will be discussed later in the chapter.

Communal control in the tuber zone is perhaps most evident in the sectoral fallow system that is found in the highlands of central Peru and Bolivia (Orlove and Godoy 1986). Under this system, community lands are divided into a number of sectors (usually five to seven), and cultivation is organized by the community in each sector. Potatoes are planted for one year, followed by other tubers (e.g., *Oxalis tuberosa*), broad beans (*Vicia faba L.*), or barley (*Hordeum* spp.) for two or more years, and then followed by fallow in which communal grazing is permitted. Participation in the sectoral rotation is encouraged by opening the sector to grazing without community support to collect damages from animals to fields that are not synchronized with the sectoral system. Such support in the form of fines does exist for plots grown within the regular cycle. Individual plots are owned in a de facto fashion within the sectors, and families are responsible for allocating labor and deciding on specific inputs on their plot. For those who wish to break the sectoral cycle, building fences and guarding the field against livestock are important labor costs.

Conflict between individual and communal management in this system is apparent in areas where commercialization, intensification, population increase, and other agricultural changes are occurring. A family with limited land and the need for greater income from agriculture may wish to grow a cash crop during the fallow cycle of the sector. Only indirect sanctions, such as community grazing policies, influence this decision, and families can build fences to protect their crops against grazing animals. The breakdown of community-managed, sectoral, fallow systems has been observed in several areas (Mayer and Fonseca 1979). It is important to note, however, that community control continues in other areas where commercialization and intensification have occurred.

As noted in the preceding section, community control is credited with stabilizing production in a risk-prone agroecosystem. The fallow period associated with sectoral rotations is especially important here. Conversely, the breakdown of community control associated with intensification and commercialization might logically be linked to environmental degradation, for instance by shortening the fallow period and thus increasing the exposure of soil to erosive influences.

Change in the Andean Agroecosystem

Andean agriculture has responded to its physical and social environment in three ways: through diversity, production zone organization, and community and individual control. These responses help to stabilize production in the agroecosystem and to limit environmental degradation. There are, however, strong pressures in the Andean region to replace traditional technology and agricultural organization with more intensive methods. There are also countervailing forces that limit the adoption of new technology and the rate of change in highland agriculture.

Many factors promote change in the Andes. Some are part of the internal dynamics of the region's economy and society, such as the accumulation of savings and differentiation among economic sectors. Others derive from external sources, such as the investment of international capital and internationally sponsored development projects. These two are, of course, intimately linked.

Several specific sources of change can be identified. Population growth has exceeded 2.5 percent per year for three decades in the general region. Although growth in the rural areas has been lessened considerably by out-migration, the growth of urban centers is a major stimulus to rural change. An active road-building program has connected once isolated highland areas to urban markets. Incentives to produce for these markets include changing consumption patterns, such as the desire to educate children or to purchase manufactured goods. Besides improved transportation, production for market has been enhanced by the availability of inputs and services to increase production. These include new crops and crop varieties, chemical fertilizers and pesticides, credit, and information. Both public and private institutions stimulate some of these changes and actively promote technological development in agriculture. Development has been a national goal in Andean nations for four decades, and has led the whole region to undertake major reforms and investment in agriculture. Agrarian reform has been undertaken throughout the Andean region with the goals of equity and greater productivity. Peru and Bolivia have both undergone radical and extensive land reforms that have reorganized agriculture away from large private enterprises.

Despite an impressive record of agrarian reform, road building, technological improvement, and market development, the rate of change in agriculture has been uneven and generally disappointing. Several Andean regions, such as the altiplano of Peru and Bolivia, have a chronic food deficit; poverty levels are highest in rural areas; and urban areas are inundated with rural migrants. In Peru, for instance, fifteen years after a radical agrarian reform, production has actually declined in the small farm sector (Alvarez 1983), and highland productivity lags far behind the coast's (Golte 1980). Factors that discourage technological change include out-migration, especially by young adults, economic disadvantages for small farmers who are distant from the urban market and who farm in more marginal environments, the high cost of inputs relative to commodity prices, and changing food habits in urban areas. In Peru's urban centers, for instance, potatoes are often replaced by rice, noodles, and bread.

The balance between factors promoting technological change and constraints to change varies greatly between regions and localities. In some areas around major urban centers in the highlands, such as Huancayo and Cuzco in Peru, modern inputs have been widely adopted, and production has been intensified and commercialized (Horton 1984; Gonzales 1984). In other areas, although modern inputs are available, traditional technology is selected (Brush 1986). In order to understand this diverse pattern of economic change, it is helpful to return to our discussion of potato agriculture and to consider how economic change affects the three adaptations described above—diversity, production zones, and communal and individual control.

For over thirty years modern potato varieties from breeding programs have been available and promoted for their specific resistance, yield potential, and commercial qualities. The precocity of some new varieties permits double cropping of potatoes and other crops in the maway zone where irrigation is available. Besides new potato varieties, the last thirty years have also offered farmers a large array of chemical subsidies to improve production. Fertilizers are important, but newly developed pesticides are critical to expanding production in the mid-altitude zones. Fungicides to control late blight (*Phytophthora infestans*) allow greater production in more humid zones. Nematicides and insecticides reduce pest populations to tolerable levels in areas where the fallow cycle has been shortened. Besides adopting new technologies, another change is production for market rather than for consumption. This includes production of seed potatoes for other farming systems as well as producing for the urban markets. In central Peru seed production for coastal potato agriculture has provided a major source of capital for the entire farming system. Improved transportation and urban growth have also stimulated investment of outside capital into rural areas.

The result of the pressures for change and the adoption of new technology has been a reorientation within Peru's highland farming system toward commercial production with reliance on capital and purchased inputs. In most of the Peruvian highlands this orientation has not completely eliminated traditional practices, such as the production of native crop varieties or communally controlled fallow.

Traditional practices are retained for good reasons, not by anachronistic behavior. To the picture of households selecting traditional technology rather than commercial technology that I have described (Brush 1986), it is important to add the concept that while adoption and change occur, traditional technology is not replaced in a simple way. Commercial agriculture may be practiced throughout the farming system of a community, but it is practiced on specific fields, while traditional agriculture is practiced on others. Thus, the farming system may actually become more complex by the addition of new subsystems, and a single family may have some of its fields under a commercial regime and others under a traditional one. It is useful to conceive of these as two subsystems or sectors, one commercial and another traditional, coexisting within a single farming system in single communities and managed by the same households. These sectors can be distinguished according to land-use intensity, inputs per hectare, productivity of land, and the goal of production. Some purchased inputs, such as fertilizers, may be used to some degree over the entire farming system of a family or village. The traditional sector is characterized by a reliance on non-purchased inputs such as labor and local varieties, by lower overall investment, and by an emphasis on subsistence production. Land in this sector is used in an extensive fashion, and productivity relative to land and labor is low. The commercial sector is characterized by reliance on purchased inputs, by higher investment, and by emphasis on market production. Land in the commercial sector is used in an intensive fashion and productivity is high.

As indicated earlier, the adaptation of Andean potato agriculture to the physical and social environment of the region has three attributes: reliance on diversity, organization into production zones, and community and individual control over production. How does the economic change characterized above as the rise of a commercial sector in Andean potato farming systems affect these three attributes?

Genetic diversity is a primary measure of overall diversity in the potato farming system. The commercial sector is distinguished from the traditional one by a higher degree of selection and genetic control. This is especially true where seed is purchased, but it is also true where it is selected from native stock. Commercial production tends to concentrate in the mid-altitude zones where environmental risks are lower, where irrigation is available, where roads are more common, and where labor is more abundant. Traditional production is not replaced by this, but it is forced into higher zones. The rise of a commercial sector may reduce diversity in two ways. First, it may reduce the amount of land devoted to diverse cultivars. This may occur because of an overall shortage of land, or because labor or other resources are scarce. Second, by occupying the optimal agricultural zones, the commercial sector may relegate traditional crops to more marginal areas where they are under more severe environmental pressure. The impact on diversity from the commercial sector is not, however, a simple function of replacement. Recent research indicates that farmers growing commercial varieties also maintain traditional varieties on separate fields at different altitudes and under different production techniques. The overall impact of commercial agriculture may be to reduce diversity, but significant efforts to retain traditional varieties and technologies are also present.

Production zone organization is affected by increased commercial agriculture as new technologies and as new sectors are added to existing ones. In the Tulumayo Valley, the addition of a commercial potato sector has increased the difference between maway and hatun subzones. Intensification and commercialization concentrates in the former, and in this zone new organization may arise because of such things as new irrigation. As traditional methods are retained in some parts of the system, so too is traditional production zone organization. Thus, in the hatun subzone, land tenure, crop inventories, levels and types of inputs, and type of control continue as before commercial agriculture. Changes within one zone also have impacts on adjacent zones. These may be direct, such as the expansion of one zone into adjacent ones. As potato agriculture has commercialized and the traditional potato sector has been pushed higher, both the maize zone below and the grazing zone above have lost territory and been otherwise reduced. Indirect impacts of expansion in one zone result from diverting labor or other resources away from adjacent zones. In sum, the reorganization of production zones for commercial agriculture has tended to break down the structure of Andean agriculture. Production zones become far more heterogeneous and more difficult to distinguish.

Communal and individual control over production shift under commercialization. The expectation is that communal control decreases with commercialization as individual households seek to maximize production. This requires greater flexibility than communal control permits, especially in shortening the fallow period. Although this is generally true, communal control appears to be remarkably tenacious in Andean agriculture. In the most commercial areas where purchased inputs, improved seeds, and market orientation predominate, communal control has been lost over field and crop rotation, but it may be strengthened for such things as irrigation. Many villages with active commercial sectors retain sectoral fallow in the higher traditional sector. Throughout the farming system, the relation and potential conflict between communal and individual control is familiar. On the one hand, individual families are cognizant of the limits imposed by communal control on their activity. On the other, they are aware of the benefits derived from the community: access to land, protection from crop damage by grazing, irrigation, and maintenance of roads, bridges, and trails. The trend under commercialization is to reduce community control over the general production system, but control is never lost altogether and may be increased in some areas.

Environmental Change

Peru's Office of Natural Resource Evaluation has applied standard land and soil classification techniques to its mountainous territory and concluded that only 3 percent of the Andes is appropriate for cultivation, 27 percent for grazing, and 5 percent for forestry (ONERN 1982). The remaining 64 percent is classified as unusable because of steep slopes and poor or highly erosive soils. Overall figures on percentage of land under cultivation and other uses in the Peruvian highlands are unavailable, but there can be little doubt that actual land use greatly exceeds these recommended limits. ONERN's figures suggest that 1,361,000 ha are cultivable, but according to Peru's 1972 Agricultural Census almost twice that amount (2,281,000 ha) is cultivated (Caballero 1981). It is possible that ONERN's classification is wrong, perhaps because of reliance on standards established elsewhere. This contrast may, however, indicate that the Andean population has discovered how to use its mountainous environment successfully in ways unimaginable to soil and land classification scientists from temperate areas. On the other hand, it may indicate that the Andean population of Peru has seriously exceeded the environmental limits of the Andes and are in the process of destroying their agricultural resource base. Although there is little evidence to support the last possibility, continued demands for greater production from highland agriculture raise the specter of environmental catastrophe.

As indicated above, traditional adaptations to the Andean environment have been affected by commercialization that typifies economic change in the region. The rise of a commercial sector in the agricultural economy of small farms has decreased diversity, broken down traditional production zone organization, and weakened community control. How have these changes affected the agroecosystem?

My early work (Brush 1977) describing traditional adaptation in Andean agriculture assumed that agricultural patterns and practices could be understood as mechanisms to stabilize production in a risk-prone environment without external subsidies and to limit environmental degradation. The stabilizing qualities of traditional agriculture have not been adequately tested, and the evidence is mixed regarding their effectiveness. On the one hand, crop failure and large-scale erosion are rare in areas of traditional agriculture. On the other, certain traditional practices, such as the tillage of traditional potato fields and animal stocking rates on communally managed pastures, seem to be environmentally degrading (Felipe-Morales et al. 1979; Lebaron et al. 1979). It was also surmised that intensification and commercialization would be destabilizing and environmentally degrading. This, likewise, has not been adequately demonstrated.

One key variable is soil loss. Fallowing reduces runoff and erosion, but the traditional practice of orienting rows downhill on steep slopes leads to substantial loss (Felipe-Morales et al. 1979). Knapp's (1984) work in northern Ecuador indicates that erosion is prevalent, especially on fields with the greatest slopes. Knapp did not find, however, that productivity was reduced by the shallow soils on eroded fields. There is, unfortunately, very little investigation and data available on the relation between agricultural practices and soil management in the Andes.

Although genetic erosion (i.e., loss of genetic variability) is occurring, its impact on production stability and on the well-being of the agroecosystem is not clear. Some scientists argue for a positive link between stability, agroecosystem quality, and diversity (e.g., Iltis 1968; Altieri et al. 1983; Clawson 1985). Others point out that the association between diversity and stability in agriculture and more general ecology is poorly defended with either theory or fact (Goodman 1975; Brown 1983). As with soils research, there is little data available on the relation between crop diversity and stability in the Andean ecosystem.

The complexity of traditional Andean agriculture compounds the theoretical and methodological difficulty of studying the environmental impact of economic and technological change. At this point it is impossible to generalize about environmental stability or degradation. The high Andean environment may be both fragile and marginal, but it has supported a dense population for millennia without agricultural subsidies. Certain aspects of traditional technology, such as diversity and sectoral crop rotations with long fallow periods, may promote stability and limit environmental degradation. Other traditional technologies, such as tillage practices, may be damaging. All in all, however, with smaller populations and the demands of subsistence economies, Andean traditional technology appears to have been successful in managing the environment.

Under current populations and commercial production for urban markets, the performance of Andean agriculture is unsatisfactory. It is underproductive relative to other areas and relative to the income expectations of Andean farmers. Increased investment and intensification have raised production, but they have not been sufficiently rewarded with increased income. Rather, they have raised the debt of Andean farmers and their sense of marginality. Continued investment and intensification is likely to increase environmental degradation. This can be mitigated by generating and promoting technologies designed with an environmental consciousness. One source of these is traditional technologies that manage environmental risk, such as tillage practices suited to different micro-niches, the communally managed system of crop rotation and fallow, and diversity in crops and varieties. From the perspective of agricultural research, these technologies are costly to investigate because they are outside of the mainstream of organized research. From a developer's and a farmer's point of view they may be inexpensive technologies because they are in place. On the other hand, they are viewed as satisfactory for subsistence production but not for more intensive commercial production. The challenge for research is how to enhance these technologies for higher production and for generating income. However, with competition between regions for urban markets, this strategy must be combined with national farm policies, such as providing research and extension services, and pricing and marketing policies, to protect Andean farmers. Without these, both the farmers and the Andean environment are likely to suffer. Farmers, researchers, and policy makers all face severe economic constraints, but none of them should shirk costs of managing the Andean agroecosystem to ensure future productivity.

Notes

1. Research for this chapter was funded by the National Science Foundation in grants to the University of California, Davis, and to the University of Illinois, Champaign/Urbana. The research has been conducted in collaboration with two co-directors, Drs. Enrique Mayer and Cesar Fonseca. The author wishes to acknowledge the contributions to this research made by field assistants: Manuel Glave, Jaime Lopez, Miriam Granados, Carlos Penafiel, Juan Perea, Alfredo Carbajal.

2. Landrace refers to the population of primitive cultivars of a crop that are maintained in its center(s) of origin and genetic diversity.

References

Altieri, M. A., D. K. Letourneau, and J. R. Davis
    1983   Developing Sustainable Agroecosystems. Bioscience 33:45–49.
Alvarez, E.
    1983   Política Económica y Agricultura en el Perú, 1969–1979. Lima: Instituto de Estudios Peruanos.
Brown, W. L.
    1983   Genetic Diversity and Genetic Vulnerability—An Appraisal. Economic Botany 37:4–12.
Brush, S. B.
    1977   Mountain, Field, and Family: The Economy and Human Ecology of an Andean Valley. Philadelphia, PA: University of Pennsylvania Press.
    1986   Who Are Traditional Farmers? *In* Household Economies and Their Transformations. M. Maclachlan, F. Cancian and M. Chibnik, eds. Philadelphia, PA: University Press of America.
Brush, S. B., H. J. Carney, and Z. Huaman
    1981   Dynamics of Andean Potato Agriculture. Economic Botany 35:70–88.
Caballero, J. M.
    1981   Economía Agraria de la Sierra Peruana Antes de la Reforma Agraria de 1969. Lima, Instituto de Estudios Peruanos.
Clawson, D.
    1985   Harvest Security and Intraspecific Diversity in Traditional Tropical Agriculture. Economic Botany: 39:56–67.

Deere, C. D.
  1978   The Development of Capitalism in Agriculture and the Division of Labor
          by Sex: A Study of the Northern Peruvian Sierra. PhD dissertation (UC
          Berkeley). Ann Arbor, MI: University Microfilms.
De Janvry, A.
  1981   The Agrarian Question and Reformism in Latin America. Baltimore, MD:
          Johns Hopkins University Press.
Dinoor, A., and N. Eshed
  1984   The Role and Importance of Pathogens in Natural Plant Communities.
          Annual Review of Phytopathology 22:443–466.
Felipe-Morales, C., R. Meyer, C. Alegre, and C. Vittorelli
  1979   Losses of Water and Soil Under Different Cultivation Systems in two
          Peruvian Locations, Santa Ana (Central Highlands) and San Ramon (Central
          High Jungle), 1975–1976. *In* Soil Physical Properties and Crop Production
          in the Tropics. R. Lal and D. J. Greenland, eds. New York, NY: John Wiley
          and Sons.
Gade, D. W.
  1975   Plants, Man and the Land in the Vilcanota Valley of Peru. The Hague:
          Dr. W. Junk B.V.
Golte, J.
  1980   Repartos y Rebeliones: Tupac Amaru y las Contradicciones de la Economía
          Colonial. Lima: Instituto de Estudios Peruanos.
Gonzales de Olarte, E.
  1984   Economía de la Comunidad Campesina. Lima: Instituto de Estudios Per-
          uanos.
Goodman, D.
  1975   The Theory of Diversity-Stability Relationships in Ecology. Quarterly Review
          of Biology 50:227–266.
Guillet, D. W.
  1978   The Supra-Household Sphere of Production in the Andean Peasant Econ-
          omy. Actes du XLII Congres International des Americanistes. Pp. 89–105.
          Paris 1976.
Harris, O.
  1982   Labour and Produce in an Ethnic Economy: Northern Potosi, Bolivia. *In*
          Ecology and Exchange in the Andes. D. Lehmann, ed. Pp. 70–96. Cambridge:
          Cambridge University Press.
Hawkes, J. G.
  1978   Biosystematics of the Potato. *In* The Potato Crop. P. M. Harris, ed. Pp.
          15–69. London: Chapman & Hall.
Horton, D. E.
  1984   Social Scientists in Agricultural Research: Lessons from the Mantaro Valley
          Project, Peru. Ottawa: IDRC.
Iltis, H. H.
  1968   The Optimum Environment and Its Relation to Modern Agricultural Preoc-
          cupations. The Biologist 50:114–125.
Jennings, P. R., and J. H. Cock
  1977   Centres of Origin of Crops and Their Productivity. Economic Botany
          31:51–54.
Knapp, G.
  1984   Soil, Slope, and Water in the Equatorial Andes: A Study of Prehistoric
          Agricultural Adaptation. PhD dissertation, Geography Department, Uni-
          versity of Wisconsin, Madison.

Lebaron, A., L. K. Bond, P. Aitken, and L. Michaelson
  1979   An Explanation of the Bolivian Highlands Grazing-Erosion Syndrome. Journal of Range Management 32:201–208.
Masuda, S., I. Shimada, and C. Morris, eds.
  1985   Andean Ecology and Civilization. Tokyo: University of Tokyo Press.
Mayer, E.
  1985   Production Zones. *In* Andean Ecology and Civilization. S. Masuda, I. Shimada and C. Morris, eds. Pp. 45–84. Tokyo: University of Tokyo Press.
Mayer, E., and C. Fonseca
  1979   Sistemas Agrarios en la Cuenca del Rio Cañete (Dpto. de Lima). Lima: Oficina Nacional de Evaluación de Recursos Naturales.
Mitchell, W. P.
  1976   Irrigation and Community in the Central Peruvian Highlands. American Anthropologist 78(1):25–44.
Murra, J. V.
  1972   El Control Vertical de un Máximo de Pisos Ecológicos en la Economía de las Sociedades Andinas. *In* Visita de la Provincia de León de Huánuco en 1562, Iñigo Ortiz de Zúñiga, Visitador. J. V. Murra, ed. Tomo II. Huánuco, Perú: Universidad Nacional Hermilio Valdizán.
Odum, E. P.
  1953   Fundamentals of Ecology. Philadelphia, PA: Saunders.
Oficina Nacional de Evaluación de Recursos Naturales (ONERN)
  1982   Clasificación de las Tierras del Perú. Lima: ONERN.
Orlove, B. S.
  1976   The Tragedy of the Commons Revisited: Land Use and Environmental Quality in High-Altitude Andean Grasslands. *In* International Hill Lands Symposium. Morgantown, WV: West Virginia University Press.
  1977   Alpacas, Sheep and Men: The Wool Export Economy and Regional Society in Southern Peru. New York, NY: Academic Press.
Orlove, B. S., and R. Godoy
  1986   Sectoral Fallowing Systems in the Central Andes. Journal of Ethnobiology 6.
Painter, M.
  1984   Changing Relations of Production and Rural Underdevelopment. Journal of Anthropological Research 40:271–292.
Troll, C.
  1968   The Cordilleras of the Tropical Americas: Aspects of Climate, Phytogeographical and Agrarian Ecology. *In* Geoecology of the Mountain Regions of the Tropical Americas. C. Troll, ed. Bonn, Germany: Ferd. Dummlers Verlag.
Vanderplank, J. E.
  1968   Disease Resistance in Plants. New York, NY: Academic Press.

14

Intensification and Degradation in the Agricultural Systems of the Peruvian Upper Jungle: The Upper Huallaga Case[1]

Eduardo Bedoya Garland

Introduction

The ecological and productivity crisis in the agricultural areas of the Peruvian upper jungle[2] has been viewed, with few exceptions (cf. Recharte 1982), to be a result of the deforestation brought about by highland settlers (Martinez 1977). Settlers are not, of course, the only agents responsible for massive deforestation and its consequent ecological disruptions. Other factors in the relationship between immigration and environmental destruction are a state that views colonization as necessary for economic development and national security, the opening of penetration roads, and the legal land tenure system. Nevertheless, the subsistence strategies of settlers from Peru's highland areas are essential elements in the situation. As one attempts to understand why settlers frequently engage in destructive production practices, a number of issues emerge that concern resource constraints imposed by the larger socioeconomic context. These include the composition of the household production unit over time, the decisions that households make regarding the hiring of wage labor, and the relationship between current agricultural prices and household production costs.

General models of soil degradation have focused attention almost exclusively on population (Boserup 1965), technological inadequacy (Sanchez and Buol 1975), or the nature of agricultural policies (Hecht 1984). While the latter perspective offers methodological advantages over the other two, studies of subsistence strategies conducted by Peruvian researchers continue to treat environmental destruction as resulting solely from the automatic response of a group of settlers to market conditions and soil quality. In this chapter, I examine the various elements that lead to environmental disturbances and show that endogenous factors, such as farmer income-earning strategies and the size of the colonist family, are especially significant.

The approach discriminates intensive and extensive systems through an index of soil use intensity. As will be discussed in more detail below, the greater the intensity of soil use, the greater the environmental degradation.

The chapter is divided into three parts: a description of the deforestation problem; a case study of the upper Huallaga valley based on results of a survey administered in 1981 by Carlos Aramburú (1982); and a synthesis and discussion of ecological degradation, including policy recommendations.

The Deforestation Problem

Several ecologists and agricultural experts have, from different viewpoints, indicated the negative effects of agricultural practices employed by immigrants in the Peruvian Amazon, especially in the upper jungle. Malleux (1975) and Martinez (1977), for example, discuss the huge area that has been deforested. In the course of the last 50 years, approximately 5,122,000 ha have been cleared. Even more serious, however, is the fact that the rate of deforestation is increasing exponentially, such that every year the area of land deforested is about 12 percent greater than the area deforested the previous year. At this rate, we can expect an additional 20 million ha of land in the Peruvian Amazon to be ruined during the period 1985–1999. In the year 2000 alone, less than 15 years from now, more than 2.5 million ha will be cleared if present trends continue unabated. José Dance (1979), more optimistic but also critical, calculates the current annual deforestation rate at 254,000 ha annually per year and projects that it will reach 339,000 ha annually by 2000. Dourojeanni (1984) predicts that over 11,000,000 ha will have been deforested by 2000.

The estimates specifically for the upper jungle are also discouraging. Approximately 3,389,000 ha have been destroyed in 50 years. In both the lower Amazon basin and the upper jungle, productive use of the cleared land is minimal: only one in every four deforested hectares currently has an agricultural use. Thus, in spite of massive deforestation, only 1,280,000 ha in all of the Peruvian Amazon are being used for agriculture, of which 850,000 ha are located in the upper jungle (Dourojeanni 1981). Despite such unproductive use of land resources, some advocates of settlement have argued that there still remain 63,588,000 forested hectares, and continue to view settlement as a way of addressing land distribution problems. This view lacks scientific justification. In the land now in fallow, huge areas are so badly degraded that they have been lost from all productive use (Agreda 1984). Of the 3,389,000 deforested hectares in the upper jungle, around 2,610,000 ha constitute an area at fallow, but not all of this area is potentially arable. The fact is that two of every five deforested hectares are not suitable even for reforestation. These were cover forests, situated on steep slopes of more than 40 degrees, which were useful as natural protection against erosion, as habitat for animals and plants, and as a defense of the Amazon's downstream hydro-energy resources (Goodland 1980).

Víctor Agreda (1984), in his recent research on the expansion of the agricultural frontiers of Peru, classifies degrees of susceptibility to soil erosion in the upper jungle. In that region, the soil not only is low in fertility due to scarce organic content (Meggers 1971) but most is also located on highly erodible slopes. According to Agreda, 47.3 percent of these lands has a high degree of susceptibility to erosion, 38.4 percent an intermediate level of susceptibility, 8.2 percent a low level, and only 6.1 percent is not susceptible to erosion. We must conclude from Agreda's classification that the upper jungle of the Amazon basin is a region at high risk. This conclusion is reinforced by the land-use classification of ONERN (Oficina Nacional de Evaluación de Recursas Naturales, the National Office of Natural Resource Evaluation), which holds that 29 percent of the soils of this region is suitable only for cover or natural protection and 40.5 percent for use in forestry. Of the 13.8 percent of the land area classified as appropriate for permanent crops, a significant sector will support only moderately light use. While 30.5 percent of the land area in the upper jungle is suitable for some form of agricultural or pastoral exploitation, as compared to only 13.7 percent in the lower basin, nearly a third of the land of the upper jungle is unsuitable for any form of exploitation (Agreda 1984:18–19).

In the interior of the upper jungle, certain basins have been affected more than others. In the Department of San Martín, 42 percent of deforested hectares is concentrated in areas classified as forest without agricultural potential, while in Amazonas it is 65 percent, in Huánuco 61 percent, in Junín 58 percent, and in Cuzco 77 percent (Dance 1979). Generally speaking, the upper jungle regions, which contain 52 percent of the Amazonian population (Lesevic 1984), suffer the most negative effects of deforestation. Moreover, in certain basins, such as Satipo, upper Urubamba, and Oxapampa, that are classified as alluvial forests with high natural suitability for farming, practically no agriculture has been developed. Instead, the bulk of agriculture is concentrated in lands of little or no agricultural potential. The consequences are evident: loss of hydroenergy potential of the upper jungle; reduction of riverine navigation; repeated destruction of roads, communication facilities, and villages by landslides; and irreparable damage to the weak balance of the tropical humid forest (Dourojeanni 1984; Agreda 1984).

Various officials of former president Fernando Belaunde's regime consider the upper Mayo region in the northern part of Peru's upper jungle, where irrigated rice cultivation has been developed during the last eight years, to be an example of effective spontaneous settlement.[3] In this basin ecological deterioration is not as great as in other areas, but problems of soil mismanagement nevertheless arise. In the upper parts of the Yuracyacu River, a tributary of the Mayo River, cover forests, or areas recommended for strict forestry use, have been cleared for annual crops. A major negative effect of this has been water filtration or evaporation at the source of the river, which has severely endangered plans for the future expansion of irrigated agriculture in the area (Bedoya 1985). The case of the Marañon basin, in the northern high jungle on the Ecuadorian border, is probably the most significant example of the use of soil unsuitable for permanent crops due to its steep slopes. Only about 37,000 ha in the basin are suitable for

permanent crops, but 47,404 ha were planted in coffee in 1980. Approximately 14,704 ha of the coffee were sown in cover forests or in soil recommended exclusively for forestry activities. Some have gone so far as to blame this indiscriminate deforestation for the sharp decline in local rainfall in 1982, when there were 700 mm of rain as opposed to the average 1,500 mm (Peñaherrera 1984; Paredes 1983a, 1983b).

Settlers of the upper jungle have traditionally been stereotyped as practitioners of shifting agriculture. According to a survey by M. Dourojeanni (1981) on the lower Mayo-central Huallaga basin, 9 percent of the total hectares cleared in 1980 was in effective agricultural use, 14 percent was made up of pastures, and the remaining 77 percent was in fallow. At that time, only 50 percent of the land classified as in agricultural use was being worked under shifting cultivation, while 40 percent was under permanent agricultural production with a fallow period and 10 percent of the land was under permanent cultivation with no fallow, growing crops that require intensive use of the soil—either annual crops such as irrigated rice, or permanent plantation crops such as coffee, cacao, coca, or tea.

With regard to shifting agriculture, not much research has been carried out and little is known. Watters' (1971) enquiries during research on peasant technology in the upper Huallaga in the 1960s include some useful indirect references to shifting agriculture, but they lack specific data (see Aramburú 1980). On the other hand, some authors have projected the figures calculated by Dourojeanni in the central Huallaga to make inferences about agricultural patterns throughout the upper jungle basins (Agreda 1984). In view of the existence of several levels of intensity of soil use throughout this region, however, these projections are not likely to be accurate. In some areas where permanent crops now dominate, shifting agriculture has been significantly reduced, especially as agricultural settlement areas begin to experience economic consolidation. For instance, a recent inquiry in the upper Huallaga indicates that only 40 percent of the settlers have cultivated one or more plots in addition to the one they are presently working (Aramburú et al. 1985).

It is, in any event, not fair to blame only those settlers who practice shifting cultivation for the deforestation of 39 percent of the jungle. Permanent as well as shifting agriculture has been carried out in areas recommended exclusively for forestry use or protection. In the Tingo María area, for example, the former large tea and coffee plantations now reorganized as production cooperatives, such as CAP (Cooperativa Agraria de Producción/ Agrarian Production Cooperative) Jardines de Té El Porvenir, and CAP Té-Café, also have occupied areas that were recommended solely for forestry use. In previous studies (Bedoya 1981; CENCIRA 1973) I have pointed out the economic unsuitability of mechanical clearing in this region. A further problem, the inappropriate locating of plantations on steep slopes, led to the destruction of tea and coffee fields in 1982, when a minor earthquake caused a landslide in the area.

From a number of sources, then, the Peruvian upper jungle has been subject to resource abuse and degradation. In what follows, I turn to an analysis of the case of upper Huallaga valley, located in the department of Huánuco, which, as has already been indicated, is one of the most deforested regions of Peru's upper jungle.

Agricultural Systems in Upper Huallaga

The upper Huallaga basin (Figure 14.1), located in the central upper jungle, contains 10.2 percent of the total population of the upper jungle— 1,221,351 inhabitants (Lesevic 1984)—and comprises 3,373,600 ha of the zone's 27,355,300 ha (Peñaherrera 1984). It represents a classic pattern of population settlement, though more recent than settlement in the basins of Chanchamayo, Jaén-San Ignacio, and central Huallaga.

Research on the upper Huallaga basin shows that there are two main agricultural systems. One is dominated by the permanent plantations of coca, tea, coffee, and cacao, which, in 1980, accounted for 61 percent of the agricultural area. The other consists of annual food crops, such as manioc, yellow corn, starchy corn,[4] and dryland rice. Annual crops accounted for 12 percent of the agricultural land under production in 1980. In 1972, eight years earlier, annual crops had accounted for 60 percent of the hectares in agricultural production. Of the remaining area (40 percent), 30 percent was covered with permanent crops (coca, coffee, tea), and 10 percent with semipermanent (banana) (CENCIRA 1973). The studies also show that each settler manages a small family garden of crops either for household consumption or for experimenting with possible cash crops.

The dramatic increase in coca (*Erythroxylon coca*) production, from about 2,228 ha in 1973 to at least 30,000 ha in 1980, explains the predominance of permanent crops that characterizes the latter year. It has been, of course, the growth of the drug trade that has stimulated these drastic changes in land use. The production of coca allows settlers to extend cultivation into more marginal areas, for it offers the possibility of exceptional profits. One hectare of coca, transformed into cocaine paste,[5] represents an income of US $30,000 per year. This return is ten times higher than the next most profitable crops, cacao or irrigated rice.

The expansion of coca production in upper Huallaga is the result of a long process of change. Since the opening of the road to Huánuco, Tingo María, and Pucallpa in the 1940s, the area has received a massive number of settlers migrating from the highlands. Large commercial estates also were established at that time, including Jardines de Té, Pra Alto, and Santa Elena (Bedoya 1982a; 1982b). Initially, the coffee and tea plantations were located in the best alluvial lands and flat gradient hills of Tingo María, while smallholder settlers from the Andean highlands were located on the most marginal areas, classified for forestry use or protection forest. Subsequently, construction in the mid-1950s of the central Huallaga road from Tingo María to Aucayacu resulted in increased colonization in this area by both Andean settlers and former Amazon riverside inhabitants who were hired to build the road. In the 1960s, the government-sponsored Tingo María-

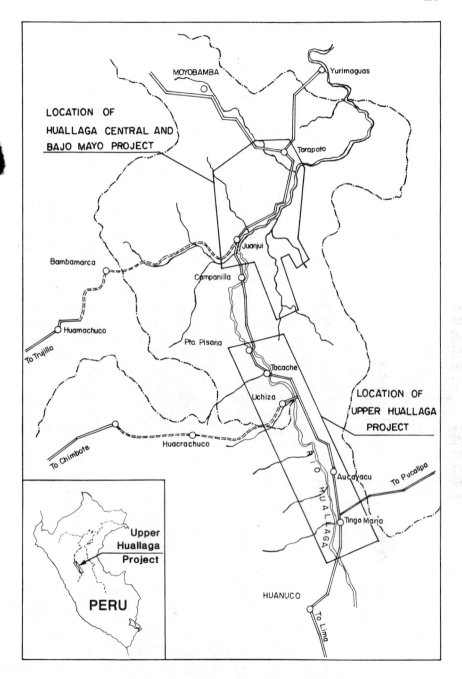

Fig. 14.1 Map of Huallaga Valley.

Tocache and Campanilla settlement program was initiated. The purpose of the effort was to locate or relocate 4,680 families, most of them spontaneous settlers, and to make use of 130,000 ha for such commercial crops as oil palm, rubber, and citrus fruits (Bedoya 1981). More recently, between the late 1960s and the early 1970s, Tocache and Uchiza zones became the regions of demographic and agricultural expansion (Aramburú 1980). As in the Aucayacu region, settlers in these two zones did not experience problems resulting from the occupation of the best soils by big plantations, as had settlers in the Tingo María region.

In summary, we can identify three settlement frontiers: the oldest one in Tingo María, where massive migratory settlements occurred in the 1940s and 1950s; a second frontier in Aucayacu during the 1960s; and a third frontier in Tocache and Uchiza in the 1970s (Aramburú et al. 1985).[6] Although large holdings were developed, particularly in Tingo María, the three regions underwent spontaneous settlement by populations from the highlands. In all three, limitations on the availability of land suitable for cultivation reproduced a peasant economy similar in many respects to what settlers had left behind in the highlands, even as the new physical environment stimulated innovations in household subsistence strategies.

During the 1960s and 1970s, however, large properties in Tingo María entered into an economic and institutional crisis. Under the provisions of agrarian reform instituted under the government of General Juan Velasco Alvarado, private estates, such as Jardines de Té, were converted into state cooperatives. Beginning in the 1960s with private firms—Saipai, for example—and continuing into the present with the state production cooperatives, commercial enterprises have experienced financial problems and economic failure. The principal cause of these difficulties has been the inability of commercial plantations and cooperatives to retain their labor supply. Throughout the upper Huallaga region, the availability of land facilitated the transformation of indebted plantation labor forces into independent smallholders managing plots outside of the plantation lands. The resulting labor scarcity impacted adversely on the production plans of commercial enterprises. Since 1978 coca production has been more profitable than tea or coffee production for cooperative members and potential hired laborers at CAP Jardines de Té. For cooperative members, the possibility of large and immediate earnings through cultivating coca was more attractive than any long-term benefits they saw accruing from participation in the cooperative. For wage laborers, wages paid by coca farmers were almost twice those paid by the tea cooperative. While CAP Jardines de Té had many financial and administrative problems, competition generated especially by coca activity led to a chronic labor deficit between 1978 and 1982. Thus, during this period, the number of workers at CAP Jardines de Té decreased from 375 to 202. This created intolerable financial pressure in the upper jungle, where large properties, under a wide range of economic conditions, have historically suffered a chronic labor shortage due to the competition generated by the economic expansion of the peasantry (Bedoya 1983). Taken together, these conditions led upper Huallaga plantations, although changed into cooperatives, almost to disappear from the region as significant agricultural systems. In the 1970s, management of the agricultural cooperatives was the responsibility of the settlers with farms of 20 to 30 ha. Except for CAP Jardines de Té, the cooperatives went out of business. In CAP Té-Café, members even substituted coca plants for coffee. With the disintegration of cooperatives, many settlers who were former members began to occupy alluvial lands or lands of better quality than those occupied by older peasants in the Tingo María region.

On the other hand, the production of crops (such as rice and yellow corn) for direct urban consumption was not promoted as strongly in the upper Huallaga region as it had been in such other areas of Peru's upper jungle, as the central Huallaga River basin and the upper and lower Mayo River basins, in spite of pricing policies implemented by the Velasco military government (1968–1975) to encourage this activity. In the first place, a large number of the settlers who moved into the central Huallaga and Mayo basins came from Bagua, in Amazonas department, and were familiar with the technology and cultural practices associated with irrigated rice production (Gonzalez 1983). Settlers arriving in the upper Huallaga area came, by contrast, from highland areas of Huánuco department. They had experience with irrigated agriculture, but with a totally different technology, based on temporary structures to manage water from rainfall (Caballero 1981).

Second, settlers in the central Huallaga and Mayo River areas benefited from higher quality soils than did their counterparts in the upper Huallaga. For example, the upper Mayo River basin has four times the amount of arable land as the lower Mayo and Huallaga basins, and fifteen times the amount of arable land as the upper Huallaga (Gonzalez 1983).[7] Such differences led to more intensive land use and more productive agriculture in the Mayo and central Huallaga basins than in the upper Huallaga. So, in 1981, the average yield of unirrigated rice in upper Mayo was 2,200 kilograms per hectare, while in upper Huallaga the overall average yield was about 1,800 kilograms per hectare, with rice yields in some areas approximating the 1,389 kilograms per hectare recorded in Tingo María. Similar differences in yields characterize the production of other important crops such as corn, manioc, and beans (Gonzalez 1983; Aramburú et al. 1985). These differences in productivity placed upper Huallaga farmers at a disadvantage in relation to farmers in other Huallaga and Mayo River areas.

A third factor responsible for the low productivity of the region was the minimal use of inputs. To a certain extent, this resulted from the differences in productivity discussed above. If yields are low, in relative terms, input costs become too expensive. Since 1976, however, the economic stabilization rules imposed by the International Monetary Fund, which removed subsidies and let the market reflect the real scarcities, have reduced effective urban demand for foodstuffs and agricultural products. Moreover, the terms of trade between agricultural prices and input costs have shown an increasingly unfavorable trend for the producer since 1973. The modern capitalist farmers were badly hurt by this, but for traditional farmers like those of upper Huallaga, the rise in relative prices of inputs was less important, since their use was already low (Alvarez 1983). In the economic crisis of 1981 to 1983, the terms of trade deteriorated even further. Overall production costs increased 2.7 times more than prices did, rising 1.6 times faster than the price of corn, 4.1 times faster than the price of manioc, and 8.1 times faster than the price of bananas (Aramburú et al. 1985).

In this context of unfavorable prices and low productivity for other crops, coca production burgeoned, but the expansion of coca has created ecological problems throughout the upper Huallaga.[8] First, as a result of its high price, coca is cultivated in large areas as a monoculture, with an almost complete lack of protection and without proper spacing or density. Second, as in other upper jungle zones, coca—like cacao, tea, and coffee—is grown on land suitable for agriculture or for forestry, removing it from other types of production. Even more ecologically damaging, due to the illegal nature of this crop settlers try to cultivate it in locations remote from roads. The hillsides are the safest alternative, but though it is a permanent crop, coca has the harmful effects of an annual crop when it is cultivated on deforested steep slopes. This is particularly true because it is typically cultivated in vertical furrows rather than in terraces that soften the damaging effects of rain.

If the current rate of increase in the area dedicated to coca production continues, the environmental destruction will be exacerbated. There are 193,600 ha suitable for annual crops in upper Huallaga, and 58,600 ha recommended for permanent and semi-permanent crops. But, as in other regions, the dynamics of development have caused land use patterns to be the reverse of those that are technically most advisable. Permanent crops like coca, coffee, and tea are the most widely cultivated, and these are encroaching upon lands best suited for annual crops.

Intensification of Soil Use
and the Process of Degradation

The production of coca and annual crops has led to ecological degradation in the upper Huallaga basin. The degree of degradation can be measured as a function of the intensification of soil use, which is reflected in the shortening of fallow periods or a decrease in fallow area. The process of intensification is measured by the formula: (permanent crops + annual crops) divided by (permanent crops + annual crops + fallow grass). For instance, for plots that have an intensity of 0.1, 6.24 hectares at fallow correspond to each cropped hectare; for farms with an intensity of 0.9, only 0.11 hectares at fallow correspond to each cropped hectare. In other words, the lowest indexes correspond to the most extensive systems, the highest indexes to the most intensive systems.

As may be seen in Figure 14.2, shorter fallow periods are not accompanied by increases in modern inputs. Official figures indicate that about 7 percent

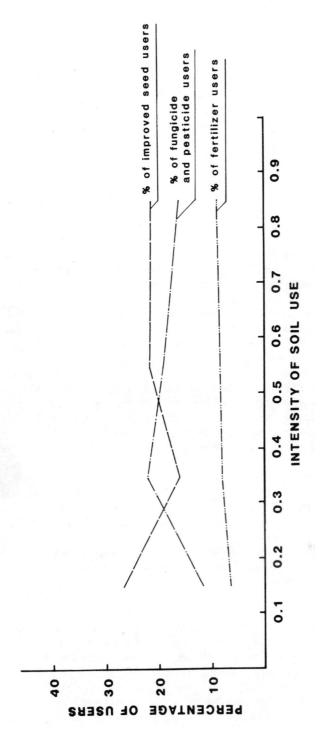

Fig. 14.2 Percentage of Modern Input Users and Intensity of Soil Use.

of settlers use fertilizers, about 16 percent use insecticides and fungicides, and 21 percent use improved seeds. The inputs are not applied as part of an overall package, however, but individually, according to what can be purchased at a particular time at a particular price. Most households in the upper Huallaga vary their economic strategies according to prevailing market conditions for agricultural products, the availability of unpaid family labor, and their need and capacity to hire wage labor. The purchase and use of capital inputs becomes part of this process only after labor requirements have been met. A household with sufficient members between the ages of 10 and 24 to carry out the bulk of its productive activities is relatively likely to use modern inputs, because it does not have to spend scarce funds on securing labor (Figure 14.3).

While abundance of household labor is accompanied by relatively high use of modern inputs, abundance of land seems to diminish their use. Thus, in regions such as Tocache and Uchiza where land is relatively plentiful, the use of modern inputs is remarkably less than in Tingo María, an area with higher population. In the former zones, two-thirds of the settlers do not use any kind of inputs, while in Tingo María exactly the opposite situation prevails. Tingo María has a population density of 52.30 inhabitants per km² —a medium-high density according to Boserup (1984)— and an average farm size of 19.50 ha (Table 14.1). Tocache and Uchiza have a medium-low density of 24.65 inhabitants per km², an average farm size of 30.07 ha. Obviously the greater availability of land is leading toward more extensive use of soil. As in the upper Huallaga, farmers who utilize modern inputs do so selectively, in a piecemeal fashion, rather than as part of a single technological package. As a result, in 1981, 68 percent of the settlers in Tingo María could not cultivate the total area of their plots due to soil exhaustion, in spite of the fact that they are relatively heavy users of modern inputs.

Several factors are related to the intensity of soil use. First, greater soil use intensity is inversely related to plot size. Figure 14.4 illustrates this relationship: while the smaller plots are concentrated on the higher indexes— 0.7 to 1.0—the larger farms are on the lower indexes—0.1 and 0.2. However, the relationship between plot size and soil-use intensity is the strongest in the older settlement areas of Tingo María, and relatively less important in the Aucayacu and Tocache-Uchiza regions. This is because the pressures to utilize the soil more intensively increase as plot size decreases, and the relationship becomes progressively stronger as the person-to-land ratio increases.

In Tingo María the smaller size of plots is a result of a dynamic land market. Although there is no information for the 1970 to 1980 period, available data show that the number of farms in the area has increased approximately 800 percent during the 1980s alone (Bedoya 1986). The rise in land value is obviously a consequence of coca's profitability. However, such an increase in the number of farms not only reduces their average size but makes the already scarce "free" land less plentiful. Intensification

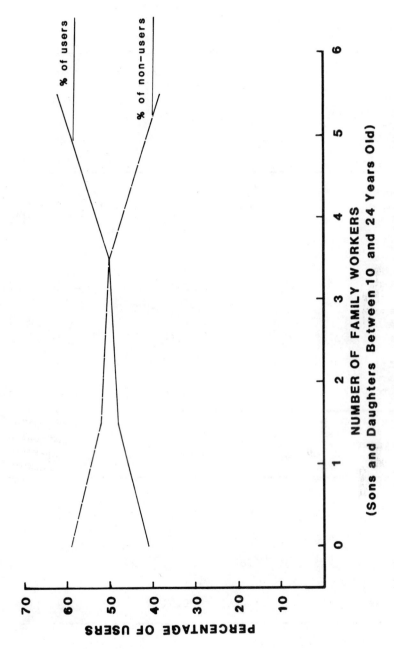

Fig. 14.3 Number of Family Workers and Use of Modern Agricultural Inputs.

Table 14.1   Population Density and Soil Use
            in Upper Huallaga Valley

Population Density (people per square kilometer)	Tingo María (older area)		Aucayacu (intermediate area)		Tocache and Uchiza (new areas)	
	52.30		18.38		24.65	
Average hectares per plot	19.5	% 100	26.75	% 100	30.07	% 100
Average hectares in permanent crops	4.73	24	3.38	13	2.34	8
Average hectares in annual crops	1.47	8	2.54	9	3.71	12
Average hectares in pasture	2.71	14	5.02	19	4.60	15
Total hectares in agriculture and pasture	8.91	46	10.94	41	10.65	35
Average hectares in fallow grass	5.09	26	7.96	30	9.22	31
Average hectares in forest	5.51	28	7.85	29	10.18	34
Intensity of soil use	0.55 (medium)		0.43 (low)		0.40 (low)	

Source: Bedoya 1986.

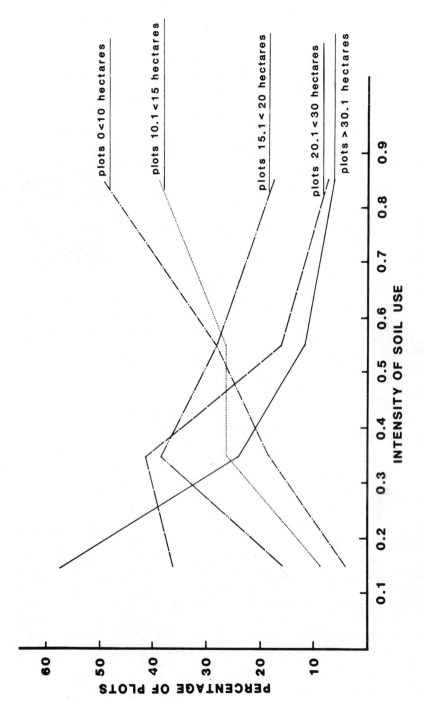

Fig. 14.4 Size of the Plots and Intensity of Soil Use.

Table 14.2   Intensity of Soil Use and Cropping and Fallow
             Periods (Annual Crops) in Tocache, Uchiza, and
             Aucayacu

Intensity of Soil Use	Number of Cropping and Fallow Years	
0.1 to 0.2 (very low)	2 cropping and 4 fallow years	3 cropping and 8 fallow years
	3 cropping and 6 fallow years	
0.3 to 0.4 (low)	2 cropping and 3 fallow years	3 cropping and 4 fallow years
	3 cropping and 5 fallow years	
0.5 to 0.6 (medium)	2 cropping and 2 fallow years	
	3 cropping and 2 fallow years	
0.7 to 0.9 (high)	2 cropping and 2 fallow years	

Source: Bedoya   1986.

is thus an immediate alternative to acquiring more land, but it results in serious degradation.

For annual crops, the relation between cultivated and fallow periods in upper Huallaga basin is an additional symptom of degradation. If land is less accessible, fallow years will be shortened and soil exhaustion will increase. As production systems have evolved on colonists' farms in Tocache and Uchiza, as well as in Aucayacu, greater intensity in soil use has accompanied a shorter fallow period (see Table 14.2). In Tingo María, however, the trend has been irregular. In the intensity indexes that run between 0.1 and 0.2 the fallow periods for annual crops are some four years longer than the cropping years. The length of fallow diminishes as the intensity index increases to 0.6, when cropped years exceed fallow. But for indexes above 0.8, cropped years decline and years in fallow again exceed cropped years. That is to say, the agricultural history of the upper Huallaga valley has been characterized by a shift away from extensive annual systems located in areas of recent occupation, toward a reduction of fallow periods in areas occupied for intermediate periods of time. But, the system finally regresses, with the reestablishment of extensive annual systems as the effects of soil degradation are felt. This pattern is similar to the one described by Recharte (1982) for the Chanchamayo region. Furthermore, in the area of Tingo María, there is evidence of profusion of "toro urco" (*Paspalum paniculatum*), a naturally occurring variety of pasture grass that is an indicator of degradation, in a higher proportion than in Tocache and Uchiza. The small size of domestic livestock that live off this grass also indicates soil exhaustion. In such a situation, coca, due to its rapid growth (eight months between planting and first harvest) and easy cultivation even on steep slopes, is the most attractive alternative. Coca has paradoxical significance for Andean agriculture and environment: on the one hand, it is a highly erosive crop because of its sowing method; on the other, it can be produced on degraded lands.

Changes in cropping patterns seem to be a factor in soil use intensification. Farms with cropping patterns based primarily on annual crops have a lower intensity than do farms where permanent crops predominate (Figure 14.5). However, the influence of the cropping pattern is perceived only at the overall regional level. In a specific area such as Aucayacu, where a dramatic transition from annual to perennial crops took place, local factors may obscure the relationship (Table 14.1).

Variations in settlers' economic strategies are also a factor underlying soil intensification. As may be seen in Figure 14.6, an orientation more linked to a market economy is associated with a greater intensification. Changes in the intensity of soil use occur simultaneously with variations in the number of crops under cultivation and the degree to which plots are dedicated to production for market or for household consumption. According to Figure 14.6, the cultivation technique of combining one commercial crop with two or more crops for family consumption is associated with relatively low intensities of soil use. However, in the medium and high ranges of the soil intensity index, the dominant pattern is a combination of two commercial crops and one subsistence—usually annual—crop. In this last period, characteristic of Tingo María, there is specialization, with permanent crops grown almost exclusively for markets, and annual crops for family consumption. This transition from subsistence to commercial production occurs in such a way that the present system is not likely to be sustainable under humid tropical conditions. The practice of simplifying the production system to include only one or two crops, usually sown in adjacent or contiguous areas, provokes biological degradation (cf. Meggers 1971; Camino 1984).[9]

Finally, family size plays an important role in determining the intensity of soil use. In the most populated areas, like Tingo María, increasing family

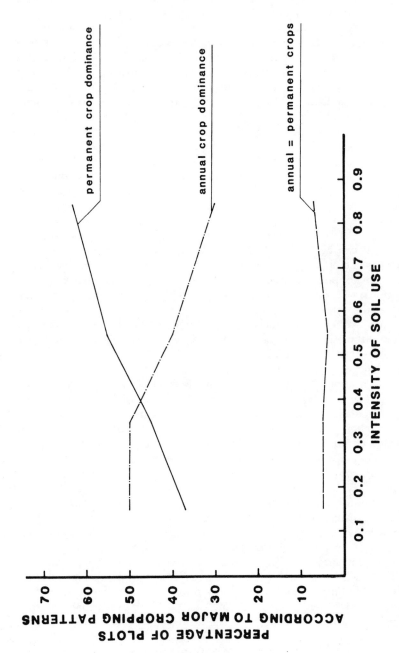

Fig. 14.5 Major Cropping Patterns and Intensity of Soil Use.

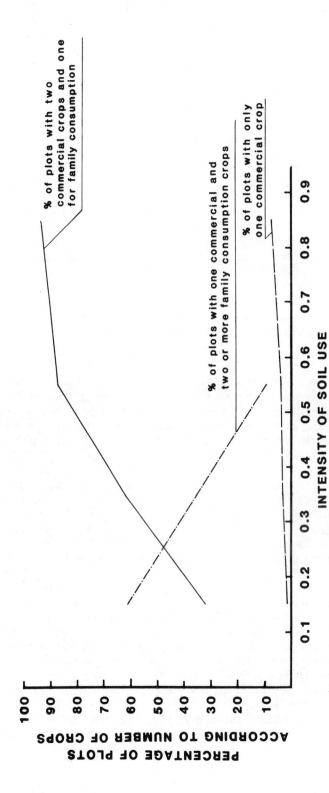

Fig.14.6 Number of Crops and Intensity of Soil Use.

size leads toward greater intensification; while in Tocache and Uchiza, where farms are bigger and land is available, the larger families enlarge their total number of cultivated hectares. This explains the fact that in Tocache and Uchiza average farm size is higher than in Tingo María (10.65 ha and 8.91 ha, respectively). A larger number of available hectares correlates positively with a larger average farm size; while fewer available hectares corresponds with greater intensification.[10] Such a trend is similar to that noted by Chayanov (1966) in reference to domestic intensification in the case of an increase of children (Figure 14.7).

In summary, four factors influence the intensification of soil use: farm size, cropping pattern, the degree of market orientation among settlers, and family size. The relative influence of each factor depends on the age of the settlement and the density of population. In any case, the Tingo María region, with greater soil-use intensity, has the worst soil exhaustion and degradation.[11]

Institutional and Ideological Factors

In addition to the physical factors underlying soil-use intensity mentioned in the previous section, variables of an institutional nature are also dynamically involved. First, for example, squatters without legal land tenure certificates are responsible for much of the accelerating process of deforestation. Squatters deforested at a rate of 1.09 agricultural hectares per year, while legal tenants or grantees did so at a rate of 0.54 ha (Bedoya 1986). The need to obtain a legal certificate to settle permanently on a plot and acquire a credit rating forces squatters who practice shifting agriculture to clear land more rapidly than colonists who already own their farms. The certificate of possession, prior to the legal title of property, recognizes only the area under cultivation, and excludes the remaining hectares, which bear fallow grass, protection forest, and so forth. At the same time, the certificate of possession is a prerequisite for legal titling of the property in the future. If only a few working hectares are recognized in the certificate of possession, the officers in charge of land concessions will not in the future give or assign to the colonist the appropriate number of hectares. Thus, at the beginning colonists will try to work the largest possible number of hectares, but after they have devoted some years to obtaining the certificate of possession, the soils will already have been used intensively. That is why the settler with a land title averages around 0.54 (medium intensity) compared to that of precarious occupants with a certificate (0.34—low intensity). Perhaps in the past, when the abundance of land did not force colonists to have a property title, soil use by squatters was more extensive. Now, however, the reduced availablity of land leads squatter colonists to intensify its use.

Second, it has been demonstrated that, given equal soil quality and equal number of years on the farm, the highland colonist utilizes significantly more intensive systems than the jungle colonist. The intensity levels in

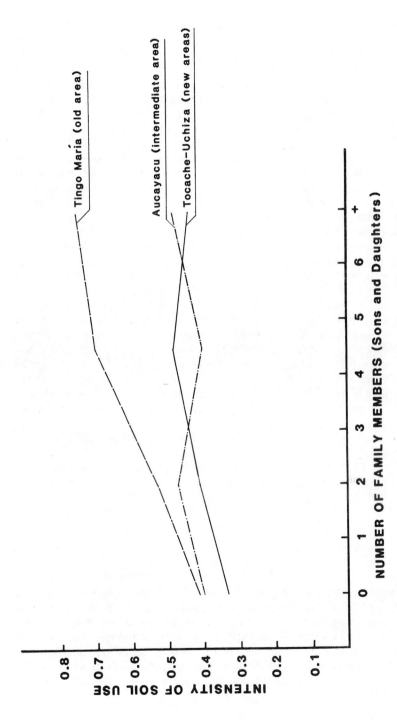

Fig.14.7 Intensity of Soil Use and Number of Family Members.

Tingo María, Aucayacu, and Tocache and Uchiza are very different for settlers from the highlands than they are for settlers from the eastern lowlands. Whereas highlanders' intensity indexes for the three regions are 0.60, 0.46, and 0.47 respectively, the jungle colonists' are 0.44, 0.33, and 0.34. Similarly, the former are much more involved in the market economy; they raise mostly permanent crops; and they usually have to face problems related to soil exhaustion after a number of years. Jungle colonists—former riverside inhabitants—develop more rational production systems: facing the fragile rainforest ecology, they have a tendency to settle on low lands, raise transitory crops for their own consumption, and remain only loosely articulated to the market economy. The differences parallel those between the adaptive system of *caboclos* (non-Indian peasants) and those of colonists coming from Brazilian regions on the Transamazonian highway, pointed out by Emilio Moran (1979).

Finally, we should consider ideological factors arising from a national government that pursues a policy of promoting lowland settlement and is reluctant to face agrarian problems in the highland regions where migrations originate. The government sees the Peruvian jungle as a territory open for settlement, where fertile lands for any kind of agriculture are abundant. In 1964, during Fernando Belaunde's first presidential term, studies carried out by the Ministry of Agriculture and the National Natural Resource Evaluation Office (ONERN) classified upper Huallaga as a region in which 51.2 percent of the soil had agricultural potential. This percentage is dramatically different from the results of studies carried out twenty years later, when colonization on tropical rainforest had proven to have serious limitations. Table 14.3 shows that in 1983 the ONERN study classified only 7.4 percent of lands as suitable for agriculture, while 58.3 percent was considered appropriate for forestry uses only. The contrast shows not only two different techniques for the study of soils, but more importantly, opposing ideologies. Marc Dourojeanni (1984) pointed out how the various soil studies in the upper jungle and Pichis Palcazu valley were similarly prejudiced and contradictory.

While the ideological reality thus prevails in state planning over the ecological, the environmental disturbances remain. The distorted judgment about the real number of cultivable hectares led in upper Huallaga to mismanagement of soils and improper intensive use of land.

Summary and Policy Recommendations

In brief, the process of intensification of land use in upper Huallaga is complicated by a series of endogenous and exogenous factors, as well as by some intermediate factors that result from the articulation of the colonists' subsistence economy with the market. Among the endogenous factors are family size, ethnic characteristics (highlanders or former jungle cultivators [*ribereños*]), the system of planting on steep slopes and/or in widely spaced rows, and peasant economic rationality, especially in the initial stages of colonization.

Table 14.3   Soil Quality in Alto Huallaga According
             to Two Studies of Potential Use

	Ministry of Agriculture ONERN* (1964)	ONERN* Peñaherrera (1983)
	Percent	Percent
Intensive annual crops	35.64	5.7
Permanent crops	15.65	1.7
Pasture	37.72	12.4
Forest without agriculture value	10.99	21.9
Forest protection	-	58.3
	100.00	100.00

*ONERN is the National Office for Studies on Natural Resources
(Oficina Nacional de Evaluación de Recursas Naturales).

Sources: Agreda 1984; Peñaherrera 1984.

As peasant production tends to evolve further into market-oriented
agriculture, bringing modifications in economic behavior (toward greater
intensification, for example), family labor allocation remains a significant
factor of economic calculation.[12] In other words, although the portion of
production dedicated to meeting consumption requirements declines, family
size continues to be a crucial factor in economic decisions because settlers
rely on labor rather than capital inputs. This seems to hold even for families
who derive relatively large earnings from coca.

I prefer to conceptualize the colonists as peasants in transition, despite
the high income generated by illegal coca cultivation. This implies that
changes are necessary in extension and titling policy in such regions of
agricultural frontier as the upper Huallaga. The size of plots granted to
peasants must be determined according to family size and needs if the
pattern of degradation, like that in Tingo María, is to be avoided.

In addition, there are exogenous factors, such as the increase in regional
population density, the unequal exchange between the city and the country,
soil quality, the legal system of land tenure, and a colonization ideology,
that lead to irrational use of the land. Government policies for human
settlement must include environmental management plans not only for rural

zones but also for urban areas, since intensification is also a result of a regional population increase.

Another factor that should regulate plot size is soil quality (see Moran in this volume). In terrains where agriculture can be more intensive, plot size could be smaller; on poor land, given the necessity of fallowing, plots should be larger. With regard to the legal system, formal recognition of the existence of shifting agriculture is imperative. Just as in the cities, where the reality of street vendors or informal family economics is often ignored, so in the jungle, the itinerant character of an important sector of colonists goes unrecognized (Dourojeanni 1984). This leads to the denial of credit, since the colonist lacks a certificate of possession or a land title. Yet in regions where shifting agriculture is abating there is a tendency toward intensification, heedless of the long-run consequences.

With regard to the ideological aspect, my technical recommendation is for more ecological training of professional agronomists in an effort to counteract the influence of university training, which is excessively oriented toward expensive, "green revolution" technology and intensive modern agricultural systems.

To complete my model of intensification leading to degradation, I include plot size and land management as factors in between exogenous and endogenous variables. The reduced size of plots, as a factor of intensification in situations like Tingo María, is the result of a dynamic land market created by the high value of coca. In other circumstances it results from the strategies of colonists, varying according to whether they are highlanders or lowlanders. While highlanders tend to have smaller plots—22.93 ha—which, in comparison to the size of their plots in the highlands seem to them a veritable estate (Shoemaker 1976), colonists of jungle origins manage larger plots—31.57 ha—because of their experience with more extensive use. However, while 23 ha could mean an immensity of land for the highlander, it also implies the beginning of the soil degradation process.

Finally, land management in the case of coca cultivation in zones of excessive slope is as much a result of highland custom—where such terrain is cultivated without major problems—as it is of the national economic context, which requires the peasant to cultivate lands that are not adequate for such use. It is not only coca cultivation that is at fault, however. As we have demonstrated, other annual and permanent crops—coffee, tea, cacao—are planted on lands of protected forest, although such lands are vital for stabilizing the soil. Therefore, credit granted in the Peruvian high jungle for agricultural purposes should be regulated according to the type of land the peasant holds. Likewise, land titles should not be granted for plots where the greatest part of the terrain is protection forest or for forestry use. The resulting forestry activity can have a double purpose: as a complement to agricultural activity, and as environmental education for the colonist.

Notes

1. I am grateful to Carlos Aramburú and INANDEP (Instituto Andino de Estudios de Población/Andean Institute of Population Studies) for permission to analyze the survey applied in upper Huallaga in 1981.

2. Upper jungle is the Spanish *selva alta,* a generally recognized ecological zone of the Peruvian tropical forest that lies between the eastern Andean slopes and the Amazon basin at an altitude of 400–800 meters above sea level.

3. The two Belaunde administrations (1963–1968 and 1980–1985) were characterized by an outstanding emphasis on colonization programs.

4. Yellow corn is *maíz amarillo duro* (hard yellow corn). Starchy corn is *maíz amilaceo,* a large grain, usually white corn.

5. Cocaine paste is *pasta basica,* an unrefined brown paste molded into 1 kg bricks for shipment to processing centers to be purified into white powder.

6. These migratory movements are reflected in the intercensus population growth rates: between 1940 and 1961, the Alto Huallaga population increased at an annual rate of 7.8 percent; between 1961 and 1972, 7.6 percent; and between 1972 and 1981, 4.5 percent. The last rate shows the start of overcrowding. At present Tingo María region shows clear signs of overcrowding.

7. Upper Mayo = Alto Mayo; lower Mayo = Bajo Mayo.

8. In addition, the clandestine nature of its production leads to economic instability for this crop.

9. The experimental station at Tulumayo, located in the upper Huallaga basin, demonstrated that a mixed cropping system yields overall returns per hectare that are superior to a monocropping system.

10. An additional example is given by comparing the average number of cultivated hectares and their respective intensities of large, usually more recently occupied, farms—30 hectares and more—with the smaller plots—less than 10 hectares. In the former, average size is 7.51 hectares and intensity 0.34. In the latter, average size is 4.11 hectares and intensity 0.64 (Bedoya 1986).

11. Other symptoms of soil degradation in Tingo María are the diminishing returns of annual crops such as corn, rice, and beans. In addition, crop performance in this area is considerably poorer than in Tocache and Uchiza, where yields are 30 percent or 50 percent higher, even though soil quality is similar (Aramburú et al. 1985).

12. In 95 percent of the cases surveyed, the principal activity of children of working age was work in the family plot.

References

Agreda, Víctor
   1984   Frontera Agrícola y Demográfica en la Selva Alta. Lima, Perú: Instituto Nacional de Planificación.
Alvarez, Elena
   1983   Política Económica y Agricultura en el Perú. Lima, Perú: Instituto de Estudios Peruanos.
Aramburú, Carlos
   1980   Estudio Social de la Colonización Tingo María, Tocache y Campanilla. Lima, Perú: United States Agency for International Development (USAID).

1982   Expansión de la Frontera Agraria y Demográfica de la Selva Alta Peruana. *In* Colonización en la Amazonía. Lima, Perú: Centro de Investigación y Promoción Amazónica (CIPA).

Aramburú, Carlos, Javier Alvarado, and Eduardo Bedoya
1985   La Situación Actual del Crédito en el Alto Huallaga. Lima, Perú: USAID.

Bedoya, Eduardo
1981   La Destrucción del Equilibrio Ecológico en las Cooperativas del Alto Huallaga. Working Paper No. l, Lima, Perú: CIPA.

1982a   Colonizaciones en la Ceja de Selva através del Enganche: El Caso Saipai en Tingo María. *In* Colonización en la Amazonía. Lima, Perú: CIPA.

1982b   Historia Económica de una Gran Propiedad en la Ceja de Selva: El Caso Saipai 1950–1970. Lima, Perú: USAID (Syracuse University).

1983   Tendencias en el Proceso Colonizador de la Selva Alta: Estudio de Siete Regiones. Labor Migrations Project. Lima, Perú: FNUAP/OIT/DGE (Fondo de las Naciones Unidas para Actividades en Materia de Población/Organización Internacional de Trabajo/Dirección General de Empleo, Ministerio de Trabajo) (United Nations Fund for Population Activities/International Labor Organization/Ministry of Labor).

1985   La Experiencia de Colonización en la Selva Alta del Perú: Racionalidad Económica y Ocupación del Espacio. Working Papers. Lima, Perú: INADE/APODESA (Instituto Nacional de Desarrollo/Apoyo a la Política de Desarrollo en la Selva Alta).

1986   Sistemas Agricolas en la Selva Alta. INADE/APODESA. Lima, Perú, forthcoming.

Boserup, Ester
1965   The Conditions of Agricultural Growth: The Economics of Agrarian Change under Population Pressure. Chicago, IL: Aldine.

1984   Población y Cambio Tecnológico. Madrid, Spain: Grijalbo Editores.

Caballero, José María
1981   La Economía Agraria de la Sierra Peruana. Lima, Perú: Instituto de Estudios Peruanos.

Camino, Alejandro
1984   La Colonización como Problemática Social. Lima, Perú: CIPA-CNP.

CENCIRA (Centro Nacional de Capacitación e Investigación para la Reforma Agraria/ National Center for Agrarian Reform Research and Training)
1973   Diagnóstico Socio-Económico de la Colonización Tingo María–Tocache–Campanilla. Lima, Perú.

Chayanov, A.V.
1966   The Theory of Peasant Economy. Homewood, IL: Published for the American Economic Association by R. D. Irwin.

Dance, José
1979   Evaluación de los Recursos Forestales del Trópico Peruano. Lima, Perú: Universidad Nacional Agraria/CEPIC.

Dourojeanni, Marc
1981   Posibilidades para un Desarrollo Rural más Integral en el Huallaga Central— Bajo Mayo. Lima, Perú: Proyecto Especial Huallaga Central (Huallaga Central Special Project).

1984   Potencial y Uso de Recursos Naturales: Consideraciones Metodológicas. Lima, Perú: CIPA-CNP (Centro de Investigación y Promoción Amazónica— Consejo Nacional de Población).

Gonzales, Alberto
1983   Colonizaciones y Patrones de Asentamiento en el Alto Mayo. Labor Migrations Project. Lima, Perú: FNUAP/OIT/DGE.
Goodland, R. J. A.
1980   Environmental Ranking of Amazonian Development. *In* Land, People and Planning in Contemporary Amazonia. F. B. Barbira-Scazzocchio, ed. Cambridge, England: Cambridge University, Centre of Latin American Studies.
Hecht, Susanna
1984   Cattle Ranching in Amazonia: Political and Ecological Considerations. *In* Frontier Expansion in Amazonia. M. Schmink and C. H. Wood, eds. Gainesville, FL: University of Florida Press.
Lesevic, Bruno
1984   Dinámica Demográfica en la Selva Alta: 1940–1981. Lima, Perú: CIPA-CNP.
Malleux, Jorge
1975   Mapa Forestal del Perú. Lima, Perú: Universidad Nacional Agraria.
Martinez, Héctor
1977   El Saqueo y la Destrucción de los Ecosistemas Selváticos del Perú. *In* Amazonía Peruana, Vol. 1, No. 2. Lima, Perú: CAAAP (Centro Amazónico de Antropología y Aplicación Práctica).
Meggers, Betty J.
1971   Amazonia: Man and Culture in a Counterfeit Paradise. Chicago, IL: Aldine.
Moran, Emilio
1979   Strategies for Survival: Resource Use along the Transamazon Highway. Studies in Third World Societies 7:49–75.
Paredes, Peri
1983a   Migraciones y Tecnología y Empleo—Agrícola. Lima, Perú: FNUAP/OIT/DGE.
1983b   Población, Colonización y Sistemas—Productivos en el Alto Mayo. Lima, Perú: FNUAP/OIT/DGE.
Peñaherrera, Teddy
1984   Aprovechamiento de los Recursos Naturales en la Selva Alta. Lima, Perú: CIPA-CNP.
Recharte, Jorge
1982   Prosperidad y Pobreza en la Agricultura de la Ceja de Selva. El Valle de Chanchamayo. *In* Colonización en la Amazonía. Lima, Perú: CIPA.
Sanchez, Pedro, and S. W. Buol
1975   Soils of the Tropics and the World Food Crisis. Science 188:598–603.
Shoemaker, Robin
1976   Colonization and Urbanization in Peru: Empirical and Theoretical Perspective. *In* New Approaches to the Study of Migration. D. Uzzell and D. Guillet, eds. Rice University Studies, Vol. 62, No. 2.
Watters, R. F.
1971   La Agricultura Migratoria en America Latina. Cuadernos de Fomento Forestal No. 17. Rome: FAO.

15

The Development Potential
of the Guinea Savanna:
Social and Ecological Constraints
in the West African "Middle Belt"[1]

A. Endre Nyerges

Introduction: Development of
the Guinea Savanna by Immigration

This chapter analyzes the ecology of the Guinea savanna from the perspective of its potential for development. My argument is that the region's prevailing conditions of low population and low production are understandable in terms of its ecology, and that recent efforts to develop the region by means of disease control coupled with immigration may fail to generate the desired results because they derive from an overly optimistic view of the resource base. Even worse, such efforts may accelerate the loss of soil and vegetation resources, which are already declining slowly under traditional management. I conclude that current proposals for development in this zone are economically and ecologically unsound. Should development occur at all, it must seek primarily to solve the management problems of local populations, and it must be predicated on the principle of conservation of renewable natural resources.

As mapped in Figure 15.1, the Guinea savanna is the West African vegetation zone bounded on the north by the sudan and on the south by the coastal forest. It is dominated by tall grasses and a fire-resistant tree cover and possesses a highly seasonal semihumid climate.[2] Sometimes called the "middle belt" of the West African savanna, the zone is characterized by an exceptionally low population density, with usually fewer than 20 persons per km[2] in comparison with populations sometimes exceeding 300 persons per km[2] in the adjacent coastal forest and sudan (Ady 1965; Gleave and White 1969; Chi-Bonnardel 1973; Onyemelukwe and Filani 1983:24–28). This condition persists despite the fact that over the last several decades most of sub-Saharan Africa has experienced an annual population growth rate in excess of 2.5 percent.

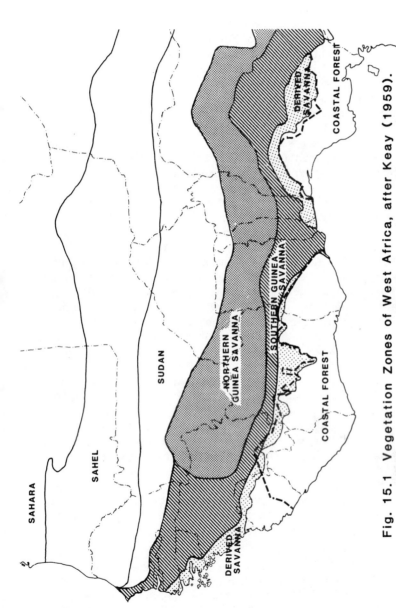

Fig. 15.1 Vegetation Zones of West Africa, after Keay (1959).

The dashed line indicates the changed position of the boundary between the coastal forest and the zone of derived savanna as drawn recently by White (1983).

Source: Adapted from *Vegetation Map of Africa South of the Tropic of Cancer*, by R. W. J. Keay (London: Oxford University Press, 1959) and from *The Vegetation of Africa*, by F. White (Paris: UNESCO, 1983), with permission from UNESCO and Oxford University Press.

Agricultural intensification has followed this growth throughout the continent, specifically in terms of shortening or even completely eliminating fallows. In a study based on earlier ethnographic reports, Morgan (1969:252–253) showed the distribution of shifting cultivation over most of West, Central, and East Africa. His map, however, can now be described as "a useful historical document, [but] not a guide to present policy" (FAO 1984:7). At present, the number of zones of population low enough to maintain long fallows has declined to some restricted and scattered locations, of which the Guinea savanna is the largest (ibid.:7–9).

The Guinea savanna's low population and apparently high resource availability have recently attracted spontaneous settlement from the drier, more densely populated zones of the north. This widely acknowledged but poorly documented migration involves FulBe herders pushed from the sudan and sahel by drought, desertification, and a shortage of grazing land, and newly attracted to the Guinea savanna by tsetse eradication. It also includes farmers emigrating from the heavily populated and intensively cultivated sudanian areas of the mouth of the Senegal River, the Mossi Plateau in Burkina Faso, the Mamprussi area of northern Ghana, and the Kano, Zaria, and Sokoto regions of Nigeria.

Spontaneous settlement, in turn, has increasingly attracted the attention of development planners, who see in the Guinea savanna a potential outlet for excess population to alleviate the pressures on the sudan and sahel. This interest in the resources of the wet savanna is readily understandable within the context of the seemingly intractable problems of overpopulation and resource decline in the drier zone, problems that more than half a billion dollars of aid have failed to resolve and that stand out among the numerous economic, ecological, and demographic difficulties of the entire African continent (World Bank 1981, 1984). A recent World Bank publication, *Desertification in the Sahelian and Sudanian Zones of West Africa*, was written "in response to growing concern, both inside and outside the Bank, that not enough was being done to tackle the desertification problem of West Africa" (World Bank 1985: preface). The paper argues that the rural population in the sahel and sudan has reached or exceeded carrying capacity, and it makes the following dismal assessment: "[t]here is not yet sufficient evidence . . . to suggest that any set of actions can do much to increase carrying capacity in the Sudano-Sahelian zone without a major technological break-through" (p. iv). The paper goes on, however, to offer this one ray of hope:

The one exception is the Sudano-Guinean zone, where actual population is far short of carrying capacity *and* proven intensive production techniques are available. People are already moving into this zone from the more densely populated parts of the Sudano-Sahelian heartland, where on-site solutions have been lacking and will be long in coming. A key element in anti-desertification strategy must therefore be further to encourage resettlement from the [Sudano-Sahelian] heartland into the Sudanian-Guinean zone, but by taking into account the difficulties encountered in this zone, notably human and animal diseases unknown in the heartland (World Bank 1985:iv).

This is an extremely interesting argument for what it says about the different potentials for agricultural expansion in the adjacent areas, but it is nonetheless open to criticism on two fronts. Similar criticisms can be made of a series of recent documents and projects that seek to solve the crisis in the sudan and sahel by resettling people to the Guinea savanna.

First, the argument suffers from an overly simplistic conception of carrying capacity: that it can be determined for a human population on the basis of resource availability (i.e., climate and soil classifications, and agricultural, pastoral, and forestry production figures), while assuming that the method of resource exploitation (i.e., technology and the system of production) remains static or inelastic in traditional communities. Such an argument, however, is problematic for human societies that possess multiple resource exploitation strategies and that can invent or borrow new techniques as the need arises. Sandford (1982), for example, has shown how economically irrational it would be to condemn people of the sahel to gear production to the carrying capacity of the worst years, particularly when they have adapted in so many ways to resource fluctuations to tide them through the worst times. While the Bank's analysis of problems of production in the sudan and sahel is sound overall, it should be recognized that an area's carrying capacity is not set for any particular human population. Rather, it is a dynamic factor that people can manipulate.

The real problem with the Bank's argument, however, is that the analysis should begin rather than end with the Guinea savanna, providing a more thorough analysis of ecology, economy, and society in the region. As it stands, the Bank study omits any close analysis of actual conditions in the zone. It simply notes that ". . . there are severe difficulties facing would-be settlers in the Sudano-Guinean zone, notably human and animal diseases as well as pests and predators unknown further north, lack of infrastructure in difficult terrain, and the relative fragility, after clearing, of soils under forest cover particularly in hilly areas" (p. 27). It argues that these problems can be dealt with and that "the unquestionable potential of the Sudano-Guinean zone to relieve population pressure further north, at least for the next two decades," can be realized by some as yet undetermined package of land-use regulations coupled with infrastructural development and public health programs (ibid.). These suggestions, however, do not adequately face the potential for resource decline and the consequent failure of economic development. Other projects and proposals that affect still larger parts of the Guinea savanna, particularly the various trypanosomiasis and oncho-cerciasis control programs, are even less adequately thought out. It remains to be specified how opening up the region to new settlement will be managed and what the ramifying social and environmental consequences will be. I find that the prevailing optimism, that "the grass is greener on the other side," needs to be tempered with a more realistic understanding of the hazards of this zone.

Climate, Resources, and People

The key social and ecological constraints to development in the Guinea savanna include:

1. a hazardous, highly seasonal climate in which rainfall is insufficiently predictable to provide the basis for increased agricultural production;
2. an environment at risk of degradation through the process of "savannization"—an apparently irreversible loss of the key agricultural resources of vegetation, soils, and water, as well as of wildlife, that follows on forest clearing and the spread of bush fires; and
3. the presence of an established, local population already dependent on the declining resources.

My examination of these problems, based on the literature and on field research, leads to the conclusion that development in the Guinea savanna is unlikely to succeed if it is imposed from outside by migrants. Instead, it should be generated on the basis of the existing ecology and the local populations that have persisted in the zone over long periods of time and that have established rights to its resources.

A preliminary step in understanding these systems is through analysis of case study materials on agriculture and ecology that I collected during 17 months of fieldwork conducted between 1981 and 1984 in the area of the proposed Outamba-Kilimi National Park (OKNP) in northwest Sierra Leone. The area's production systems are based on a highly efficient swidden technology, yet they also have significant shortcomings with respect to their adaptation to the environment. In particular, while the rate of resource decline is slower under traditional management than it would be under currently proposed development interventions, the established system is nonetheless causing degradation of the environment. Therefore, development in the Guinea savanna, whether based on new or existing settlements, will require exceptionally careful, region-wide planning and an emphasis on the conservation of resources, or else it will run the risk of ecological disaster. This situation raises questions about the relationship between development and conservation that I will return to at the end of the chapter.

Climate

The perceived potential for development in the Guinea savanna depends on the abundance and reliability of rainfall relative to the sahel and sudan. Yet the assertion that the rainfall is less risky in the Guinea savanna is an unproven and unwarranted assumption and probably reflects observer bias. One of the key aspects of climate in this region is extreme seasonality, which is reflected in the rapid onset and decline of the rains. Figure 15.2

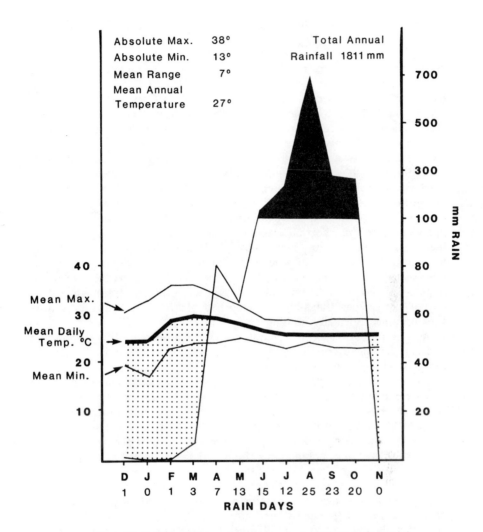

Fig. 15.2 Kilimi Temperature and Rainfall Record
Dec. 1981 to Nov. 1982.

Shaded Area: Rainfall in excess of 100 mm is shown at 1/10 scale.
Speckled Area: The period of relative drought.

charts this pattern over the course of one year for one location, the Kilimi portion of the OKNP. Virtually complete drought from November through March is followed by heavy, often extreme rainfall from April through October (see also the climate-diagram maps in Walter, Harnickell, and Meuller-Dombois 1975).

Unanticipated precipitation shortfalls, particularly in the sense of a delayed beginning or premature end to the rains, may severely affect production and constitute drought conditions. As Cox (1981:6) has argued, the worst food shortfalls are typically phenomena of highly seasonal climates. Studies by Oguntoyinbo and Richards (1978) and Wetherell, Holt, and Richards (1979) show that farmers in the semihumid zones of Nigeria and Sierra Leone are able to recall a long series of droughts in this century, and that their recollections accord with rainfall records. Furthermore, in 1973 very damaging droughts were recorded in both areas when early rainy-season precipitation deficits of as much as 30 to 50 percent of the mean had disastrous consequences for foodcrops. In the area of the OKNP in Sierra Leone, I recorded a 20 percent rainfall deficit in 1983 as compared to the previous year. This shortfall was particularly evident in an erratic end to the rains, in which a 60 percent rainfall deficit occurred (Figure 15.3). The week-long rainless periods prompted a steady stream of local farmers into the research camp, who would point to the weather station and worriedly inquire if indeed the rains had ended. Their concerns were realized at harvest time, when those farmers who had planted rice in strictly rainfed sites harvested virtually nothing.

As Sandford (1979:34) points out, drought is a relative phenomenon that depends on the demand for and expectation of water; it is "a rainfall-induced shortage of some economic good brought about by inadequate or badly timed rainfall." Rainfall deficits are especially hazardous in the sahel because rainfall is already low, and rainy seasons are short. In the wetter zones to the south, the more abundant rainfall and longer seasons would seem to allow for greater flexibility in a population's response to below-average precipitation. This perception, however, is in a sense false: in the sudan the dependent population is high and the requirement for rainfall is concomitantly high. People are adjusted to higher expectations and thus experience drought with a relatively smaller deficit. In the still sparsely populated Guinea savanna, droughts are already a serious problem for the production of such preferred but water-demanding crops as rice. Certainly, rainfall variability in the Guinea savanna is not as radical as in the sudan and sahel, but it is nonetheless significant and its significance will undoubtedly increase with increased demand as populations and production rise.

A second major problem associated with the extreme seasonality of the Guinea savanna is that it presents severe logistical difficulties for development and agriculture (see Chambers, Longhurst, and Pacey 1981). The heavy rains that give the savanna its natural productivity also greatly impede travel for half the year, as roadways become flooded in some places and overgrown with tall, almost impenetrable grasses in others. In the dry

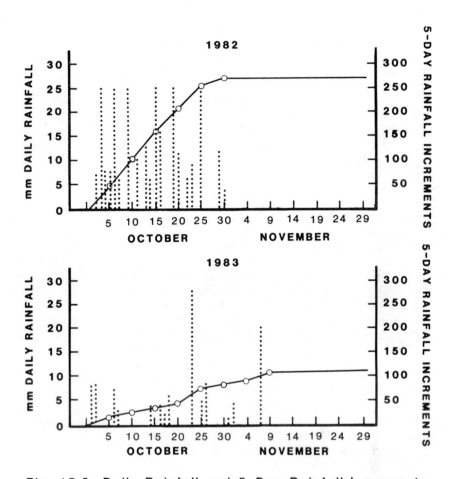

Fig. 15.3 Daily Rainfall and 5-Day Rainfall Increments
at the End of Rains. 1982 and 1983
for Kilimi, Outamba-Kilimi National Park, Northwest Sierra Leone.

The end-of-the-rains 1983 deficit from the 1982 figure is
162mm, or 60%. Data from two stations in Outamba and
Kilimi show a rainy season deficit of 20% in 1983
compared to 1982.

season, the rampant savanna fires commonly set to clear paths and roads may injure people, destroy villages, and damage crops. Solving these problems will require the establishment of all-weather roads and the suppression of bush fires. Without these improvements, controlling immigration, managing the exploitation of resources, and educating immigrants to new productive techniques will be virtually impossible. Creating such a physical infrastructure far inland in Guinea savanna countries, however, will be extremely difficult and costly. Moreover, the consequence of such development would be further environmental degradation as spontaneous settlers enter the zone along the new roads, bringing with them maladapted production techniques and displacing the local population. The region's seasonality, like its disease burden (see below), has long protected its resources from over-exploitation. Incautious removal of these barriers to development may result in a dramatic decline in resources.

Wildlife

Opening the Guinea savanna to settlement will necessitate resource destruction if for no other reason than to solve the problem of crop raiding by wildlife. Currently, the Guinea savanna supports a diverse fauna including many avian crop raiders such as the red-headed dioch (*Quelea erethrops*), a regional variant of the sudanic black-faced dioch (*Q. quelea*) that has been referred to as "the most destructive and possibly most numerous bird in the world" (Ward 1965:173). These birds are serious pests on rice, millet, and sorghum. While individually small (sparrow-sized), their flocking behavior, number, and granivorous habit make them extremely damaging. In northern Sierra Leone, as each rice variety produces grain, farmers are obliged to remain in the fields for weeks on end, chasing off the persistent birds with slings and shouts. This problem is especially severe for early-maturing varieties, often introduced as "improved," that are planted as a hunger stopgap before the main crop is harvested. These varieties may mature during a time when guard labor is scarce because farmers are engaged elsewhere in gathering and fishing activities. At the same time, savanna grass seeds may not yet be sufficiently developed to provide an alternate food source for birds. Predation at this early-harvest season may destroy entire patches of desperately needed grain.

Mammalian crop raiders include Guinea baboons (*Papio papio*), green monkeys (*Cercopithecus sabaeus*), warthogs (*Phacochoerus aethiopicus*), and hippopotamus (*Hippopotamus amphibius*) (see the distribution maps in Dorst and Dandelot 1969). A recent wildlife survey in northern Sierra Leone indicated that baboon densities alone exceeded human populations by a factor of two or three to one (Harding 1984). Local concentrations may increase this ratio still further, making defense of fields during the growing season a formidable task. Labor demands are especially high for such long-term crops as cassava which may be uprooted by warthogs and baboons and require guarding year around. Furthermore, the labor problem involved in guarding is particularly severe for part-time herders, who are caught between the need to tend flocks and the need to guard fields, often against the depredations of their own stock. Delgado (1979), in research in Burkina Faso, has shown that attempts to develop the zone through a combination of livestock production and agriculture are unlikely to succeed because of the excess demand that guarding places on labor.

Crop raiding by wildlife will undoubtedly increase as increasing production presents new opportunities. Unfortunately, such techniques as fencing and other deterrents are rarely effective against primate and bird pests. Recent efforts by primatologists (Forthman-Quick 1986) to solve the baboon crop-raiding problem by such inventive means as learned taste aversions have met with only limited success in field trials. These studies have demonstrated the possibility of protecting small, scientifically valuable populations of monkeys from the dire consequences of becoming known crop raiders. The method, however, remains impractical for large-scale application to the problem of crop protection as yet, as it requires trapping and injecting the crop-raiding animals individually. Killing crop-raiding animals is also only a temporary expedient as emptied habitats can be rapidly recolonized. In fact, the only effective solution to the crop-raiding problem (and not always a pragmatic one) is to eliminate the wildlife population by habitat destruction. The habitat that supports crop raiders, however, also supports species rarely considered to be pests. In the region of the OKNP in Sierra Leone these include such primates as chimpanzees (*Pan troglodytes*), black-and-white colobus (*Colobus polykomos*), red colobus (*C. badius*), sooty mangabeys (*Cercocebus torquatus*), mona monkeys (*Cercopithecus campbelli*), and spot-nosed monkeys (*C. petaurista*), along with ungulates such as forest buffalo (*Syncerus caffer nanus*), waterbuck (*Kobus ellipsiprymnus*), bushbuck (*Tragelaphus scriptus*), bush pig (*Potamochoerus porcus*) and duikers (*Cephalophus* spp.). The risk to these and other animals brings up the issue of conservation: is it acceptable to alter irreversibly one of the least-disturbed portions of West Africa when, in fact, a better, more economical use of the region might be to conserve its resources for wildlife habitat and for sustainable use as swidden fallow?

Disease

The inhabitants of the Guinea savanna bear a tremendous burden of parasitic disease: onchocerciasis, schistosomiasis, trypanosomiasis, dracunculiasis, and malaria. Do we invite people to migrate to this region and simply write off mortality and disease as a cost to the immigrant population? The standard response is to eliminate the diseases. But the disease burden at present acts as a check on human and livestock populations. As the eradication of tsetse (*Glossina morsitans* and *G. tachinoides*), black fly (*Simulium damnosum*), and other disease vectors proceeds through such means as habitat destruction, the extermination of alternate hosts, and the application of insecticides, we can predict an inevitable rise in the human and livestock populations with serious ecological consequences.

Trypanosomiasis, for example, is a disease of cattle that is transmitted by the bite of the tsetse fly. Although absent from the drier sudan and sahel, tsetse breed readily in the fringing or riparian forests of the Guinea savanna. Historically, tsetse and trypanosomiasis have had the effect of restricting the exploitation of the Guinea savanna for grazing to very limited populations of the small, trypano-tolerant n'dama breed of cattle, which is herded locally by farmers. FulBe flocks of nonresistant zebu, which are tended most of the year in the sudan and sahel, may also be brought to the Guinea savanna in the dry season when the pastures are temporarily tsetse-free (Ford 1971:377–378).

This situation has maintained a heavier pressure of grazing on the sudan and sahel than in the Guinea savanna. However, as overpopulation and resource degradation proceed in the north, and as—in oil-rich Nigeria at least—measures are applied to clear forest and control tsetse, the situation has been changing to a greater dependence on the savanna. Even without a substantial increase in the Nigerian cattle population following tsetse eradication (see B. K. Na'isa, quoted in Haskell 1977), the decline of the sudanian and sahelian pastures means that former relationships between zones no longer obtain. The possibility now arises of serious overgrazing in the once-protected Nigerian middle belt and elsewhere in the Guinea savanna. As Ormerod (1976) has argued convincingly, the benefits of easing grazing pressure in the higher latitudes by opening a new area of pasture to the south must be weighed against the potential environmental cost of a spread of the sahelian problem of desertification to the Guinea savanna.

Further problems related to tsetse eradication include the fact that try-panosomiasis can be transmitted by other, as yet unknown vectors, and may not be effectively eliminated by this means (Ormerod 1979). Also, since the cattle being moved into the savanna are mostly nonresistant zebu, they are at great risk when, as may happen, tsetse reinfest an area following the regrowth of cleared bush where the prophylactic program is not maintained. And finally, should the pasture be depleted by overgrazing, even trypano-tolerant breeds will be at risk because malnourished animals become susceptible to the disease.

Onchocerciasis provides a second example of the complex environmental problems that may be associated with efforts at disease control in the Guinea savanna. The vector for this disease, the black fly, breeds in rapidly flowing rivers and streams and may range approximately one kilometer from water. Persons born and raised in stream-side villages are subject to a progressively increasing burden of the disease throughout their lives, as they accumulate infected bites, with blindness as the ultimate result. As analyzed by Duke (1974), the effect of this has been to restrict the duration and degree of settlement along rivers in the Guinea savanna, because villages with a high level (5 to 10 percent) of adult blindness are not viable and are abandoned as a consequence.

A major effort, the multidonor-supported Onchocerciasis Control Program (OCP), has been underway for more than a decade to eradicate the parasite's vector. Although costly, it has proven highly successful in arresting transmission of the disease throughout the Guinea savanna regions of Benin, Burkina Faso, Ghana, Ivory Coast, Mali, Niger, and Togo, and it is now being expanded to additional countries (WHO 1984). The burden on the human population of blindness and associated premature deaths has been reduced. In addition, the program has had the further beneficial impacts of returning affected adults to the labor force, opening water resources to safer exploitation, and decreasing the pressure on neighboring, overpopulated lands. Yet the program strongly reflects its basis in humanitarian and public health concerns and characteristically lacks a set of comprehensive follow-up development plans to manage the new ecological situation (Walsh 1986).

Brown and Dash (1986:C-19), in an AID evaluation of the OCP, indicate that the rural population of the OCP lands is generally aware of the problem of resource decline, but they nonetheless find that ". . . opportunities for safeguarding the environment are not being taken full advantage of throughout the program area." For example, the major resettlement project in OCP lands, the Volta Valley Development Agency/Autorité des Aménagements des Vallées des Volta (AVV) in Burkina Faso, has been plagued with problems of environmental change that efforts at reforestation cannot contain. In the AVV, the large numbers of spontaneous immigrants, though directed by the authorities to farm intensively along rivers, choose to farm extensively instead, often selecting too-young fallows. Results of this failure to police and control settlers effectively are:

(1) deforestation and uncontrolled bush fires resulting in the extermination of animals; (2) overgrazing; and (3) the predominance of extensive cultivation, the lack of efficient cultivation methods, and the cultivation of marginal lands, practices that contribute to the "sahelization" of the area (Brown and Dash 1986:C-19).

This recent AVV experience of settlement leading to environmental decline accords with the historical evidence, cited below, that large-scale migration to this zone only too often leads to the degradation of vegetation and soils, necessitating further movements south into the wetter, still-forested zones.

Deforestation

While exploitation of the Guinea savanna for pasture has been restricted until recently, its woodlands and forests have long been exploited for swidden farming and for the production of charcoal required for iron smelting. Where swiddeners maintain forest and bush fallow rotations, the vegetation demonstrates a great capacity to regenerate, although its resilience in the face of farming should not be overestimated. Any heavier use of the vegetation, such as in more intensive farming or in the combination of charcoal production with swiddening, has proven devastating for the environment (Goucher 1981). The history of the southern Guinea savanna, in fact, is one of constant chipping away at the forest edge. In the Fouta Jallon highlands, for example,

Susu-speaking farmer-smiths cleared the forest by the 18th century. This not only destroyed their own resource base but also degraded the forest into pasture, thereby opening the way for FulBe cattle-herder incursion and, ultimately, domination (Brooks 1985). The FulBe, in turn, are often held responsible for the further deterioration of this environment through overgrazing and burning that has resulted in the denuding of extensive lateritic hardpans, or bowé (Church 1980:67). As evidence from Central America (Myers 1981; Nations and Komer 1983) and elsewhere strongly suggests, pasture produced from degraded tropical forest and exploited for livestock production is susceptible to further disruption and loss of fertility within a very few years.

The zones of "derived" savanna or forest-savanna mosaic frequently marked on vegetation maps reflect this process of savannization—in which disturbed forest sites are invaded by grasses that subsequently burn and prevent or retard the regrowth of forest and the redevelopment of soil. Characteristics of this zone, which imply a history of degradation, include a sharp forest-savanna boundary, the presence of forest outliers and emergents in savanna, and the mosaic pattern of primary forest, secondary forest, farmland, and tall grass savanna that constitutes the transition between the forest and savanna zones (Schnell 1976:697).

A comparison of the zones of derived or mosaic savanna marked on the two UNESCO vegetation maps of Africa drawn twenty-four years apart by Keay (1959) and White (1983) indicates a significant change for the westernmost extension of the forest in Sierra Leone, which has been entirely converted to savanna over the years since World War II (see Figure 15.1). All available reports suggest that large zones, particularly of deciduous forest on the rainforest edge, are now being converted to a mixture of grassland and species-poor secondary forest by complex ecological processes generated by human activity (Myers 1980). Although still poorly documented, degradation may also be assumed for the woodlands of the savanna (Church 1980:67). The simple fact is that the Guinea savanna cannot support even its present low population without causing an erosion of its southern, deciduous forest boundary, because disturbance of forest sites by farming often leads to the establishment of a fire climax.

Land Rights

Although sparsely populated, the Guinea savanna is not an open frontier awaiting the arrival of settlers. It is already occupied, and existing social groups have tenure rights. These groups historically have encouraged immigration, in response to a high demand for labor, but immigrants or "strangers" who come without special skills are commonly incorporated at the bottom of the social ladder. They are often denied the right of access to land, and they may be progressively impoverished as population grows and the inheritance of rights to prime land becomes increasingly important (see Haswell 1975).

On the other hand, the populations of the Guinea savanna are and have been numerically and politically weak. If large groups of settlers arrive, they would rob them of their resources, mimicking, in a sense, the past relationship of exploitation in which the powerful and populous Muslim emirates of the sudan raided the pagan, militarily weaker middle belt for slaves (Adeleye 1974). Oxby (1985) and Gooch (1979) review the slow progress of efforts to settle FulBe pastoralists in the savanna. Oxby finds the reasons in a "failure to recognize the range of previous uses of areas allocated to projects, and of the different categories of users" (p. 224). Thus,

> [p]rojects in the subhumid zone are usually implemented on the basis that the land allocated to them is empty, unused. This is invariably a misleading assumption. Land may be used on a seasonal basis, or as a resource for bad years; it may be used for shifting cultivation, for hunting game, for collection of fruits and other forest produce, or for grazing. The administration of the projects has thus been severely hampered as the project authorities have gradually become aware of the various patterns of land-use in the allocated areas, and have been unable to deter people claiming long-standing use rights from farming within the grazing areas or grazing their animals on a seasonal basis within the ranch boundaries, with no reference to the project authorities (Oxby 1985:224).

There are, then, two opposing points of view reflected in the process of settlement in "new" lands (for example, Lopez in this volume). One is that of the immigrant or development planner who sees in the Guinea savanna abundant land for farm and pasture. The other is that of the resident who requires the land for swidden fallows, sees resources as constrained, and fears displacement.

The Ecology of Established Populations

I have argued above that characterizing the Guinea savanna as a zone of high potential for development because of its rainfall is a dangerous oversimplification. Furthermore, efforts at the development of the zone through immigration would inevitably result in habitat destruction, resource decline, and loss of land by resident populations. The history of the Guinea savanna is replete with population movements, often from north to south, yet the contemplated large-scale resettlement to the area of sahelian and sudanian peoples would be a radical departure from previous processes that would culminate in overall loss of resources. While this could cause the failure of new settlements, it would most substantially affect established local populations. These groups have long-standing rights in the resources of this zone, which should be recognized. While their adaptations to this environment are problematic, given the history of resource decline cited above, the indigenous production systems nonetheless offer the only realistic basis on which ecologically sound management can ultimately be generated.

What follows is a brief case study of agriculture and ecology among Susu swidden farmers in the area of the OKNP in northwest Sierra Leone. It is based on a preliminary analysis of research results and is summarized from Nyerges (1985). In it I present some of the elements of an "insider's" ecology (see Spooner in this volume), in which resource goals of the local actors are emphasized and contrasted to the environmentalist's goal (see Janzen 1973) of long-term sustained agricultural production.

Susu Ecology in Sierra Leone

The feature of West African rural life that most affects the exploitation of resources is the gerontocratic and patriarchal social system that has been documented as an economic process by Meillassoux (1964) and analyzed in terms of the cultural principle of "rights-in-persons" by Kopytoff and Miers (1977) and Kopytoff (1986). This system of social and economic control exercised by the elder men over the women and young men produces a significant social demand for persons. It is expressed in what amounts to a competitive scramble for available labor, and it has caused the evolution of social forms by which some members of society exercise control over labor. Because of this social environment, some farmers, particularly young men attempting to farm on their own, are unable to mobilize sufficient labor and therefore cannot produce adequate yields. Other farmers, particularly the elder men with greater access to and control over labor, are led to intensify production, interact with the cash economy, and take greater farming risks in order to maintain their positions. The Susu of northwest Sierra Leone, as an example of a West African swidden system, face myriad problems of production that may frequently result in food shortage, including rainfall vagaries; soil poverty; weed, pest, and disease burdens; and ecosystem fragility. Perhaps the severest problem faced by the farmers, however, is the impact of the social system on the organization, availability, and exploitation of labor. This situation, in turn, has significant consequences for ecology.

Because of the social system, cultural adaptations that sacrifice yields to conserve resources cannot be expected. Rules and practices that function to conserve forest can evolve only if they increase yields, as by farming in old fallows, or save labor, as through minimal clearing and tillage. The environmental impact of Susu farming in the western Guinea savanna thus appears to be primarily the result of an imbalance in the distribution of labor that is brought about by the social system and demand for persons.

Briefly, an examination of the swidden work cycle among Susu reveals that, if possible, a farmer will choose for his swidden a healthy, vigorous forest fallow of some 30 years in age, generally on a hillside or streambed with groundwater discharge. Such sites are considered to be best for the production of rice and intercrops, and they are also most likely to regenerate vigorously after the standard one year of farming—particularly given the Susu practice of minimal clearing and tillage.

As I have suggested, however, the production system is characterized by forms of labor control. The elder men command the labor of women through the practice of polygyny, and they control the labor of boys and young men through their domination of the organization and activity of the young men's cooperative work group. Thus, while virtually every adult member of Susu society is a farmer in his or her own right, control of the labor necessary for farming is concentrated in the hands of the elder men.

Lacking control over household and work-group labor, young men often depart from the standard, ecologically adaptive, one-year rice farm in old fallow. Young men farming independently for the first time tend to select young-fallow sites on the basis of ease of clearing and nearness to the village. Such young-fallow "farms of convenience," of course, have low fertility and high weed and pest burdens relative to older sites, and are also unlikely to regenerate successfully when subsequently returned to fallow.

The elder men, despite their relatively greater access to labor, have their own labor and production problems that stem from their interaction with the cash economy. While young men gather honey for sale or barter, the elder men plant a cash crop of chili peppers. The men who intercrop pepper in their rice farms, however, encounter two problems. In the first place, peppers are a two-year crop, not yielding substantially until the second year. In order to have a good pepper yield the farm must be weeded in the second year, yet spare labor is not available for this work. The only way to get the pepper weeded is to institute a two-year rotation, in which women put their groundnut farms in last year's rice farms, weeding the pepper at the same time as clearing for the groundnuts. The groundnut farms, however, are small, and only a limited portion of rice farmland can be refarmed for groundnuts and weeded for pepper in the second year. The system, then, presents a significant labor bottleneck, and only wealthy elders with many wives and local female kin have a chance of successfully growing peppers for cash. Even the elders must compete among themselves for access to the scarce labor. In particular, in order to get the women to weed a farm and clear it for groundnuts, the farmer must choose a relatively dry site— groundnuts and peppers will rot if there is groundwater in the field. That means choosing rainfed as opposed to rain- and groundwater-fed rice sites. This need to farm rice rather inappropriately in the flat, pluvial sites puts the better-off elder men at great risk of crop failure. The risk may be worth it because of the potential cash payoff, but the potential for disaster in terms of subsistence yields is also substantial.

These farming variants—in age of fallow at time of clearing (young versus old bush) and in the pattern of rotations (one versus two years of farming)—have significant consequences for the environment. Fallows treated either of these ways are subject to grass invasion. Because the grasses subsequently burn annually, the sites may recover a forest canopy only very slowly, if at all; they are very likely to be converted to savanna.

In summary, the Susu economy at present is based on the exploitation of a forest vegetation that is degrading slowly under the pressures of production. Although lineage institutions organize and control farming, this control is not exercised to conserve the vegetation. This pattern—of a failure to control environmentally destructive variants in farming—is a consequence of the problem of labor organization and control in a competitive, gerontocratic social system that obliges farmers to act as short-term managers of resources.

Conclusions: Conservation and Development

This chapter has identified two systems of "bounded rationality" (the human incapacity to understand fully and to solve rationally the problems presented by the real world—Simon 1957:198–200) in relation to the exploitation of resources in the Guinea savanna. The first is that of the development planner, whose proposals to alleviate population pressures in the sudan and sahel by encouraging emigration to savanna regions would result in the rapid exhaustion of savanna resources, to the detriment of both settlers and native populations. The second is that of the local farmer, who is concerned with the management of resources but whose capacity to do anything other than maintain production, at whatever the long-term environmental cost, is also limited.

People in this environment are simply unable to conserve resources at present, except possibly by default through the use of minimal cultivation techniques, and I suggest that future prospects are potentially worse. Given the social system described above, people will compete for any new technology or addition of labor as economic change and development proceeds. This will result in a further imbalance in the distribution of the means of production, for example between elders and juniors, with predictable consequences for the environment as individuals struggle to achieve or maintain position. And as people come to depend more on the larger political economy than on local resources, they will have less reason, and still less freedom, to try to conserve them.

Development alternatives that avoid worsening the situation are limited, as they would require the reorganization of labor and consequent serious social disruption. I would, in fact, argue that we do not know enough at present to manage or develop successfully the resources of the Guinea savanna, although we seem to know a great deal about how to destroy them. Above all, we do not yet know how to institute the right kinds of social change. Consequently, the most significant problem for the Guinea savanna now is the need for time in which to study and plan for development.

Given the rapid economic change in Africa, however, it seems likely that, unless strong steps are taken, the resources of the Guinea savanna will be gone before the measured development of local systems will have had time to occur. On the one hand, conservationists concerned with the maintenance of plant and wildlife populations might reasonably argue that some areas of the savanna should be preserved in their present state as examples of natural habitat. The value of this, to science and local economies, however, would have to be weighed in each case against the costs of excluding people from land and resources and the resultant intensification of exploitation and degradation of the remaining space. On the other hand, an economic argument might be made that through prudent husbandry it should be possible to conserve the savanna's resources and ensure their continued availability until such time as region-wide planning, study, and experimentation will have revealed how to exploit them on a sustainable basis.

The first step in a development process based on conservation of resources for sustained use and future availability must be to abandon the goal of solving the sudano-sahelian crisis by plundering the Guinea savanna. Spontaneous resettlement will undoubtedly continue, but it should be controlled and restricted as a matter of state policy insofar as is possible. The second step should be to examine carefully how best to conserve and exploit for the long term the Guinea savanna's most significant resources. These include such highland areas as the Fouta Jallon watershed, as well as the swidden fallows: A body of data on fallows in the OKNP is currently being analyzed (Nyerges in preparation) and should contribute substantially to our understanding of the vegetation successions initiated by the practice of swidden farming. With this material in hand, it should be possible to devise plans to modify the existing technology and social organization of local populations, better to take advantage of their farming skills, labor, and knowledge. By conserving local resources, and developing ways in which they may be exploited on a sustained basis by local populations, it may ultimately be possible for enhanced production in the Guinea savanna to compensate in some degree for the resource constraints of the sudan and sahel.

Notes

1. Research in Sierra Leone discussed in this chapter was partially supported by the Charles Lindbergh Foundation and by the Department of Anthropology, University of Pennsylvania. I am grateful to Michael Horowitz, Peter Little, Brian Spooner, Rebecca Huss-Ashmore, Tom Painter, Vivian Carlip, Sylvia Horowitz, and Lee Blonder for their critical comments and suggestions on earlier versions of the text.

2. The Guinea savanna falls roughly between the 1,000 and 1,500 mm isohyets; its transitions with adjacent zones extend it further to the 800 and 2,000 mm isohyets. Church (1980:67–79), following Keay (1959), describes it as a wooded grassland, interspersed with lines of fringing forest along watercourses, which is subject to annual fires during the four-to-six-month dry season. For convenience, the zone may be divided into northern and southern belts, although it must be understood that these zones grade into one another and into the adjacent forest and sudan as well. The northern Guinea savanna supports medium to tall grass and is wooded with fire-resistant trees such as *Isoberlinia* and *Uapaca*. It represents the western extension of the *miombo* woodlands of East Africa. The southern Guinea savanna is wetter and supports tall grass and a cover of trees including *Daniellia* and *Lophira*. Here, the annual fires act to prevent the invasion of forest trees. It grades into the coastal forest in a transitional mosaic of suppressed forest or "derived" savanna.

References

Adeleye, R. A.
  1974   The Sokota Caliphate in the Nineteenth Century. *In* History of West Africa.
          Vol. II. J. F. Ajayi and Michael Crowder, eds. Pp. 57–92. London: Longman.
Ady, P. H.
  1965   Oxford Regional Economic Atlas—Africa. Oxford: Clarendon Press.
Brooks, George E.
  1985   Western Africa to c/1860 A.D.—A Provisional Historical Schema Based
          on Climatic Periods. Indiana University African Studies Program Working
          Papers Series, No. 1.
Brown, Antoinette B., and Larry Dash
  1986   Appendix C: Socioeconomic Impact. *In* Impact Review of the Onchocerciasis
          Control Program, Ouagadougou, August 1985. Jim Kelly, Clive J. Shiff,
          Howard C. Goodman, Larry Dash, Antoinette B. Brown, and Ali Khalif
          Galaydh. AID Project Impact Evaluation Report No. 63. Washington, DC:
          USAID.
Chambers, Robert, Richard Longhurst, and Arnold Pacey, eds.
  1981   Seasonal Dimensions to Rural Poverty. London: Frances Pinter.
Chi-Bonnardel, Regine
  1973   The Atlas of Africa. New York, NY: Free Press (Jeune Afrique).
Church, R. J. Harrison
  1980   West Africa—A Study of the Environment and Man's Use of It. 8th ed.
          London: Longman.
Cox, George W.
  1981   The Ecology of Famine: An Overview. *In* Famine: Its Causes, Effects, and
          Management. John R. K. Robson, ed. Pp. 5–18. New York, NY: Gordon
          and Breach.
Delgado, Christopher L.
  1979   Livestock Versus Foodgrain Production in Southeast Upper Volta: A Resource
          Allocation Analysis. Monograph 1. Livestock Production and Marketing
          in the Entente States of West Africa. K. H. Shapiro, ed. University of
          Michigan: Center for Research on Economic Development.
Dorst, Jean, and Pierre Dandelot
  1969   A Field Guide to the Larger Mammals of Africa. Boston, MA: Houghton
          Mifflin.
Duke, B. O. L.
  1974   The Ecology of Onchocerciasis in Relationship to the Ecology of Man. *In*
          Proceedings of the First International Congress of Ecology: Structure,
          Functioning, and Management of Ecosystems. Pp. 323–329. Wageningen:
          Pudoc.
FAO (Food and Agriculture Organization)
  1984   Institutional Aspects of Shifting Cultivation in Africa. (Written by Mary
          Tiffin.) Rome: FAO.
Ford, John
  1971   The Role of the Trypanosomiases in African Ecology. Oxford: Clarendon
          Press.
Forthman-Quick, Debra L.
  1986   Controlling Primate Pests: The Feasibility of Conditioned Taste Aversion.
          In Current Perspectives in Primate Dynamics. David M. Taub and Frederick
          A. King, eds. Pp. 252–273. New York, NY: Van Nostrand Reinold.

Gleave, M. B., and H. P. White
 1969 The West African Middle Belt—Environmental Fact or Geographer's Fiction? The Geographical Review 59(1):123–129.
Gooch, Toby
 1979 An Experiment with Group Ranches in Upper Volta. Overseas Development Institute (London). Pastoral Network Paper 9b.
Goucher, Candice L.
 1981 Iron Is Iron 'til It Is Rust: Trade and Ecology in the Decline of West African Iron-Smelting. Journal of African History 22(2):179–189.
Harding, R. S. O.
 1984 Primates of the Kilimi Area, Northwest Sierra Leone. Folia Primatologica 42:96–114.
Haskell, P. T.
 1977 Problems of Land Use and Tsetse Control. Transactions of the Royal Society of Tropical Medicine and Hygiene 71(1):12–14.
Haswell, Margaret
 1975 The Nature of Poverty—A Case-History of the First Quarter-Century after World War II. London and Basingstoke: Macmillan.
Janzen, D. H.
 1973 Tropical Agroecosystems. Science 182:1212–1219.
Keay, R. W. J.
 1959 Vegetation Map of Africa South of the Tropic of Cancer. London: Oxford University Press.
Kopytoff, Igor, ed.
 1986 The African Frontier: The Reproduction of Traditional African Societies. Bloomington, IN: Indiana University Press. In Press.
Kopytoff, Igor, and Suzanne Miers
 1977 Introduction. In Slavery in Africa. Suzanne Miers and Igor Kopytoff, eds. Pp. 3–81. Madison, WI: University of Wisconsin Press.
Meillassoux, Claude
 1964 Anthropologie Economique des Gouro de Côte d'Ivoire. Paris: Mouton.
Morgan, W. B.
 1969 Peasant Agriculture in Tropical Africa. In Environment and Land Use in Africa. M. F. Thomas and G. W. Whittington, eds. Pp. 241–272. London: Methuen.
Myers, N.
 1980 Conversion of Tropical Moist Forests. Washington, DC: National Academy of Sciences.
 1981 The Hamburger Connection: How Central America's Forests Become North America's Hamburgers. Ambio 10:3–8.
Nations, James D., and Daniel I. Komer
 1983 Rainforests and the Hamburger Society. Environment 25(3):12–20.
Nyerges, A. Endre
 1985 Swidden Agriculture and the Savannization of Forests in Sierra Leone. Paper presented at the 84th Annual Meeting of the American Anthropological Association. Washington, DC, December 4–8, 1985.
Oguntoyinbo, J. S., and P. Richards
 1978 Drought and the Nigerian Farmer. Journal of Arid Environments 1(2):165–194.
Onyemelukwe, J. O. C., and M. O. Filani
 1983 Economic Geography of West Africa. London: Longman.

Ormerod, W. E.
   1976   Ecological Effect of Control of African Trypanosomiasis. Science
            191(4229):815–821.
   1979   Environmental and Social Consequences of Tsetse Eradication. Overseas
            Development Institute (London). Pastoral Network Paper 8b.
Oxby, Clare
   1985   Settlement Schemes for Herders in the Subhumid Tropics of West Africa:
            Issues of Land Rights and Ethnicity. Overseas Development Institute
            (London). Pastoral Network Paper 19f. Originally published in Development
            Policy Review 2(2):217–233 (1984).
Sandford, S.
   1979   Towards a Definition of Drought. *In* Proceedings of the Symposium on
            Drought in Botswana. Madalon T. Hinchley, ed. Pp. 33–40. Hanover, NH:
            The Botswana Society and Clark University Press.
   1982   Pastoral Strategies and Desertification. *In* Desertification and Develop-
            ment—Dryland Ecology in Social Perspective. Brian Spooner and H. S.
            Mann, eds. Pp. 61–80. London: Academic.
Schnell, Raymond
   1976   Introduction à la Phytogéographie des Pays Tropicaux. Vol. 3. La Flore et
            la Végétation de l'Afrique Tropicale. 1re partie. Paris: Gauthier-Villars.
Simon, Herbert
   1957   Models of Man—Social and Rational. New York, NY: Wiley.
Walsh, John
   1986   River Blindness: A Gamble Pays Off. Science 232:922–925.
Walter, H. E., D. Harnickell, and D. Mueller-Dombois
   1975   Climate-Diagram Maps of the Individual Continents and the Ecological
            Climatic Regions of the Earth. Berlin: Springer.
Ward, P.
   1965   Feeding Ecology of the Black-faced Dioch *Quelea quelea* in Nigeria. Ibis
            107:173–214.
Wetherell, H. I., J. Holt, and P. Richards
   1979   Drought in the Sahel: A Broader Interpretation with Regard to West Africa
            and Ethiopia. *In* Proceedings of the Symposium on Drought in Botswana.
            Madalon T. Hinchley, ed. Pp. 131–141. Hanover, NH: The Botswana Society
            and Clark University Press.
White, F.
   1983   The Vegetation of Africa. Paris: UNESCO.
WHO (World Health Organization)
   1984   Onchocerciasis Control Programme in the Volta River Basin: Progress
            Report of the World Health Organization for 1984. JPC. 2 (OCP/PR/84).
            (Cited in Walsh 1986).
World Bank
   1981   Accelerated Development in Sub-Saharan Africa: An Agenda for Action.
            (Written by Elliot Berg). Washington, DC: World Bank.
   1984   Toward Sustained Development in Sub-Saharan Africa—A Joint Program
            For Action. (Written by Stanley Please). Washington, DC: World Bank.
   1985   Desertification in the Sahelian and Sudanian Zones of West Africa. (Written
            by David Steeds). Washington, DC: World Bank.

16

Rehabilitation Efforts and Household Production Strategies: The New Halfa Agricultural Scheme in Eastern Sudan

Muneera Salem-Murdock

Recurrent if unintended consequences of large-scale irrigation development in the Third World include the erosion, salinization, and waterlogging of soils. The New Halfa Agricultural Production Scheme in eastern Sudan is no exception. The problems in New Halfa are compounded by (1) an extensive canal network that is frequently choked with a vigorous growth of water hyacinths clogging turbines and water control structures; (2) association with a dam and a large reservoir whose capacity is rapidly being decreased through siltation; (3) location in a country that has for years suffered severe financial crises with resultant scarcities of machinery, fuel, other agricultural inputs, and trained personnel; and (4) a management system largely unresponsive to the needs and demands of its tenant farmers.

In this chapter I examine the transformation of a rural economy based largely on subsistence production to one increasingly based on commodity production, and explore relationships between rural socioeconomic differentiation and environmental degradation. In the first section I provide an analytical description of production systems on the New Halfa Agricultural Production Scheme at the household, community, and regional levels, including materials on land and wealth accumulation, increased social differentiation, and economic diversification. I suggest that although diversification is a strategy common to all tenants, the poor are obliged to diversify to provide an adequate subsistence, while the more affluent elect to diversify to increase profit.

In the second section, I speculate on the relationships between land and wealth accumulation and the progressive deterioration of the Scheme in terms of environment and productivity. I suggest, on the basis of preliminary evidence, that accumulation and increased social differentiation on the Scheme are positively correlated with increased degradation. My argument is based on the observation that the long-term concerns of affluent tenants are not primarily in agriculture. Although most of them are farmers, they aspire to educate their children for other careers. Furthermore, most of the land these people farm is rented, not owned, and they see it in their best interest to use the land for short-term gains without concern for longer sustainability.

In the third section I consider rehabilitation efforts, currently being undertaken on the Scheme with World Bank funding, that call for the production of fodder and livestock rather than the current cotton, groundnuts, and wheat rotation. Although the recommended shift to local crops and animal herding is justified in terms of conserving resources, as planned it will increase the already widening gap between the affluent few and the poor majority. If my argument concerning the correlation between social differentiation and land deterioration is correct, the rehabilitation effort is likely to fail because the group that will benefit the most has little or no long-term interest in conservation.

Production Systems on the New Halfa Scheme

The New Halfa Agricultural Production Scheme is a large-scale irrigated agricultural project along the western bank of the Atbara River, a Nile tributary, in the semiarid Butana plain in eastern Sudan. It is about 96 km long and from 20 to 35 km wide. The soil is mainly heavy clay and the annual rainfall ranges between 250 and 300 mm.

The Scheme covers an area of about half a million feddans (1 feddan = 0.42 hectares), of which 436,500 are designated for irrigation, distributed as follows: 330,000 feddans divided into 22,000 tenancies or farms of 15 feddans each; a sugar estate of 41,000 feddans; 24,000 feddans of freehold lands; 19,000 feddans as reserved area; 2,500 feddans for afforestation; and 20,000 feddans for research substations. The population of the Scheme is estimated at 300,000 persons, of whom 35,000 reside in New Halfa Town, the administrative and commercial center. Another 41,000 persons form a semipermanent agricultural labor force (and its dependents) for the government-run sugar estate, and also provide supplementary farm wage labor on the tenancies (Agrar 1980b). The remaining 224,000 persons are Scheme tenants and their families.

The New Halfa Scheme was launched in 1965 for the resettlement of 50,000 Sudanese Nubians whose Wadi Halfa lands and villages were inundated by the reservoir of the Aswan High Dam in Egypt. Although the Nubians were promised their choice of any of six sites for resettlement, Khashm el-Girba (now known as New Halfa) was ultimately forced upon them (Dafalla 1975). Like all the other areas considered for relocation, Khashm el-Girba was not without prior claimants. The area constituted part of the Butana plain, the traditional grazing lands of the Shukriya Arabs and their allies. Although inclusion of pastoralists on the Scheme was an afterthought, the attempt to incorporate them fit well with the then-current ideology that regarded the sedentarization of nomads as desirable and progressive (Abou-Zeid 1959; Amiran and Ben-Arieh 1963; Awad 1954; Musham 1959). Accordingly, although the Scheme was initially intended for Nubian resettlement, ultimately two-thirds of its tenants were of nomadic Arab and Hadandawa origin.

Nubian tenants of the Scheme were settled in 25 planned villages, with cement housing and an array of social services. Nubians who had owned agricultural land in Wadi Halfa were granted, in addition to their 15-feddan tenancies, freehold lands of twice the acreage they had lost. In contrast to government tenancies, where managerial decisions lie entirely in the hands of the New Halfa Corporation, on freehold lands farmers decide what, how, and when to grow, and the kind and number of animals to keep. The Shukriya and other pastoralists received nothing more than the privilege of becoming Scheme tenants—not even the improved housing and planned villages provided to Nubians. Furthermore, the project made no attempt to incorporate their significant traditional skills in animal husbandry and rainfed production of sorghum.

To justify the very high cost of large-scale irrigated agricultural Schemes per settler household and per unit of land, donor agencies and host governments alike pressure tenants to grow what are considered high-value crops. In New Halfa the chosen crops were cotton and groundnuts to increase export earnings, and wheat (plus sugarcane on the state-owned sugar estate) to decrease national import dependency. In making this decision it was not considered that two of the three crops introduced (cotton and groundnuts) were alien to the Nubians, or that all three crops were alien to the Arabs. Moreover, tenant householders, including Arabs, were allowed to keep only one animal unit (defined as one cow plus two sheep or goats) on their government tenancies. In contrast, the better-off Nubians, with freehold lands, were allowed to keep as many animals as they pleased. This encouraged Nubians with little background in livestock raising to incorporate animals in their daily agricultural activities, while animal husbandry was effectively denied to its traditional practitioners, the Shukriya and other pastoral groups.

Household Production Systems on the Scheme

Accumulation on the Scheme. Tenancy and wealth accumulation among affluent New Halfa tenant households and the resultant increased social differentiation are complex phenomena, embedded in historical processes. The initial inequalities that result in subsequent differentiation are particularly clear among the Shukriya.

Shukriya presence in eastern Sudan dates back to the fourteenth century, when Shakir, their eponymous ancestor, is reputed to have crossed the Red Sea from Saudi Arabia along with his brother Bashir, the ancestor of the Bawadira and Um Badriya. Shakir's seven sons founded the Shukriya clans in the Butana: 'Ifeisat, Fteisat, Mheidat, Rutamat, Nawayma, Nazzawin, and Zeidan. The Zeidan is the largest Shukriya clan and includes more affluent persons than the others in the project area.

Eastern Sudan, including the Butana plain, was formally incorporated into the Turko-Egyptian political system in 1820. The Turks sought the support of influential tribal elders, and Shaikh Ahmad bin 'Awad el-Karim Abu Sin, a Zeidan Shukriya, became one of their most trusted allies. For his support he was rewarded with the title "Bey" and was given large land grants east of the Blue Nile (Hillelson 1920:60). Shaikh Ahmad was later made governor of Khartoum, remaining in office for ten years (Holt 1976:9). Under the leadership of Shaikh 'Awad el-Karim, Ahmad's son, the Abu Sin family held "a general overlordship over all the nomads of the Blue Nile, the Gezira and the Atbara, and tithes were paid to the Abu Sin family on the crops of nearly every *wadi* in the ancient Island [sic] of Meroe" (MacMichael 1967:252). The position of the Shukriya faltered under the Mahdia (1881–1898), since Shaikh 'Awad el-Karim, the chief of the tribe, despite his imprisonment by the Khalifa (the Mahdi's follower and successor), remained loyal to the Turko-Egyptian regime (Salem-Murdock 1979).

The fortunes of the Shukriya reversed again with the 1899 Anglo-Egyptian conquest of the Sudan. British indirect rule, as practiced in the Sudan under the Native Administration, involved a hierarchy of chiefs—*nazirs, shaikh khats, umdas,* and local *shaikhs*—appointed to facilitate government administration. Although the tribes were already hierarchical, the political functions of the newly appointed chiefs, almost all of whom were established tribal shaikhs, differed markedly. The new chiefs acted as formal linkages between the central government and the local tribes: the umdas reported to the shaikh khats, the shaikh khats to the nazir, and the nazir to the British District Commissioner. Shaikh Muhammad 'Awad el-Karim Abu Sin was appointed nazir of the Butana tribes. The nazirate of the Butana remained with the Abu Sin lineage until 1972, when the new Sudanese government replaced the Native Administration with locally elected rural councils.

The allocation of New Halfa Scheme tenancies to pastoralists, from 1966/1967 through 1969/1970, was left entirely in the hands of the Native Administration. Since fewer tenancies were available for distribution than the number of potentially eligible households, some had to be excluded. The process by which households were recruited involved the application of locally understood values, which meant favoring relatives over strangers, political allies over political opponents or neutrals, and reinforcing one's support base (Salem-Murdock 1979:20). Accordingly, Scheme tenancies were largely absorbed by the elite and their supporters and followers. The principle of one man (supposedly the household head)/one tenancy had to be formally observed, but tenancies were frequently assigned to all male members of elite households—whether they were present or absent, adult or children. In a few cases involving very influential and affluent men, multiple tenancies were awarded to the same person. For example, among 39 interviewed household heads from an Arab village on the Scheme, tenancy distribution is shown in Table 16.1[1] (Salem-Murdock 1984:276).

Among the household heads with no certified tenancies, three (37 percent) identified farming as their main occupation, while two (25 percent) identified

TABLE 16.1   Tenancy Distribution in an Arab Village

Number of tenancies	Number of household heads	Percent
None	8	20
One	28	72
Two	2	5
Nine	1	3
Total	39	100

it as their second major occupation. Two others (25 percent) identified themselves as herders. The initial distribution of tenancies had already set the stage for increased tenancy accumulation among the Shukriya at the onset of the Scheme.

Because of compensation issues, land distribution among Nubians followed entirely different lines, which nevertheless allowed for accumulation. Tenancy and freehold land distribution for Nubians were based on a population and landholding survey. Households that possessed a dwelling in Wadi Halfa were granted a house and a 15-feddan tenancy in New Halfa, as were those with commercial lands and shops; people with agricultural land were granted twice their former amount in privately owned freehold land. Since many Nubian households never moved to the Scheme, or moved there but never cultivated because of other occupations, tenancy accumulation was already under way among the Nubians, too, at the inception of the Scheme. Most of the non-occupants either rented out or loaned their lands. In one Nubian village in 1980–1982, an affluent tenant had 15 tenancies under his control, of which only one was in his own name. The rest were in the names of his dead father, brother, and other relatives. This number does not include rented freehold and tenancy lands, or tenancies "borrowed" from the New Halfa Corporation on a seasonal basis.

Tenancy ownership is only one aspect of the unequal access to resources that the New Halfa Scheme manifests. Tenant households are further differentiated by their access to additional material resources such as other types of land (e.g., grazing and freehold land), livestock, and money, and to socioeconomic and political resources such as kinship, tribal and ethnic affiliation, political and social position within the household, education, and influence.

Money is one of the most important differentiators:

Persons with money are able to hire labor at certain critical points during the agricultural cycle, and the increased production from this labor usually more than compensates for its cost. Those without funds and without sufficient labor resources find themselves in a descending spiral of lowered production, yielding smaller cash returns and rendering it more difficult to obtain additional labor. Such persons, after selling off their livestock, often lose effective control over their tenancies and end up joining the ranks of the wage-laboring class (Salem-Murdock 1984:208).

Money is used to acquire other agricultural inputs such as improved seeds, fertilizer, and insecticides; to hire or purchase tractors and pay for their fuel; and to offer hospitality, a very important resource in acquiring goods and services:

> Hospitality is a virtue, much admired in the Sudan. But it is not its own reward. For hospitality, for those who can afford it, is an essential component of building influence. It brings *ma'rifa* and *wasta* ("connections"), and thereby administrative and political access. On the Scheme, critical inputs, including water, are often in short supply, and any advantage in their allocation may strongly benefit the recipient. One of the wealthy Halfawi [Nubian] settlers responded to my questions about the rumor that some tenants bribe water guards (*ghafeer*) to increase their share of irrigation water. He confirmed the rumor, but added that only those who are "stupid" would resort to such a strategy. "I would never do a thing like that," he said. "What can a ghafeer do? He does not control that much. When I have a problem with [the lack of] water, I go to the chief engineer himself. You see how I have been running around for the last few days because of water shortages. I knocked at the chief engineer's door at 3:00 a.m. and woke him up to have him give me a letter to the ghafeer to turn the water on for my *hawashat* [tenancies]." I said he must agree that the majority of the tenants are not in a position to go knocking at the chief engineer's door any time, let alone at 3:00 in the morning, that one must know a person fairly well before one can do that. "I agree," he said, "but no one has entered this town [meaning New Halfa] who has not eaten a meal at my house" (ibid.:211–212).

The increasing differentiation among tenants is further exacerbated by the very high cost of production and, for many tenants, increasingly low returns. This is clearest in the case of cotton. Table 16.2 shows the increase in the cost of cotton production, which is shared equally by the Scheme administration and the cultivating tenants, from 1975/1976 through 1980/1981. The cost of production per feddan has increased every year except 1980/1981 (insecticides were largely unavailable that year but all other costs continued to rise).

The situation resulted in two categories of tenants. A few tenant households, through their better access to resources—including multiple tenancies—could provide adequate capital, labor, and water inputs to their Scheme fields. Most of these households were able to do reasonably well, and some very well, because productivity on their lands was high.

The great majority of households, however, were without such access to resources and could not make it on the Scheme because their returns were inadequate. In order to survive development these households had no option but to diversify their economic activities, whether in rainfed sorghum

TABLE 16.2   Cost of Cotton Production from 1975-1976
through 1980-1981 (in Sudanese Pounds)

Season	Costs per 5-feddan tenancy	Cost of spray per tenancy	Total
1975/76	190	240	430
1976/77	221	286	507
1977/78	259	301	560
1978/79	259	305	565
1979/80	312	368	680
1980/81	422	72	494

Source: Salem-Murdock 1984:79.

cultivation, pastoral herding, or wage labor. The fact that Arab tenant households were not allowed to grow sorghum on the Scheme until 1981 intensified their off-Scheme interests.[2]

Two lines of seemingly contradictory arguments account for peasants' off-Scheme interests. The first is that poor peasants, involved in a capital- and labor-demanding economic enterprise, are caught in a cycle of un-profitability. To survive development, they must seek additional off-Scheme sources of income; this results in decreased productivity on the Scheme that in turn leads to greater dependence on off-Scheme activities (Hoyle 1977; Sørbo 1973, 1977a, 1977b, 1985).

The second argument is phrased in terms of the articulation of capitalist and noncapitalist modes of production, where the profitability of the capitalist enterprise itself rests on the viability of traditional social structures that supplement the poor wages received in return for labor (Barnett 1975, 1977; Foster-Carter 1978a, 1978b; Meillassoux 1981). Both arguments can be made validly in the New Halfa context. The poor are frequently caught in a vicious circle: low returns from labor force them to seek alternatives, which in turn negatively affect the productivity of the main economic activity. It is also true that poor societies in transition are not totally dependent on the capitalist enterprise, because of the existence of other social and economic structures that can supplement earnings. This relieves the capitalist sector of the need to provide for the full costs of physical reproduction of labor.

A third argument is that the New Halfa tenancies were seldom regarded by Shukriya as an exclusive source of income, but rather as an additional one. This is not to minimize the severe financial problems that most tenants regularly face, but to place the problem discussed here in a more realistic context.

Economic diversification is by no means a strategy only of the poor. Affluent farmers also engage in a wide range of economic activities. However, while the poor diversify to improve their survival chances, the affluent diversify to increase their wealth.

Accumulation, Increased Social Differentiation, and Scheme Deterioration

Have accumulation and increased social differentiation themselves accelerated the problems of soil erosion, salinization, and waterlogging on Scheme tenancies? Although it is difficult to arrive at firm conclusions regarding this issue, the indications of accumulation and increased differentiation, the presence of degradation, the negative relationship between degradation and land ownership, and the fast turnover of land among elite tenants, strongly support this line of argument.

I have shown that a key factor in the increased social differentiation of the New Halfa Scheme is the accumulation of land in the hands of the elite. Nubian and Arab elites share two important characteristics: (1) they have limited long-term interest in cultivation, as their children are rarely brought up to be farmers; (2) since the formal principle of one tenant household/one tenancy still applies, although it is frequently circumvented in practice, accumulation generally involves the short-term use of lands that are borrowed or rented from others. Short-term users frequently find it in their interest to mine the soil to depletion and then move on to other lands. This is evident in the fast turnover of land on the Scheme and in the frequent haggling between tenancy-holders and renters, with the former usually interested in longer-term arrangements to assure a steady income, while the latter are usually interested in short-term leases. One Nubian farmer, however, has been renting 25 freehold farms, which total 125 feddans, on a regular basis for several years. His reasons for this unusual interest in long-term arrangements are instructive:

> I rent them every year and never exhaust the soil. Although I never cultivate all of them in any one year, I nevertheless pay the rent to make sure that they do not go to somebody else. I never cultivate the same piece of land more than twice a year, mostly only once. People in the village know that they are better off with me than with a stranger who would intensively cultivate the land for the whole year and leave it utterly exhausted so that no one would want to rent it the following year (Salem-Murdock 1984:320–321).

Being conscious of soil quality is not the only reason that this Nubian farmer was willing to make long-term arrangements with the owners. The entire area referred to above was in freehold lands, hence much more valuable than government tenancies, since all managerial decisions are in the hands of cultivating farmers. In addition, all the farms were near his village, making for easy transportation. In contrast, taking the same farmer as an example, let us look at instances of his rental and borrowing of tenancies. Before the completion of the Scheme in 1968/1969, he was granted a request for 65 tenancies (340 feddans) in a section of the Scheme that was designated for Arab resettlement. In succeeding years, however, he cultivated from 20 to 25 tenancies, since no more were available. He worked on a sharecropping basis under which he supplied all inputs and received four-fifths of the produce (ibid.:320).

In 1981/1982 he farmed 75 rented feddans in tenancies for groundnuts, 45 feddans of them cultivated in partnership with the brother of a senior-level New Halfa Corporation official. He also farmed 180 feddans in wheat, of which 15 tenancies, or 75 feddans, were under his direct control, while 21, or 105 feddans, were granted to him by the Corporation for that season:

> The twenty-one tenancies granted to him by the Corporation had been left uncultivated by the villagers because they felt that the land was not well-suited for watering since they were too high, and considering water shortages, they were afraid the crop would die of thirst. [He] . . . went to the Corporation where he has many friends who come and see him several nights a week, and for whom he provides food and drinks, and asked to be allowed to cultivate the fields saying that he was willing to take the risk (ibid.:326).

In 1980/1981, an affluent Arab tenant persuaded the Corporation to open eight new tenancies of five feddans each for wheat cultivation for the benefit of the village school, since soil depletion and weeds rendered the old lands no longer profitable. Among nine other tenancies under his direct control, this man put four into sorghum cultivation. He had intended to grow wheat in the remaining five but changed his mind since he considered the land unsuitable because of poor soils and a high weed burden. The Corporation, with whom he had excellent relations—facilitated by his former position as an *umda* under the Native Administration—found it justifiable that this farmer be compensated. He was, therefore, granted two newly opened tenancies that he considered in excellent condition.

This pattern of increased accumulation and fast turnover of land among the elite is complemented by evidence of widespread environmental degradation, exemplified by soil erosion, salinization, waterlogging, and pest and weed invasion. The serious difficulties facing the Scheme were recognized by the Sudanese government as early as January 1976, when the Minister of State for Agricultural Production approached the World Bank for technical and financial assistance to rehabilitate the Scheme (Salem-Murdock 1984:50). This resulted in a two-phase New Halfa Rehabilitation study initiated in February 1977 and supported by an International Development Association credit to the Sudanese Ministry of Plan. Phase I of the study, conducted between January and May 1978, covered such topics as soils, irrigation and drainage, crop and livestock production, forestry, health, sociology, marketing, agricultural engineering, pollution, domestic water supply, power, agricultural economics, organization and management, and market prospects and prices. Among the production constraints identified by the study team were reservoir siltation; poor water management and poor maintenance in minor and field canals; shortages of agricultural machinery, spare parts and fuel; serious

TABLE 16.3 Cotton Cultivation and Average Production

Season	Area in feddans(a)	Ave. big qantar(b) per feddan
1964/65	15365	3.50
1965/66	32965	2.50
1966/67	53375	3.60
1967/68	70755	4.90
1968/69	91605	4.68
1969/70	102475	4.80
1970/71	107385	4.52
1971/72	108025	4.11
1972/73	109000	2.62
1973/74	109151	3.88
1974/75	108960	4.02
1975/76	81290	1.77
1976/77	109105	3.70
1977/78	99120	4.10
1978/79	85560	2.02
1979/80	63290	0.96
1980/81	53535	2.00

(a) 1 feddan = 0.42 hectares.
(b) 1 big qantar = 315 pounds of seed cotton.

insect problems; public health problems; pollution of the drinking water supply; and pollution from sugar factory drainage (Agrar 1978:22–23). The study concluded that the original storage capacity of the Kashm el-Girba reservoir, 1.3 billion m³, had declined to 0.775 billion m³ by 1977, and predicted that the reservoir's capacity will decline further to 0.550 billion m³ by 1997.

Scheme deterioration is also reflected in the continuing decline in average production per feddan and in area under cultivation. Table 16.3 presents information on cultivated area and average yield for cotton from 1964/1965 through 1980/1981. The table indicates the tremendous increase in the area cultivated through 1969/1970, due to the incorporation of the remainder of nomadic tenants into the Scheme in its final phase. Declines in area under cultivation reflect either the Scheme administration's decision regarding the unsuitability of certain fields for cultivation, or machinery and fuel shortages (Salem-Murdock 1984:80). The high cost of production combined with recurrent declines in yields led to several confrontations between the tenants and the government.[3]

The Rehabilitation Effort

The New Halfa Scheme rehabilitation effort, sponsored mainly by the World Bank, is based on evidence of a continuous decline in irrigation water supplies, and is designed for conditions of reduced water supply. The restoration of full water supply would require the construction of a new dam on the Upper Atbara River, for which no financing is foreseen.

Under reduced water-supply conditions rehabilitation has two phases, one for the short term, another for the longer term. Recommendations for the short term are based on the 1980 finding that irrigation efficiency on the Scheme was at 37 percent of original. The rehabilitation effort is supposed to increase that efficiency to 48 percent through some basic technical improvements, such as the use of heavier machinery and the introduction of different irrigation methods and better inputs. Starting about five years after the rehabilitation effort was launched, the consultant team predicted that reservoir siltation will produce a new continuous decline in water availability. Groundnut cultivation area will be reduced to zero and cotton to 7,600 feddans by the year 2010. Shortly thereafter sugar production will also begin to decline. Agrar (1980a and 1980b) recommended an immediate replacement of irrigated wheat by rainfed sorghum. The New Halfa Corporation, however, has not applied this recommendation strictly because of the strong Nubian commitment to wheat cultivation. Instead, the choice of grain was left up to the farmers, in the expectation that at least the Arab two-thirds of the tenants would be glad to shift.

Because of siltation problems, long-term measures have had to focus on a closer integration of animals on the Scheme. However commendable the idea, the three models for livestock raising proposed under the reduced water-supply situation are far removed from production realities in the area, because they assume stall feeding rather than grazing (Agrar 1980b).

- Model 1. Tenants breed cattle for sale (for fattening purposes) and for milk production (mainly for household consumption). The fodder base will be a sorghum/legume mixture, in addition to groundnut stover, as long as the declining water supply makes the production of groundnuts possible. In this model, animals are to be confined within enclosures all year with feed brought to them. The model foresees the participation of 4,106 tenants in year 1 and 7,400 at full development.
- Model 2. This model differs from the previous one in that tenants will be allowed to purchase and fatten animals in addition to breeding them. The feed will be the same except that tenants will buy concentrates for fattening animals from proposed feed plants at the sugar estate. When the groundnut stover supplies decline under reduced water supply conditions, tenants will have to substitute industrial ready-mix con-

centrates. The model foresees the participation of 1,270 tenants in year 1 and 7,391 at full development.

- Model 3. In this model tenants fatten sheep instead of cattle, purchasing the animals on the open market. A total of 2,500 tenants is planned for year 1 and 3,100 at full development.

All planned livestock models anticipate the keeping of animals near the tenant's house.

The great financial and human resource efforts that the World Bank and the government are putting into the rehabilitation of an existing agricultural Scheme in favor of a more visible and attractive—although perhaps less rewarding—alternative of initiating a new project is commendable. The attempts to shift Scheme focus from cotton, groundnuts, and wheat to local crops and animals are socially and ecologically sound. As planned, however, the effort is likely to undermine the very structure that is being rehabilitated. By still perceiving the Scheme as a closed, export-oriented system in which individual household decisions are minimized, the World Bank and the Scheme administration are subverting the very conservationist principles they are formally advocating. What seem like efforts to accede to the desires of poor households for the incorporation of sorghum and animals are likely to widen the already increasing gap between the rich and the poor. Farmers never proposed raising grain for animal feed and never saw animals as primarily export products rather than as elements of domestic subsistence and local commercialization. The new program is insensitive to:

1. the ability of households to control the factors of production;
2. the microecology of individual holdings;
3. the goals, aspirations, and production objectives of individual household units; and
4. the fundamental social problems behind resource decline.

Were the state to permit integration of on-Scheme and off-Scheme activities by allowing each production unit to make its own decisions about the allocation of land, labor, and capital, it would more likely benefit a larger number of households and, accordingly, the Scheme itself.

Notes

1. The table represents official holdings that appear on the books under a certain tenant's name. It does not reflect actual control that tenants might have over tenancies registered under someone else's name. For example, one of the household heads reported as having two tenancies under his own name also had direct control over seven others in 1980/1981 and eight others in 1981/1982.

2. Poor tenants in New Halfa, especially those of pastoral origin, have for years sought permission to diversify production by incorporating sorghum in the crop rotation of the Scheme, and in fact grew sorghum illegally wherever they could. The irony of this is that, as the capacity of the reservoir in Khashm el-Girba was reduced

through siltation, rehabilitation experts recommended a production shift in the direction favored by Arab tenants: gradually replacing the water-demanding rotation of cotton, groudnuts, and wheat with sorghum, livestock, and fodder crops.

3. Adverse relations between tenants and the state are exemplified in the following letter, dated April 29, 1979, from the president of the New Halfa Farmers' Union to the Minister of Agriculture:

> With much respect, we submit to Your Excellency this memorandum of ours with great hopes that it will find attention from you. Your Excellency, the results of the present season 1978-1979 in the New Halfa Agricultural Production Scheme have been the worst this Scheme has seen since the beginning, and the reasons are many and we will brief Your Excellency about the circumstances of each crop separately:
>
> 1. The groundnut crop—the area cultivated has been reduced this season to 32,000 feddans and production dwindled to an average of nine qantar per feddan.
> 2. The cotton crop—the productive section of the area cultivated went down to 85,000 feddans, and production went down to less than two [big] qantar per feddan.
> 3. The wheat crop—the cultivated area went down from 120,000 feddans to 42,000 feddans, on which the productive area was 30,000 feddans, and production went down to less than one ton for a five feddan tenancy.
>
> Your Excellency, seasons are passing by the tenant; production has been continuously dwindling for years, with a continuous increase in the cost of production, leading to tenant's low spirits, and his disbelief in the utility of agricultural work, and its reliability in meeting the living expenses which are continuously increasing because of the financial crises that the world, of which we are a part, is suffering from. Add to this the clear shortages the Scheme is suffering from, especially in machines, lack of fuel, transportation bottlenecks, in addition to many other problems that are well known to Your Excellency . . .
>
> Your Excellency, because the reasons are many, as we mentioned above, the reasons that we have mentioned here are given as examples and not to cover all. Cultivation in this situation, if we may use the example, is like ploughing the sea. The tenants are convinced of the uselessness of agriculture because the results are known in advance. What drives this very important element, the tenant, to stay on the Scheme are the hopes for the future, despite the hard conditions that he presently suffers from. . . . (Salem-Murdock 1984:86–87, author's translation).

References

Abou-Zeid, A. M.
   1959   The Sedentarization of Nomads in the Western Desert of Egypt. International
           Science Journal 11(4):550–558.

Agrar und Hydrotechnik
  1978   New Halfa Rehabilitation Project. Phase I. Main Report. Project Preparation
          Unit, Ministry of Planning. Democratic Republic of the Sudan.
  1980a   New Halfa Rehabilitation Project. Phase II. Main Report. Project Preparation
          Unit, Ministry of Planning. Democratic Republic of the Sudan.
  1980b   New Halfa Rehabilitation Project. Phase II. Feasibility Study. Animal
          Husbandry. Project Preparation Unit, Ministry of Planning. Democratic
          Republic of the Sudan.
Amiran, D. H. K., and Y. Ben-Arieh
  1963   Sedentarization of Bedouins in Israel. Israel Exploration Journal 13(3):
          161–181.
Awad, Mohamed
  1954   The Assimilation of Nomads in Egypt. Geographical Review 44:240–252.
Barnett, Tony
  1975   The Gezira Scheme: Production of Cotton and the Reproduction of Un-
          derdevelopment. *In* Beyond the Sociology of Development: Economy and
          Society in Latin America and Africa. Ivar Oxall, Tony Barnett, and David
          Booth, eds. Pp. 183–207. London: Routledge and Kegan Paul.
  1977   The Gezira Scheme: An Illusion of Development. London: Frank Cass and
          Company Limited.
Dafalla, Hassan
  1975   The Nubian Exodus. Khartoum: Khartoum University Press.
Foster-Carter, A.
  1978a   The Modes of Production Controversy. New Left Review 107:47–77.
  1978b   Neo-Marxist Approaches to Development and Underdevelopment. *In* So-
          ciology and Development. Emanuel de Kadt and Gavin Williams, eds. Pp.
          67–105. London: Tavistock Publications.
Hillelson, S.
  1920   Historical Poems and Traditions of the Shukriya. Sudan Notes and Records
          3:33–75.
Holt, P. M.
  1976   A Modern History of the Sudan: From the Funj Sultanate to the Present
          Day Third edition, fourth rpt. London: Weidenfeld and Nicolson.
Hoyle, S.
  1977   The Khashm el-Girba Agricultural Scheme: An Example of an Attempt to
          Settle Nomads. *In* Landuse and Development. Phil O'Keefe and Ben Wisner,
          eds. Pp. 116–131. International African Institute.
MacMichael, H. A.
  1967   A History of the Arabs in the Sudan. 2 vols. Reprint. London: Frank Cass
          and Company.
Meillassoux, C.
  1981   Maidens, Meal and Money: Capitalism and the Domestic Community.
          Cambridge: Cambridge University Press.
Musham, H. V.
  1959   Sedentarization of the Bedouin in Israel. *In* Nomads in the Arid Zones.
          International Social Science Journal 11(4):539–549.
Salem-Murdock, M.
  1979   The Impact of Agricultural Development on a Pastoral Society: The Shukriya
          of Eastern Sudan. IDA Working Paper No. 17. Binghamton, NY: Institute
          for Development Anthropology.
  1984   Nubian Farmers and Arab Herders in Irrigated Agriculture in the Sudan:
          From Domestic to Commodity Production. Ph.D. dissertation. Department
          of Anthropology, State University of New York at Binghamton.

Sørbo, G.

1973   Scheme- and Off-Scheme Interests. Unpublished M.A. thesis. University of Bergen.

1977a   How to Survive Development: The Story of New Halfa. Monograph No. 6. Development Studies and Research Centre. University of Khartoum.

1977b   Nomads on the Scheme: A Study of Irrigation Agriculture and Pastoralism in Eastern Sudan. *In* Landuse and Development. O'Keefe and Wisner, eds. Pp. 132–150. London: International African Institute.

1985   Tenants and Nomads in Eastern Sudan: A Study in Economic Adaptations in the New Halfa Scheme. Uppsala: Scandinavian Institute of African Studies.

17

The Local Impact of Centralized Irrigation Control in Pakistan: A Sociocentric Perspective[1]

Douglas J. Merrey

The body of accumulating knowledge on civilizational growth in the past (and in the present?) testifies to the instability rather than the stability of large-scale socionatural systems and the increasing uncertainty, rather than control, resulting from technoeconomic growth.

Bennett 1976:147

Introduction

Investment in irrigation to increase agricultural production has been an economic development strategy in many regions of the world for thousands of years. In ancient times, large-scale publicly constructed and managed irrigation systems were fundamental to the existence of centralized states in Mesopotamia, China, India, Sri Lanka, Egypt, Mexico, Peru, and elsewhere. In modern times, both developed nations and the poorer developing countries assisted by international donors are investing heavily in irrigation development. They hope that this will lead to higher agricultural production, development of industries and markets, generation of revenues for the state, and improved well-being for the presumed beneficiaries. Although such investments in new construction continue, there is increasing concern among both developing country governments and international donors that the investments in irrigation are not providing economic returns at the rates assumed during project planning. Far more attention is therefore being given to questions of how to improve the management and productivity of irrigation systems, and how to increase the rate of cost recovery from beneficiaries in response to the spiraling recurrent costs of irrigation systems.

One of the first efforts in modern times to use massive irrigation investments to promote economic development was the British construction of large-scale irrigation systems in India, particularly Punjab, in the 19th and 20th centuries. The British were pioneers in developing many of the technical criteria used in irrigation design today. They were relatively successful in constructing very large irrigation systems in a timely manner, without major cost overruns, and were able to finance the construction by raising funds in private markets and paying off the investors using funds generated from high irrigation fees charged to the water users. Huge tracts of land in what is presently the Province of Punjab in Pakistan were transformed from sparsely populated deserts and herding grounds into heavily settled intensively cultivated areas. For several decades in the early 20th century, Punjab was a major exporter of food and fiber.

Today, however, Pakistan is counted among the poorest countries in the world, with a per capita income of under US$400 in 1982 (World Bank 1985). Agricultural productivity is very low both by world standards and its own potential. From the late 1940s until the early 1980s, Pakistan has had to import about 25 percent of its annual wheat requirements, and as much as 90 percent of its cooking oils. The Government of Pakistan, with assistance from international donors, has been investing billions of dollars in upgrading, extending, and improving the irrigation system it inherited from the British colonial government, and such massive infusions of aid will continue in the foreseeable future.

All of these investments, at least until recently, have been predicated on the assumption that the problems to be solved are primarily technical, and thus purely technical solutions are required. There is widespread agreement that the return on these investments has been less than anticipated. Some recent development programs do address organizational issues, but they are focused at the local level, on promoting Water Users' Associations, and involve at best very limited tinkering with the local organization of the system. This limited approach is unfortunate, since it seems increasingly clear that the problems are fundamentally organizational and political, and not exclusively—or even primarily—technical. Thus, as Spooner argued recently, a "socio-centric" theoretical approach, taking account of the centrality of human activity, is essential if the problems are to be clearly identified and appropriate solutions formulated (Spooner 1984).

The present chapter builds on earlier work on social organizational problems in Pakistan's irrigation system. I previously analyzed the inappropriateness of village-level social organization and values for carrying out the tasks necessary to make efficient use of the irrigation system imposed by the British colonial government (Merrey 1982). A second work provides a detailed historical study of the impact of the British land settlement policies and the later imposition of the large-scale canal irrigation system on one village and its region in Pakistani Punjab (Merrey 1983). That study attempts to explain why the "beneficiaries" of one of the largest development projects in modern times are still about as poor today as they were at the turn of the century when the irrigation system was built. The answer proposed relates to government policies since the 19th century which both strengthened an unproductive local organization of production, and facilitated the extraction of much of the surplus produced by farmers under the new irrigation system.

In this chapter I analyze changes in local resource management strategies, and the environmental impact of centralized irrigation management since the mid-19th century. These changes are viewed primarily as responses to increasing interventions of the state, and the co-opting by higher-level bodies through centralization of what had been local functions. This in turn has led to an inability to respond to local level problems before they reach crisis proportions. I draw upon a systems-theory model of the evolution of the state originally developed by scholars interested in the demise of Mesopotamian civilization, to interpret the trends and identify key problems and issues.[2] This analysis provides the basis for a short critique of present development programs, and for identifying several key research questions.

Pakistan's Irrigation System[3]

The Indus Basin is a huge plain crossed by six major rivers, the Indus, Jhelum, Chenab, Sutlej, Ravi, and Beas. The climate is arid to semiarid, with rainfall that is both low and extremely unreliable, thus necessitating some form of irrigation as a basis for stable agriculture. Since the implementation of the Indus Waters Treaty of 1960, Pakistan has been using the water from the three western rivers (Indus, Jhelum, Chenab), while India diverts for its own use most of the flow of the other three rivers. The flood plains were, and still are, subject to monsoon flooding. The higher land between the rivers was covered by grassy and woody vegetation before the construction of the canals, but today is intensively cultivated.

The British began planning canal projects even before formal annexation of the Punjab in 1849. The first canal, the Upper Bari Doab, began irrigating in 1861. Thereafter, the British continued building increasingly sophisticated and large-scale canals, with stock-taking interludes between them, until the end of their rule. Since 1947, Pakistan with the aid of international donors has remodeled, expanded, and integrated the systems. Aside from several new canal projects, two major dams, Mangala and Tarbela, have been constructed, and huge link canals completed to carry water from the western to the eastern river beds and canals. Thus systems that were originally constructed as separate canal systems are today components of the largest single integrated irrigation system in the world. About 63,000 km of canals and distributaries carry water to some 90,000 watercourses, irrigation channels under farmers' control that lead to their lateral ditches and fields. About 14 million hectares are irrigated by the system.

To divert water from the rivers into the canals, the system uses barrages designed for continuous operation at or near full capacity. The amount of flow cannot be regulated on demand, except within very narrow parameters, though it may be interrupted during floods or repair work. Water flows continuously from canals into distributaries, then through ungated concrete modular outlets (*mogha*) into watercourses, and finally into farmers' ditches and fields. The mogha is designed to deliver a fixed quantity of water when the canal is flowing at full capacity, based on the area commanded. Each watercourse commands about 225 ha, cultivated by about 50 farmers, though there is a great range of variation in area irrigated and number of farmers. The Provincial Irrigation Department is directly responsible to the mogha for the operation and maintenance of the barrages, canals, and distributaries. Operation and maintenance of the watercourse is legally the joint responsibility of the farmers owning land in the commanded area.

Each farmer has a right to water proportional to the size of his landholding. Water is distributed on a weekly rotation basis, with each farmer allotted a period of time to take all of it. Although these rotations were originally established by the farmers themselves, most have been replaced by formal rotations devised by the Irrigation Department. Farmers get water for a fixed period of time every week regardless of crop water requirements. Water trading is common although illegal under formal rotations. The system was designed by the British deliberately to command the maximum area possible (about 350 acres per cusec, or 0.21 litres per second per ha) with a minimum of management necessary up to the mogha. Despite the major remodeling of the system at the macro level, canals are still operated according to the principles established originally by the British.

This rather straightforward description does not convey the magnitude and impressiveness of the engineering achievement that is the basis of Pakistan's irrigated agriculture system, sometimes referred to as the "Indus Food Machine." The early British engineers were proud of their work, and that pride continues in Pakistan's Provincial Irrigation Departments. A non-engineer viewing the huge tree-lined canals flowing through the green intensively cultivated countryside has little difficulty understanding that pride.

Nevertheless, from the earliest years severe problems have plagued the system. Waterlogging and salinity are not new—they date back to the mid-19th century, on the first large canal constructed by the British. Despite some research and various investigative committees, the British never seriously addressed this issue. They found it cheaper or more profitable to continue expanding the system rather than embark on major efforts to solve its problems (Johnson 1982).

In 1947 at independence, Pakistan discovered itself to be a major food-deficit country, and has had to import large quantities of wheat during the past 38 years.[4] Further, a series of studies and commissions during the 1950s and 1960s made clear that Pakistan's irrigation system was facing a major crisis.[5] During that period it was estimated that 20,000 to 40,000 ha were going out of production annually from waterlogging and salinity (White House 1964:63–64). Further, the productivity of the system has remained low compared to other countries with similar conditions, and compared to the demonstrable potential of the Indus Basin.

The combination of low productivity, major food deficits, severe waterlogging and salinity, and the general poverty of the country have led to massive external investments since the 1950s further to develop and improve the irrigation system. In addition to dams and link canals, major investments have been made in large public tubewells to provide vertical drainage in waterlogged and saline areas. Referred to as the Salinity Control and Reclamation Program (SCARP), these wells have had some impact in controlling the water table and increasing cropping intensity by making more irrigation water available to farmers; but the program has proven so costly that its continuation is now being seriously questioned.[6]

More recently, in addition to continuing SCARP programs and new canal construction such as the Chashma Right Bank, donors have been investing large amounts in watercourse improvement programs, rehabilitation of major canals (deferred maintenance), and a scheme referred to as "Command Water Management," basically an Integrated Rural Development activity focused on irrigated agriculture. All told, up to 1977, the U.S. Government alone had invested about $1 billion. Present donor pledges to Pakistani irrigation development total over $1.15 billion, not including recent decisions to go ahead with a huge left bank drain project and with a major new dam on the Indus (Peterson 1984:9–10).

To implement these large-scale water, hydropower, and reclamation projects, the Water and Power Development Authority (WAPDA) was established in 1958. Several of the foreign advisory reports since then have recommended even more centralization of planning and management at this high level, for "better coordination" (White House 1964:179–84; Lieftinck et al. 1969[2]:186–91). Based on such high-powered external recommendations, donor pressures, and the bureaucracy's own predilections, all of the policies and "solutions" to Pakistan's irrigation programs since independence have shared these characteristics: "an orientation toward purely technical solutions, designed and implemented from the top down, with the financial and advisory aid of foreign organizations; and an assumption that the 'experts' know best what the problems are and how to solve them" (Merrey 1982:91). None has addressed the most fundamental question of all: how should the Indus irrigation system be organized and managed?

Processes of Evolution:
A General Systems Model

The experience of other "hydraulic societies" suggests that Pakistan's concern about the problems of its irrigation system is not misplaced. Similar problems have had profound consequences for large-scale irrigation systems in the past. The dependence on a centrally managed canal irrigation system was as characteristic of ancient Mesopotamian civilization as it is of modern Pakistan. Despite technological innovations like power-driven tubewells and reinforced concrete dams, I suggest that the same mechanisms, processes, and "pathologies" characterize the organization and development of both modern and ancient large systems.

The conventional wisdom used to be that there was a direct relationship between successful irrigated agriculture and the presence of a strong stable central government in ancient civilizations (Wittfogel 1957; Adams 1974; Jacobsen 1958). According to this view, it was only when government controls weakened that the irrigation system and thus the whole agricultural regime collapsed.

Some years ago, this argument was reversed. For example, Gibson (1974:7) argues "that, on the contrary, in Mesopotamia the intervention of state government has tended to weaken and ultimately destroy the agricultural basis of the country." Using the data contained in an anthropological study of a contemporary group in southern Iraq (Fernea 1970), as well as archeological data, Gibson hypothesizes that the cyclical rise and fall of kingdoms in Mesopotamia from the fourth century B.C. to the present is related not to the breakdown of administration (this is a later stage in the cycle of decline) but, first, to the state-managed irrigation projects that increased waterlogging and salinity and undermined long-term agricultural productivity; and "more deleterious," the government's intervention at the local level which resulted in violating the fallowing essential to maintenance of the productivity of Mesopotamia. This intervention had the same origin in both Mesopotamia and Pakistan—rising demand for food by growing urban populations, and the need for revenues by the state.

Whitcombe's (1972) study of the disastrous impact of British irrigation schemes and agricultural policies in the Ganges River Valley (present-day Uttar Pradesh) shows that Mesopotamia is not an isolated case; the Ganges, Mesopotamian, and Pakistani systems share many features, which suggests they may be analyzed under one theoretical approach.

Flannery, building on Rappaport (1969; 1971) and others, has suggested a useful theoretical model based on systems theory for the evolution of the state. Flannery (1972:409) points out that human societies may be regarded as one class of living systems, and the state as a very complex system whose complexity can be measured in terms of two processes: the degree of *segregation,* "the amount of internal differentiation and specialization of subsystems"; and the degree of *centralization,* "the degree of linkage between the various subsystems and the highest order controls in society." An explanation of the rise, and decline, of a state would focus on the processes of increasing segregation and centralization, and their consequences. Flannery distinguishes among "processes," "mechanisms," and "socio-environmental stresses." He suggests the processes and mechanisms are universal characteristics of complex systems, while socio-environmental stresses that select for these processes vary over time and space.

A complete exposition of Flannery's model is not appropriate here. I focus on just one of Flannery's "processes" (centralization), one "mechanism" by which centralization occurs (linearization), and two "system pathologies" which, in conjunction with socio-environmental stresses, lead to progressively greater stress and instability of systems. These are "meddling" and "hyperintegration."

Systems respond to stress by either breaking down or changing (evolving). Under stress, new institutions or control levels may emerge (*segregation*) or higher-order controls may be extended and strengthened (*centralization*). A major mechanism by which these processes occur is *linearization* (ibid.:413), in which lower-order controls in the system are repeatedly or permanently bypassed by higher-order controls, usually after the former have failed to maintain relevant variables within the "proper" range.[7] Flannery offers the example of central authorities taking over local irrigation regulation from local institutions.

Linearization as a response to stress may lead to evolutionary change, but may also lead to new problems (ibid.:413–14). Linearization, for example, often destroys the intervening controls that buffer one subsystem from perturbations in another. Such internal changes may lead to what Flannery, citing Rappaport, calls "systemic pathologies," which subject the system to further stresses leading to progressively greater centralization—"the process is one with many positive loops." Two of the pathologies identified are *meddling*, which means "to subject directly to a higher order control the variables ordinarily regulated by lower order controls"; and *hypercoherence* (or *hyperintegration*), which refers to the over-integration of a system. This is a highly centralized and therefore potentially unstable condition that results from the breakdown of the autonomy of subsystems in a larger system, and their tight integration, such that change or perturbation in one rapidly and directly affects the others (ibid.:420). Thus, in this multi-variant model,

> we might see the state evolving through a long process of centralization and segregation; brought about by countless promotions and linearizations, in response not only to stressful socio-environmental conditions but also to stress brought on by internal pathologies (ibid.:414).[8]

The intention of Flannery's paper is to contribute to the development of a "generative model" for the origin and evolution of state systems, but its relevance is not limited to ancient civilization. Lees (1974a; 1974b), for example, has used Flannery's (1972) and Rappaport's (1969) models in discussing increasing involvement of the government of modern Mexico in local irrigation systems in the Valley of Oaxaca. Government intervention ("meddling") in what used to be independent local irrigation systems has led to increased agricultural productivity in the short run, but is also leading to insensitivity to local conditions and problems as the system responds to non-local perturbations, and increasing "hypercoherence" among the various subsystems. Lees (1974a; 1974b) suggests the system is potentially unstable, and increasing environmental degradation as a result of the state's intervention is leading to diminishing returns from investment in hydraulic development. The short-run response to this degradation (mainly decreasing availability of water) has been further centralization: higher order controls have been strengthened as increasingly sophisticated and expensive technology has been required to extract more water from the environment. However, this centralization, as in Mesopotamia, leads to further degradation; "centralization will not correct the disturbance to the system but may exacerbate it" (Lees 1974b:174).

Lees observes that so far only short-term processes are observable in the contemporary Oaxaca system. Since the Indus Basin system has been in operation for only 130 years, relatively little time has passed from an evolutionary perspective. Nevertheless, the system has grown rapidly and trends are emerging. The mechanisms, processes, and pathologies that constitute Flannery's model appear to characterize Pakistan's irrigation system. Therefore, analyzing the problems from the perspective of this model should provide important insights. My original research was focused on a particular village community in historical perspective. Although I have a lot of data on local management strategies and social organization, there has been little research on the larger bureaucratic organizations that control the irrigation system. Thus, the remainder of this chapter is somewhat programmatic, suggestive rather than definitive, leading to a series of questions that might be addressed through further research.

Changing Resource Management Strategies in Gondalpur[9]

The Pre-Canal Period

Gondalpur (a pseudonym) is a village about three miles from the Jhelum River, on the Chaj Doab, the interfluve between the Jhelum and Chenab Rivers. Politically, Gondalpur is in southern Gujrat District (Punjab), on the border with Sargodha District. Since 1904, its land has been irrigated by water from the Lower Jhelum Canal. Although there are many "colony" villages in the region—new settlements created as part of the canal development project in which people from East Punjab were settled—Gondalpur is an older village that predates the canal system. Historically, this region has been a backwater, a center of neither political nor cultural development in Punjab.

At the time of the first British survey in 1857, a total of 67 people were counted as inhabitants in Gondalpur. Subsistence was based primarily on cattle herding supplemented by some agriculture. There was one recently constructed Persian wheel well[10] irrigating about 7.3 ha, and about 19 ha of rainfed cultivation, along with at least a hundred head of cattle. The inhabitants were recent settlers on this land, though some claimed to trace their genealogy many generations back to a "founder" whose name is the real name of the village today. The cattle herders on the uplands had very close symbiotic relations with the people in the flood plains, where settled populations practiced intensive irrigated agriculture, and where a number of small towns were located.

On the active flood plain, which is flooded during the summer monsoon, wheat and other crops were cultivated on the residual moisture during the winter. In addition, on the less active portions of the flood plain, the water table was fairly high (9 to 15 meters), and there were a large number of Persian wheel wells used for irrigation. There were also inundation canals that carried summer flood waters to land away from the rivers, enabling an irrigated summer crop on the inactive flood plain. The wells were owned by individuals or small groups of people; the inundation canals were generally constructed and managed by local landlords with control over the requisite capital and manpower. However, the British survey in the middle of the 19th century followed a long period of political and economic uncertainty, so that most of the inundation canals were not operational. Gondalpur itself is located on the crest separating the upland from the flood plain. Its one Persian wheel well was marginal because the water table was almost too low (17 meters) for the lift technology of the period.

It is clear, then, that local resources were controlled at the local level during the pre-British period. In this area and indeed in most of Punjab, there were no large-scale public works such as state-controlled canal systems. Although empires based in Lahore sometimes were able to extract tribute from the Gondalpur area through local centers of power, this was probably not done consistently even during the height of the Mughal Empire.

With the extension of direct British rule, all of this changed. The British carried out detailed surveys of land, people, and resources, and demarcated land into individual revenue villages (*mauza*), and within each mauza, individual holdings, in order clearly to define and record responsibilities for payment of land revenue to the state. This process of defining and assigning rights is called "settlement." The settlement process in Gondalpur created a village community with a legal basis where none had existed before. It created a "brotherhood" of land proprietors sharing an official genealogical charter, and provided brotherhood members with individual rights in land. The differential possession of land rights, and the exclusion of a significant portion of the community from such rights, created a totally new basis for social relationships and social differentiation. It also initiated the process of "centralization," since a higher level and rather remote entity, from the point of view of Gondalpur's residents, took over the right to regulate land use. As part of this process, land not assigned to individuals became government land, and the government then restricted the right to graze cattle or cultivate thereon. This centralization of control over land use rights, in conjunction with other factors, had a profound impact on local resource management strategies.

The restrictions on use of land not one's own, and assignment of land rights to specific individuals or the state, along with other changes at the time (relative peace, increases in interregional trade, population growth) led to a shift on the uplands from seminomadic cattle keeping supplemented by casual agriculture, to a great expansion in rainfed agriculture, and attempts to expand irrigated agriculture as well. Before the end of the 19th century, two more Persian wheel wells had been constructed in Gondalpur, although one of them never worked properly because of the low water table. As part of this process, tenancy relationships became more formalized, and about 50 percent of the land was being cultivated by tenants around 1900.

What was more serious in the long run was that speculators began purchasing land in anticipation of the building of the canal. This occurred during a period in the 1890s when there was a series of local droughts and epidemics, forcing villagers to sell land to survive. As a result, on the eve of the introduction of canal irrigation, over half the land in Gondalpur was controlled by town-based landlords living outside of the village. Overall, the contrast between the upland and flood plain adaptive strategies had nearly disappeared, with the rapid population increase and the agricultural intensification on the uplands. Upland agriculture, however, being primarily rainfed, was far more unstable and uncertain than flood plain cultivation.

On the flood plains there was also a process of agricultural intensification, through construction of more Persian wheel wells and more inundation canals. The British made it public policy during this period to encourage private investment in such improvements, including inundation canals. One can say, then, that until about 1900 in this region, water resources continued to be locally managed and controlled, as a matter of public policy and fact. However, as a state whose finances were dependent on revenues from cultivated land, the British colonial government had centralized control over land, providing specific rights to certain persons over specific plots of land, and reserving a large portion of the land completely under government control.

The Post-Canal Period[11]

Construction of the Lower Jhelum Canal (LJC) was begun in 1897, and completed in 1917. Irrigation began along the upper reaches of the canal in 1901, and in 1904 Gondalpur began receiving irrigation water. Today the net command area of the LJC is about 628,000 ha. Maximum design discharge at the head (Rasul Barrage) is 151 cubic meters per second, or about 0.24 liters per second per hectare. Actual discharges vary widely by season and year, and often exceed the maximum when sufficient water is available (Bottrall 1978:4–8; the LJC is one of the anonymous cases in Bottrall 1981).

Developments during the decades before 1904 had prepared the residents of Gondalpur and its region for irrigation, because the response was immediate: within just a few years, the area cultivated in the village more than doubled, all of it irrigated. As emphasized in Merrey (1983), the immediate impact of the introduction of canal irrigation was not radical. Rather, it intensified trends already evident during the pre-canal period: increasing dependence on agriculture with a continuation of a mixed rather than a mono-cropping strategy, a shift from grazing to stall-feeding animals using fodder crops and residues from grain crops, an increasingly complex and hierarchical community social structure, and retention of a basically subsistence orientation toward farming, despite the (forced) necessity of growing more cash crops to pay land revenue, irrigation fees, various illicit charges levied by the bureaucracy, and to buy a few basic necessities.

Nevertheless, in the longer run, the impact of the introduction of canal irrigation was profound, radically changing the environment, local social structure, resource management strategies, and relationship of the villagers with institutions and forces outside the community. I have discussed these changes in detail (Merrey 1983). Here I concentrate on land and water control, and the impact of changes in these two areas on the environment, as responses primarily to increasing centralization through linearization, and "pathological" tendencies toward meddling and hypercoherence.

Despite post-independence legal changes ostensibly designed to protect tenants' rights, and two attempts at land reform, it is fair to say that there have been no drastic changes in land laws during the 20th century having a major impact on land use in Gondalpur, with two qualifications. One is that the threat of land reform laws has led large landlords to move tenants around more, lest they develop squatters' rights, and, in recent years, some tenants have been turned into daily wage laborers or annually engaged agricultural "servants" on land directly managed by the landlord (Merrey 1983: Chapter IX). The other partial exception is the impact of land consolidation laws. The government attempted to implement a land con-solidation scheme in Gondalpur in 1977, with very mixed results (Merrey 1983: Chapter XII).

As the LJC was extended, most of the government-owned land was allotted to settlers from East Punjab, effectively eliminating the remaining grazing areas. In Gondalpur itself, as mentioned above, over half the land was acquired by absentee landlords during the decade or so before irrigation began.[12] Much of the area acquired by absentees was prime land during the pre-canal period because it was relatively low, being located on the periphery of the inactive flood plain. This area was particularly valuable because well irrigation was possible, though just barely, since the water table was higher than in the rest of the village lands. More important, the area caught runoff from the rains, facilitating the successful cultivation of rainfed crops. Ironically, within about 25 years of the introduction of canal irrigation, most of this land became severely waterlogged and somewhat saline. Today, although only a portion of this area is officially classified as waterlogged, much of it is in fact not very productive. Much of it is still owned by absentee landlords and cultivated by very poor tenants who cannot make a living on it. I return to this below.

A major consequence of the implementation of the LJC was of course the complete loss of local control of water. On the other hand, the quantity and predictability of water compared to the pre-canal period increased manyfold, enabling a shift from rainfed agriculture with some well irrigation, to a largely irrigated regime. However, given the design of the system, with minimal latitude for manipulating water supplies except at the headwork (still within very limited parameters), the supply of water to the local users depends on decisions made at the headworks by the Executive Engineer. His decisions are based primarily on instructions from Lahore, the provincial capital, and available water supply in the Jhelum River, and not on conditions or demand for water in the command area. The system is supply driven, not demand driven. That is, whatever water is available is distributed according to fixed procedures whose objective is to spread water as equitably as possible over as large an area as possible, regardless of crop water requirements or farmers' demand at any given time.

Very detailed data are available on cropping patterns since the beginning of canal irrigation in Gondalpur (Merrey 1983: Chapter VII). While there have been adjustments in the relative importance of particular crops, and the addition of new crops such as rice and sugarcane in recent decades, the overall management strategy has not changed greatly. Gondalpur farmers, like most Punjab farmers, pursue a mixed cropping strategy, avoiding dependence on a single crop. During the summer (monsoon) season, the major crops in the early decades of canal irrigation were *bajra* (spiked millet), then a staple grain, but now primarily a fodder crop, cotton (a cash crop), and miscellaneous fodder crops. Today, paddy and sugar cane have become extremely important as cash crops. During the winter season, wheat is the major crop (for cash in the past, primarily subsistence now), along with mustard, spinach, clover, and alfalfa (all fodder crops).

Cultivators' first priority is fodder for their cattle, followed by wheat for their own subsistence, and finally a cash crop in order to buy clothes and other necessities, and pay taxes and other "fees." Farmers use rotations and manuring to maintain soil fertility, but in 1977, at least, they were using minimal amounts of commercial fertilizer.

From the beginning, the intensity of agriculture along the LJC and in Gondalpur has been greater than the "design" intensity. That is, whereas the system was designed on the assumption that only 75 percent of the total command area would be irrigated in a year, from the beginning the actual sown area was around 96 percent, and the harvested area 85 percent. When supplementary water from the SCARP tubewells became available in 1965, the average cropping intensity for Gondalpur went to 140 percent, but had dropped to 120 percent by 1975–76 because of increased waterlogging again (Merrey 1983:341).

Since the timing and quantity of water supplied is relatively fixed, and cannot be influenced by the cultivators, farmers attempt to match their cropping pattern to the water supply. Using rules of thumb, they plan the mix and acreage of their crops based on what they think they can irrigate during the season. They tend to stretch water at peak times, thus under-irrigating; but there are periods when the crops need less water than supplied, leading to over-irrigation in an attempt to store extra water in the root zone. Both over-irrigation and under-irrigation are considered to be among the major causes of the waterlogging and salinity faced by Pakistan today: to oversimplify, over-irrigation contributes to waterlogging by raising the water table; under-irrigation contributes to salinization by leading to movement of salts upward in the soils, through capillary action and evaporation, and by failure to leach salts downward, below the root zone (Merrey 1983:141–45; Lowdermilk, Freeman, and Early (1978[2]:56–57).

When the canal was opened in 1904, the Persian wheel wells were immediately abandoned. This was generally true throughout the region, and has been reported as a key impact in 19th-century Uttar Pradesh as well (Whitcombe 1972). In addition, the British and modern Pakistan governments as a matter of policy incorporated all the inundation canals into the larger system. These former inundation canals are now operated on a non-perennial basis: they receive water during the summer (monsoon) season when water in the system is plentiful.

The whole area was thus made completely dependent on one massive canal operated by engineers residing over 200 km from the tail of the system, and responding more to commands from above than to demands and conditions communicated from below. The implementation of the LJC is a clear case of centralization through linearization, to use Flannery's terms, in which local control centers were bypassed as a higher level of the state took over control of the water supply.

Environmental Stress:
Responses to Waterlogging and Salinity

Since independence, waterlogging and salinity have come to be recognized as the most dangerous "menace" facing the irrigation system of Pakistan, but the problem has a long history. Within a few years of its opening in the 19th century, the Western Jumna Canal in Uttar Pradesh was threatened by waterlogging and salinity. In the 20th century it became a major concern as canal irrigation expanded, because in some areas, including the Chaj Doab itself, it was serious enough to threaten the viability of the canals. A Waterlogging Inquiry Committee began examining the problem in the mid-1920s, and the British experimented with various technical solutions, including drainage, lining of canals, restriction of canal supplies and even canal closings, and the first attempt at vertical drainage through tubewells on the LJC itself.

There is considerable controversy over the actual extent and modern trends of waterlogging and salinity, but in the late 1970s some authorities claimed that as much as 50 percent of the canal-irrigated area of the country had a water table of less than three meters, and was thus waterlogged or "potentially" waterlogged; and as much as a third of the country's irrigated land was "strongly saline or sodic" (Malik 1978; Lowdermilk, Freeman, and Early 1978[2]:56–63).[13] The causes have to do with both environmental factors and the design and operation of the canal system.

A very flat terrain with low gradients, combined with very heavy rains during the summer monsoons, creates drainage problems that are difficult to solve. Design and operation factors include the lack of lining in main canals and in the newer link canals, even in porous soils or where the canals are elevated above the ground; inadequate drainage facilities at all levels; and farmers' irrigation practices (which are responses to the design and operation of the larger system [Merrey 1983:141–45 and references cited therein]).

By the 1920s waterlogging had become a serious problem on the LJC. In the area around Gondalpur the water table rose by as much as 18 meters above the pre-canal depth, to within less than a meter of the surface in some areas. Gondalpur and a neighboring village are mentioned specifically as having several hundred hectares of land thrown out of production from waterlogging. The Mona Drain, which began functioning in 1928, was expected to drain this area (Merrey 1983:174–75, 328, and references cited therein). The water table had stabilized before the installation of the SCARP II tubewells in the mid-1960s, and operation of these tubewells is said to have lowered the water table in the area one to two meters, where it has again allegedly stabilized. However, the quality of the water being pumped was declining by the late 1970s, and the whole SCARP program was facing severe cost and management constraints (Merry 1983; Johnson 1982).

The Gondalpur records reflect the impact of waterlogging, and the closure of canals as a "solution," beginning in the early 1920s. During the 1920s and 1930s the area defined in the records as "rainfed," i.e., not receiving irrigation water, rose slowly from about 3 percent of the total cultivated area in the first five years of irrigation, to over 50 percent in the early 1930s. It dropped slowly thereafter to around 5 percent of the total cultivated area in the mid-1970s. It seems most likely that the high percentage of rainfed land in the 1920s and 1930s was the result of canal closures and waterlogging. The official figures on waterlogged and saline land per se in Gondalpur are not very clear, but during this period they were approximately 120 ha, or about a third of the total cultivable land in Gondalpur. Waterlogging was sufficiently serious that at least five landowning families were given new land in southern Punjab under a government scheme to compensate people whose land was put out of production by waterlogging and salinity.

The records indicate that in conjunction with the worldwide depression in the 1930s, the high level of waterlogging and conversion of much of the land to rainfed by the government (by reducing and stopping canal water supplies) had a drastic impact on the productivity and incomes of Gondalpur farmers. The annual estimated amount of wheat produced in the village fell by 78 percent between the 1909–1917 average and the 1933–1936 average. Whereas selling 33 percent of the wheat crop was sufficient to pay the annual irrigation and land revenue "taxes" in 1909–1917, by the 1933–1936 period, these taxes were equivalent to 157 percent of the cash value of the wheat crop (Merrey 1983:439, Table 8.7).

The official response to the waterlogging crisis in the Gondalpur area in the 1920s and 1930s illustrates several points. First, one of the consequences of over-centralization, especially in the absence of any effective communication upward in the system, is an inability to identify and respond to local problems until they become crises. Thus, it was not until the situation was very bad—there was standing water on large tracts that had previously been cultivated—that the government recognized the problem. Part of the solution was to build a drain, a necessary but insufficient action by itself. Another part was to reduce or stop canal irrigation supplies to large areas, including areas that were not waterlogged, thus reducing both the productivity of a very large area and the incomes of many people.

This response is a case of "hyperintegration" or "hypercoherence," one of the pathologies discussed by Flannery and Rappaport. When a system is hyperintegrated, such that disturbances or crises in one part of the system have negative impacts on other parts, that system becomes more vulnerable and unstable. Here the system "survived" (in the short run), but at the expense of a large (but indeterminable with present data) number of cultivators who had become dependent on the LJC.[14]

The official figures give the impression that waterlogging and salinity in Gondalpur declined during the 1940s and 1950s. There is a wide gap, however, between the official figures for waterlogged and saline land and farmers' perceptions of the extent of these problems in the village today, and I am sure this is not a new phenomenon. In fact, this region was chosen as the second SCARP site, and large capacity tubewells operated by the government were installed in the area, including one on each of Gondalpur's three watercourses, in the mid-1960s. These tubewells have lowered the water table somewhat, and enabled both a substantial intensification of cultivation and the cultivation of crops requiring more water, such as paddy. However, the area uncultivated due to waterlogging in Gondalpur, according to official figures, has increased by a factor of three since the installation of the tubewells. Based on our household survey, and farmers' and our own observations, it is clear that waterlogging and salinity continue to have an important impact on the productivity of about 60 percent of the land in Gondalpur, far beyond what is recognized by the official figures, though further research would be needed to quantify the impact.[15]

The SCARP tubewells are intended not only to lower the water table, but also to provide supplementary irrigation. They are operated by government employees according to schedules made up in a central office. Electrical engineers base these schedules on expected electric supply (which is short), and not on local irrigation or drainage needs. Thus, SCARP water is often not available when most needed (for example in the early weeks of the paddy crop, before the monsoon starts), and then comes when less water is needed, contributing to the over-irrigation blamed on farmers.

This is "meddling," in Flannery's and Rappaport's terms, i.e., control by higher order entities of variables (water supplies) normally under lower level entities' control. The SCARP system is a second imposed over-centralized system, whose operation is apparently not coordinated with the operation of the canal system even where the Irrigation Department controls both.[16] By operating in a way that ignores local demands, the SCARP tubewells exacerbate the very problem they are designed to reduce, that is, waterlogging and salinity, inducing further instability in the larger system in the long run. Evidence for this was noted above: after initially allowing a rise in cropping intensity to 140 percent in Gondalpur, increased waterlogging had reduced this to 120 percent a few years later.

Conclusion

During the British period, a number of large-scale irrigation systems were constructed on the various interfluves of Punjab, each managed from a central point by officials responsive primarily to directives from above, but having little capacity to respond to demands from below. The British began linking different interfluves into larger systems, a process that reached its culmination in the 1960s and 1970s, with the completion of the major dams and link canals. These integrated a number of already large, but separate, systems into one huge system. In order to manage this new system and the construction tasks involved, WAPDA was created in 1958. Since then, WAPDA has expanded its role from major construction to include operation of major dams, operation of the national electric grid, construction of the SCARP tubewell schemes and management of some of them, and research into water management and land reclamation at the farm level.

During the 1970s, when the government became very concerned about alleged mismanagement of water by farmers at the watercourse level, a new organization was set up within the Agricultural Department, the "On-Farm Water Management Directorate" (OFWM), to take the lead in inducing farmers to rehabilitate watercourses and do precision land leveling. New legislation was adopted in each province, ostensibly enabling the establishment of "Water Users Associations," but in fact strengthening the power of the state over the watercourse, since farmers are now obliged to carry out maintenance or repay the costs if the government does it (OFWM officials also have special roles in these associations).

More recently, under a concept referred to as "Command Water Management" (CWM), there is an attempt underway to integrate—hyperintegrate if you will—institutions responsible for fertilizer supply, seed supply, extension, watercourse reconstruction, and the Irrigation Department itself. CWM is presented ostensibly as a decentralization project, to develop a degree of "self-management" at a more localized level (James Wolf, personal communication). There is provision for farmer "participation" in this program, but as under the OFWM program, such participation will be based on the above legislation, which defines a long list of "duties," and sanctions which the government can impose on associations not carrying these out. Government officials delegated to project areas by the Provincial Government will retain control of water and other resources and will continue to respond to directives from the provincial capital, not from local farmers. All of these activities are directed at trying to impose state wishes at the local level, but they do not address the fundamental organizational issues in Pakistan's irrigation management structure.

With the financial and technical support of the major international donors, Pakistan is proceeding along a path in its irrigation development policies that began with the British colonial government. That is, the processes of segregation (creation of additional institutions) and linearization (co-opting lower-order control institutions' functions by higher-order control institutions) are leading to higher degrees of state control over irrigation water, i.e. centralization. But the system's problems are not solved, and additional new problems are created, by the technical "solutions" implemented by the state, as well as by the performance of the new institutions. These lead to further centralization, and in Flannery's and Rappaport's terms to pathological tendencies such as meddling with lower-order affairs and hyperintegration. The state response is further centralization, so that the process is a positive feedback loop. The more centralized the system becomes, the less able it is to respond to local-level problems until they become crises threatening the viability of the system; and the responses to such local crises often have negative impact on other components of the system since the autonomy of local subsystems has been destroyed.

This chapter raises questions about the direction Pakistan is taking in developing its irrigation system. More is known about farmers' management strategies than about how the system works—how state institutions operate, relate to each other, and relate to farmers. I have applied an analytical framework to identify key questions and research issues. Much research is already under way in Pakistan, primarily, however, on very technical issues, and to a lesser extent on local organizational issues, with the support of USAID, World Bank, and others, but the following questions are not being systematically explored:

1. To what extent has the proliferation of agencies (segregation) and concentration of control at high levels of the state (centralization) led to inappropriate intervention at local levels (meddling), inability to respond to local problems until they reach crisis proportions, vulnerability of the larger system to crises that get out of hand and reverberate throughout the system (hyperintegration), and a tendency for institutions created for particular systemic purposes ("system-serving institutions") to become "self-serving institutions"?[17]

2. What management changes are feasible, given the design of the present physical system, that would allow for a greater capacity to respond to local-level demands and problems, including an enhanced capacity for local-level institutions to take back from higher-level institutions some degree of control over local affairs? To what extent, and at what level, could the system be converted from a supply-driven system to a demand-driven system?

3. What changes could be made in the present physical system that would allow greater flexibility in management, greater responsiveness to local demand, and greater autonomy of discrete subsystems, including an enhanced ability for local groups to take responsibility for local-level management? For example, the watercourses are far larger than most authorities think can be managed effectively and directly by farmer groups (Uphoff et al. 1985). Would replacing these watercourses with a larger number of small watercourses be feasible, and enable greater local capacity to organize and manage the irrigation system (Merrey 1983:762–64)?

4. What changes can be induced in the irrigation agencies themselves, perhaps through a bureaucratic reorientation process successful elsewhere (Korten and Uphoff 1981), that would assist them to decentralize and become more responsive to local needs and problems, while still maintaining an overall systemic perspective?

5. If some combination of specific action research activities were undertaken to explore the above questions, what difference could be made in the productivity and long term viability of the system, and the well-being of the people dependent on the system?

The chapter began with a quotation from John Bennett, which notes the instability and uncertainty, rather than stability and greater control, resulting from the growth of large-scale socionatural systems. A better understanding of Pakistan's irrigation system, from a systematic sociocentric perspective, would test the validity of Bennett's observation, and could lead to strategies for achieving the potential productivity of the Indus Food Machine.

Notes

1. The field research upon which this chapter is based was supported by the Social Science Research Council, New York, in 1976–1977. The first draft of this chapter was written while I was employed by the US Department of Agriculture Graduate School, under a contract with the Agency for International Development. I revised it into the present version after I joined the staff of the International Irrigation Management Institute (IIMI). I am grateful for the support of all these institutions, but none of them are to be held responsible for the contents of this chapter. I am also grateful for the useful critical comments made by Mark Svendsen, Hugh Plunkett, Robert Wade, James Wolf, and Thomas Wickham on an earlier draft. That earlier draft, presented at the symposium, "Lands at Risk in the Third World: Local Level Perspectives," had a different title: "Local Level Management Strategies and the State in the Indus Food Machine."

2. The idea for this chapter was inspired by my reading of two papers by Susan Lees (1974a; 1974b), in which she took a similar approach to analyzing local trends in water resource management in Oaxaca, Mexico; in one paper (1974b) she notes specifically the similarity of processes in the Indus Basin.

3. This section is based on the brief description of Pakistan's irrigation system contained in Merrey (1982). See also Merrey (1983) and Michel (1967) for more complete discussions of the history and present characteristics of the system. Many changes have occurred since Michel (1967) was published, so a new comprehensive analysis of the system would be a valuable addition to the literature.

4. Pakistan has produced enough wheat to satisfy internal demand in only two of the past 38 years; in the most recent year, the country has reportedly had to import $250 million of wheat—in a period when it cannot sell its surplus cotton (Remarks of a senior Government of Pakistan official in a USAID meeting, Washington, DC 1985).

5. Johnson (1982) provides a discussion of some of the strengths and weaknesses of these reports. The most important are the so-called "Revelle Report" (White House 1964) and the "World Bank" report (Lieftinck et al. 1969). More recent

development strategies are set out in the "Revised Action Plan for Irrigated Agriculture" (WAPDA 1979), which has been endorsed by all the major donors (Peterson 1984).

6. See Johnson (1982) for a thorough discussion of the major issues from the point of view of an economist. It should be noted that there has been a large expansion in private tubewells, to an estimated 200,000 (Peterson 1984).

7. Flannery (1972) does not consider a situation in which higher levels of the system change the expectations or standards for judging lower order controls, for example when the state presses for rapid increases in production.

8. In "promotion," an institution may rise to a higher level in a control hierarchy, or a new institution may arise out of a single role of a previously existing institution.

9. This section is based on data presented in Merrey (1983: Chapters IV–VI).

10. A Persian wheel well is a continuous chain of pots or buckets for raising water from a well using animal power.

11. This section is based largely on data presented in Merrey (1983: Chapters VII–IX).

12. By the late 1930s, a few villagers had re-acquired about half of this land, all from one landlord. Today about a quarter of Gondalpur's land is owned by non-residents.

13. The Punjab government estimates that seepage from the large link canals is causing the loss of 607 to 810 ha per day to waterlogging—this would amount to 221,000 to 296,000 ha per year, if correct (remarks by a senior Government of Pakistan official, in USAID, Washington, DC 1985).

14. Merrey (1983) argues that extraction of much of the surplus production from small farmers in these early decades of canal irrigation had a fundamental and lasting impact on the system's capacity to respond to development opportunities today; if that argument has any merit, British policies in dealing with waterlogging were a major contributing factor.

15. In addition, in our survey farmers reported 93 ha as seriously affected by waterlogging and salinity, a total of 27 percent of the cultivated land in the village. This does not include another third of the land at one end of the village, constituting another 33 percent of the total cultivated area, which is owned by outsiders and cultivated by very poor tenants, floods periodically, and has lost production in recent years as the water table has crept upward. That area did not get into our census.

16. It is also a case of "hyperintegration" of the electricity grid, in which local areas suffer as a result of constraints imposed elsewhere. Through its control of the dams (water supply) and the whole electricity production and distribution system, WAPDA presents an interesting case for further exploration of "centralization" issues.

17. Flannery (1972:423) suggests that the evolutionary trend of institutions generally is from system-serving to self-serving (general purpose), a trend that is visible in Pakistan.

References

Adams, Robert McC.
    1974   Historic Patterns of Mesopotamian Irrigation Agriculture. *In* Irrigation's Impact on Society. Theodore E. Downing and McGuire Gibson, eds. Anthropological Papers of the University of Arizona Number 26. Tucson, AZ: The University of Arizona Press. Pp. 1–6.
Bennett, John W.
    1976   The Ecological Transition: Cultural Anthropology and Human Adaptation. Oxford: Pergamon Press.

Bottrall, Anthony
    1978   Field Study in Pakistan: Lower Jhelum Canal and SCARP II Circles, Sargodha District, Punjab. Comparative Study of Management and Organization of Irrigation Projects. Report No. 7. World Bank Research Project No. 671/34. Unpublished paper.
    1981   Comparative Study of the Management and Organization of Irrigation Projects. World Bank Staff Working Paper No. 458. Washington, DC: The World Bank.

Fernea, Robert A.
    1970   Shaykh and Effendi: Changing Patterns of Authority among the El Shabana of Southern Iraq. Cambridge, MA: Harvard University Press.

Flannery, Kent V.
    1972   The Cultural Evolution of Civilizations. Annual Review of Ecology and Systematics 3:399–426.

Gibson, McGuire
    1974   Violation of Fallow and Engineered Disaster in Mesopotamian Civilization. In Irrigation's Impact on Society. Theodore E. Downing and McGuire Gibson, eds. Anthropological Papers of the University of Arizona Number 26. Tucson, AZ: The University of Arizona Press. Pp. 7–20.

Jacobsen, Thorkild
    1958   Salinity and Irrigation Agriculture in Antiquity. Diyala Basin Archeological Project, Report on Essential Results, June 1, 1957 to June 1, 1958 (mimeographed). Baghdad. Cited in Gibson (1974).

Johnson, Sam H., III
    1982   Large-Scale Irrigation and Drainage Schemes in Pakistan: A Study of Rigidities in Public Decision Making. Food Research Institute Studies 18(2):149–180.

Korten, David C. and Norman Uphoff
    1981   Bureaucratic Reorientation for Participatory Rural Development. NASPAA Working Paper No. 1. Washington, DC: National Association of Schools of Public Affairs and Administration.

Lees, Susan H.
    1974a   The State's Use of Irrigation in Changing Peasant Society. In Irrigation's Impact on Society. Theodore E. Downing and McGuire Gibson, eds. Anthropological Papers of The University of Arizona Number 26. Tucson, AZ: The University of Arizona Press. Pp. 123–128.
    1974b   Hydraulic Development as a Process of Response. Human Ecology 2: 159–175.

Lieftinck, P., A. R. Sadove, and T. C. Creyke
    1969   Water and Power Resources of West Pakistan—A Study in Sector Planning. Three volumes. Baltimore, MD: Johns Hopkins University Press.

Lowdermilk, Max K., David M. Freeman, and Alan C. Early
    1978   Farm Irrigation Constraints and Farmers' Responses: Comprehensive Field Survey in Pakistan. Six volumes. Water Management Technical Report No. 48. Fort Collins, CO: Colorado State University.

Malik, Bashir A.
    1978   Some aspects of Concept and Practice of Land Reclamation. The Pakistan Times (Lahore Edition), October 24, 1978.

Merrey, Douglas J.
    1982   Reorganizing Irrigation: Local Level Management in the Punjab (Pakistan). In Desertification and Development: Dryland Ecology in Social Perspective. H. Mann and B. Spooner, eds. London: Academic Press. Pp. 83–109.

1983   Irrigation, Poverty and Social Change in a Village of Pakistani Punjab: An Historical and Cultural Ecological Analysis. Ph.D. dissertation, Department of Anthropology, University of Pennsylvania. Ann Arbor, MI: University Microfilms.

Michel, Aloys Arthur
1967   The Indus Rivers: A Study of the Effects of Partition. New Haven, CT: Yale University Press.

Peterson, Dean F.
1984   Pakistan USAID Long-Range Strategy Options for Water Resources. Islamabad. Unpublished paper.

Rappaport, R.A.
1969   Sanctity and Adaptation. Prepared for Wenner-Gren Symposium, The Moral and Esthetic Structures of Human Adaptation. New York, NY: Wenner-Gren Foundation. *Cited in* Flannery (1972).
1971   The Sacred in Human Evolution. Annual Review of Ecology and Systematics 2:23–44.

Spooner, Brian
1984   Ecology in Development: A Rationale for Three-Dimensional Policy. Tokyo: The United Nations University.

Uphoff, Norman, Ruth Meinzen-Dick, and Nancy St. Julien
1985   Getting the Process Right: Farmer Organization and Participation in Irrigation Water Management. A State-of-the-Art Paper for the Water Management Synthesis II Project prepared at Cornell University. Draft.

WAPDA (Water and Power Development Authority)
1979   Revised Action Programme for Integrated Agriculture. Master Planning and Review Division, WAPDA.

Whitcombe, Elizabeth
1972   Agrarian Conditions in Northern India. Volume 1. The United Provinces under British Rule, 1860–1900. Berkeley, CA: University of California Press.

White House
1964   Report on Land and Water Development in the Indus Plain. The White House-Department of Interior Panel on Waterlogging and Salinity in West Pakistan. Washington, DC: Superintendent of Documents, U.S. Government Printing Service.

Wittfogel, Karl A.
1957   Oriental Despotism: A Comparative Study of Total Power. New Haven, CT: Yale University Press.

World Bank
1985   The World Bank Atlas 1985. Washington, DC: The World Bank.

18

Conservation and Society in Nepal: Traditional Forest Management and Innovative Development[1]

Donald A. Messerschmidt

Introduction—The Himalayan Resource Crisis

In nature there is, strictly, no such thing as an environmental crisis because nature always reacts to restore an equilibrium. Thus, the global ecosystem is simply what mankind in societies fashions it to be.

Riddell 1981:46

For more than a decade, alarm over the natural resource crisis in the Himalayas has been loudly sounded.[2] The landed resource base of Nepal and of its neighbor states is at great risk. Forest resource degradation is perhaps the most well documented for Nepal, but basic soil and water resources have also declined, with concomitant negative impacts on the quality of life among virtually all Himalayan and adjacent lowland populations.

A 1979 World Bank analysis outlines the potentially disastrous state of Nepalese forestry. Demands on forest and land resources have created serious problems of soil erosion, loss of potential agricultural land, drying up of mountain streams, and severe downstream flooding and sedimentation. The report estimates that, in 1964, 45.5 percent of Nepal's land area was covered by forest. By 1971 it was reduced to 34 percent; by the end of the decade to 29 percent. Overall, the loss in hill forest cover for the decade of the 1970s was 25 percent. Continuing pressure, the report predicts, will cause "the complete disappearance of all the accessible forest in the Hills in the next 15 years and in the Terai (lowlands) in 25 years unless reforestation programs are initiated on a massive scale" (World Bank 1979:i; see also NAS 1981).

Recognizing the severity of the problem, national and international agencies in Nepal have initiated a concerted effort to ameliorate the crisis through development aid. Much of that aid comes in the form of reforestation programs, usually linked with efforts to improve soil conservation and watershed management.[3] While much of the potential of these costly aid efforts has yet to be realized, some of the lessons learned so far are noteworthy.

This chapter treats both the local perspectives on environmental decline and on conservation development work, as well as on the practical and theoretical interrelationships and implications of those two things. It high-lights a successful strategy for involving local people, knowledge, and custom in resource planning and action. The data are drawn from the author's recent experience in Nepal (1981–1984) as the social science advisor to the Resource Conservation and Utilization Project (RCUP).[4]

Discussion of the Himalayan resource crisis begins with a brief examination of its multifaceted causes. There is, however, one caveat—that while the discussion of contending opinions about the crisis is necessarily brief, the issues are tremendously complex and contentious. Not all observers agree about the nature of the crisis, and some even question whether there is a crisis at all. Thompson and Warburton (1985a, 1985b) and Hatley and Thompson (1985), for example, question the whole basis on which the concept of a Himalayan "crisis" is identified and dealt with in the literature and in conservation programs. Though I tend to sympathize with much of their perspective, I am nonetheless convinced that environmental problems do exist—in the minds of scientists and developers and, not the least, in the perceptions of the Himalayan folk themselves.

People and Nature—The Causes
of Environmental Decline

Whether it takes place little by little or in one swift calamity, soil erosion is generally attributed to man's careless greed, his idleness or neglect. It would not, I think, be fair to blame the people of these valleys on the Himalayan fringe for the frequent landslips which occur here. In turning the steep slopes into fruitful fields they have neither been lazy nor neglectful. . . . One might say that on such hillsides the forest should never have been cleared, in which case the country must be left uninhabited. . . .

Tilman 1952:126–127

Not everyone agrees with Tilman's sympathetic view of human use of the mountain resources. The Indian Himalayanist, A. D. Moddie, for example, implies an element of human neglect behind the decline of the mountain environment: "In bygone ages the Himalaya seemed eternal," he writes, but "man's onslaught has rendered them among the most fragile eco-systems of the earth" (1981:342).

Some observers seek further explanation of the cause of what is clearly, to them, an ecological disaster in the making if not already in fact. The blame is variously attributed to several historical "causes" including forest policy, population pressure, nature, and human neglect.[5] Each major cause is examined in turn.

Forest Policy

Deepak Bajracharya's treatise on the causes of the demise of the Himalayan forest (1983a) is especially informative. He divides Nepalese forest history into three periods. The first covers the century preceding the 1950s, under the Rana government of Nepal. Rana forest policy was based on the assumption of unlimited abundance. Guided by advice from officers of the British India Forest Service from 1925 onwards, the Ranas "encouraged the indiscriminate clearing of forests for both timber and agriculture" (1983a:232). Nepal's forests were believed to be infinite, an assumption that encouraged exploitation and greed, and fostered long-range disastrous results.

The second period, from the mid-1950s to the mid-1970s, was heralded by the enactment of the Private Forests Nationalization Act of 1957. But even this new policy of centralized control resulted in further negative consequences. One forestry official has concluded:

the Nationalization Act . . . hastened the process of forest depletion, especially in the hills and the mountains. Where previously traditional forest management systems allowed many rural people to satisfy their basic forestry related needs without overly depleting the resource base, the new Act made such arrangements illegal. As long as enforcement was lacking the people tended to overexploit forest resources which they no longer felt were their own (Manandhar 1982:8).

Similarly, Chapagain (1984:173–174) reports the widespread belief that the Act of 1957 hastened deforestation by prompting individuals to convert as much private forest to agricultural land as possible before it was nationalized. Where there had previously been clear incentives to preserve private forest for local benefit, the only logical action from the standpoint of many individuals, when faced with the risk of losing forests to nationalization, was to overexploit them. This situation has been characterized by Rieger as the "tragedy of the hills" (1978/79:179), mirroring Garrett Hardin's theme of the "tragedy of the commons" (1968).

The contemporary period of Nepal's forest history began in the mid-1970s with legislation designed to reverse the deleterious effects of nationalization through enactment of the National Forest Law of 1976 and the Panchayat and Panchayat Protected Forest (PF/PPF) Rules of 1978 (and later amendments). Nepalese forestry is now in a period of relative enlightenment, looking to reengage a community spirit by encouraging local involvement and stressing more decentralization of authority and control. This move toward decentralization, with more local participation and community or collective management of the forests, was followed by the enactment of the more wide-ranging Decentralization Act of 1982.

When Bajracharya examined the initial effects of this change in the early 1980s, he concluded that it was much too soon to speak of successful implementation (1983a). A more recent examination, however, sees positive results from the collective management of hill forests in the work, for example, of HMG's Community Forestry Development Project (Arnold and Campbell 1986; Pelinck and Campbell 1984).[6]

Population Pressure

In considering the causes of resource degradation, many observers tend to identify population growth as the underlying culprit, coupled with the very human inclination to meet basic survival needs by overusing available resources (Bajracharya 1983a, 1983b; cf. Thompson and Warburton 1985a, 1985b). The World Bank's list of causal factors, for example, includes population increase, the scarcity of agricultural land, overstocking, and increasing demand for fuelwood, fodder, and building materials (World Bank 1979).[7]

Following the theme that population pressure is one (if not the ultimate) culprit, Cool notes that:

> Historical and demographic assessments would suggest that during the past century the impact of human intervention [in the Himalaya] has increased as a proportion of the whole, and that the rate of that increase continues to accelerate. . . . In an important sense, it is the growth of human population . . . which lies at the heart of our current dilemma (1984:29).

But are misguided policies, demographic pressures, human neglect, and even development interventions wholly sufficient causes? Do not natural factors also play an important role in the decline of forest and other natural resources? The answer is, of course, that they do; and further, that various natural *and* sociopolitical factors, in combination, provide the most reasonable explanation of overall environmental decline.

Natural Causes

Extreme altitude and steep slope, combined with tectonic and climatic forces (particularly the annual monsoon) make the Himalaya a "high energy environment" (H. B. Gurung 1982a:6). These forces are observable in glacial scouring, landslides, and soil erosion. Together, they create what Gurung calls a "conveyor belt for material transport." This geomorphic combination of elevation, slope, and angle combined with other natural and cultural disturbances to the fragile ecosystem causes the steady flow of materials downslope towards the Gangetic plain (H. B. Gurung 1982a:6–7; see also 1981a).

Gurung, in effect, asks where the people of the lowlands would be without the natural forces of the mountains that continue to create the fertile plains? Ironically, but for the combination of natural processes of degradation and "the transport of vast quantities of sand and silt by Himalayan rivers over millions of years, there would be no Gangetic plain and no developed [downstream] economies to contrast with the poverty of the hills" (1982a:7; see also Cool 1977a, 1977b; and Ives 1984).[8]

Human Neglect (and Potential)

In contrast to these on-going natural forces, the human role in the changing natural landscape of the Himalayas is relatively recent and considerably less formidable. From a sociological perspective, Campbell describes the neglect in these terms:

> A number of widespread practices—such as over-collection of fuel and fodder, over-grazing, shifting agriculture, and regeneration of fodder grasses through annual burning—are well known. These ecologically unsound activities are not new; but in recent years they have caused an unprecedented amount of environmental damage and now threaten to virtually destroy the Himalaya's natural resources (1979:11).

Another observer puts it into a colder economic perspective:

> While the degree of farmers' awareness of the environmental problems . . . varies according to the severity of the problems in each micro-area, ignorance of basic ecological processes is not a primary determinant of land-use behavior. Rather, the factors which do appear to underlie present land-use behavior relate to increasing resource scarcity, the propensity of farmers to maximize their individual household productivity through exploitation of public land resources, and the patterns of farmer decision-making which balance short-term productivity gains against a high degree of risk avoidance on private lands (USAID 1980:25–26).

Many factors help to explain why the resource base of the Himalayas is, indeed, at great risk. But since a major theme of this book is anthropological application, I propose in the remainder of this chapter to go beyond cause and effect, to discuss avenues for human-centered ameliorative development action. I now turn away from the negative role of human involvement in the ecological decline in the Himalayas, to explore the potential for environmental rejuvenation. That is, I look not so much to human interventions that have accelerated environmental decline, but prefer, instead, to examine the potential role of traditional knowledge and social custom available to assist in producing positive natural resource development action.

There is nothing new in considering the potential value of recognizing and incorporating people's participation and human and social resources into development (see Altieri 1983; Hatley and Thompson 1985; Uphoff et al. 1979; and USAID 1984). All too often, however, despite this "common sense" approach and the fact that the people are the single "common denominator"—indeed, the most important "resource" we have to work with—the essential humanity of development is often neglected in the rush to find one or another technological "fix."

Extrinsic Resources

Rural communities often have profound and detailed knowledge of the ecosystems and species with which they are in contact and effective ways of ensuring that they are used sustainably. Even when a community is growing in numbers and is clearly destroying a part of its environment it should not be assumed that all

of this knowledge has disappeared or become invalid or that the traditional ways
of regulating use have atrophied. . . .

IUCN 1980: Section 14, No.10

In speaking of conservation development, or "eco-development," I find
it useful to divide the universe of resources into four broad categories (cf.
Riddell 1981; SCSA 1982):

1. *Non-Renewable*—physical (geological) in nature, manifest as minerals
   and fossil fuels;
2. *Continuing*—physical, as gravity and solar energy;
3. *Renewable* (sometimes considered *Convertible*)—biological, as water,
   flora, and fauna; and
4. *Extrinsic*—sociocultural, in both cognitive and non-cognitive forms (of
   human behavior).

Of these four resources classes, I concentrate in this chapter on the last,
the class of "people resources," particularly indigenous technical knowledge
and social organization.

People and their cultural resources and practices are at once malleable,
educable, expressive, and sensitive as well as potentially aggressive and
destructive. For these reasons, people (and I speak here principally of people
on the land and in the forest) are among the most important factors to
take into account in discussing lands and forests at risk, and in planning
and implementing actions necessary to ameliorate the risk.

These extrinsic resources fall into two categories, "cognitive" and "non-
cognitive." The former include the resources of human behavior, speech,
and thought. The latter include the resources of our making. Both kinds
encompass the traditional knowledge of our species, in many varieties of
expression. The cognitive resources of the mind are incorporeal or intangible
"mentifacts" (mental facts, thoughts, ideas), while the non-cognitive resources
of matter are manifest as the tangible "artifacts" (physical things designed
or modified by humans).

Cultural knowledge includes systems of kinship, economy, control, common interest, religion, knowledge, and expression. Cultural experience encompasses a vast encyclopedic range of rules, customs, expectations, and
things that tend simultaneously to order and reflect the ways in which we
manage ourselves in societies. It also conditions how we manage, for better
or for worse, the natural resources on which we depend for life and
sustenance. And, just as biologists and geneticists are concerned with the
rapid loss of genetic resources world wide (Frankel 1974; IUCN 1980; NAS
1980), so too are social scientists concerned with the potential loss of sociocultural resources as a tragedy to be avoided at all cost.

Traditional Knowledge
for Forest Management in Nepal

Rationality and scientific knowledge on the one side and traditionality and ignorance on the other were set against each other as antitheses.

Shils 1981:5

The hill farmer, with his . . . culturally and biologically based knowledge and skills [is] absolutely crucial to the design of development work. We should stress that we are not saying that the villager is the repository of all wisdom, only that he is the repository of *some* wisdom. He is not an empty vessel; and to work on the assumption that he is, is to risk some nasty and wasteful surprises. . . . The local is the expert on his locality, and that local expertise is as important as (but very different from) global experience.

Hatley and Thompson 1985:368; original emphasis

In the global experience there are two sets of knowledge: "science" and "folk." Too often they are considered opposite and hence incompatible, but both are precious human resources. The social scientist in development should explore ways to retain and use folk knowledge in combination with established science and technology to produce resource development action systems that are sensitive to the needs of local people (Howes 1980).

Concern for conserving traditional sociocultural resources of the world should not be merely a concern over loss for their own sake, but loss of their potential for usefulness and good. It is local technical knowledge that informs indigenous systems of natural resource management, which in turn hold considerable potential for use in sensibly and sustainably managing the environment. The task at hand in the Himalayas, and the world, is to determine what they are, to understand them, and to incorporate them into conservation development.

Local systems of forest management in Nepal are, in some instances, very effective but not often well known beyond the immediate locality. Some are of an old vintage, reflecting the needs and conditions of ancestral populations operating under significantly lower demographic pressures and using technologically less sophisticated tools. Others are management systems of relatively recent invention, but which tend, nonetheless, to reflect acceptable preexisting patterns of social organization, custom, and use. Each is an expression of the close relationship among people, and between people and nature.

Anthropologists and others have recorded numerous examples of effective indigenous forest management in the mountains of Nepal (e.g., Campbell 1979; C. P. Gurung 1981; Messerschmidt 1981, 1984; Molnar 1981). They include drinking water and irrigation systems, communal forestry, and highland pasture management. The following examples are drawn from my own observations in the village panchayats of Nepal, while engaged in social forestry and resource development work with the Resource Conservation and Utilization Project (RCUP) during the early 1980s. A village panchayat (*gaun panchayat*) is the smallest political and administrative unit and averages from 3,000 to 6,000 people in an area of from 10 to 60 sq km. Village panchayats are organized into districts (*jilla*) of which there are 75 in Nepal.

Ghatan Panchayat

In 1983 at Ghatan Panchayat (a predominantly high caste Hindu village in Myagdi District, west Nepal) RCUP staff engaged villagers in an exercise to inventory local resources (both biophysical and socioeconomic), in preparation for drawing up plans for local resource development. A guiding principle was to elicit local knowledge of the resource base, and to document indigenous systems of resource management for incorporation into village panchayat and district plans.

Most of Ghatan Panchayat's slopes resemble a close-shaven head, devoid of their once flourishing forest cover—an overcut, overgrazed, denuded brushland. In one small part of the panchayat, however, there is a history of community involvement in reforestation and forest conservation.

According to local account, some three generations ago a folk-hero and local visionary persuaded his neighbors to close approximately 75 ha of degraded local pine forest from further use and abuse, to allow it to regenerate naturally. In time, the Big Pine Forest (*thulo saleri ban*) was reopened to controlled cutting of dead and fallen trees, for a small fee. The fees plus small donations of grain from the users paid for a watchman to keep the forest paths clear of pine litter and to watch for fires. This system continued for decades as the forest matured. With the enforcement of forest nationalization rules, and more recently as the demand for construction timbers has risen in response to a building boom in the nearby district headquarters town, traditional management fell into decline. In 1983 under the new community forest initiatives, RCUP staff, district forest officers, and villagers began discussing plans to formalize some of the earlier management practices under the nation's new community forestry rules.

When the first RCUP-initiated community planning session was held in Ghatan, it was convened under one of the few remaining trees on an otherwise denuded mountain slope. During the session an articulate farmer spoke of the rich forest resources of bygone years. He drew on local knowledge and the practice of using descriptive place names based on naturally occurring phenomena. The farmer admonished his audience to recall the old familiar locales—where the walnut trees (*okhar bhot*) and kaphal berry trees (*kaphal bhot*) grew, the place where the water used to flow among the birch trees (*saur pani*), and the place where wild goats rested (*goral bas*). "But look around you now," he implored, "none of these natural things remains." Each such place, now devoid of the trees, ground water, and wildlife, had been important for its resources to earlier generations. Now, however, the once rich resource base is remembered only by the place names.[9]

For lack of sufficient forest, Ghatan villagers must now travel great distances to collect firewood and fodder. A delegation of village women, well aware of their resource poverty, requested the project to help them develop an all women's fuelwood and fodder tree plantation. As a group, they wanted to establish a user committee to manage and harvest the trees, but without the meddling of their menfolk. They said it is they, the women—and not the men—who bear most of the burden of collecting firewood for the home and fodder to feed the farm animals.[10] The district forester agreed to help.

Chhoprak Panchayat

At Chhoprak Panchayat (a Hindu caste village in Gorkha District, central Nepal), yet another form of participatory forest management exists. In 1960, 46 households of mixed ethnicity (high caste Brahmin and Chhetri, and artisan castes) organized a forest watchman system involving members of all user households in rotation (*ban palo-garne*) to protect a neighborhood forest called Tarke Ban (*ban* = forest). Use rights include controlled access for firewood collection, fodder cutting, grazing, and timber felling for construction and house repair. The forest also serves as a water source for the village and as the abode of a local tutelary goddess. This forest is unfenced.

Each user household sends a watchman (*pale*) to the forest by turn, so that there are regularly two watchmen on duty by day and two by night. While there are no restrictions on collecting dead or broken twigs for fuel or grasses for fodder (even by households not participating in the watchman services), the cutting of green timbers and poles for house construction or repairs is strictly controlled. The user group meets annually to assign permits and regulate timing. Fines are levied against households that neglect to send a watchman in their turn, and against unpermitted intruders.

The villagers say that they developed this system and have maintained it despite the forest nationalization laws that technically disenfranchised them from control over the resource. They considered it important enough that in the absence of effective controls by the government they quietly developed a local management strategy to protect the resource by themselves. As community forestry began to be rejuvenated in the 1980s, knowledge of the Tarke Ban management system spread to neighboring villages. Recently, 45 other households in a predominantly Brahmin community took Tarke Ban as a model and established a reforestation and management initiative for their own highly degraded Gaire Ban. Both Tarke Ban and Gaire Ban have subsequently come under the new rules of panchayat-managed community forests.

The relative leniency at Chhoprak regarding access to community forests for some uses, and strict controls for others, follows a general pattern described by researchers for other villages of Nepal. According to Bajracharya (1983b) and Fox (1983), for example, two types of fuelwood are recognized by the users: *jikra* and *daura*. Jikra includes old fencing and agricultural residue (stalks, cobs, etc.) found around the villages or households. It is collected without restriction any time of the year, but most often in summer and autumn before the winter period of daura collection. Daura refers to wood in its more natural state. It includes dead wood (dry twigs and branches) found on private lands and the forest commons and is, like jikra, usually free for the taking. But fresh daura (wet or green wood) growing on communal or public lands is more carefully controlled and managed.

Lete Panchayat

Another example of traditional community forestry is seen in Lete Panchayat at Ghasa (a Thakali ethnic village in the predominantly Buddhist district of Mustang in north-central Nepal). Ghasa villagers recognized in the 1960s that their local pine forest was rapidly being depleted by over-cutting, indiscriminate grazing, and general abuse. They closed off approximately 5 ha to allow regeneration. Access is controlled and the forest is patrolled by members of a community forest committee. While this committee functions within the modern panchayat system, it is of an older style dating to pre-panchayat times (pre–1960s) when the Thakali people exercised much more control over local affairs.

Since 1974, access to the Ghasa forest has been strictly forbidden for sheep and goat grazing. Cattle, water buffalo, horses, and pack mules, however, are allowed to graze. Similarly, cutting fuelwood and building materials is prohibited, although cutting poles and timber for public use (e.g., school construction, bridge repair) is permitted on request to the committee. Fines are levied on violators.

Each winter the householders of Ghasa are required to collect debris and litter within the forest. Two persons from each of approximately 50 households are allowed to collect up to five large basket loads of pine needles and litter daily, over a nine or ten day period. This serves to reduce the risk of forest fire and provides bedding for cattle stalls. The litter ultimately becomes a valuable mulch and compost for the fields. The forest is also home to a tutelary Thakali deity.

In the early 1980s, under the RCUP project, forest officers recommended that a formal management plan be prepared following the new rules for panchayat-protected forests. The villagers expressed reluctance, however, in the belief that by changing current management practices, they would lose all local control. Currently, national involvement is limited to district forest officers assigning permits for thinning the forest, and there are plans to permit cutting of large timber at maturity. As of 1984, no further action had been taken to change the old system.

Reluctance to change the old ways of resource management is a common theme among the ethnic peoples in the northern border districts of Nepal. Elsewhere in Mustang District, for example, similar traditional systems for managing local resources have been documented (Messerschmidt 1986b). In some instances, villagers go along outwardly with new schemes promulgated in the name of the nation-wide panchayat system, but quietly maintain their own social traditions behind the scenes. As Devkota et al. (1983) have observed: "The traditional system is the underlying strength of the communities; the panchayat system serves as the community mouthpiece to the outside."

Three Conclusions

Based on these examples, and others like them, three conclusions can be drawn about traditional Nepalese forest management systems; that (a) *they reflect a rich body of indigenous technical knowledge* of the bio-physical resource base and of the social resources and conditions necessary to maintain and manage natural resources effectively; (b) *they closely involve the local people* on a daily and seasonal basis; and (c) *they appear to be flourishing at the local level.* Some of them show remarkable residual strength even in the face of significant changes in national conservation priorities and rules and/or as pressures mount and conditions change regarding local and national demand on a particular resource.

Theoretical Basis
for Innovative Development Action

Innovation is . . . "a non-mechanical concept [in which] the new is born from the old through the creative transformation emerging from advanced technology *combined* with the empirical methods of the peasants."
Bajracharya 1984:330, quoting Friere 1973:130; original emphasis

A major question confronting the RCUP in Nepal, and other projects and programs dealing with forest and other landed resources at risk in the Third World, is this: how do we sensitively and successfully incorporate traditional knowledge and custom into conservation development action? The RCUP's approach to the answer is informative.

Intervention vs. Innovation

We began with a simple dichotomy between what (in international development parlance) is called "intervention" (sometimes called the "penetration model," i.e., top down "technology transfer"), and a more participatory approach, which I prefer to call "innovation."[11]

Intervention is an unfortunate but all too common term used uncritically in the jargon and implementation strategies of large-scale donor-assisted international development. Picture intervention as a wedge or funnel driven into existing social and resource systems in the Third World. Into this funnel, development agents (mandated by policy makers and national planners) pour new and presumably "better" technologies ostensibly designed to improve local conditions. My colleague, Deepak Bajracharya, describes the process in these terms:

Contrary to the purported aim of 'people's participation,' the normal route followed in conceptualization, planning and implementing rural development programs remains in the top-down model as follows: (a) researchers assess the 'state of knowledge' and recommend 'policies' and 'action plans' based on 'feasibility studies'; (b) policy makers then identify 'interventions' and 'set the targets' as part of the planning process; (c) action agents 'meet the targets' in the course of 'implementation'; (d) people in the rural areas receive the bullets in the form of 'interventions' (personal communication, 1983).

In defense of my sociologically sensitive development colleagues, I must hasten to say that many—and the number seems to be growing—are more enlightened than they receive credit for (cf. Cernea 1983, 1985b; Garcia-Zamor 1985). Nonetheless, many attempts at incorporating a more "bottom-up" approach are insufficiently grounded in a working knowledge of local systems and are rarely tested against the realities of village life and need. "At best," Bajracharya notes elsewhere (1984:279), "local people's interests and needs are intellectualized by the planner and plans that supposedly embrace people's needs are assumed to be 'appropriate.'"

In large conservation projects it is as if the goal is principally to improve the resource base, not the resource users. Quite often and despite planning rhetoric to the contrary, it seems, conservation development interventions are pursued from the center, without due concern for their short or long term effects on the *total* resource base—including the people. Interventions are often pursued without concern for their relationship and compatibility with existing systems of knowing and doing.

A more innovative people-centered approach, by contrast, has the potential to turn the orthodox development process around, and open it up to the constructive and appropriate involvement of the extrinsic resources of the "native . . . *homo ecologicus*" (Nowicki 1985:271).

By innovation, I mean here not a single thing nor the diffusion of things, but a process of dialogue. Without question, innovation means change, but with the incorporation of extrinsic human resources, by linking appropriate changes to local knowledge, custom, and need, there exists a greater potential to ameliorate the innate intrusiveness of outside assistance.

According to Barnett's definition, an innovation is "any thought, behavior, or thing that is new because it is qualitatively different from existing forms" (1953:7; see also 1983). Its "newness" is rooted in the old, in the sense of reorganizing that which already exists and making it compatible with other resources. It can, of course, be argued that *any* development action is an intervention, and that we delude ourselves if we think otherwise. But the point is that innovative change involves the local people and the resources that they, as culture-bearers and social beings, can martial to help effect a more rational and appropriate change.

Among the underlying assumptions of conservation development are that some things or conditions in nature are either in danger and need to be assiduously protected, or are in need of repair or improvement, or both. In Nepal, as elsewhere, many of the traditional resource management systems are no longer appropriate, given such systemic aberrations as increased demographic pressures, state encroachment, and catastrophic natural disasters. Innovative conservation development implies, however, that we look to the old, and reorganize or modify it to address the changed circumstances of the present. It implies that we address the problems not only by introducing technological "fixes" from outside, but rather by combining new technologies in ways compatible with old and traditional ones. Communities alone may not be able to accomplish all that is necessary to effect the desired results of conservation development (Cool 1983). The innovation model allows for technological involvement from both directions, inside and outside. In it the "extrinsic" human resources now become "intrinsic" to the solution of the problem; local inputs are allied in newly appropriate ways with other extrinsic resources from outside the local community.

Practical Application
in the RCUP Project, Nepal

Not only are social factors primarily responsible for the deterioration of Nepal's natural environment, but realistic solutions require an unprecedented degree of local participation. The success or failure of the RCU Project is thus mainly contingent on the degree to which local people can be effectively mobilized to conduct their own conservation activities on a massive scale. Fortunately, there are strong grounds for optimism which suggest that a properly designed and implemented project can indeed enlist the support of many local people in managing the natural resources upon which their livelihood depends.

Campbell 1979:1

Based on the theory of innovative participatory development action, social scientists and planners engaged by the RCUP set out, in 1982–1983, to develop an acceptable and appropriate strategy for natural resource planning, implementation, and management. One mandate in the RCUP's original project paper (USAID 1980) was that we work with, among others, the local village people in the planning and implementing of resource development action. The preparation of these plans is commensurate with the goal of improving the degraded resource base by implementing certain direct resource development actions (e.g., reforestation, soil conservation measures, improved cropping, and land hazard controls) and by setting in place long-term systems of resource management and maintenance.

Conservation Committees

Prior to implementing RCUP activities in the affected watersheds, district-level Catchment Conservation Committees (CCC) were formed under the direction of the district chairperson. These committees were composed of government officials from the principal line agencies including the Catchment Conservation Officer from the Department of Soil Conservation and Watershed Management, the District Forest Officer, the district's Agriculture Development Officer, and the Local Development Officer, along with chairpersons of the district's women's and farmer's organizations, the vice chairperson of the district panchayat, and village panchayat representatives. The Catchment Conservation Officer serves as the CCC's member-secretary. The CCC meets quarterly to formulate annual programs under the RCUP, select sites and project activities, conduct budget analysis, carry out program review and problem analysis, encourage interagency coordination, and mobilize local resources and participation in support of development activities.

At the level of the village panchayat, the RCUP promotes the establishment of Panchayat Conservation Committees (PCC), chaired by the panchayat chairperson. PCC members include the panchayat vice chairperson, a representative from each of the panchayat's nine wards, two farmers, at least one women's representative, two Junior Technical Assistants (one each from agriculture and livestock extension) and a Soil Conservation Assistant who serves as secretary. The PCC serves as a sub-committee to the regular village assembly and its members advise on resource conservation and RCUP-related project development and management issues. In some instances, the PCC is further divided into specific resource subcommittees (e.g., forestry, irrigation). A principal objective of the PCC is to prepare an annual Panchayat Resource Development Plan with assistance from central RCUP staff.

Dialogue for Local Involvement

For purposes of preparing the plan, RCUP personnel set out in 1982–1983 to develop a strategy for local involvement and innovation called *Gaun Sallah* or "Village Dialogue."[12] This activity requires at a minimum, social scientists, natural scientists (forestry, soil conservation, etc.), agriculturalists, and economists. While expatriate advisors may be needed, the core team should be national in composition. Our team consisted of a social scientist, an agricultural economist, and a livestock pasture specialist, assisted by project staff, district development staff, an expatriate advisor, and American Peace Corps volunteers familiar with forestry, soils, hydrology, range management, and hazards (landslide) mapping.

The Village Dialogue strategy has three steps. Each is briefly outlined here:

Step 1. The first step is to survey and inventory the existing socioeconomic and biophysical resources in each panchayat. Because local participation and understanding are fundamental goals, this step begins with a training activity, to familiarize local leaders and their constituents with the nature, purpose, potentials, and limitations of the RCUP project. At the same time, team members are educated in typically or uniquely local conditions and needs, potentials, and constraints. The ability to listen is important for dialogue success.

A major component of the resource assessment is fully to document pre-existing systems of resource management, in addition to the biophysical elements (Messerschmidt 1985). This, in turn, requires an intimate understanding of and appreciation for local forms of social organization. The examples of indigenous forest management described above represent some of the data we recorded during initiation of the dialogue process. In later stages of the planning dialogue, we (developers and villagers together) noted the most appropriate pre-existing organizations and determined, together, how they might be incorporated into a long-range resource management strategy.

Step 2. This actually begins during the inventory phase to expand the already established dialogue. The dialogue is a two-way conversation between developers and villagers. Planning discussions are conducted in the villages. A village venue allows development agents a closer look at local conditions, and promotes more open communications from the local people. Many villagers are simply afraid to speak up under the unfamiliar and culturally uncomfortable and insensitive surroundings of cold, formal district or project offices, away from their homes and farms.

A common criticism of decentralized planning is that it is easily co-opted by the local elite. To prevent this from happening while testing the Village Dialogue strategy, the planning team encouraged local villagers to divide into representative groups for discussion. In Ghatan Panchayat, for example, the wealthier male leaders and principal farmers met in one group, women in another, and representatives of the lower classes in a third. In this way, the normal practice of letting the village elite speak for all was agreeably circumvented and a wider variety of comment and opinion was heard and recorded. This had the effect of creating a stronger sense of accountability among the elites and fostered a better understanding of resource issues affecting *all* levels of the local society. When the village assembly reconvened and compared notes, leaders commented that local resource issues and their potential solutions were more widely representative of the whole than ever before. More importantly, they supported the concerns expressed by the women and the lower classes and proposed that they be fully addressed in the plan (Messerschmidt et al. 1984; RCUP 1983).

With data about local resources, needs, and priorities, the planning team again brings the district development officers and extension agents together with the village assembly to discuss local problems and issues, and to formulate specific plans for their solution. At approximately this point planners and technicians visit proposed local project sites in the company of villagers to determine feasibility and to assure the further participation of as many local individuals and groups as possible. Following the site tours, the core planning team, district development officers, and the villagers convened once again at a central location in the panchayat to discuss findings and to draft a preliminary plan.

Step 3. The third step is performed mostly by the core members of the planning team in consultation, as necessary, with district development officers and staff. The list of local resources, needs, and priorities are matched with existing and planned development programs. This step is usually conducted in the district project office, and is refined and further developed at the project's central office.[13]

To conclude, a semifinal Panchayat Resource Development Plan is drafted and returned to the Panchayat Conservation Committee for final modification and ratification. It is then forwarded through the Catchment Conservation Officer to the district-level Catchment Conservation Committee. Finally, it is incorporated into the District Development Plan.

Discussion

There are several thousand village panchayats in Nepal, only 60 of them within the current jurisdiction of the RCUP project. During the initial experimental period of the Village Dialogue methodology, we were able to complete plans for only nine panchayats. Recognizing the slowness of the dialogue approach, we modified it in the field by considering several contiguous panchayats grouped together in units called *ilakas*. (An ilaka is a service area unit established between the district and the village panchayat.) Using the ilaka approach helped us to consolidate and speed up the process.

Following the initial field tests of 1983, my Nepali colleagues intended to modify the approach further by training teams of district-based development technicians and extension workers to continue the process. The process should be reiterated in the future at periodic intervals to reflect changing conditions and need, and to feed into each future planning activity. During the initial tests of the Village Dialogue, however, the longer-term aspects were not well addressed.

By modifying the Village Dialogue to work at the *ilaka* level, and by training district technicians and extension agents, my colleagues and I addressed some of the critical constraints commonly voiced about Third World development—time and manpower shortages and insufficient training and experience in community action techniques. Other constraints include resistance to innovation by project staff trained in narrow technical specialties and the relatively high recurrent costs that national agencies are typically expected to bear after the donor agencies terminate outside assistance. These issues are described and discussed in greater detail elsewhere (Messerschmidt 1986a; Messerschmidt et al. 1984; Simmons et al. 1983; cf. Cernea 1985a).

While, admittedly, this method of engaging local people to plan and implement innovative development plans is time-consuming and resource intensive, its payoffs far outweigh such constraints. The result is a much greater potential for constructive engagement with and by local people at the grass roots, using their knowledge in tandem with newer, more "scientific" technologies and other outside resources (e.g., partial funding from donor funding agencies). As Norman Uphoff has put it:

> the problems of changing and improving resource management in the hills are *so* immense, that size and cost are not relevant quarrels *if* the approach works, if it gets the change process started on a sound footing . . . as long as you can show results (personal communication, 1983; original emphasis).[14]

A Global Afterword

The challenge is enormous, but we like to believe that the human intellect is infinitely resourceful.

Cool 1983:47

Concern has been expressed worldwide about the dangers caused by the loss of genetic diversity and the extinction of species, but much less is heard about the loss of cultural diversity and the demise of social systems and traditional knowledge. The reasons for maintaining indigenous knowledge and diversity are clear, among them being that diversity provides a cushion against disaster. By maintaining and preserving a broad range of local sociocultural variety, just as by preserving a large gene pool, options and solutions to crises and conditions not yet perceived are kept alive. The Village Dialogue is a tested and innovative method for maintaining sociocultural diversity and variety. It works by incorporating the local villager into the dialogue for development.

Mankind's attempts at managing nature, our tinkerings with the environment, are still relatively primitive and imprecise. We do not know many answers, nor even the range of questions that should be asked. What is known is that many local populations bear with them enviably simple ways of surviving in harmony with the natural environment. Traditional management practices and technologies provide locally appropriate models of stewardship for the resources and the environments that need to be enhanced and protected. It is in the best interest of all to retain, protect, encourage, and use those human resource systems that still exist, and which are recoverable and replicable. Too many modern development actions and modern technologies fail for lack of understanding of local peoples, lack of compatibility with pre-existing social and natural systems, and a consequent lack of acceptability by those for whom success is most critical—the toilers on the lands at risk in the Third World.

Notes

1. Much of the material for this chapter was developed while I was a fellow at the International Centre for Integrated Mountain Development (ICIMOD) in Kathmandu, Nepal, in 1984. The basic data are derived from the Resource Conservation and Utilization Project (RCUP), and are backed up by my international development experience in the Himalayas over a period of two decades. I wish to thank my colleagues and associates at ICIMOD, the RCUP, and other Nepal government agencies and organizations who assisted in the design and development of the Village Dialogue strategy. While they are too many to name, these few deserve recognition: Deepak Bajracharya, Udaya Gurung, Marilyn Hoskins, and Vijaya Shrestha. I also thank Peter D. Little at the Institute for Development Anthropology, in Binghamton, New York, for his editorial comments and suggestions for improvement, most of which have been incorporated into the text. Responsibility for the final result is, of course, all my own.

2. These alarms are found in the popular media and environmentalist literature (e.g., Eckholm 1975, 1976, 1984; Nichols 1982; Sterling 1976) and in scientific assessments and development project papers (e.g., Bhattarai 1983; Macfarlane 1976; Moddie 1981; NAS 1981; Rieger 1981; Thompson and Warburton 1985a, 1985b; and World Bank 1979).

3. Basic policy is also being addressed, for example, through work on a Nepal Conservation Strategy (Nepal and IUCN 1983). Efforts to address national conservation strategies and policies affecting the greater Himalayan-Hindukush region and adjacent foothills are also in progress for Bangladesh, India, and Pakistan (IUCN 1980, 1985). International interest is also demonstrated in the establishment of the new International Centre for Integrated Mountain Development (ICIMOD) in Kathmandu, with which most nations of the Himalaya-Hindukush region are associated.

4. The Project was funded mainly by the Agency for International Development (AID) through His Majesty's Government (HMG), Ministry of Forest and Soil Conservation.

5. Another "cause" cited in the literature is development aid itself. Schaller, for example, makes this questionable and unsubstantiated observation: "Although Nepal's midlands were once covered with forests, over half of the land has been cleared in the past twenty-five years to provide more space to grow food and to produce lumber as a 'significant contribution to the national economy,' in the words of a United States AID program which encouraged such stripping" (1980:177).

6. Funded by the United Nations Development Programme (UNDP) and executed in Nepal through the United Nations Food and Agriculture Organization (FAO).

7. The population of Nepal currently exceeds 16 million, at an annual growth rate of 2.6. The population increase during the decade of the 1970s was 30 percent, adding 346,446 persons every year on the average (Goldstein et al. 1983; H. B. Gurung 1981b, 1982b; see also Macfarlane 1976; Nepal, Central Bureau of Statistics 1977; and Tuladhar et al. 1975). For comparative purposes, the official recorded census figures for the past half century in Nepal are as follows:

1930	5,532,565
1941	6,283,649
1952/54	8,473,478
1961	9,799,820
1971	11,555,983
1981	15,020,541

(H. B. Gurung 1971, quoted in Poffenberger 1980:28, and H. B. Gurung 1982b).

8. The larger "Himalayan-Ganges Problem" was the subject of a recent international conference sponsored by the International Mountain Society (IMS) and the United Nations University (IMS n.d.).

9. Systems of indigenous environmental knowledge have not been widely studied in Nepal, but for comparison of indigenous technical knowledge and response to environmental hazards in Nepal, see Johnson et al. (1982). For a wider ethno-ecology literature, see, for example, Brokensha et al. (1980) and McNeely and Pitt (1985).

10. The role of Nepalese women in the household economy and resource utilization is well documented in the exemplary work of Acharya and Bennett (1981).

11. The distinction between "intervention" and "innovation" is not new. Based on conceptual deliberations about people's involvement when we worked together in the RCUP, Bajracharya (1984) began to develop the practical distinctions in terms of appropriate rural energy development through his work at the University of

Hawaii's East-West Resource Systems Institute. Friere (1973) has written a classic work on this subject.

12. The Gaun Sallah, or "Village Dialogue," strategy for resource planning traces part of its conceptual lineage to the SONDEO and other forms of Rapid Rural Appraisal (Hildebrand 1981; Longhurst 1981; Pearce and Jones 1981; see also Chambers 1983, 1985.) At the time of designing and testing the Gaun Sallah dialogue in Nepal, I was unaware of a similar participatory planning program in Mexico. The PIDER program (Programa Integral para el Desarrollo Rural, or Integrated Program for Development) is structurally quite similar to the Gaun Sallah strategy. See Cernea 1983 for details; for a short review of PIDER, see Uphoff 1985.)

13. Ideally, the Village Dialogue process should occur before project targets and budgets are established, but the reality of the RCUP project was otherwise. Many targets and budgets were fixed in the project-planning phase, in an infamous set of "yellow books" (APROSC 1979) well before the dialogue fieldwork was begun. Nonetheless, there was sufficient flexibility to advise reorienting some activities to meet local and immediate contingencies. In other instances, where local needs do not match pre-planned and budgeted programs, other ways of implementing them are advised. For example, some priority needs may have to be put off for a year or more as new targets, incorporating local needs, are planned. And some are more appropriately addressed through other local projects or development programs. The planning process takes these suggestions into account. It was strongly recommended by Village Dialogue designers and advisors that the lead agency for the RCUP project (the Department of Soil Conservation and Watershed Management) invert the order of procedure and incorporate village level inputs at the start of all forward planning.

14. The introduction of the Village Dialogue planning method met with some initial resistance from other development strategists in the RCU Project. Later, however, after it had been successfully implemented, support for it was more evident, and its use was subsequently praised in the 1985 evaluation of the project's first phase (1980–1985). In terms of the project's overall goal of *integrated development*, the 1985 evaluation notes that the Village Dialogue method for local level planning was "the only real integration . . . observed in RCUP." But, while "local people did have a voice in adjusting line agency targets," the constraints imposed by the RCUP's overall "line agency, target-driven approach" made integrated resource management *after* planning virtually impossible (Meiman et al. 1985:26, 128).

The methodology, however, also attracted attention outside of the RCUP, and outside of Nepal. One recent iteration of it appears in the Community Information and Planning Systems program adopted for use in nine South and Southeast Asian countries by the Centre on Integrated Rural Development for Asia and the Pacific, headquartered in Dhaka, Bangladesh (CIRDAP 1984). Similarly, associates of the Institute for Development Anthropology of Binghamton, New York, have recently adapted the dialogue strategy for use in a forestry assistance project in Malawi, in southeast Africa (Thomas, Brokensha, Little, and Riley 1985).

References

Acharya, Meena, and Lynn Bennett
    1981   The Rural Women of Nepal: An Aggregate Analysis and Summary of 8 Village Studies. The Status of Women in Nepal. Vol. II, Part 9. Kathmandu: Centre for Economic Development and Administration (CEDA).

Altieri, Miguel A.
  1983   Agroecology: The Scientific Basis of Alternative Agriculture. Berkeley, CA:
          University of California, Division of Biological Control.
APROSC
  1979   Resource Conservation and Utilization Project. 5 vols, with annexes.
          Kathmandu: Agricultural Projects Services Centre.
Arnold, J. E. M., and J. Gabriel Campbell
  1986   Collective Management of Hill Forests in Nepal: The Community Forestry
          Development Project. Proceedings of the International Conference on
          Common Property Resource Management, Annapolis, Maryland, 21–27
          April, 1985. Washington, DC: National Academy of Sciences. In Press.
Bajracharya, Deepak
  1983a   Deforestation in the Food/Fuel Context: Historical and Political Perspectives
          from Nepal. Mountain Research and Development 3:227–240.
  1983b   Fuel, Food or Forest? Dilemmas in a Nepali Village. World Development
          2(12):1057–1074.
  1984   Organizing for Energy Need Assessment and Innovation: Action Research
          in Nepal. *In* Rural Energy to Meet Development Needs: Asian Village
          Approaches. M. Nurul Islam, Richard Morse and M. Hadi Soesastro, eds.
          Pp. 279–336. Boulder, CO: Westview Press.
Barnett, H. G.
  1953   Innovation: The Basis of Cultural Change. New York, NY: McGraw Hill.
  1983   Qualitative Science. New York, NY: Vantage.
Bhattarai, Sushil
  1983   State of the Environment in Nepal. Environment Management Project,
          Publication No. 2. Environmental Impact Study Project. Kathmandu: De-
          partment of Soil Conservation and Watershed Management.
Brokensha, David W., D. M. Warren, and Oswald Werner, eds.
  1980   Indigenous Knowledge Systems and Development. Lanham, MD: University
          Press of America.
Campbell, J. Gabriel
  1979   Community Involvement in Conservation: Social and Organizational As-
          pects of the Proposed Resource Conservation and Utilization Project in
          Nepal. Resource Conservation and Utilization Project. Prepared by the
          Agricultural Projects Services Centre for the U. S. Agency for International
          Development. Vol. V, Annex Mb. Kathmandu: Agricultural Projects Services
          Centre (APROSC).
Cernea, Michael M.
  1983   A Social Methodology for Community Participation in Local Investments:
          The Experience of Mexico's PIDER Program. World Bank Staff Working
          Papers, No. 598. Washington, DC: The World Bank.
  1985a   Putting People First: Sociological Variables in Rural Development. London
          and New York: Oxford University Press, for the World Bank.
  1985b   Sociological Knowledge for Development Projects. *In* Putting People First:
          Sociological Variables in Rural Development. Michael M. Cernea, ed. Pp.
          3–21. London and New York: Oxford University Press, for the World Bank.
Chambers, Robert
  1983   Rural Development: Putting the Last First. London: Longman.
  1985   Putting 'Last' Thinking First: A Professional Revolution. Third World Affairs
          1985:78–94.

Chapagain, Devendra Prasad
  1984   Managing Public Lands as a Common Property Resource: A Village Case
          Study in Nepal. PhD dissertation, Land Resources Department, University
          of Wisconsin.
CIRDAP
  1984   Regional Workshop on Community Participation in IRD [Integrated Rural
          Development] through Community Information and Planning System (CIPS),
          Comilla, Bangladesh, August 13–19. Workshop Report. Dhaka: Centre on
          Integrated Rural Development for Asia and the Pacific.
Cool, John C.
  1977a   The Great Indus Food Machine. Islamabad: Ford Foundation. Mimeograph.
  1977b   Stability and Survival: The Himalayan Challenge. Islamabad: Ford Foun-
          dation. Mimeograph.
  1983   Population Growth and Unequal Access to Resources in Asia. *In* Agriculture,
          Environment and Rural Development. Amrit Man Shresthha, ed. Pp. 35–
          47. Kathmandu: Agricultural Projects Services Centre (APROSC).
  1984   Factors Affecting Pressure on Mountain Resource Systems. *In* Mountain
          Development: Changes and Opportunities. Proceedings of the First Inter-
          national Symposium and Inauguration, December 1983. Pp. 28–33. Kath-
          mandu: International Centre for Integrated Mountain Development
          (ICIMOD).
Devkota, Bharat, Bhimendra Katwal, and Udaya Gurung
  1983   RCUP Social Science Fieldtrip Report No. 18. Kathmandu: Resource Con-
          servation and Utilization Project.
Eckholm, Erik P.
  1975   The Deterioration of Mountain Environments. Science 189:746–770.
  1976   Losing Ground. New York, NY: W. W. Norton.
  1984   Nepal: A Trek Through a Forest in Crisis. New York Times, February 14,
          pp. C1, C5; February 21, p. C2.
Fox, Jefferson M.
  1983   Managing Public Lands in a Subsistence Economy: The Perspective from
          a Nepali Village. PhD dissertation, University of Wisconsin.
Frankel, O. H.
  1974   Genetic Conservation: Our Evolutionary Responsibility. Genetics 78:
          53–65.
Friere, Paulo
  1973   Education for Critical Consciousness. New York, NY: Seabury Press.
Garcia-Zamor, Jean-Claude, ed.
  1985   Public Participation in Development Planning and Management: Cases
          from Africa and Asia. Boulder, CO: Westview Press.
Goldstein, Melvyn C., James L. Ross, and Sidney Schuler
  1983   From a Mountain-Rural to a Plains-Urban Society: Implications of the 1981
          Nepalese Census. Mountain Research and Development 3:61–64.
Gurung, Chandra Prasad
  1981   People's Participation in Local Level Planning: A Case Study from Nepal.
          M.Sc. thesis, Asian Institute of Technology, Bangkok, Thailand.
Gurung, Harka B.
  1971   Demographic Aspects of Development in Nepal. Paper presented at the
          seminar on Population and Development, Centre for Economic Development
          and Administration, Tribhuvan University, Kirtipur, Nepal.

1981a   Ecological Change in Nepal: A Native Interpretation. New ERA Occasional
         Paper No. 1. Kathmandu: New ERA.
1981b   Study on Inter-Regional Migration in Nepal. Study prepared for the National
         Commission on Population, National Planning Commission, HMG Nepal.
         Kathmandu: New ERA.
1982a   The Himalaya: Perspective on Change. Kathmandu: New ERA.
1982b   Population Increase in Nepal 1971–1981. New ERA Occasional Paper No.
         4. Kathmandu: New ERA.

Hardin, Garrett
1968   The Tragedy of the Commons. Science 162:1243–1248.

Hatley, Thomas, and Michael Thompson
1985   Rare Animals, Poor People, and Big Agencies: A Perspective on Biological
         Conservation and Rural Development in the Himalaya. Mountain Research
         and Development 5:365–377.

Hildebrand, Peter E.
1981   Combining Disciplines in Rapid Appraisal: The SONDEO Approach. Ag-
         ricultural Administration (Special Issue on Rapid Rural Appraisal) 8(6):
         423–432.

Howes, Michael
1980   The Uses of Indigenous Technical Knowledge in Development. *In* Indigenous
         Knowledge Systems and Development. David W. Brokensha, D. M. Warren
         and Oswald Werner, eds. Pp. 341–357. Lanham, MD: University Press of
         America.

IMS
n.d.   Proceedings of the Mohonk Mountain Conference on the Himalayan-Ganges
         Region: Problem Definition, Analysis, and Research and Policy Recom-
         mendations; April 1986. Boulder, CO: International Mountain Society,
         forthcoming.

IUCN
1980   World Conservation Strategy: Living Resource Conservation for Sustainable
         Development. Gland, Switzerland: International Union for the Conservation
         of Nature and Natural Resources.
1985   World Conservation Strategy in Action. IUCN Bulletin Supplement 1/
         1985 (March): 4–5.

Ives, Jack D.
1984   The Himalaya-Ganges Problem in the Context of Peace and Resource-Use
         Conflict Management. Mountain Research and Development 4:363–365.

Johnson, Kirsten, Elizabeth Ann Olson, and Sumitra Manandhar
1982   Environmental Knowledge and Response to Natural Hazards in Moun-
         tainous Nepal. Mountain Research and Development 2:175–188.

Longhurst, Richard, ed.
1981   Rapid Rural Appraisal: Social Structure and Rural Economy. IDS Bulletin
         12(4). Brighton: Institute of Development Studies, Sussex University.

Macfarlane, Alan D. J.
1976   Resources and Population: A Study of the Gurungs of Nepal. Cambridge:
         Cambridge University Press.

Manandhar, P. K.
1982   Introduction to Policy, Legislation and Programmes of Community Forestry
         Development in Nepal. Field Document No. 19. Kathmandu, Nepal: HMG/
         UNDP/FAO Community Forestry Development Project.

McNeely, Jeffrey A., and David Pitt, eds.
1985   Culture and Conservation: The Human Dimension in Environmental Planning. London: Croom Helm.
Meiman, James R., et al.
1985   Resource Conservation and Utilization Project, Nepal. Evaluation Report submitted to the U.S. Agency for International Development/Nepal. Washington, DC: International Science and Technology Institute.
Messerschmidt, Donald A.
1981   *Nogar* and Other Traditional Forms of Cooperation in Nepal: Significance for Development. Human Organization 40:40–47.
1984   Using Human Resources in Natural Resource Management: Innovations in Himalayan Development. Watershed Management Working Paper, WSM I/1. Kathmandu, Nepal: International Centre for Integrated Mountain Development.
1985   Commentary on: Agricultural Land Evaluation for National Land-Use Planning in Nepal: A Case Study in the Kailali District, by P. B. Shah and H. Schreier. Mountain Research and Development 5:137–146.
1986a   "Go to the People": Local Planning for Natural Resource Development in Nepal. Practicing Anthropology 7(4):12–15.
1986b   People and Resources in Nepal: Customary Resource Management Systems of the Upper Kali Gandaki. Proceedings of the International Conference on Common Property Resource Management, Annapolis, Maryland, 21–27 April, 1985. Washington, DC: National Academy of Sciences, in press.
Messerschmidt, Donald A., Udaya Gurung, Bharat Devkota, and Bhimendra Katwal
1984   Gaun Sallah: The 'Village Dialogue' Method for Local Planning in Nepal. Kathmandu: Resource Conservation and Utilization Project.
Moddie, A. D.
1981   Himalayan Environment. *In* The Himalaya: Aspects of Change. J. S. Lall, ed. Pp. 341–350. Bombay: Oxford University Press.
Molnar, Augusta
1981   The Dynamics of Traditional Systems of Forest Management in Nepal: Implications for the Community Forestry Development and Training Project. Report to the World Bank/International Finance Corporation. Washington, DC: World Bank.
NAS
1980   Research Priorities in Tropical Biology. Washington, DC: U.S. National Academy of Sciences.
1981   Proceedings. Workshop on Management of Renewable Resources: Problems, Strategies, and Policies. Kathmandu, February 6–13, 1981. Washington, DC: U.S. National Academy Press.
Nepal (HMG of), Central Bureau of Statistics
1977   The Analysis of the Population Statistics of Nepal. Kathmandu: HMG Central Bureau of Statistics.
Nepal (HMG of), and IUCN
1983   National Conservation Strategy for Nepal. Gland, Switzerland: International Union for Conservation of Nature and Natural Resources.
Nichols, S.
1982   The Fragile Mountain (film). Franklin Lakes, NJ: Nichols Productions, Ltd.

Nowicki, P.
  1985   Cultural Ecology and "Management" of Natural Resources or Knowing
          When Not to Meddle. *In* Culture and Conservation: The Human Dimension
          in Environmental Planning. Jeffrey A. McNeely and David Pitt, eds. Pp.
          269–282. London: Croom Helm.
Pearce, John, and Gwyn E. Jones, eds.
  1981   Rapid Rural Appraisal. Agricultural Administration (Special Issue) 8(6).
          Essex: Applied Science Publishers.
Pelinck, E., and J. Gabriel Campbell
  1984   Management of Forest Resources in the Hills of Nepal. Paper prepared
          for the Franco-Nepalese Seminar on Ecology and Development, HMG/
          UNDP/FAO Community Forestry Development Project, Kathmandu.
Poffenberger, Mark
  1980   Patterns of Change in the Nepal Himalaya. Boulder, CO: Westview Press.
RCUP
  1983   Panchayat Resource Development Plans, Ghatan Panchayat (Myagdi Dis-
          trict). Kathmandu: Resource Conservation and Utilization Project.
Riddell, R.
  1981   Ecodevelopment: Economics, Ecology and Development, An Alternative to
          Growth Imperative Models. Hampshire: Gower.
Rieger, Hans Christophe
  1978/79 Socio-Economic Aspects of Environmental Degradation in the Himalayas.
          Journal of the Nepal Research Centre (Kathmandu) 2/3:177–184.
  1981   Man versus Mountains: The Destruction of the Himalayan Ecosystem. *In*
          The Himalaya: Aspects of Change. J. S. Lall, ed. Pp. 351–375. New Delhi:
          Oxford University Press.
Schaller, George B.
  1980   Stones of Silence: Journeys in the Himalaya. New York, NY: Viking.
SCSA
  1982   Resource Conservation Glossary. 3rd edition. Ankeny, IA: Soil Conservation
          Society of America.
Shils, Edward
  1981   Tradition. Chicago, IL: University of Chicago Press.
Simmons, Frederick F., Charlotte Miller, Prachanda Pradhan, and David B. Thorud
  1983   Special Evaluation of the Resource Conservation and Utilization Project.
          Submitted to USAID/Nepal. Arlington, VA: Development Associates, Inc.
Sterling, Claire
  1976   Nepal. Atlantic Monthly (October) 238(4):14–25.
Thomas, Garry, David Brokensha, Peter D. Little, and Bernard Riley
  1985   Understanding Tree Use in Farming Systems. Rome: FAO.
Thompson, Michael, and Michael Warburton
  1985a   Uncertainty on a Himalayan Scale. Mountain Research and Development
          5:115–135.
  1985b   Knowing Where to Hit It: A Conceptual Framework for the Sustainable
          Development of the Himalaya. Mountain Research and Development 5:
          203–220.
Tilman, H. W.
  1952   Nepal Himalaya. Cambridge: Cambridge University Press.
Tuladhar, Jayanti, B. B. Gubhaju, and John Stoeckel
  1975   The Population of Nepal. *In* Workshop-Conference on Population, Family
          Planning and Development in Nepal. Pp. 50–61. Berkeley, CA: HMG

Nepal and the University of California Family Planning/Maternal and Child Health Project.

Uphoff, Norman
1985   Fitting Projects to People. *In* Putting People First: Sociological Variables in Rural Development. Michael M. Cernea, ed. Pp. 359–395. New York and London: Oxford University Press, for the World Bank.

Uphoff, Norman, John Cohen, and Arthur A. Goldsmith
1979   Feasibility and Application of Rural Development Participation: A State-of-the-Art Paper. Rural Development Committee Monograph Series No. 3. Ithaca, NY: Cornell University.

USAID
1980   Resource Conservation and Utilization Project, Project Paper. Kathmandu, Nepal: U.S. Agency for International Development.
1984   Local Organizations in Development. AID Policy Paper. Washington, DC: U.S. Agency for International Development, Bureau for Program and Policy Coordination.

World Bank
1979   Nepal Forestry Sector Review. Report No. 1952-NEP. Washington, DC: World Bank, South Asia Projects Department.

Notes on Contributors

James N. Anderson is a Professor of Anthropology at the University of California, Berkeley, and Director of the Program for Philippine Studies in the University's Institute of East Asian Studies. He has carried out research on economic, social, and ecological change among peasant and tribal peoples in the Philippines and Malaysia for almost three decades. His scholarly interests also include human ecology, land tenure, indigenous agroecosystems, and medical anthropology. He has long involved himself in applied research relating to rural development with special concern for local organization and participation. Between 1973 and 1975 he worked with the Institute of Medical Research in Kuala Lumpur, Malaysia. From 1977 to 1979 he was a Project Specialist for Resources and Environment for the Ford Foundation at the University of the Philippines, Los Banos, working with forest and water resource programs focusing principally on the uplands. Anderson has served as a consultant to the United Nations Institute for Economic Development and Planning, the Fulbright-Hays Program in the Philippines, the UNESCO Man in the Biosphere Program, the International Rice Research Institute, the National Economic Development Authority of the Philippines, the Agency for International Development, the United Nations Centre for Regional Development, and the World Bank.

Eduardo Bedoya Garland is the principal investigator at the Centro de Investigación y Promoción Amazónica (CIPA). He obtained his Master's Degree from the Pontificia Universidad Católica del Perú in Lima in 1982, and his principal areas of activity include economic anthropology, agricultural production systems in tropical areas, and human settlement. He has recently completed field research on agricultural production systems in the high jungle on behalf of Peru's Institute Nacional de Desarrollo (INADE) and the office of Apoyo a la Política del Desarrollo de la Selva Alta (APODESA), and on the impact of the market economy on Native Communities in the Urubamba, Satipo, and Madre de Dios regions of Peru on behalf of CIPA. He is the editor of the journal *Amazonía Peruana* published by the Centro Amazónico de Antropología y Aplicación Práctica (CAAAP), as well as of CIPA's journal, *Extracta*.

Stephen B. Brush received his doctorate in anthropology from the University of Wisconsin, Madison in 1973. He taught at the College of William and Mary in Virginia and served as Program Director for Anthropology at the National Science Foundation. He is currently Administrator for International Agricultural Development at the University of California, Davis. His teaching and research interests concern agricultural and environmental change in the Third World.

Jane L. Collins is Assistant Professor of Anthropology, State University of New York at Binghamton. She has conducted research on the impacts of agrarian reform and on smallholder productive strategies and migration in Peru, and has written on labor scarcity, resettlement, and small farm agriculture. She has produced numerous articles addressing these issues and a monograph entitled *Unseasonal Migrations: The Social Construction and Ecological Effects of Rural Labor Scarcity in Peru,* to be published later this year by Princeton University Press. She received her Ph.D. in Anthropology from the University of Florida.

Michael M Horowitz, Professor of Anthropology at State University of New York at Binghamton and Director of the Institute for Development Anthropology, has carried out research among farming and pastoral peoples in Senegal, Niger, Mali, Burkina Faso, the Sudan, Zaire, Rwanda, Zimbabwe, Tunisia, Jamaica, and Martinique. He has been an advisor and consultant to the United Nations Development Programme, the U.N. Environment Programme, the U.N. Sudano-Sahelian Office, the Food and Agricultural Organization, the World Bank, the Agency for International Development, the Overseas Liaison Committee of the American Council on Education, the Overseas Development Council, the Board on Science and Technology for International Development of the National Academy of Sciences, and the U.S. Congress Office of Technology Assessment. In 1974–1975 he served as regional anthropologist and director of applied social science research for AID's Regional Economic Development Services Office for West Africa, and from 1979 to 1984 he was senior social science advisor to AID's Office of Evaluation. He received the Ph.D. in anthropology from Columbia University.

Fouad N. Ibrahim is Professor of Geography at the University of Bayreuth, Federal Republic of Germany. Since April 1986 he has been Senior Economist at the U.N. Development Programme in Khartoum. He did his D.Sc. on the social and economic analysis of handicraft in Tunisia at the University of Hannover in 1975, and his "Habilitation," at the University of Hamburg, on desertification in Darfur, Sudan. His most recent research is on rural-urban migration in the Sudan. His publications are mainly concerned with ecological problems in the arid and semi-arid zones of Africa as well as with the socioeconomic consequences of drought and desertification. Among recent publications are *Ecological Imbalance in the Republic of the Sudan* (Bayreuth 1984) and "Savannenökosysteme" in *Geowissenschaften in unserer Zeit* 2(5):145–159 (1984).

Peter D. Little received his Ph.D. in 1983 from Indiana University. He is a Senior Research Associate at the Institute for Development Anthropology and an Adjunct Assistant Professor at SUNY-Binghamton. He has served as consultant to the United Nations, the World Bank, the Agency for International Development, and the Office of Technology Assessment, U.S. Congress. Dr. Little is the IDA Project Director of the Cooperative Agreement on Human Settlement and Resource Systems Analysis (SARSA) between Clark University and the Institute for Development Anthropology. He has carried out research on pastoral ecology and production systems, regional marketing, and irrigated agriculture in Kenya and Pakistan, and is currently conducting research on livestock and grain marketing in Somalia. He has published widely in edited books and professional journals, including *Africa, American Ethnologist* (forthcoming), *Human Ecology,* and *Human Organization.*

Maria Elena Lopez, Ph.D., Anthropology, Harvard University (1986), is Assistant Professor of Anthropology at Ateneo de Manila University, Philippines. As a research associate at the Institute of Philippine Culture (1973–1977), she carried out sociological analyses of projects in population, nutrition and urban settlement. Her current research deals with ethnicity and land tenure.

Douglas J. Merrey is a social anthropologist on the staff of The International Irrigation Management Institute (IIMI) in Sri Lanka. His previous position was as

Senior Social Scientist in the Office of Rural and Institutional Development, Bureau for Science and Technology, AID. After working as a Peace Corps Volunteer in North India, he did his Ph.D. in anthropology at the University of Pennsylvania. The data on which the article in this collection is based are from his dissertation research in Pakistan. Following this fieldwork, he worked for nearly two more years on an AID-funded research project on on-farm water management in Pakistan, looking into the organization of farmers' irrigation associations. He also spent 18 months as an Institutional Advisor on the Gal Oya Project, a recently completed irrigation system rehabilitation project in which important organizational innovations have been introduced in Sri Lanka. With IIMI, his research is focused on the decision-making and implementation processes in irrigation management agencies, and communications and interactions between farmers and agencies, both in day-to-day irrigation system management, and in implementing a rehabilitation and modernization project.

Donald A. Messerschmidt is a development anthropologist with the Department of Anthropology at Washington State University. He has conducted extensive research on social systems and resource management in the Himalaya. He first went to Nepal as a Peace Corps Volunteer in 1963. Recently he has been an advisor and consultant to the Food and Agriculture Organization of the United Nations, the Agency for International Development, the Board on Science and Technology for International Development of the National Academy of Sciences, the Smithsonian Institution, and the South East Consortium for International Development. In 1981–1984, he served as social scientist with the USAID-funded Resource Conservation and Utilization Project (RCUP) in Nepal, and in 1986 he consulted on community forest management, monitoring and evaluation with the U.N.-funded Community Forestry Development Project (CFDP) in Nepal. He received his Ph.D. in anthropology from the University of Oregon.

Emilio F. Moran is Professor and Chairman of the Department of Anthropology, and Professor in the School for Public and Environmental Affairs at Indiana University, Bloomington. He is a specialist in ecological anthropology, tropical agriculture, and rural development. He is on the Scientific Advisory Board of the Soil Biology and Fertility Programme of the International Union of Biological Sciences, and a Fellow of the American Association for the Advancement of Science. He is the author of numerous articles in professional journals and of several books, among them: *Human Adaptability* (Westview 1982); *The Ecosystem Concept in Anthropology* (AAAS 1984); *The Dilemma of Amazonian Development* (Westview 1983); and *Developing the Amazon* (Indiana University Press 1981).

A. Endre Nyerges is a Senior Research Assistant at the Institute for Development Anthropology and a doctoral candidate in anthropology at the University of Pennsylvania, Philadelphia. His master's thesis, presented in 1977, was based on a field study of the ecology of sheep and goats under traditional pastoral management in the Turan Biosphere Reserve, Iran. Mr. Nyerges' dissertation focuses on the exploitation of forest fallows by swidden agriculturalists in northwest Sierra Leone. At IDA he is involved in the planning of pastoral and agricultural development projects throughout North and West Africa. He is particularly interested in the environmental impact of development and in the integration of traditional resource management practices in development efforts.

Michael Painter is a Research Associate at the Institute for Development Anthropology and an Adjunct Assistant Professor in the Department of Anthropology of the State University of New York at Binghamton. He has conducted research on food and agricultural policy and natural resource management in Peru, Bolivia, and Ecuador, and he has taught and written extensively on these topics.

Thomas M. Painter is Program Associate with the Social Science Research Council in New York. From 1983 to 1986 he was a Research Associate at the Institute for Development Anthropology, managing or co-managing most of the Institute's programs in West Africa. He has conducted sociological analyses, and has participated in the design and evaluation of development projects in the areas of human resources, agriculture, extension, and literacy training. In addition he has assisted with the long-term implementation of programs for village well construction, adult literacy, and cooperative training programs in Niger, and has participated in advanced training programs for literacy workers in West Africa. He received his Ph.D. in sociology (development studies) with supporting work in development anthropology at the State University of New York, Binghamton, in 1986. His recent publications include "In Search of the Peasant Connection: Spontaneous Cooperation, Introduced Cooperatives, and Agricultural Development in Southwestern Niger," in a collection he co-edited with Michael Horowitz entitled *Anthropology and Rural Development in West Africa* (Westview 1986), and "Making Migrants: Zarma Peasants in Niger, from 1900 to 1920" in *African Population and Capitalism: Historical Perspectives*, Dennis D. Cordell and Joel W. Gregory, eds. (Sage 1986).

Muneera Salem-Murdock is Executive Officer and Senior Research Associate at the Institute for Development Anthropology. She received her Ph.D. in social anthropology from the State University of New York at Binghamton in 1984. Dr. Salem-Murdock has carried out research on household production systems among agrarian and pastoral communities in the Sudan, Tunisia, and Jordan and has directed IDA development activities in Tunisia, Somalia, Liberia, and Pakistan. Among her other research interests are river basin development, irrigation, farming systems, and women.

Marianne Schmink is Associate Professor of Latin American Studies and Executive Director of the Amazon Research and Training Program (ARTP), Center for Latin American Studies, University of Florida. Since 1980 the ARTP has stimulated research and training on the Amazon region and facilitated interactions between researchers in different fields and countries. Dr. Schmink's research on settlement and frontier change in the Brazilian Amazon region began in 1976 and she received her Ph.D. in anthropology from the University of Texas in 1979. She has served as a member of the Directorate for Tropical Forests of the U.S. Man in the Biosphere program since 1981. She is also a development consultant (to the Ford Foundation, the Population Council, and USAID), and since 1981 has been co-manager of a Population Council/USAID project entitled "Women, Low Income Households, and Urban Services" in Mexico, Peru, and Jamaica. The project supports local expert groups who experiment with models of service provision. She served as Co-Director of the Women in Agriculture program (University of Florida) and as an elected member of the Board of Directors, Association for Women in Development.

Brian Spooner, who teaches anthropology at the University of Pennsylvania, where he is also Director of the Middle East Center, received his D.Phil. from Oxford in 1967. Since then he has conducted ecological research related to development issues in a number of countries, most especially in Iran, Afghanistan, and Pakistan. He was Senior Advisor to the Secretary-General of the United Nations Conference on Desertification and has acted as consultant to a number of international development agencies. His recent publications include "Who are the Baluch? A Preliminary

Investigation into the Dynamics of an Ethnic Identity for Qajar Iran" in *Qajar Iran: Political, Social and Cultural Change 1800–1925,* edited by Edmund Bosworth and Carole Hillenbrand (Edinburgh University Press 1983) and "Weavers and Dealers: The Authenticity of an Oriental Carpet" in *The Social Life of Things: Commodities in Cultural Perspective,* edited by Arjun Appadurai (Cambridge University Press 1986).

Gilbert F. White is Gustavson Distinguished Professor Emeritus of Geography in the Institute of Behavioral Science at the University of Colorado, Boulder. He has worked on problems of water management and natural hazards, and is an executive editor of *Environment.*

J. B. R. Whitney, Professor of Geography and Associate of the Institute for Environmental Studies at the University of Toronto, teaches in the areas of environmental assessment, East Asia and Africa. From 1979 to 1981, he worked with the Ford Foundation in the Sudan helping to establish the Institute of Environmental Studies at the University of Khartoum. During the time there, he conducted research on rural energy problems of the Sudan and served as a member of the Sudan National Energy Administration's committee on Household Energy. He is currently conducting similar research in China. He also acts as coordinator of the Asia Region for Project Ecoville, an international project examining the environmental impacts of urbanization in twenty-five countries of the world and sponsored by the International Federation of Institutes of Advanced Studies, Stockholm.

Charles H. Wood is an Associate Professor in the Department of Sociology and an affiliate member of the Center for Latin American Studies at the University of Florida, Gainesville. After finishing a degree at the Population Research Center at the University of Texas in Austin in 1975, he was a visiting professor for three years at the Center for Economic Development and Regional Planning (CEDEPLAR) at the Federal University of Minas Gerais, Brazil. He has been involved in three research projects: a longitudinal study of frontier expansion in the Brazilian Amazon; a project on the impact of the Brazilian style of economic development on differential fertility and mortality rates in Brazil; and an analysis of seasonal migration from the Caribbean to Florida.

Index